Remaking Madrid

REMAKING MADRID

CULTURE, POLITICS, AND IDENTITY AFTER FRANCO

Hamilton M. Stapell

First published in 2010 by
PALGRAVE MACMILLAN®
in the United States – a division of St. Martin's Press LLC,
175 Fifth Avenue, New York, NY 10010.

Where this book is distributed in the UK, Europe and the rest
of the world, this is by Palgrave Macmillan, a division of Macmillan
Publishers Limited, registered in England, company number 785998,
of Houndmills, Basingstoke, Hampshire RG21 6XS.

Palgrave Macmillan is the global academic imprint of the above
companies and has companies and representatives throughout
the world.

Palgrave® and Macmillan® are registered trademarks in the
United States, the United Kingdom, Europe and other countries.

ISBN: 978–0–230–10641–3

Library of Congress Cataloging-in-Publication Data

Stapell, Hamilton M., 1971–
    Remaking Madrid : culture, politics, and identity after Franco / by
Hamilton M. Stapell.
      p. cm.
    ISBN 978–0–230–10641–3 (alk. paper)
    1. Madrid (Spain)—History—20th century. 2. Madrid (Spain)—
Politics and government—20th century. 3. Urban renewal—
Social aspects—Spain—Madrid—History—20th century.
4. Regionalism—Spain—Madrid—History—20th century. 5. Group
identity—Spain—Madrid—History—20th century. 6. Popular
culture—Spain—Madrid—History—20th century. 7. Spain—
History—1975– 8. Spain—Politics and government—1975–
I. Title.
    DP362.S73 2010
    946'.41083—dc22
                                                    2010009168

A catalogue record of the book is available from the British Library.

This book is printed on paper suitable for recycling and made from fully
managed and sustained forest sources. Logging, pulping and manufacturing
processes are expected to conform to the environmental regulations of the
country of origin.

Design by MPS Limited, A Macmillan Company

First edition: September 2010

10 9 8 7 6 5 4 3 2 1

For Ana who twice opened my eyes to the world

CONTENTS

LIST OF TABLES

Acknowledgments

Many individuals and institutions helped bring this book to fruition. I am especially grateful to my former graduate advisor, Pamela B. Radcliff, for the best comments, questions, and criticism anyone could ask for. I am also grateful to have had the opportunity to work with David R. Ringrose, whose words of encouragement were only matched by his words of wisdom. This project would not have been possible without financial research support from the following institutions: the University of California, San Diego, Department of History; the United States Military Academy, West Point, Office of the Dean; and the State University of New York, New Paltz, Office of the Provost. It is my pleasure to acknowledge the *Bulletin of Spanish Studies* and the *International Journal of Iberian Studies* for granting me permission to use some previously published material here. My thanks goes as well to my fellow SUNY New Paltz colleagues–especially Katherine French, Andrew Evans, and Michael Vargas–for their very gracious assistance at every stage of this project. And I need to make a special salute to my former colleagues Colonels María del Pilar Ryan and Lance A. Betros at the United States Military Academy. Their assistance, inspiration, and camaraderie will not be forgotten. I would also like to thank Donald Wallace at the United States Naval Academy for his always expert advice.

In Spain, I accrued innumerable debts, the greatest of which I owe to Marina Arredonda Crecente and Manuel Fuentes Losa. Without the kindness and constant assistance of these two very special people, all aspects of my experience in Spain would have been far poorer. I also owe a special debt of gratitude to Marina Fuentes Arredonda and Diego San Roman Mendiguren, who not only have shown me the true meaning of the word *generosidad*, but also first set me off on what turned out to be a long and marvelous Spanish journey. Finally, I wish to express my humble thanks to my dear friend Don Joaquín Santa María Lopéz and to all of the *camareros* at the "Cruz Blanca" for making sure I was never thirsty in that wonderfully frustrating city caught somewhere between earth and the heavens.

PREFACE

I left for Europe in January of 2002 with the idea of writing about Americanization in Spain. I went looking for signs of cultural imperialism, for suggestions of cultural insecurity, and for evidence of either the rejection or embrace of America and the American way of life. After settling down in Madrid, I began examining some of the specific connections between American culture, on the one hand, and Spanish film, fashion, music, and media, on the other. I eventually came to focus on Madrid's colorful cultural explosion of the 1980s, known as the *movida madrileña*. Specifically, I was interested in how Andy Warhol and American popular culture in general influenced both the form and the content of the movida.

But as I learned more about "Madrid's Movement," I quickly discovered that the effects of Americanization were limited and that it was influenced as much by European cultural trends—especially those from England—as by American culture. More importantly, all of the frantic cultural activity associated with the 1980s—all those public festivals, all those gallery openings, all those packed bars, all that new music—seemed to suggest something more than just a desire to stay out all night and have a good time. It suggested a deeper and more profound change in the capital.

This was not, however, the way the movida madrileña had been understood by scholars or the popular press. Most often it was seen as part of a nationwide cultural renaissance that swept all of Spain after the end of the Franco dictatorship in 1975. Many also viewed the movement as a kind of belated 1960s counterculture, flowering two decades late in a perpetually backward Spain. And others tried to place it within the international context of a lively and sometimes notorious youth culture. While I came to recognize how each of these three interpretive trends explained certain aspects of the movida, I also noticed that none of these perspectives was rooted in the specific context of Madrid. In other words, despite obviously being called the movida madrileña the relationship between the movement and the capital itself had been overlooked.

As fate would have it, in May of that year I took a break from my work and set off on the *Camino of Santiago*, or the Road of St. James, across northern Spain from Roncesvalles in the East to Santiago de Compostela in the West. It was on that medieval pilgrim's road that the very contemporary questions about the movida madrileña, Madrid, and the connections between the two

came surprisingly into focus. Along my month-long journey I expected to
see evidence of Basque nationalism—as Basque separatists have waged a
decades-long and sometimes bloody campaign for independence against the
central government. But I did not expect to see regionalist demands scrawled
on overpasses, on viaducts, and on abandoned buildings in every region
I walked through, from Navarre and La Rioja, through Castile-Leon, and
on to Galicia. And, more importantly for me and my work, in each of these
regions, the culprit or the spoiler was always the same: Madrid. Simply put,
everyone blamed the capital for everything. Depending on the location and
the age of the graffiti, Madrid was home to either fascists, or no-good *rojos*
(reds), or thieves, or to things that can not appear here in print. At the same
time, everyone appeared to be defining themselves—or *re*-defining themselves
since the death of Francisco Franco and the transition to democracy—against
Madrid, against the capital, against the center. Madrid was, in other words,
the "other." By the time I reached the Cathedral of Santiago, I was left with
an obvious question: If Madrid was always *the* problem, the "other," what was
going on in the capital?

So witnessing those very real and sometimes crude reminders of regionalism, forced me to reconsider what was happening in the center. And it
especially made me question what had happened in Madrid since the end
of the dictatorship—since 1975. How had madrileños tried to define or
redefine themselves? And, against whom? Who did they blame? Who could
they blame? Did Madrid experience its own form of regionalism? And, was
the movida madrileña somehow a part of this? More specifically, I became
interested in how ordinary residents of Madrid dealt with the legacy of the
Franco dictatorship in the 1980s, and how the process of democratization
had worked in the capital—especially since the capital was literally the home
of repression and centralism for almost 40 years. Put another way, I wanted
to find out if Madrid was populated by something other than "no good
nationalists."

Exploring these questions about the center—which had first occurred to
me when I was on Spain's northern periphery—turned out to be a sometimes difficult journey that included some ups and downs. As for one of the
downs, not everyone was receptive to any change in Madrid's identity, even
during the 1980s. A case in point was a letter I received from the head of
Madrid's main municipal archive, regarding a request I made for documents
relating to cultural subsidies. In a very polite letter, the director informed
me: "No authority ever has changed, nor ever will change, the identity of
Madrid." In other words, according to this very distinguished gentleman,
Madrid's identity has remained essentially static since King Philip II made
it the capital almost 500 years ago. To support this claim, his letter quotes
a seventeenth-century text by Luís Vélez de Guevara and a line from *Doña
Francisquita*, a zarzuela from the early twentieth century. Needless to say, he
never produced the documents I was looking for. Nor was his opinion about
the unalterable nature of Madrid's identity uncommon among the residents
of the capital.

Despite the resistance and the occasional setback, I was also spurred along at times by some small and unexpected discoveries. Like one day when I was waiting to cross one of the busiest boulevards in Madrid, Paseo de Recoletos, which happens to be right in front of the Biblioteca Nacional (National Library). Out in front of that massive library there stands a curious little statue of two figures reading a book together. I had first noticed it many years earlier, but never paid attention to its date or inscription. It happens that Madrid's well-known mayor, Enrique Tierno Galván, dedicated the statue at the height of the movida madrileña in 1984, and it was funded in part by the city hall. After realizing its context the apparent symbolism of the statue made more sense to me, and it became one of the images that helped guide me through the rest of my work. The statue depicts two young people, possibly a boy and a girl, literally fused or joined together, symbolizing—for me at least—the notion of *convivencia*, or coexistence. And what helps join them together? A book, a physical representation of culture, and, through the process of reading, of cultural activity. In many ways, these two ideals—peaceful coexistence and active cultural participation—sum up for me what Madrid's remarkable democratic transformation in the 1980s was all about.

INTRODUCTION

By 1985, word had spread to the rest of the world that something was happening in Madrid.[1] Something clearly had been going on in the decade since Francisco Franco's death in 1975. The mid-1980s, in particular, were years of elation, almost euphoria, for the citizens of Madrid. Simply put, things had changed. That change could be heard on the local airwaves, seen in exhibition halls, experienced in neighborhood bars, and felt especially on the street. The city was alive with art, music, and a newfound sociability. The term movida madrileña, or "Madrid's Movement," became the catchall phrase to describe the apparently magical transformation of Spain's capital city.

Seemingly overnight, Madrid had transformed from a dull, provincial capital into a vibrant, modern city. It was as if someone turned on the lights after 37 years of dark and dreary dictatorship. In June of 1985, *Rolling Stone Magazine* announced that, since the death of Franco, "Madrid has been having itself one ongoing coming-out party. The kind you have when the folks are away for the weekend. Only this time the Old Man isn't coming back."[2] The article went on to describe how

> Madrid has been transformed into a cultural oasis, where new music, crafts, intellectualism, drugs, free love, all-night clubs and boundless idealism have all become part of the daily scene—much like San Francisco in the Sixties. A city reborn to run.[3]

While these radical changes may have appeared to an outsider as a kind of throwback to the counterculture of the 1960s, the transformation of the capital actually had much more to do with the particular political, social, and cultural context of Spain itself at the time. After nearly four decades of a centrally imposed vision of an antidemocratic, Catholic, and conservative "Spanishness," Spaniards were faced with the task of redefining themselves and those around them in the decade following the end of the dictatorship.

The historian Michael Richards has succinctly summed up the situation: "The challenge facing Spaniards in the period after the death of Franco was nothing less than the reinvention of Spain as a state and as a nation."[4] In other words, the challenge was to create a new democratic Spain— populated by democratic Spaniards—and to secure the formal political transition to democracy, which had taken place between the death of the dictator in 1975 and the creation of the new constitution in 1978.

This challenge of consolidating Spain's democracy was met in part through the creation of new geographically based identities. In other words, Spaniards increasingly identified with a geographical region—or regions—other than that of the Spanish nation-state. In fact, decentralization, rapid social change, and globalization, along with the breakdown of an officially imposed national identity, all came together to create a new spectrum of democratic loyalties—ranging from the local to the supranational. Of course, these affiliations were not fixed, nor were they equal. In general, a singular national identity has remained weak and fragmented since the 1970s, while regional identities have flourished across Spain. In addition, supranational affiliations have surged after 1986 with Spain's integration into the European Union.

Despite the tendency to equate Madrid with "the national" and with a kind of "eternal" Spanishness, the central premise of this book is that *madrileños* too reinvented or remade themselves after 1975, and that the remarkable transformation that occurred as a result of that reinvention helped secure Spain's transition to democracy. Specifically, there was a moment in the first half of the 1980s when the local political and cultural elite was able to undertake a project to distance the capital from its authoritarian past and create a new democratic sense of place for all of Madrid's residents. As in the other areas of the country, this process of establishing new democratic affiliations came in the form of a new *regional* identity project mainly because all forms of official nationalism were seen as illegitimate, or at least highly suspect, after the experience of the dictatorship.

Reinvention, however, was no simple or insignificant task in the capital. Unlike other areas of the country, Madrid had no usable cultural, ethnic, or linguistic traditions to look back on. The language of Madrid, *castellaño*— what English speakers typically call "Spanish"—was quite literally the language of the dictatorship. In other words, there was no unique linguistic tradition to revive. And for decades the Franco regime had appropriated and distorted many of the capital's traditional cultural symbols in an effort to create its own official national identity. A return to Madrid's pre–civil war popular culture—what's known as *lo castizo*—was not a possibility either, mainly because of the need to forget the traumatic memory of polarization that had led the war. As the political scientist Paloma Aguilar has convincingly argued, this "forgetting" was necessary in order to secure the peaceful transition to democracy after 1975.[5] Finally, the capital's large and diverse population made the task of creating a new post-Franco collective identity even more difficult. While these challenges were great, what was at stake was even greater. Failure to transform Madrid would mean the persistence of a kind of "authoritarian hangover" in the middle of Spain. As the country's largest city and as the former center of the authoritarian regime, the remaking of Madrid was essential for the ultimate success of Spain's democratic transition.

Using archival sources, the press, and sociological data, this book shows how Madrid's local political elite implemented an ambitious regionalist agenda and successfully transformed the capital in less than a decade.[6] Madrid's new Socialist mayor, Enrique Tierno Galván (1979–1986), led this project to rehabilitate the city and return a sense of civic pride to all of its residents. To accomplish this goal, the local administrations stressed the values of peaceful coexistence (*convivencia*) and active participation—two prerequisites for a successful democracy. The wide-ranging program included the physical transformation of Madrid, the renovation of the capital's historical patrimony, and the reform of the city's administration. The combination of these changes altered the physical landscape of the capital and, more importantly, changed the way Madrid's residents from all walks of life understood themselves and their relationship to the capital. Or, in other words, the program helped madrileños "imagine," or identify, themselves as new democratic citizens.

But the goal of creating a participatory and inclusive "civic" identity (as opposed to an exclusionary "ethnic" identity) that could unify its diverse population was something that would not be achieved simply by physically altering the capital. Broad cultural activity and the movida madrileña came to play a critical role in the process. The promotion of this colorful, and at times chaotic, artistic movement, which produced the likes of the film director Pedro Almodóvar, proved to be an essential ingredient in the development of a new democratic regional identity. Even though rock and roll concerts, bar-hopping, and a socially active street life may not have constituted traditional methods of teaching democratic principles and civic engagement, they nevertheless provided a definitive break from the undemocratic past and created the means by which new habits and affiliations could be formed, specifically in the capital.

The project to create a distinctive regional identity in Madrid, along with the movida madrileña, did not last forever. It came to an end shortly after Enrique Tierno Galván's death in 1986. This resulted from the fact that the specific project in Madrid, which focused on culture and cultural mobilization, was increasingly at odds with the national goals of economic development and European integration in the second half of the decade. Specifically, the political and institutional space that had allowed for the articulation of a unique madrileño identity was closed after 1986 as the national leadership of Spain's Socialist party, the PSOE, consolidated its power and reappropriated Madrid, once again, as the "capital" of Spain.[7] Nevertheless, by the beginning of the 1990s, Madrid's tie to the Franco regime had been permanently severed and madrileños still retained much of their newfound self-confidence and pride.

Recognizing the changes that occurred in Madrid over the course of the 1980s as part of the process of democratic consolidation (i.e., creating democratic Spaniards within the context of a newly created democratic political framework), rather than as a series of isolated, albeit exceptional, changes related only to the capital itself, demonstrates four broader conceptual and historiographical points. First, regionalism in Madrid calls into question the dominant center-periphery model of identity formation in the Spanish context and answers the missing "center" question, posed by such scholars as Mary K. Flynn and Xosé Núñez.[8] The recognition of a regional movement in the center shows that there was more to Madrid than some kind of vague or "monolithic" national identity against which peripheral regions defined themselves. It also demonstrates that new democratic affiliations were formed specifically on the sub-national level all around Spain after 1978. And, as a result, Madrid becomes less of an exception at the center and more a part of a common process of "local" democratization that emerged in every region of the country. At the same time, it dispels the notion that the "center" is somehow intrinsically linked to the national identity of a country, when in fact national identity is a product of power, represented through an ideological program and transmitted through state institutions.

Second, by seeing the specific changes in Madrid between 1979 and 1986 as an expression of regionalism, a clearer understanding of that transformation, and what it was not, emerges. The project to create a new participatory and inclusion civic identity, of which the very contemporary movida madrileña was a part, demonstrates that the past does not necessarily need to be called upon to construct a new geographically-based collective identity in the present. It also shows—in contrast to much of the existing scholarship on nationalism in Eastern Europe—that culture and official cultural policies can be used to promote an inclusive civic identity, and not just narrowly defined ethnic identities. In other words, "culture" does not have to be synonymous with "ethnic difference."

Third, by contrasting the specific regionalist project in Madrid (1979–1986) with the PSOE's national political and economic program of the late 1980s, Spain's particular path to democratic consolidation after the dictatorship comes into clearer focus. It was ultimately a road—one consciously chosen by the national leadership of the PSOE—toward a more formal model of liberal democracy (neoliberalism) and away from a more participatory form of radical or social democracy. Evidence in the capital of a successful alternative to this more formal and passive model suggests that there is not a single road to a stable democracy; instead, there are multiple paths to democratic consolidation after the end of an authoritarian regime.

Finally, this examination of Madrid within the broader context of Spain's democratic consolidation helps illustrate the position of the contemporary nation-state and official national identities at the end of the twentieth century. It informs us about the devolution of European nation-states, the emergence of a multiple (or "postmodern") identity, and about what those developments might mean for conceptualizing nationalism and regionalism in the future. There is evidence that points to the nation-state's resilience and adaptability, as well as to fragmentation and new hybrid identities within that traditional model.

* * * * *

Beginning with the first democratic municipal elections of 1979 and ending with Madrid as the Cultural Capital of Europe in 1992, the following eight chapters explore Madrid's transformation from the gray and lifeless home of the former dictatorship to the open and proud place that came to be known around the world for its excitement and enthusiasm. They also explain exactly how and why Madrid's transformation was primarily the product of regionalism, and how that project fit into the broader effort to create democratic Spaniards after the formal transition to democracy was over. Finally, they explore the ultimate failure of regionalism in the capital after 1986 and ask whether or not Madrid's unique form of participatory and inclusive civic identity might have been transferred to the rest of Spain as a kind of alternative path to democratic consolidation for the country as a whole.

Chapter 1 examines the construction of new geographical identities in Spain after 1978 and presents a critique of the almost universally accepted center-periphery model of identity creation. Based on the presence of Madrid's regional identity project in the "center," the chapter makes the case for the development of a Spanish multiple, or postmodern, identity in the 1980s. It also argues that new forms of democratic affiliation had to be constructed specifically on the sub-national level after 1978 on account of the perceived relationship between Francoism and Spanish national identity.

Chapter 2 analyzes both the need and the opportunity to foster new forms of identification in the capital after almost four decades of dictatorship. It first explores the problem of defining a new democratic identity for Madrid in the face of no reclaimable linguistic or local cultural tradition. Then it shows how the capital's local political elite eventually overcame this problem between 1979 and 1986 by taking advantage of a new political and institutional space that opened in Madrid from both "above" and "below." The lack of a coherent national project direct by the central administration from above, coupled with the absence of a popular grassroots movement from below, allowed for the promotion of a new kind of *madrileñismo*, or "Madridness," in the capital.

Chapter 3 then describes in detail the official plan to transform both Madrid and its residents. Through a wide variety of programs and initiatives— from the construction of new libraries and sports centers to the cleaning of the Manzanares River and the restoration of historic buildings—both the municipal government and the new regional administration (created in 1983) worked to instill civic pride, to educate the citizenry, to restore public confidence, and to promote civic engagement. The chapter also argues that, in contrast to the many "ethnic" identity projects of the late twentieth century, these efforts in Madrid symbolized the creation of a new "civic" identity based on democratic habits and institutional allegiances.

However, the promotion of a series of civic values that could draw all residents into a common project only represented part of the official plan to transform the capital. Chapter 4 shows how culture and cultural activity,

in particular, were used to redefine madrileños and promote a new democratic feeling of community. Even though "culture" and state-sponsored
cultural policies are commonly associated with the creation of exclusivist
ethnic identities, this chapter describes how massive cultural mobilization—
including the revival of popular street festivals—was used to reinforce a
particularly inclusive sense of place. Such a program not only distanced the
capital from its undemocratic past by instilling the values of active participation and peaceful coexistence, but also provided an alternative path to democratic consolidation in a context in which traditional political mobilization
was seen as dangerously divisive.

While broad cultural mobilization encouraged all madrileños to come
together and actively participate in the capital, Chapter 5 demonstrates that
Madrid's political elite increasingly focused cultural participation and a new
kind of "official cultural identity" specifically on the symbols of the movida
madrileña. From this perspective, the music, films, magazines, and nightlife
of the movement became a critical part of the project to define a new democratic identity for Madrid between 1979 and 1986. Representing a distinct
break from the past, the movida's modern symbols were far more effective
at redefining Madrid as an open, democratic, and proud region than were
traditional symbols recovered from the capital's tainted past. While Madrid's
political elite eventually co-opted the movida to serve its own ends, this
chapter also demonstrates that the movement was not simply manufactured.
Instead, the movida madrileña developed spontaneously at first, and was
only later officially adopted after its inclusive, participatory, optimistic, and
modern characteristics were fully recognized.

Chapter 6 investigates the impact, or reception, of the plan to transform Madrid and create a new democratic regional identity in the capital.
In other words, it tries to gauge how successful the program was in changing
the actual attitudes and behaviors of all madrileños. Specifically, the chapter
details the changes related to four different aspects of the plan: increased
levels of cultural mobilization, the development of a new feeling of democratic coexistence, growing madrileño pride, and a greater sense of regional
association. While no elite-driven project designed to create an "imagined
community" turns out exactly the way it was envisioned, there is evidence to
suggest that the goal of transforming the way residents identified with each
other and with the place they lived was at least partially achieved. In fact,
acceptance for, and inclusion within, the project was significant because both
the plan itself and actual changes that occurred as a result of the plan were
not understood at the time as highly partisan or politicized. Rather, they
were seen as the "natural" outcome of the formal transition to democracy
(executed between 1975 and 1978).

Despite the project's success between 1979 and 1986, the attempt to
create a unique regional identity in the capital was ultimately short lived.
Chapter 7 argues that the project came to an end because the political and
institutional space that had originally allowed for its articulation closed in
the second half of the 1980s. After the death of Tierno Galván in 1986,

the national leadership of the PSOE was able to consolidate its power on both the national and local level, and readopt the newly transformed Madrid as the capital of a "Europeanized" Spain. As a result, the notion of Madrid as a culturally mobilized and independent region had to be left aside by the end of the decade. This chapter highlights both the disappearance of that more participatory form of democratic identity in Madrid, which had developed during the first half of the 1980s, and the emergence of new forms of local and supranational identification as the priorities of economic neoliberalism and Europeanization increasingly came to dominate the capital in the second half of the 1980s. Nevertheless, by the beginning of the 1990s, Madrid's connection to its undemocratic past had been permanently broken.

While both the movida madrileña and Madrid's experiment with regionalism clearly faded away after 1986, Chapter 8 explores the possibility that Madrid's experience could have served as a model for the rest of the country. It shows that the project symbolized a model for greater civic engagement, social equality, and popular participation that might have offered a possible alternative to Spain's eventual centralized and less mobilized path to democratic consolidation. Ultimately, however, a new civic identity, based in part on the symbols of the movida madrileña, never made the transfer to the national level because of resistance both from other regions articulating their own exclusivist regional identities and from the national leadership of the PSOE, whose tendency toward neo-liberalism and European convergence favored centralization and stability over greater mobilization. Despite the fact there was no transfer to the national level, the existence of an alternative project in Madrid highlights the fact that there was more than one possible road to Spain's democratic consolidation after the end of the dictatorship.

CHAPTER 1

CONSTRUCTING GEOGRAPHICAL
IDENTITIES IN DEMOCRATIC
SPAIN AFTER 1978

Across Europe, the momentous and sometimes unexpected changes at the end of the twentieth century placed tremendous pressure on the structure of the traditional nation-state and profoundly altered the way individuals understood themselves and those around them.[1] The end of the Cold War, the collapse of longstanding dictatorial regimes, and the emergence of new states in Eastern Europe, on the one hand, and economic globalization and the growth of international organizations such as the European Union, on the other, led to the rise of both new subnational and supranational affiliations. The Spanish nation-state, rather than representing the exception, experienced just such an alteration as well. The end of the Franco dictatorship and the new possibilities that came with the transition to democracy, along with the dramatic social changes accompanying the dual processes of urbanization and modernization that began in the 1960s, opened the door for a variety of new identities to form in Spain. It was also a time during which new forms of identification were in constant flux and competed in an ongoing struggle for legitimacy. Out of this disorientation emerged a new kind of identity in Spain—one that was capable of simultaneously incorporating a variety of loyalties.

Put another way, it could be said that a Spanish national identity, in any kind of a monolithic nineteenth-century sense, no longer existed by the end of the 1980s. The social, political, and economic developments mentioned above all combined to fundamentally alter the structure of the nation-state and create new forms of collective identity around the country. While the strength of subnational movements has varied across Spain since 1978, scholars typically highlight the fact that many of the same tools were used in different areas to construct new forms of geographical identification. Both new regionalist projects, ranging from Andalusia to Cantabria, and the programs of the three historical nationalities (Catalonia, the Basque Country, and Galicia) have used propaganda, cultural promotion, educational policies, and the claim of "Madrid's guiltiness" to consolidate new democratic identities since the end of the dictatorship. This final aspect, that of using Madrid as the "other," has been the focus of a great number of scholars wishing to explain the formation of subnational, or regional, identities in Spain after 1978.[2] As a result of this reliance on Madrid as the "other," the center-periphery model of regional development has become, by default, the standard analytical model used to explain the creation of new geographical identities after the end of the dictatorship.

In contrast to this standard approach, this chapter uses the example of Madrid to expose the many inadequacies of the center-periphery model, at least in the Spanish context. To accomplish this task, the rest of this chapter proceeds in three parts. Part one briefly discusses the origins of the center-periphery model and its original application to Spain. Part two highlights the serious shortcomings of this model when applied to Spain in the period between 1978 and 1992. Part three, then, offers some possibilities for reconceptualizing regional and national identity formation in the post-Francoist period. Contrary to the center-periphery model, which posits regional identities forming in response to a strong national center, an examination of Madrid finds no unified national identity, or Spanishness, articulated in the capital during this period. At the same time, there is evidence to suggest a more global process of regional identity formation that escapes the constraints of the center-periphery model and points to the creation of a multiple, or postmodern, identity after the dictatorship.

Part I: Origins of the Center-Periphery Model

Starting in the 1970s, scholars began proposing different theoretical models to describe the apparently oppositional character of regionalism and nationalism.[3] The two most important models to develop in this period were the center-periphery model and, a variation of that model, the internal colonialism model. In both models, regionalism or nationalism, on the "periphery" of an nation or empire, creates a unique new identity in response to economic exploitation by the center. Based originally on André Gunder Frank's dependency theory, Tom Nairn was among the first to employ the center-periphery model in the 1970s to analyze the birth of nationalist movements on the periphery of the British Empire. Nairn argued that imperialist exploitation, based on modern capitalism, reduced overseas regions to a condition of dependency and underdevelopment. Faced with these circumstances, the political and cultural elite of such peripheral dependencies attempted to resist this imperialist exploitation though the mobilization of the masses. In Nairn's analysis, mobilization was based on a nationalist program that was popular, cross-class, and usually offered a romanticized view of local cultural traditions.[4] Nationalism, and the invention of new and separate forms of collective identities, was thus used as a tool on the periphery to resist imperialism and to compete with the core for resources.

Around the same time, Michael Hechter offered the idea of "internal colonialism" as a variation to Nairn's center-periphery model. Based on England's relationship with Wales, Ireland, and Scotland, Hechter argued that the rise of regional separatism was a response to internal colonization and economic deprivation by the core. Although Hechter's model stressed the importance of industrial capitalism in creating the economic dependence of the periphery on the core, his internal colonialism model also highlighted cultural discrimination. Hechter explained, "There is national discrimination on the basis of language, religion or other cultural forms."[5] This discrimination, however, was based on aggregate economic difference due to unequal industrialization, and not merely on cultural chauvinism. Nevertheless, regionalism on the periphery of a nation was understood as a response to perceived economic and cultural exploitation by the core.

Published in the mid-1970s, the works of Nairn and Hechter arrived on the scene at the moment when scholars were trying to understand the development of new sub-nationalisms in Spain, particularly in the Basque Country.[6] While the center-periphery model's new emphasis on "internal colonialism" may have served the political ideology of many of the scholars employing the model, especially those on the left and the nationalists on the periphery who have undertaken most of the work on nationalism in Spain, the application of the model to the Spanish case has been problematic. Despite the fact that Nairn's and Hechter's models originally focused on underdeveloped regions in the first half of the twentieth century and earlier, both models have been applied to the case of Spanish regionalism and nationalism since 1975, including to the highly developed regions of Catalonia and the Basque Country. While Nairn's internal colonialism model of subordination neatly fits within the context of the former oppressive dictatorship, the fact that economic development and industrialization were actually greater on the periphery than in the core has never been adequately explained. Likewise, the rise of regionalism around the country after the *end* of the repressive dictatorship contradicts the internal colonialism argument in the period after 1975. Moreover, the Spanish state's newly decentralized autonomous structure largely removed the dominant core from the model after 1978.

Rather than working out these contradictions, scholars tried to resolve these issues by adjusting the model in order to fit the specific Spanish context. By focusing mainly on the oppositional aspect of the model, the appearance of regional identities has subsequently been explained through a more generalized center-periphery model. Thus, rather than concentrating on economic exploitation, subnational identities came to be explained through cultural, economic, or political conflict with the state. Or, in the words of one scholar, regionalism in Spain is caused by the "inequitable distribution of economic or political power."[7] While this generalized model appears, on the surface, to explain the formation of regional identities after the Franco regime, another major flaw has developed since the mid-1970s. That is academic emphasis has focused almost exclusively on the periphery, leaving the center unexplored and undefined. A closer look at the notion of the center reveals the further inadequacies of the center-periphery approach in the Spanish context.

PART II: QUESTIONING THE CENTER-PERIPHERY MODEL IN THE SPANISH CONTEXT

The problem begins with the fact that both the center-periphery model and the use of the term "peripheral nationalism" in the Spanish context imply a core. However, as just mentioned, little work has been done on Spain's core. Specifically, neither "official" Spanish nationalism in the post-Francoist period nor the specific collective identity of madrileños has been adequately researched or debated. As a result, the center-periphery model of identity formation describes peripheral identities forming in opposition to something completely undefined in the period after 1978. To fully develop this key point, it is first necessary to look more closely at Spanish nationalism in the post-Francoist period, and then turn specifically to the formation of collective identities in the center, or Madrid.

Turning first to the question of Spanish nationalism and Spanish national identity in the post-Francoist period, it is impossible to overstate the lack of research on the subject since the end of the dictatorship. There has been so little research, in fact, that several years ago Juan Linz asserted that "there doesn't exist one book about Spanish nationalism and I must confess that I am not able to think of anyone in Spain or abroad who, at present, may have assumed this project."[8] This trend has been more fully analyzed separately by both Justo Beramendi and Xosé Núñez.[9] And, more recently, Núñez has succinctly summed up the state of the field: "At present one of the least researched areas in Spanish politics is the ideological, political, and social presence of Spanish nationalism [as opposed to peripheral nationalisms]."[10] In addition, this lack of attention extends beyond the specific arena of historical inquiry. Again, Núñez explains:

> The purported non-existence of Spanish nationalism also constitutes a common belief which is currently reproduced by prominent intellectuals, politicians and the mass-media. Even for most Spanish opinion-makers, as well as for a large part of the Spanish academic community, Spanish nationalism is virtually a non-existent phenomenon, dissolved at the end of Francoism and the birth of the democratic Monarchy established by the 1978 Constitution.[11]

Of course, one of the major reasons that post-1978 Spanish nationalism has received less attention is due to the fact that the bulk of Spanish historiography on the national question has concentrated on the study of new peripheral subnationalist movements, and not specifically on Spanish national identity. Up until the mid-1990s, academic emphasis has been mainly on the three so-called peripheral national identities. Specifically, Catalan nationalism, followed by Basque and Galician nationalisms, has received the most attention.[12] Other regions, such as Andalusia, Valencia, and Aragón, have only recently started to receive more limited attention. Much of this work on subnational identities has been promoted by the respective autonomous communities, with universities in Catalonia, the Basque Country, and Galicia, in particular, sponsoring numerous studies of their respective autonomous communities.

In addition, scholars both inside and outside of Spain have neglected the core, or Spanish nationalism and national identity, because of what might be called "the bad reputation of Spanish nationalism at the end of Francoism" and because of the desire to embrace a new democratic "nation" of autonomies after the dictatorship.[13] In other words, the scholarly rejection of any kind of post-1978 "official" Spanish nationalism was rooted in the assumption that it could have no role in the new democracy.[14] As a result, Spanish nationalism after 1978—through its association with the delegitimized legacy of Francoist nationalism—was felt to be irrelevant by most scholars. Also, the obvious lack of regard for Spain's formal national symbols (e.g., the flag, national anthem, etc.) in the 1980s and early 1990s is another likely reason why Spanish nationalism has been discounted in the years after the dictatorship. These national symbols, decided upon during the transition, are too closely associated with Franco and the right to be valued by the majority of the population, especially those on the left. Finally, the only political parties and organizations that "have adopted the label of 'Spanish nationalist' have been Fascist-oriented parties (such as Albiñana's *Partido Nacionalista Español* during the 30s, or Calvo Sotelo's monarchist party *Renovación Española*)."[15] Hence, the prevailing impression is that Spanish nationalism only manifests itself through reactionary or conservative ideological programs, and is thus unlikely to be found in the period after the transition to democracy.

Developments during the transition to democracy are not typically understood as fostering national unity, or Spanish nationalism, either. After the forcible suppression of regional identities for nearly forty years, the Spanish territory was divided up into 17 autonomous communities, each with its own statute of autonomy and regional assembly, making the unity of the Spanish nation even more problematic. In addition, because of Franco's link to official Spanish nationalism, opposition to dictatorship and democratic forms of identity became synonymous with regionalist politics. Most scholars have traditionally called on the combination of these factors to make the case for a weak Spanish national identity and its irrelevance to democratic consolidation in the period since 1978. In fact, Stanley Payne has even argued that Spanish nationalism after the dictatorship "is weaker than ever and has for all practical purposes disappeared."[16]

Now returning specifically to the limitations of the center-periphery model, it would seem that the perceived "disappearance," or at least weakness, of Spanish nationalism after 1975 clearly poses a difficulty for the model: without the clear articulation of Spanish nationalism, the center-periphery model describes peripheral identities forming in opposition to literally *nothing*. Mary K. Flynn has described the construction of peripheral identities in exactly this context as "*deus ex machina*, almost self constructing in the present day, perhaps in opposition or affiliation with the state, but with little consideration of the national identity at the state's heart."[17] Thus, in the center-periphery model, regional identities in the Spanish context are created in opposition to something that does not exist, or at least to something that has not been clearly defined. Or, put another way, we have only seen one side of the center-periphery coin. Flynn sums up this problem:

> If it is accepted that the creation of national [or regional] identities is due, to a large extent, to the codification of difference—between the "us" and the "them"—then the near absence of the Spanish nation from the analytical equation of ongoing national [or regional] construction on its periphery provides, at best, a lopsided picture.[18]

In this quote, Flynn implies that the remedy to this "lopsided picture" is located at the state's "heart." However, as was just discussed above, Spanish nationalism has received, and continues to receive, scant attention in the post-Francoist period. And, probably not coincidentally, questions regarding identity formation specifically in the capital of Spain have received little attention as well.

As the capital of the nation-state of Spain, and as the former center of the dictatorship, Madrid *should* hold a special place of interest for scholars interested both in the creation of new forms of democratic identity and in the fate of Spanish nationalism after 1975. In addition to the capital's importance for the center-periphery model, the region of Madrid is one of the most important in Spain in its own right. The city of Madrid is the largest metropolitan area in terms of population in the country, and the region of Madrid claimed 12.3 percent of the country's population in 1987, while the Basque Country and Catalonia claimed 5.6 percent and 15.6 percent, respectively.[19] Economically, it is one of the richest regions in the country. Madrid's political importance is even more obvious. As the capital of Spain, it is the focal point for both national and international politics. Nevertheless, Madrid, both as a separate locality and as the center of Spain, has almost completely escaped the attention of scholars interested in regional and national identity formation in the post-Francoist period.

It is curious that Madrid has been so neglected, despite its obvious significance. Perhaps scholars have been reluctant to investigate collective identity in Madrid because of its relationship to the centralism and repression of the Franco regime, just as there has been resistance to the exploration of Spanish nationalism. It is also possible that Madrid's association with the "nation" has created a kind of a blind spot for scholars interested in regional or subnational identities. Regardless of the cause, Madrid remains one of the least researched regions in this area. Although there are quite literally hundreds of studies investigating the collective identities of Catalonia, the Basque Country, and Galicia, there is not a single study related to the specific collective identity of the residents of Madrid.

In fact, in Xosé Núñez's masterful review of Spanish nationalism and regionalism, *Historical Approaches to Nationalism in Spain*, there is information related to works on every region of Spain, including Castile, but there is not a single reference to the region of Madrid: neither with regard to its current identity, nor about the development of either nationalism or regionalism in the capital itself.[20] The nature of Madrid's collective identity simply has not been seriously considered by scholars up until this point. However, similar to Flynn, Núñez does implicitly place Madrid at the center of Spanish national identity by calling on historians interested in the capital to tackle "the national question from a Spanish point of view."[21] Or, in other words, to investigate Spanish nationalism in the capital of Spain. And, again implicitly linking the capital with national identity, Núñez also states that "Madrid-centered historiography . . . is still paying attention to the traditional thinkers of liberal nationalism in the XXth century, such as Ortega y Gasset," instead of working to develop a broader model of Spanish nationalism.[22] In both examples, Núñez consciously—or, possibly more significantly, unconsciously—associates Madrid with Spanish national identity.

This assumption highlights the central difficulty of the center-periphery model when applied to Spain. Taken together with the perceived weakness of Spanish nationalism since 1978, this tendency to link the center, or Madrid, with Spanish nationalism leads to what should be an obvious paradox. On the one hand, almost everyone agrees that there is no coherent national identity or Spanish nationalism after the end of the dictatorship.[23] On the other hand, no one has identified a collective identity in Madrid that is separate from Spanish national identity.[24] If both of these assertions are true, then what forms of geographical identification are found at the center? In the absence of any concrete answer, "Madrid" has simply been assumed to represent some kind of vague yet monolithic national identity against which peripheral regions define themselves.

PART III: RECONCEPTUALIZING IDENTITY FORMATION AFTER 1978

Contrary to this assumption, however, Madrid may not represent Spain's "heart," at least not in the late 1970s and early 1980s. In sharp contrast to the Franco regime, the transition governments of Adolfo Suárez and, later, Leopoldo Calvo Sotelo were too preoccupied with ensuring the stable political transition from dictatorship to democracy to pay much attention to the specific management of Madrid. In addition, it was too early in the process of the transition to democracy for either of the two new moderate center-right governments to articulate any kind of new national identity for the country as a whole or specifically for the capital. Rather than embodying a kind of Spanish national identity, it is now clear that, in the first decade after the dictatorship, the capital saw the emergence of its own unique democratic regional identity. Chapters 3, 4, 5, and 6 describe this project to remake Madrid and examine its impact on ordinary madrileños.

This evidence of both a conscious regionalist project directed by the capital's political elite and new feelings of regional affiliation among ordinary madrileños suggests that the process of defining new democratic forms of identity on a regional level occurred all across Spain in the 1980s. Put another way, every region in Spain appears to have experienced a period of regionalism after the dictatorship, including the so-called center. Thus, in contrast to much of the existing scholarly analysis, there is in fact no fundamental distinction between the three historical nationalities, the other examples of regionalism on the periphery (Andalusia or Valencia for instance), and the project to create a new democratic collective identity in the capital.[25] While it appears that the same basic process occurred everywhere, the characteristics of each manifestation did of course vary from place to place. Some new regional identities were based on well-established historical artifacts, others invented a past, and at least one, Madrid, created a new identity out of symbols found mainly in the present. Nonetheless, in each case, the processes of democratization, decentralization, and social upheaval created a similar context in which new regional identities could be formed. And, in each case, these new forms of regional identification worked to mark an important break from the nondemocratic past.

In addition, while the regionalist project in Madrid may not have been as strong or as well recognized as those in Catalonia or the Basque Country, it is nonetheless clear that the promotion of this new sense of place in the capital between 1979 and 1986 did not represent official Spanish nationalism, a monolithic national identity, or a new Spanishness. And, despite the ultimate failure of regionalism in Madrid (discussed in Chapter 7), the disconnect between the interests and motivations of the capital—articulated as a unique region—and the interests of the national political elite, represented first by Suárez and Calvo Sotelo and later by the team of Felipe González and Alfonso Guerra in the mid-1980s, demonstrates that an official Spanish national identity and the center are not naturally or inexorably linked. Once again, evidence of regionalism in Madrid demonstrates that every area of Spain, not just those on the so-called periphery, sought to define new forms of democratic identification specifically on the regional level. In this way, the capital was part of a broad, parallel process that affected every region in the country, and that helped define a new series of democratic identities after the dictatorship.

But why were new democratic affiliations promoted specifically on the regional level during this period? Of course, the roots of regional identification and self-determination in the three historical nationalities reach back to the nineteenth century, with some arguing for their origins in the early modern period. And, certainly, both the motivations of regional economic elites and the decentralized framework of autonomous communities—created in part to satisfy the demands of the Catalans—contributed to the emergence of new regional identities after 1978. Nonetheless, new forms of democratic affiliation in Madrid, and elsewhere in the country, were created specifically on the regional level primarily because of the negative relationship between Spanish nationalism and the experience of the Franco regime. In fact, for almost forty years the dictatorship propagated a repressive and traditionalist version of Spanish nationalism. In addition, Francoism, with its repression of minority nationalities, served to associate authoritarianism with official state nationalism and, by extension, promoted a connection between decentralization and democracy. Thus, the negative experience of the dictatorship, and, especially, the imposition of an official national identity, convinced Spaniards almost everywhere to define themselves as something other than the "national" after 1978. In short, Spanish nationalism and national identity acquired antidemocratic connotations because of their association with the authoritarian regime.

Regionalism, on the other hand, was free of the legitimacy problems from which Spanish nationalism suffered. In fact, regionalism was closely associated with democracy in the Spanish context. The identification of Spanish nationalism with authoritarianism and repression pushed almost all political parties to defend regionalist claims and to see decentralization and devolution as the surest road to democracy during the transition. This linkage of nationalism with authoritarianism and regionalism with democracy had important implications for the creation of new forms of identity in the capital after 1978. In an environment where all forms of nationalism were seen as illegitimate, or at least suspect, and where regionalism was generally understood as a democratic phenomenon, the formation of new local and regional affiliations became the most practical path to a new democratic identity.

As a result, the formation of democratic affiliations occurred on the regional level (as opposed to on the national level) everywhere in the country after 1978, not just in the three historical nationalities or on the "periphery." While the same process occurred everywhere, the characteristics of each manifestation did, obviously, vary from place to place. Rather than simply forming in binary opposition to an imagined center, new forms of identity and representation were dictated by the specific context in each region. In fact, regional difference depends on a variety of variables: the perception of geography, the ability to appropriate and reuse symbols and traditions from the past, the strength of local institutions, and the individual motivation of local or regional elites. Of course, in most regions new democratic affiliations were built upon a shared linguistic, cultural, or historical tradition and were seen by local elites as a vindication of those formerly repressed traditions. However, this use of a shared past was not necessarily a prerequisite, as the case of Madrid suggests.

Clearly, though, geographical identification in Madrid, or in any of the other regions for that matter, was not exclusively "regional." Instead, regionalism became one axis of a multiple set of overlapping geographical identities. Thus, rather than displacing all preexisting forms of identifications in Madrid, a new regional sense of place made up one part of a multiple identity that included both local, or neighborhood, and national affiliations. In other words, the residents of Madrid came to identify with at least three distinct layers of geographically-based identities in the early 1980s. So, like the rest of Spain, Madrid's new democratic regional identity coexisted with both local and national affiliations and, increasingly after 1986, with supra-national sentiments. A close examination of Madrid then does not resolve the problem of the lopsided center-periphery model by simply shining the spotlight on the center or by uncovering a previously unidentified national identity at the core. Rather, evidence of regionalism around the country, including in Madrid, calls into question the validity of applying the model to Spain altogether—at least in the decade-and-a-half after 1975. Instead of using the center-periphery model to explain regional identity formation, it is better to understand regionalism in Spain as a general response to the legacy of the Franco regime and to the pressures of "modernity" at the end of the twentieth century. Specifically, social transformation, beginning in the 1960s and accelerating with the transition to democracy, and the discrediting of Spanish nationalism generated a new series of plural identities across the country, which linked people together on a variety of geographical levels.[26]

From this perspective, Spanish identity after the end of the dictatorship might be understood as a group of overlapping circles of collective identity, produced through the process of constant contestation and negotiation, and not simply as a binary or "dual" identity specific to some regions. These various circles of geographical affiliation, however, are not equal, nor have they been static. In some parts of the country, identification with the region has come to dominate, while solidarity with the nation is less important. In other regions, this relationship is reversed. And, since Spain's integration into the larger European community in the mid-1980s, supranational affiliations have increasingly been added to this mix.

Following the postmodern perspective, the coexistence of these multiple identities in Spain should not be seen as an impossible or contradictory phe-nomenon, for it has become increasingly clear that the local and the global are connected in complex ways. For Jo Labanyi, "the two are not in opposi-tion but are enmeshed through the processes of late capitalism, which have mapped onto the model of the nation-state (which still remains in place) new macro and micro groupings."[27] In the Spanish context, these regional and supranational loyalties have come to coexist alongside national sentiments after 1978 because the processes of modernization, decentralization, and Europeanization have combined to wipe out the possibility of any mono-lithic form of geographical identity, be it regional, national, or supranational. Spain's postmodern identity at the end of the twentieth century is thus more a result of social change and disorientation than of historically weak Spanish nationalism or the resurgence of age-old ethnic antagonisms.[28]

Formulated in this way, the creation of multiple identities is not a sign of failed nation-building or a flaw in the country's democratic consolidation. Furthermore, this development does not demonstrate Spain's exceptionalism, but instead its similarity with the rest of Europe. Following Eric Hobsbawm, the emergence of multiple identities in Spain should be understood as a consequence of the refiguring of the Spanish nation-state—brought about by both the end of the dictatorship and rapid social change—at the end of the twentieth century, rather than as a cause of it.[29] In this way, Spain's development between 1979 and 1992 very much coincides with the rest of the West. Likewise, the lack of a strong, unifying national identity in the period following the dictatorship should not be interpreted as a failure of Spanish nationalism or of the Spanish state.[30] Nor should the emergence of new regionalisms after 1978 be seen as a "contradiction" within the new democratic system.[31] Rather this is the expected, and possibly even desired, condition of European nation-states in the late twentieth century. As a result, those searching to find, or even resurrect, a singular Spanish national identity in this period will be disappointed. Due to political and cultural diffusion, revolutions in communication and transportation, freer and more open markets, and a global neoliberal economic system, it is no longer feasible to create a single national identity, in the nineteenth century sense. A unified national identity is simply no longer viable within a context of such subnational and supranational influences.

Finally, one could argue that postmodern pluralism is both a more viable and a more desirable alternative to nineteenth- and early-twentieth-century nationalism. Without question, though, problems have arisen with the creation of Spain's "nation of nations": constant competition between regions for both resources and prestige, redundant layers of administration and bureaucracy, and ever greater demands for autonomy by some regions. Yet, with the exception of the radicalization regional sentiment, as in the Basque case, plural identities and multiculturalism have the ability to create greater tolerance, openness, and acceptance of democratic principles. Eric Hobsbawm again reminds us that "cultural freedom and pluralism at present are almost certainly better safeguarded in large states which know themselves to be plurinational and pluricultural than in small ones pursuing the ideal of ethnic-linguistic and cultural homogeneity."[32] Measured by this standard, Spain's multiple democratic identity in the post-Francoist period should be considered as a success. Since 1975, both the nation and the state have developed in such a way as to satisfy almost all regional desires, preserve national unity, and allow for the integration of supranational affiliations along with the rest of Europe.[33] The history of Madrid's regionalist project in the 1980s provides one such an example of how all parts of Spain saw the development of these multiple identities and how new regional affiliations, in particular, were used to redefine Spain as a modern, democratic nation-state after the experience of the dictatorship.

CHAPTER 2

RECOVERING FROM THE PAST: THE
PROBLEM OF REMAKING MADRID
AFTER THE DICTATORSHIP

Probably more than any other part of Spain, there was a need to remake Madrid and change the way madrileños saw themselves after the experience of the dictatorship, as the capital had literally been the center of Francoism. Decades of centralism and repression also produced a unique set of constraints on the capital. So for those wishing to redefine themselves and the capital after the dictatorship, the possibilities were quite limited. Unlike Catalonia or the Basque Country, Madrid had no local cultural traditions to look back on, because they had been tainted by Franco. In addition, neither a pre–civil war madrileño identity, based on *lo castizo*, nor the civil war's *"no pasarán"* resistance movement could serve as the model for a new Madrid because of the consensual settlement of the formal transition to democracy and its accompanying collective memory, which was committed to forgetting the chaotic, divisive past. As a result, something else had to serve as the basis for a new sense of madrileño identity after the dictatorship. In the absence of a usable local tradition, and because of the inability to return to the capital's pre-Francoist past, a uniquely new democratic identity—focused mainly on the present—ultimately had to be found for Madrid.

But what shaped the particular contours of this project to remake Madrid? This chapter explains the complex set of factors that created both the necessity and the opportunity for a new regional identity in the capital between 1979 and 1986. Put another way, this chapter examines the specific need for a renovation of the capital after the experience of the dictatorship and also the new democratic context in which this change took place. The first part of the chapter explores the problem of redefining Madrid in the face of no reclaimable linguistic or local cultural tradition. The second part of the chapter then goes on to describe how Madrid's political elite overcame this problem by taking advantage of a new political and institutional space that opened within the democratic state between 1979 and 1986.

PART I: THE PROBLEM OF A NEW DEMOCRATIC IDENTITY FOR MADRID

While the feelings of pride and affiliation that eventually formed the foundation of a new democratic identity came rather easily in the mid-1980s when Madrid—with its refurbished infrastructure, blossoming cultural activity, and seemingly boundless energy—was the envy of much of the West, such an environment had not always existed in the capital. In fact, less than a decade earlier, life in Madrid was close to the opposite. By the mid-1970s, Madrid had lost much of its former appeal and unique personality from earlier in the century. A place once known for its clean air, pure water, and compact urban structure, the capital had become the sprawling, generic, and polluted center of the dictatorship. With a lack of facilities, a deteriorating environment, and a widening social and economic gap between the center and the periphery that suggested a divided city, Madrid was a place that sparked little affection or pride.

From the very beginning of the Franco regime, Madrid began deteriorating from a vibrant, democratic city to the swollen and gray authoritarian center of Spain. In 1936, the slogan from the barricades of Madrid, "*no pasarán*" ("They shall not pass!"), became the chant for the antifascist world. Three years later, however, the rebels did *pasaron* and Madrid was declared by Franco to be both the actual and the symbolic capital of his own vision of a centralized imperial regime. For a long time afterward, Madrid embodied that defeat, and came to stand for that vision of imperial centralization.

In the period immediately following the war, Madrid was characterized by its misery, repression, and strict censorship. The streets and plazas of the city were especially dominated by hunger, black markets, and the language of victorious Francoism. Faced with such conditions, the capital suffered both socially and culturally. David Gilmour has summed up the situation in the postwar period: "Madrid in the post–civil war epoch was undoubtedly a boring and provincial place. It had lost its intellectuals and many of its most talented people and had retreated into one of its hermetic periods."[1] Life in Madrid has also been defined as "a color, gray; a feeling, sadness; and a sound, silence."[2] It also should be remembered that between 1936 and 1937 some of the Civil War's fiercest and most sustained fighting took place around the capital, leaving much of the city physically in ruins. After suffering through close to two decades of hunger and repression immediately following the civil war, the capital never returned to the cultural and political vibrancy that was characteristic of the prewar period.[3]

The second half of Franco's regime proved just as detrimental for Madrid, but for different reasons. Twenty years of unchecked development and mismanagement had left the capital overcrowded, segregated, and centralized. In order to satisfy the desire for autarky after the civil war, greater industrial development was called for by the Franco regime, especially in the capital. In 1946, the *Plan de Bidagor* (Plan Bidagor) turned the traditional administrative city of Madrid into a base for industrial development. This plan for a *"Gran Madrid"* (Grand Madrid) set the course for economic expansion and large-scale immigration in the decades to follow. By the early 1960s, mass immigration created the need for a new plan. In 1963, the regime created the *Plan General de Ordenación Urbana del Area Metropolitana de Madrid* (General Plan for the Urban Organization of the Metropolitan Area of Madrid) and, in 1964, the central administration, through the organization COPLACO (Ministerio de Obras Públicas y Urbanismo, Comisión de Planeamiento y Coordinación del Area Metropolitana de Madrid), assumed responsibility for the planning of all of the localities incorporated in the metropolitan area of Madrid.

These changes enormously increased the size of the capital and greatly extended administrative control, with towns such as Colmenar Viejo (30 kilometers north of the city) incorporated into the metropolitan area. Unlike many other large metropolitan areas, however, Madrid did not primarily grow by absorbing adjacent urban centers; instead it grew like an "oil stain [*mancha de aceite*]," spreading out in all directions from the center.[4] In 1930 Madrid had less than one million residents and in 1950 only one-and-a-half million. By 1970, however, the city was on its way to four million inhabitants. Hastily built and unregulated middle and lower class neighborhoods and bedroom communities sprang up around the city, especially in the south. By the mid-1970s, mismanagement, favoritism, and unimpeded real estate speculation furthered the capital's problems. The result was greater social segregation between the center and the periphery and between the rich neighborhoods of the north and the poor neighborhoods of the south, a deteriorating infrastructure, a lack of affordable housing, the expulsion of the popular classes from the center of the city, the indiscriminate destruction of historical buildings, the invasion of the automobile, and the increased degradation of the environment.

In contrast to the period prior to the civil war, the cultural situation in the capital under Franco was also bleak.[5] Madrid, along with the rest of the nation, suffered from direct and indirect censorship, investment in only officially approved cultural projects, blacklisting, state-control, a culture of evasion, and general cultural apathy. The capital was also largely excluded from the international cultural circuit of expositions, theatre companies, and musicians during the Franco years. Moreover, because of the desire to impose an official "Spanishness" on Madrid, "local cultures and popular traditions were deliberately exterminated."[6] These physical and cultural conditions coupled with the stigma associated with living in the authoritarian center of Spain left little room for many madrileños to be proud of their city or to identify closely with one another.

At the same time, other areas in the country became more closely associated with democracy and tolerance during the dictatorship. Barcelona, for example, with its close proximity to censored materials just across the French border, became the beacon of cultural and political hope, especially for those on the left. Barcelona was often seen as the "good" city, separated from the repressive regime. In direct contrast, Madrid was the symbolic "bad" dictatorial stepsister. The capital was literally the home of Franco's power and his center of authoritarian control. In addition, the images and symbols of Madrid and of the surrounding area of Castile, such as the proud and pious wheat farmer, were appropriated by the Franco regime to create a uniformly imposed Spanish national identity, or official Spanishness, between 1939 and 1975.

At the core of this national identity project was the acceptance of the centrality of Castile to the shaping of the Spanish nation. In working to solidify this nineteenth century nationalist construct of "Castile as Spain," the Franco regime suppressed all forms of regional difference, with Catalonia, the Basque Country, and Galicia facing especially harsh discrimination.[7] In the place of regional differentiation, Franco imposed a "Castilian hegemony glorifying 'España' and its 'sacred and indestructible unity.'"[8] This particular brand of nationalism sought centralization, but was neither unifying nor integrative; "[R]ather it sought to Castilianise, by replacing all traces of Spain's liberal past with an intolerant, anti-secular, anti-foreign Catholic conservatism."[9] Franco's supposedly "integrative" national identity was thus specifically constructed around the Castilian language and traditions:

> [T]his cultural representation provided a symbolic foundation myth for Spanish society that not only differentiated Catholic Apostolic Spain from the religious decadence of the other beyond its borders, but also provided the internal differential markers of the Castilian language and cultural traditions that excluded the internal others: laic or "un-Christian" Spain, freemasons, Catalans and Basques, from the national community.[10]

And Madrid itself was made the center of this "national community" and became the first victim of the Franco regime's authoritarianism.

In fact, nowhere in the country was Franco's authoritarian state more centralized than in Madrid. For almost forty years, "cultural traditions were curbed and local autonomy ignored."[11] As Deborah Parsons has shown, the Franco regime appropriated Madrid's local traditions, especially the city's fiesta culture and religious festivals, for the purpose of constructing a universal national culture and a commercially marketable image to be sold both at home and abroad.[12]

It was in this context that the capital increasingly came to embody the ideal of centralism for the rest of the country. While Madrid has symbolized unification and centralism to a certain degree since Philip II selected it as the seat of government in 1561, the creation of Franco's Castile-dominated state greatly solidified this perception. At the same time, the capital also served as the regime's political and administrative hub, with all the major lines of transport and communication reaching out from the capital like spokes on a wheel. As a result, when people outside of the capital referred to the national government, they said, "In Madrid it was said . . ." and, "Madrid decided that . . ." In other words, in the minds of many Spaniards, Madrid simply represented the dictatorship and vice versa.

It should come then as no surprise that many of the citizens of Madrid—particularly the newly empowered political and cultural elite of the left—desired to distance themselves and the capital from the defunct regime after 1978. But again how could they do this? What options did they have given the lasting association between the symbols of the capital and Francoism? As for contemporary models outside of Spain, there were few. The other side of the Atlantic did not provide a particularly attractive model. Many large American cities at this time were experiencing a crisis of poverty, intellectual and capital flight, and dilapidation. In Europe, the prospects were not much brighter in the late 1970s and early 1980s. The Cold War had polarized the continent's capitals into either the American or Soviet camp, leaving few viable models for Madrid's new political elite who leaned heavily toward neutrality and nonproliferation. A feeling of local pride and a desire to chart a separate course for the capital also kept the new Socialist leaders from turning exclusively to Europe. As a result, a uniquely "madrileño" sense of place was needed to remake Madrid.

So, if contemporary foreign models were not very attractive, and if Franco had left the symbols of the surrounding region of Castile unusable, why not return to Madrid's past? This, however, was not a possibility either. A return to a pre–civil war Madrid meant a return to the conflict and disorder of the Second Republic. And as Paloma Aguilar has argued, the traumatic memory of the civil war ensured that such a return to the past was not possible after 1975.[13] In Spain's "collective memory" of the 1970s, the Second Republic was associated with social disorder and violence that eventually erupted into a kind of "collective madness." In this way, the memory of the Second Republic's failure was associated with the tragic experience of the civil war. During the transition, Spaniards wanted to avoid the mistakes of the Second Republic at all costs, embracing consensus over conflict and disorder. This emphasis on peace, stability, and public order made the return to any kind of prewar society impossible. As a result, a strict revival of *lo castizo*, or Madrid's turn-of-the-century urban and typically working-class culture, was not possible either.[14]

As just mentioned, Aguilar has described how the formal transition to democracy was allowed through a collective forgetfulness, based on the recognition of collective guilt. In other words, because of the belief that both sides were to blame for the civil war, it was better to forget the terrible and shameful past rather than to point fingers at the guilty party, reopening old wounds. But, at the same time, as Michael Richards reminds us, this "'forgetting' had to be supplemented (even compensated for) by political and ideological representation, especially of the 'historic regions.'"[15] In other words, if the past had to be forgotten, and thus could not be called upon to serve as a model for the present, then new forms of democratic representation had to take its place. For the three historical regions referred to by

Richards, representation was of course based on newly developed *regional* identities. This came to be true for Madrid as well.

Thus, in part because of the need to "forget" the past and in part because of the direct association of Francoism with Spanish nationalism (discussed in the previous chapter), the process of creating a new madrileño identity had to focus on the present and be based specifically on the promotion of local—or regional—attachments. So, in contrast to other areas, regionalism in the capital did not find a basis for its argument in its history, old cultural traditions, or even the "people's will." Instead, Madrid's unique position as the former home of the dictatorship required the invention of a new "civic" identity that would break its links with authoritarianism and incorporate all of its young and heterogeneous population. In the beginning, this program—described in Chapters 3 and 4—was focused more on the physical and broad cultural transformation of the capital. However, modern symbols, specifically those related to the movida madrileña, increasingly came to play an important role in the process after 1983. As Chapter 5 demonstrates, the music, art, and general aesthetic of the movida madrileña were incorporated into the official project in order to more clearly redefine the capital and differentiate it from its recent undemocratic past. The movida's modern symbols were far more effective at fostering new feelings of pride and redefining Madrid as a contemporary, democratic region, than were traditional symbols recovered from the distant past.

PART II: OUT WITH THE OLD AND IN WITH THE NEW: A NEW SPACE IN THE CAPITAL

But need alone was insufficient to remake Madrid and create a new democratic regional identity. There had to be an opportunity at the local and regional level in order to successfully articulate a new collective identity in the capital. Why and how did such a space open up? The articulation of a regionalist project in Madrid, and the subsequent creation of a new sense of place, was made possible by several interrelated factors that came together to form both a political and institutional space within the new democratic state. The three main institutional factors included the removal of national control over the capital, the creation of an independent municipal administration after 1979, and the formation of the official region, or autonomous community, of Madrid in 1983. Furthermore, there was a lack of competing political projects from both above and below in the capital between 1979 and 1986. The combination of these institutional and political factors created the opportunity to fully remake the former home of the dictatorship.

First, the demise of the old authoritarian administration slowly brought an end to national control over Madrid. In the period before 1975, through the combination of political repression and excessive bureaucratic centralism, the Franco regime presided over the effective demise of local government in the capital. Local institutions, such as the *Ayuntamiento*, or City Hall, of Madrid, "were basically instruments for administering the policies of central government and enjoyed no real autonomy."[16] Such was the degree of control in the capital that the mayor was appointed directly by Franco himself, and not by a minister for home affairs or by a civil governor.[17] In addition, like elsewhere in Spain, local elections in the capital were strictly controlled by the country's only political party, the *Movimiento Nacional* (National Movement), which ensured that only officially sponsored candidates were elected.[18] With regard to the actual administration of the capital, the mayor of Madrid governed by simple decree according to the will of the Francoist national administration, leaving very little room for debate or compromise. The connection between the national and local was so close, in fact, that the last Spanish president appointed by Franco, Carlos Arias Navarro, had previously served as mayor of Madrid.

Despite the death of Franco in 1975, the municipal administration of Madrid remained in the control of former Franco elites until democratic elections were held four years later. During the transition to democracy, King Juan Carlos, in April 1976, named Juan de Arespacochaga to replace Miguel García Lomas, the last mayor of the Franco regime. Less than two years later, by Royal Decree, the mayor's office was given first to José Luis Álvarez in February 1978 and then later that year to Luis María Huete—who would be remembered as "the mayor of 100 days."[19] At the same time, however, the disintegration of the old regime and the installation of a new center-right government, led by Adolfo Suarez, also brought some important reforms that affected the municipal administration: the disbanding of the National Movement, the legalization of political parties, and the introduction of new electoral laws. This last reform finally cleared the way for local elections in 1979. The ultimate demise of the old central administration, coupled with the process of decentralization outlined in the 1978 Constitution, left a vacuum in which new forms of identification could be promoted by a democratically elected municipal administration and, later, by a new regional government.

The new elections of 1979 led to the second necessary factor: the establishment of an independent municipal administration. As just described, before 1979, the Ayuntamiento of Madrid was a weak, ancillary institution that had little control over the city's management and planning. The democratic elections of that year brought to power a municipal administration that self-consciously wanted to regain control of the capital from the national administration.[20] In the words of the new administration, "For the first time in 40 years, the Ayuntamiento had the awareness of being an institution *per se*, not something secondary or dependent on the government of the nation."[21] Some of the most important new figures included the lieutenant mayor, Ramón Tamames; the Concejal de Cultura (Councilor of Culture), Enrique Moral; the head of the Centro Cultural de la Villa, Antonio Gómez Rufo; the Concejal de Area de Urbanismo (Councilor of Urban Development), Jesús Espelosin; and the Concejal de Hacienda (Councilor of Finance), Joaquín Leguina.[22] While these and many other individuals and organizations helped transform the capital, Madrid's mayor, Enrique Tierno Galván, was by far the dominant force behind the project. The "old professor" ("*viejo profesor*"), as the mayor was commonly known, dominated this process because of his educational formation, political prestige, intellectual prowess, and personal charisma.[23]

Tierno Galván was not, however, a typical politician. Nor, ironically did he ever have any intentions of becoming Madrid's mayor. After years of political activism during the dictatorship, Tierno Galván would have much preferred to have been elected the new democratic president of Spain. His position as mayor was also atypical because, even though he had been involved in opposition political activity for decades, Tierno Galván had little administrative experience. In fact, it has been said that "Tierno was a man that knew almost everything, except municipal politics."[24] In addition, while other Socialist politicians at the time wore jeans and leather jackets, Tierno Galván stood out because he wore gray three-piece suits. He also stood out because of his remarkable intellectual background.[25] After a short period of internment in a concentration camp for his service in the Republican army during the Spanish Civil War, Tierno Galván received a doctorate in law and masters degrees in philosophy and literature. As a professor of law and philosophy at the universities of Murcia and Salamanca during the 1950s and 1960s, Tierno Galván translated the works of Locke, Hobbes, Hume, Montesquieu, Krause, and Wittgenstein, and published dozens of books and hundreds of articles on a variety of topics related to Western civilization.[26] However, his official academic career was cut short by his opposition political activities.

Tierno Galván's formal political activism began in the late 1950s. He was jailed in 1957 for belonging to the Asociación de la Unidad Funcional de Europa, an organization that he helped to found. In 1959, Tierno Galván joined part of a group of Socialists and Monarchists that met to plan an opposition movement to the dictatorship.[27] After being cited for participation in this conference, he taught at Princeton University for a short time, which represented the first of several periods of self-imposed exile. After returning to Spain in the early 1960s, Tierno Galván openly criticized the regime and voiced his support for student protests. Suffering increasingly from administrative persecution, he was finally arrested and expelled—along with José Luis López Aranguren, Augustín García Calvo, and Santiago Montero Díaz—from his professorship at the University of Salamanca in 1965. In the late 1960s and early 1970s, between periods of self-imposed exile in the United States, where he again taught at Princeton and Bryn Mawr, Tierno Galván practiced law and, at one point, spent another month in jail. Despite these obstacles, he continued to work toward democracy, launching the Interior Socialist Party in 1968, which later became the Partido Socialista Popular (PSP) in 1974.

While the PSP was a small but well-respected party, filled with mainly intellectuals and professionals, it had few connections to the working class. And, despite efforts to promote the party, the PSP remained on the sidelines until the mid-1970s. Increasing the party's profile during the transition,

Tierno Galván signed the Moncloa Pacts in October of 1977, along with Felipe González, Adolfo Suárez, Manuel Fraga, and Leopoldo Calvo Sotelo. However, after a disappointing showing in the national elections that year, the PSP joined with the PSOE in April 1978.[28] While this merger forced him to give up larger political aspirations, it did concede the mayorship of Madrid to the old professor in the first democratic municipal elections, a position he held to his death in 1986.[29] Faced with the task of governing madrileños, instead of all Spaniards, Tierno Galván's new administration instituted a broad state-centered program to wipe away the old dictatorship and return Madrid to democracy.

Even though the official legal reform of local government did not come until 1985 when the PSOE approved the *Ley Regulador de las Bases de Régimen Local* (Basic Law on Local Government), this process of making an active and independent Ayuntamiento in Madrid began immediately.[30] In fact, the administration's efforts to provide a full range of services could be held up as a model for the list of local services eventually enumerated in the 1985 Basic Law on Local Government. The new administration first assumed responsibility for city planning, whereas that responsibility had been formerly controlled by the national organization COPLACO, and reclaimed jurisdiction over such basic services as sanitation and the city's metro. In a symbolic move, the Ayuntamiento also regained control of the crumbling Teatro Español, traditionally under the jurisdiction of the city since the seventeenth century, after a 40-year parenthesis.[31] The creation of the independent Instituto Municipal de Deporte (Municipal Institute of Sport) was another indication that the administration no longer "understood its function as something decorative or auxiliary with respect to the state."[32] While discussed more in-depth in the next chapter, a few of the other major projects that symbolized the Ayuntamiento's new independence included the reappropriation and eventual transformation of the old Cuartel de Conde Duque into Madrid's most important cultural center, the renovation of the symbolic Puerta del Sol, and the recovery of the capital's long-neglected river, the Manzanares. For the first time since the Second Republic, the capital's local administration, instead of the national government, was able to take the initiative and create a vigorous political program that addressed all aspects of Madrid's governance and development.

The third factor that allowed for the construction of a new democratic identity in Madrid was the formal creation of the autonomous community, or *Comunidad*, of Madrid. When in March 1983 the immediate area around the city of Madrid was granted an official regional status it was, in theory, equivalent to other regions such as Catalonia and Andalusia. With the granting of its own officially designated regional boundaries, the opportunity for more than just a local or municipal madrileño identity opened up, as the newly designated Comunidad produced a broader sense of territorial distinctiveness. In this way, the creation of a new physical region helped create new regional feelings, and not the other way around. Even though it was initially a national political decision to transform the area around Madrid into an autonomous community, the new region became a useful symbol to further promote a unique madrileño identity and to distance the capital from its authoritarian past.

As just suggested, the Comunidad of Madrid was originally created out of political expediency, and not out of popular demand, or even out of a demand by the region's political elite. There was simply no loud cry for regional status before 1983. In this sense, the creation of the region was not a historical, linguistic, or geographical vindication. The making of Madrid into a region had more to do with the practical problems of completing the new autonomous framework of the nation set out by the 1978 Constitution. Madrid posed a problem for the national government because no other region in Spain wanted to deal with the city's problems or its close association with the former regime. Nor did they want to compete with its political weight. Other regions feared that the inclusion of the capital into their autonomous communities would dominate the politics of that region. At first, Madrid was to be part of the Comunidad of Castilla-La Mancha, but when representatives from that region balked at the idea of including a 500-pound gorilla (the population of Madrid was greater than the two Castillas combined) into their community, a new solution had to be found. Because the Constitution did not allow for the creation of a federal district—like Washington D.C., for example—to solve the problem of Madrid, the only other solution was the creation of a uniprovincial autonomous community.[33]

This new region of Madrid, however, had to be created practically from scratch. A triangular shaped area, just less than 8,000 square kilometers (7,995 km²), was cut out between the regions of Castilla-León and Castilla-La Mancha to provide the territory for the new region. With the capital in the center, and incorporating 183 other municipalities, the Comunidad of Madrid included mountains in the northwest and agricultural zones in the south. The process to create the autonomous region of Madrid began on June 25, 1981. The first assembly was formed on June 14, 1982, and the statute of autonomy was published on March 1, 1983.[34] To create its political framework, the Comunidad acquired responsibilities, and personnel, from the former *Diputación Provincial* of Madrid and from the central administration. However, the region lacked all manner of official symbols and institutions, and, most importantly, a sense of regional identity.

It was exactly this lack of identification that further increased the need to foster a new sense of place in the capital. And the creation of this ready-made regional structure provided Madrid's political elite, including the Comunidad's new president, Joaquín Leguina, the tools to help broaden a new madrileño sense of place into a wider regional identity. However, because the regional administration was not fully functional until the end of 1983, this institution played less of a role than Madrid's municipal government in the articulation of the capital's new democratic identity. Nevertheless, the establishment of this new autonomous community did reinforce the creation of a unique madrileño identity in and around the capital.

1979–1982: THE ORIGINS OF THE SPACE
FROM ABOVE AND BELOW

In addition to the three institutional factors just discussed, there was a political opening from both above and below that allowed for the articulation of a new madrileño identity in the capital. That opening began in 1979 and continued all the way up to 1986. First, in the period between 1979 and the end of 1982, during the administrations of Adolfo Suárez and Leopoldo Calvo Sotelo, Tierno Galván's democratically elected administration was able to articulate a new socialist program independent of those center-right transition governments on the national level (from above). In this early period, the disintegration of a popular citizen movement in Madrid also cleared the way (from below) for a new regionalist project directed from the municipal level.

Later, after 1982, Madrid's local political elite continued to chart an independent course, even after the PSOE's landslide election victory in the general elections of that year. Despite their formal incorporation into the PSOE in 1978, Tierno Galván and his followers were never fully integrated into Spain's dominant Socialist party, thus leaving the local administration of Madrid free to pursue a separate program between 1982 and 1986. In addition, national institutions, such as the Ministry of Culture, exerted little influence over the creation of new forms of identity in the capital, even under the administration of Felipe González.

One of the main reasons why the project in Madrid initially succeeded was because of the lack of attention paid to the capital from above in the early years of Tierno Galván's administration. Specifically, there was no coherent program of official nationalism directed toward Madrid during this period. As a result, Madrid's local political elite had more room to pursue a regionalist agenda.

While Adolfo Suárez's slowly deteriorating center-right party, the Unión de Centro Democrático (UCD), was busy orchestrating Spain's political transition to democracy, Socialists won the majority of Ayuntamientos across the country in the municipal election of 1979. In general, these newly elected local governments of the left, the first of their kind since the Second Republic, struck out on a course of reform and renovation that was more radical than the negotiated reform being articulated on the national level. At the same time, and in sharp contrast to the Franco regime, the transition governments of Adolfo Suárez and, later, Leopoldo Calvo Sotelo were too preoccupied with ensuring the stable political transition from dictatorship to democracy to pay much attention to the specific management of Madrid. In addition, it was too early in the process of the transition to democracy for either of the two new moderate center-right governments to articulate any kind of new democratic national identity for the country as a whole or specifically for the capital. This lack of a coherent program from above first opened the space that allowed Madrid's political elite to freely undertake a program to reinvent Madrid outside of a national agenda.

In addition to benefiting from the lack of attention from above, Tierno Galván's program to transform Madrid also initially benefited from a lack of a coherent project articulated from below. Like many large urban areas in Spain during the mid-1970s, the region of Madrid saw an increase of popular mobilization and the consolidation of a diverse citizen movement built around local neighborhood associations. As described further in the next chapter, the citizen movement in the capital represented an alternative model of democracy based on direct political action by ordinary citizens. However, after 1979, this grassroots movement entered into a period of crisis.

To date, Manuel Castells has offered the most detailed examination of grassroots mobilization in Madrid. In his study, Castells offers the argument that Madrid's citizen movement was instrumental in bringing about the end of the Franco regime and in initiating significant urban change in Madrid immediately following the dictatorship. However, Castells also describes the decline of the movement, beginning first in 1977 and accelerating after 1979. Generally speaking, Castells argues that the new formal political structures of democracy, such as political parties and elections, pushed the grassroots movement aside after 1979.[35] As a result, Madrid's citizen movement, which had previously sought changes in the areas of housing, clean water, green spaces, public health, popular celebrations, schooling, and transportation, entered into a period of rapid decline. Echoing Castells, Angel del Rio argued in 1989 that, with many of its leaders in positions of responsibility in the new municipal government and with the domination of a handful of political parties in Madrid, "the citizen's movement entered into one of the most escalating [*galopantes*] crises of its short history."[36] In fact, it was a crisis from which the movement never recovered, opening the way for the creation of new forms of association and identification in the capital.

In this way, the task of articulating a new regionalism project from the level of the Ayuntamiento was made easier by the absence of grassroots interests competing from below. Thus, after 1979, Madrid's new political elite did not have to contend with competing projects from either the grassroots level or from the center-right national administration, as just discussed. Stated another way, there was a unique political space in the capital, created by an opening from both above and below, in which a new regional identity could be constructed by Madrid's local political elite. And, despite the Socialists' victory in the national elections of November 1982, the capital's local administration, along with Madrid's newly created regional government, was able to continue the promotion of a separate madrileño identity in the capital up until 1986 because of an ongoing split between Tierno Galván and the national leadership of the PSOE.

1982–1986: As Close as Oil and Water: Madrid's Political Elite and the National PSOE

With the PSOE's resounding national election victory in 1982, it would be logical to expect a high degree of cooperation between the Socialists on the national level and the Socialist administrations (municipal and regional) of Madrid, thus bringing an end to the capital's independence from above. Even one of the most knowledgeable observers of Madrid, Bernard Bessière, has assumed that the three layers of socialist administration in the capital were working together during this period for a common goal in the capital: the revitalization of Madrid.[37] Bessière has argued that "political harmony" characterized "State-Comunidad-Ayuntamiento relations over the length of the decade."[38] This, however, was not the case.

While the capital was home to all three levels of political power, there was very little cooperation or coordination between the Socialist administrations of Madrid and the Socialist central administration between 1982 and 1986. The national leaders of the PSOE may have resided in Madrid but they operated on a different level and addressed issues and problems facing the country as a whole, most specifically the country's high level of unemployment. In addition, coming from southern Spain, the national political leadership was more preoccupied with Andalusia than with the capital itself, at least before 1986. Madrid's link to the centralism and oppression of the Franco regime may have also produced an initial reluctance by Felipe González and Alfonso Guerra to associate too closely with the capital. Furthermore, the prevalence of centralist ideology within the PSOE made the party's leadership generally more dismissive of local government. Finally, and most importantly, the lack of coordination between the PSOE's national political leadership and Madrid's political elite was the result of Tierno Galván's failure to be fully integrated into the PSOE. While Spain's dominant Socialist party usually accepted no dissent within its ranks, Tierno Galván represented one important exception. The Spanish historian Santos Juliá stresses that the mayor's criticism and dissent was unusual in a "party that was disciplined and unified and in which any critical voices were swallowed up in the self-satisfaction of the majority."[39]

Even though Tierno Galván's old party, the PSP, and the PSOE originally merged in 1978, the mayor and his followers were never fully incorporated into the fold of the PSOE. Many of the top officials of Tierno Galván's administration, including Enrique Moral and Antonio Gómez Rufo came from the former PSP. In many ways, Tierno Galván and Madrid's other local political elite represented a party within a party during the first half of the 1980s. In fact, while Tierno Galván never publicly expressed regret for the integration of his party into the PSOE, the differences between Madrid's mayor and the two leaders of the PSOE, González and Guerra, were nonetheless an open secret almost from the beginning of the unification in 1978.[40] The fundamental split between Tierno Galván and the national leadership of the PSOE first occurred in 1979 when most of the Marxist ideology was purged from the PSOE's political platform in favor of a more pragmatic program in line with Europe's other Socialist parties, including François Mitterrand's in France, Willy Brandt's in West Germany, and Bettino Craxi's in Italy.[41] Tierno Galván strongly disagreed with the dropping of Marxism from the PSOE's political platform and both publicly and privately criticized the party's leadership for choosing political expediency over ideological loyalty.[42] Such criticism led to Tierno Galván's marginalization from the internal decision-making process within the PSOE after 1979, and even led to the threat of official censure.[43]

In part because of the party's official abandonment of Marxist ideology and Tierno Galván's marginalization within the PSOE, the local administration in Madrid was able to independently present a program of renovation and reform that remained more faithful to socialist principles and to the central notion of popular participation. Even as the PSOE's national political leadership increasingly shifted to the right, more so González than Guerra, Tierno Galván remained firmly on the left. In addition, the mayor also put the interests of Madrid before the political demands of his party that controlled the national government. For example, beginning in 1979, the mayor chose to form a governing pact with the Spanish Communist Party (PCE) instead of with the UCD, in spite of the center-right party's willingness to work with his administration.[44] Tierno Galván even designated the Communist leader Ramón Tamames to serve as his first lieutenant following the first municipal elections in 1979. When asked about the collaboration between both parties, Tierno Galván responded, "[W]e have worked together without a moment of disagreement. It has been an *Ayuntamiento* equally [*a la par*] Socialist and Communist, although with a Socialist majority."[45] This willingness to work with the far left, particularly with the Communists, was simply never displayed by the national PSOE.[46]

Even after the PSOE's overwhelming national election victory in 1982, Madrid's independent path remained unaltered. In fact, Tierno Galván openly announced in October 1982 that his administration would remain independent from the newly elected Socialist government on the national level.[47] The mayor almost seemed to delight in his independence within the PSOE during this period. He continually offered what he considered to be constructive criticism of his own party, serving as a kind of voice of conscience of the PSOE. Tierno Galván believed that the PSOE's shift to the right had created "great contradictions within it."[48] Specifically he felt that the party's increasingly open embrace of neoliberal economic policies was not doing enough to help workers and the lower classes. For Madrid's mayor, the promotion of economic development at the cost of higher unemployment stood as an obvious contradiction within a Socialist government. Equally condemning, Tierno Galván frequently maintained, "[T]he PSOE is left empty of content [*vacío de contenidos*]."[49] In other words, political and economic reforms were solely based on pragmatism rather than on real Socialist ideology. The old professor even went so far as to accuse his own party of hypocrisy; he criticized the PSOE for not being open to criticism when the party itself had fought for the right to criticize the former regime when it had been the opposition.

While not to the same degree as his counterpart in the Ayuntamiento, Joaquín Leguina also set the regional government on an independent course after the creation of the Comunidad of Madrid in 1983. At the same time, there was also an important link of continuity between the municipal administration and the new regional government, as many of the new regional administrators came from the Ayuntamiento of Madrid. For instance, Joaquín Leguina served as the Councilor of Finance in Tierno Galván's administration before being elected president of the new Comunidad in 1983. Such connections ensured that the local and the regional administrations shared many of the same policies and goals, including the desire to maintain a degree of autonomy from the national PSOE.

Despite the collaboration necessary to complete the transfer of responsibilities from the central administration to the newly-created regional administration, Leguina constantly sought the expansion of administrative power and financial resources for the Comunidad of Madrid. Furthermore, the first president of the new Comunidad was preoccupied with separating both the abstract notion of "Madrid" and the actual political direction of the capital from that of the national administration. In fact, for Leguina, one of the most important objectives of the region of Madrid was to "end the false myth of *madrileño* centralism, which is confused, or that some want to confuse, with the repressive centralism imposed by the previous regime."[50] By distancing the new region from "the national," Leguina wanted to show that the capital had been the victim of centralism and not its perpetrator: "[I]n the last few years [with the development of the autonomous community of Madrid] it has been recognized that the first victims of centralism were the people of Madrid."[51] In other words, the granting of an official regional status to Madrid helped demonstrate that the capital was not inherently linked to centralism; rather, centralism was a product of the previous regime. It also showed that the capital, and its immediate surroundings, was just like any other part of Spain, and thus worthy of the same rights and responsibilities.

According to Leguina, Madrid deserved an independent regional government with the same level of autonomy and responsibility as the other regions, "not out of a desire to emulate the rest [of the Comunidades]," but to provide the citizens of Madrid the same level of representation.[52] Separate representation, and the possibility of creating a distinct regional identity, was a question of "civil rights."[53] In other words, all citizens of Spain, even those falsely perceived as responsible for centralism and repression, deserved equal representation on the regional level. And the Comunidad of Madrid would be able to respond to the region's problems and necessities more efficiently and effectively than the national government. From this perspective, it was only fair that the residents of Madrid were afforded that kind of separate representation as well.

Unique regional representation for Madrid, along with an independent political program, was also justified by the idea that the region of Madrid constituted a distinct group of people. The regional administration maintained that the residents shared a common history, suffering together through the Franco regime, and held many of the same needs and desires. It was also believed that the people of Madrid shared common characteristics. According to Leguina, madrileños represented a region that was "cultured, united, [and] tolerant."[54] In this way, Madrid was unique because it was open to people from all places, yet retained its own distinct identity. Openness and the incorporation of others did not deny a distinctive regional identity; instead, they were part of its very essence. Such distinctiveness was exactly the reason why the residents of Madrid deserved regional representation and a political program that was not administered strictly from the national level.

Accordingly, the focus of the new regional government was not on the national issues, but on the unique problems, circumstances, necessities, and issues of the region. This led to a constant struggle between the regional administration and the central government for greater autonomy, funding, and political freedoms. And, once again, even though both the regional and national administrations were part of the same Socialist party—the PSOE—there was not a close working relationship between Joaquín Leguina and the national leaders at Moncloa. In fact, the president of the Comunidad was not afraid of criticizing the national political leadership, frequently complaining of the central administration's discrimination against Madrid and favoritism toward *other* autonomous communities, such as Catalonia.[55] In short, like the new municipal administration, the regional government identified exclusively with the region of Madrid and worked to differentiate itself from the national administration whenever possible.

CONCLUSION

After the experience of the dictatorship there was an acute need to redefine the capital. In fact, as the former home of centralism and repression, Madrid was probably the region most closely associated with the undemocratic past. However, between 1979 and 1986, there was more than just the need to transform the way madrileños perceived themselves; there was also the opportunity. A complex set of factors created both the new institutions and the political space necessary for the articulation of a new regional identity project. While there was an opening from both above and below after 1979, the distance between both the local and regional administrations and the national administration was especially important for developing a regionalist project in the official capital of Spain.

This gap between Madrid's local political elite and the national PSOE was underscored particularly well at the time of the mayor's death. Highlighting Tierno Galván's reputation for dissent and his ideological consistency, opposition leader Manuel Fraga said of the old professor at the time of his funeral: "He maintained the ideological tradition of the left in Spain, at a moment in which the majority of Socialists oriented themselves toward technocratic positions."[56] In fact, when Tierno Galván died in 1986, he was one of the few active politicians who openly labeled himself a Marxist. While the mayor's project in the capital did not represent a classic Marxist, or even Socialist, revolution, such a designation did clearly demonstrate his distance from the national leadership of the PSOE. The great divide between Tierno

Galván and the rest of the PSOE was summed up at the time in an editorial in Spain's leading newspaper, *El País*:

> While those Socialists [the national PSOE] installed in the central government and in the Congress carried out a political program for the most part enigmatic and closed, Tierno gave explanations to whoever asked for them, never hid his intentions, gave explanations about his most unpopular decisions, and maintained around him complete freedom of opinion about the divine and the human . . . Tierno preserved his old habits, did not change his form of living, and continued breathing with normalcy the citizen air [*aire ciudadano*].[57]

In addition, the argument was made that even the residents of Madrid recognized the separation that existed between Tierno Galván and the PSOE:

> It is possible that the emotional farewell by *madrileños* to the "old professor" contained a nostalgic recollection of other more transparent times and a veiled rebuke to other Socialists who also used to come out to the streets, shared the problems of the people, and were capable of speaking the same language as their voters.[58]

Such comments at the time of Tierno Galván's death reflected the space— both political and institutional—that Madrid's political elite enjoyed during the first half of the decade. It was in this space that a regionalist project could more easily be promoted and new identifications could be formed. The following chapter details how an independent regional project was specifically designed to create a new democratic sense of place and overcome Madrid's authoritarian past by promoting civic, rather than ethnic, affiliations. The eventual result was a fundamental change in the way madrileños identified with each other and with the place they lived.

CHAPTER 3

FROM A "FORTRESS" TO A "PLAZA": THE TRANSFORMATION OF MADRID AND THE FORMATION OF A NEW CIVIC IDENTITY

By all accounts, between 1979 and 1986, Madrid transformed from the gray and lifeless former home of the dictatorship to an open and proud place that was known around the world for its vibrancy. Part of the reason why Madrid's transformation stands out is because it was so complete. The capital's parks, monuments, and historical buildings were cleaned and repaired, and its once empty streets were filled with festivals, parades, footraces, open-air theatres, and concerts. Painters, singers, theatre companies, and artists from around the world came to Madrid to exhibit their work or to perform. The residents of Madrid were also transformed from subjects of the dictatorship into active participants, engaging in all manner of social activities around the clock and creating traffic jams at 3:00 a.m. Most importantly, madrileños were on their way to becoming democratic citizens, with a greater appreciation for government institutions and with a closer connection to each other and to the place in which they lived. In other words, Spain's democratic transition had been peacefully consolidated, at least in the center.

In no way, however, was this transformation somehow predestined or the natural outcome of the formal political transition to democracy executed between 1975 and 1978. Instead, change in the capital was the result of a conscious effort by Madrid's democratically elected political elite to distance the capital from its authoritarian past and create a new collective identity for all madrileños. Taking advantage of both the need and the political and institutional space (discussed in the previous chapter), the local governments purposely instituted an ambitious program to remake Madrid and renovate the "signs of identity" of madrileños.[1] As Socialists who believed in reason, progress, and a utopic destiny, Madrid's political elite went about the project like a group of enlightened *philosophes*. They held conferences to debate the issues, they drew up plans, they revised the plans, and they acted rationally and methodically. But they also acted with a decisiveness and intensity that came from an unquestioned faith in reason and progress. The results were remarkable by any standard: the physical and cultural transformation of the largest city in Spain and its inhabitants in less than a decade. After first describing the political and philosophical ideals behind Madrid's transformation, the majority of this chapter analyzes that change as a project to create an inclusive "civic" identity. Specifically, Madrid's political elite promoted civic pride, civic education, civic confidence, and civic participation to forge a common sense of place and a feeling of democratic community among all madrileños.

POLITICAL AND PHILOSOPHICAL FOUNDATIONS: A DIFFERENT KIND OF "CULTURAL REVOLUTION"

Like most efforts to forge a new common identity, the project in Madrid was achieved in opposition to some conscious "other." While the other is usually described in spatial terms, "us" located here versus "them" located over there, the other for Madrid was a temporal matter. Madrid's other was Madrid itself. Specifically, it was the gray, repressed capital under the Franco regime that served as the object against which a new Madrid was defined. This process, then, did not involve the creation of a new or an "invented" entity, as is often described in the work on collective memory.[2] Instead the very recent experience of the dictatorship left a clear impression of what life was like in the capital under the authoritarian regime. It was this impression that was employed as the other. The project to transform Madrid was thus specifically defined against Franco's swollen and dysfunctional capital: where there had been centralization, there would be decentralization and democracy; where there had been a "culture of evasion," there would be civic participation; where there had been cultural elitism, there would be a genuine popular culture; where there had been intolerance, there would be openness; and where there had been an officially imposed national identity, there would be a new madrileño sense of place.

In order to completely wipe away the old dictatorship and create a new democratic Madrid, a complete overhaul of the capital was necessary. The wide-ranging project to transform Madrid included urban renewal and the physical transformation of Madrid, the renovation of the capital's historical and cultural patrimony, reform of the city's administration, and a broadly defined renewal of Madrid's culture. More specifically, the entire city was cleaned from top to bottom. Symbolic monuments, such as the Puerta del Sol, were restored. The capital's long-neglected river was cleaned and populated with wildlife. Streets and boulevards were renamed. Major roadways were rerouted. New museums, athletic centers, and cultural centers were opened. Virtually every act of artistic expression was officially supported. Ordinary madrileños returned to the streets to participate in newly inaugurated open-air theaters and movies, footraces, bicycle festivals, and neighborhood fiestas. Madrid's books were balanced for the first time in the capital's recent history. City services were automated and computerized. Every city block was even scrutinized and, if necessary, a plan of restoration was created. The combination of these changes altered the physical landscape of the capital and, more importantly, changed the way Madrid's residents from all walks of life understood themselves and their relationship to the capital.

While it is clear that Madrid's political elite, led by Enrique Tierno Galván, undertook an ambitious plan to transform the capital between 1979 and 1986, the ideology behind that plan is not quite as obvious. In fact, at the time of his death, the mayor's longtime friend and colleague, José Luis López Aranguren, commented, "[N]either myself, nor perhaps anyone, sufficiently knew a personality like him, as complex, ironic and, in its depths, hidden [oculto]."³ Rather than representing any single ideology, Tierno Galván's program is best understood as a combination of often contradictory lines of leftist political and philosophical thought: utopianism, libertarianism, Marxism, elitism, and populism. Overall, however, the program is probably best defined by Tierno Galván's unwavering belief in an egalitarian utopia, which for him symbolized peace, liberty, and equality. When asked about his belief in a Marxist utopia in 1979, Tierno Galván responded:

> I believe that if we lose our utopic horizon we have lost everything. What moves me and many other companions is that we are ants that carry our grain of sand to the mountain of progress, in whose summit we see peace, liberty, and equality. If we get rid of the conviction that we are going to make this mountain, which direction are we going to carry our grain of sand?⁴

However, because of the consensual settlement of the transition, this utopia was not going to be reached through a classic political Marxist revolution. Nor was it going to happen through an entirely state-centered project, as popular participation was part of the plan as well. Instead, Tierno Galván wanted to set in motion a kind of "cultural revolution" to transform both the capital and its residents.

This cultural revolution, however, had nothing to do with Chairman Mao in China. Rather, it represented the desire to voluntarily transform society's existing set of values in order to change the system and, ultimately, to change madrileños themselves.⁵ In this way, Tierno Galván's cultural revolution did not rely on formal politics. Nor did the discourse of the administration emphasize the terms "utopia" or "revolution." Instead the program—which appeared apolitical on the surface—sought to change society's underlying values and attitudes through new forms of participation and civic education. In the words of one of its participants, Antonio Gómez Rufo, this change was supposed to replace "quantification with qualification, competitiveness with solidarity, and hypocrisy with sincerity."⁶ Within the specific context of the capital, that meant a transformation from passivity to activity, from spectatorship to participation, and from a state monologue to a dialogue.

The end result would be a change in individual and collective habits that would secure the transition to democracy and ultimately lead to greater peace, liberty, and equality.

While Tierno Galván never formally laid out his idea for this cultural revolution in a political tract, he did summarize the relationship between culture, participation, and democracy in a 1983 interview with *El País*. When asked what his dream for Madrid that guided the local administration was, Tierno Galván responded:

> The main thread has been, above all, to foment culture as much in the meaning of culture as spectacle as in the academic meaning of culture . . . understanding both meanings of culture as something external to us, what surrounds us, everything is culture. A hoe is culture because man made it in order to try to dominate the world, and our own ideas are culture.[7]

As was usually the case in his interviews and speeches, Tierno Galván employs both meanings of the word "culture" here. First, "culture as spectacle" refers to the more traditional artistic meaning of the term. Second, "the academic meaning of culture" suggests the word's broader anthropological definition.[8] Based on this dual definition of the term, Tierno Galván sought an all-encompassing program of "cultural" change in order to transform—or perhaps more accurately, to enlighten—madrileños:

> To foment culture is to foment the conscience and to foment the conscience is to foment education. In that way, we have taken a position that I would say in many cases has been enlightened [*ilustrada*] . . . that corresponds more to the Enlightenment than to the Baroque. We have tried to enlighten the people, to cultivate the people, we enlighten and cultivate ourselves in that we are people, and in this sense we have made an enlightenment without despotism.[9]

Using the dual definition of culture, the mayor logically understood that all aspects of the program to remake Madrid contributed to this cultural revolution or transformation. In fact, the mayor claimed, "A new facility, a new recreation center, new gardens, more services, this is enlightenment [*ilustración*], this contributes to culture."[10] And, as seen in the next chapter, "culture as spectacle"—i.e., expositions, popular festivals, open-air theatre, and other artistic activities that promoted collective encounters and popular participation—came to play a particularly important role in Madrid's transformation. Summing up the project, Tierno Galván concluded the *El País* interview with: "Culture and participation have been the basic ideas from which I have tried to guide the *Ayuntamiento*."[11]

How can this emphasis on participation through cultural promotion be understood? Tierno Galván's desire for more popular participation partially reflected a wider shift in European Socialist political thought during the 1970s away from classic Marxism and toward greater mobilization and active citizenship. For example, as discussed in the previous chapter, in the period just prior to Madrid's first democratic elections, the capital had seen the development of a strong grass-roots movement that symbolized such an alternative model of radical democracy. Clearly, however, Tierno Galván's state-centered project did not represent a totally decentralized, or bottom up, model of democracy. Even though the mayor's project focused on greater civic participation, it was not dictated exclusively by grass-roots input. In other words, Tierno Galván's program represented a shift toward greater mobilization, but it did not symbolize the continuation of a radical democratic alternative either, symbolized by the earlier citizen movement.[12]

The reliance on more of a state-centered project stemmed, in part, from a feeling of paternalism, or perhaps "professorialism," within the administration. Because of the absence of civic involvement and participation under the dictatorship, Tierno Galván believed madrileños were a "young" people in need of an education. In his first official statement after taking office in April 1979, Tierno Galván announced: "*[M]adrileños* constitute a young people [*pueblo*], made up of young people who are young and of old people who are young, and this youth is defined above all by a desire for knowledge."[13] To fill this desire, Tierno Galván and the other members of the administration conceived of an Ayuntamiento that was, "in a certain sense, an institution that has a pedagogical function."[14] In the way all teachers believe they can shape and transform their students into something better, Tierno Galván hoped to do the same for the citizens of Madrid. Thus, in addition to the administration acting as a kind of "vanguard" for the capital, Madrid also became Tierno Galván's own personal classroom. He had been, after all, a professor for most of his professional life. However, there were few formal lectures on democratic political principles. Nor did the mayor engage in the fiery political rhetoric that characterized many of the exchanges between the PSOE and the conservative Alianza Popular (AP) in the 1980s, particularly between Manuel Fraga and Alfonso Guerra. Instead, the administration presented a nonconfrontational civic education.[15] The mayor's *Bandos*, written proclamations posted around the city, were to be the textbooks, and the lessons were to include: civic pride, civic education, civic confidence, and civic participation. Together with the broad cultural transformation just described, these lessons would offer madrileños a new sense of place based on a shared commitment to where they lived—Madrid. In this way, and this is a key point, the main purpose of creating a new regional identity in the capital was not the vindication of local linguistic, cultural, or historic traditions, but rather to provide madrileños with a new democratic identity and promote new democratic habits after the experience of the dictatorship.

As discussed in the previous chapter, this new identity had to fit within the framework of the 1978 Constitution and within the formal political transition mediated from above. Thus, in addition to a feeling of professorialism, the project to transform Madrid also came in the form of a top-down model because of the limitations of the consensual transition to democracy. In fact, Tierno Galván was himself a member of the transition elite, signing the Moncloa Pacts in October 1977, which represented the broad-based consensual effort to socially and economically stabilize the country so the political transition could continue. In addition, although not officially a member of the commission designated by the Congress to create the 1978 Constitution, Tierno Galván also wrote the new Constitution's Preamble.[16] As a member of the transition's political elite, Tierno Galván was well aware of the need for coexistence and "consensual unity": "This [transformation of Madrid] has to be done in the context of democratic coexistence, from there we will have increased popular confidence and participation."[17] In other words, political mobilization and polarization, which could jeopardize the democratic transition negotiated from above, could not be part of the program to transform the capital.

It is important to note that while the political and philosophy ideals behind the transformation of Madrid did not represent a radical or direct model of democracy, they also did not represent—as the second half of the previous quote suggests—the model of complete demobilization that eventually came to dominate Spain's democratization process in the second half of the 1980s either. As described in the previous chapter, after 1982 the national leadership of the PSOE increasingly followed another European Socialist trend and pursued a centralized model of democracy that led toward neoliberalism and decreased mobilization. This model emphasized the election of representatives who would protect citizens, rather than empowering them. As a result, Spain's democratic consolidation came to be characterized by a more formal definition of democracy, stressing political parties and the election of representatives, rather than direct participation. In contrast, Tierno Galván offered an alternative form of participatory democracy based not on the traditional model of partisan politics or political mobilization, but on cultural mobilization. Thus, rather than demobilize the capital's residents to ensure political stability and economic growth, Madrid's local political elite wanted to *expand* opportunities for collective encounters and popular participation through such cultural initiatives as the restoration of Madrid's public festivals and the sponsorship of art expositions. As Chapter 4 demonstrates, both the local and regional administrations invested heavily in Madrid's cultural infrastructure—building new libraries, recreation centers, and museums— and sponsored a wide range of specifically "madrileño" cultural activities in order to promote greater popular participation in the capital. While this participation, of course, privileged the cultural over the political, it also made the project a unique alternative in this regard. This leads to a second key point: at a time when many people on both the left and the right feared mass political mobilization, broad cultural participation offered another path to civic activity and engagement. The mayor believed that such an alternative democratic model would not only secure the consensus-driven transition to democracy in the present, but also ensure the continuation of democracy in the future by changing society's underlying attitudes and behaviors. And while not everyone in the capital directly supported the new democratic administrations, the project to transform Madrid was purposely designed to appeal to and affect all madrileños.

Changes such as the restoration of a public monument, the reinstatement of a formerly banned public festival, or the cleaning of a neighborhood park transcended differences based on class, age, and political loyalties. In other words, change was not limited to, or directed at, a small percentage of the population. Instead, Madrid's renovation was meant to benefit and transform everyone, and to make them feel part of a common project. And because of the nonconfrontational approach, the transformation of Madrid was often perceived as apolitical. As a result, the possibility of affecting residents across the political spectrum, including those on the right, was greater. This desire to transform the capital in a way that would specifically include all madrileños was poetically summed up by Madrid's mayor in 1983: "Municipalities were fortresses. We dismantled those fortresses, we filled in the moats, lowered the drawbridges, destroyed the walls, and where there had been a fortress, today there is a plaza in which we all join together in order to talk."[18]

Creating a New Civic Identity in the Capital

More than a physical transformation, the rest of this chapter shows that the effort to transform Madrid from an authoritarian "fortress" to a democratic "plaza" actually represented the creation of a new "imagined community" in the capital.[19] And even though Madrid's transformation employed both culture, which is often associated with the formation of ethnic identities, and the idea of equal "citizenship," which can ultimately be guaranteed only by a nation, the project to create a specific madrileño sense of place between 1979 and 1986 is best understood as an effort to include all residents within an inclusive "civic," rather than an exclusive "ethnic," regional identity.

But what exactly is the difference between a civic identity and an ethnic identity? And why is that difference important in the case of Madrid? On the one hand, civic identity, or civic nationalism, offers "a vision of a community of equal citizens."[20] In the case of a nation such as France in the early nineteenth century, a civic national identity stemmed from a concept of popular sovereignty that was based on the "voluntary association of equal and free citizens, who enjoyed membership of the community by virtue of their residence on national soil, irrespective of their ethnic origins or religious beliefs."[21] Thus, free from attachments based on culture or race, civic nationalism creates an "open, voluntaristic community based on rational choice."[22] In short, the fundamental logic of a civic identity is universal inclusiveness. On the other hand, ethnic identity, or ethnic nationalism, offers "a vision of a community united by a belief in common ancestry and ethno-cultural sameness."[23] Between 1870 and 1914, and again at the end of the twentieth century, ethnic nationalisms forged collective identities and community bonds through "seemingly objective qualities, such as history, language and culture and often, by connotation, blood ties."[24] In other words, ethnic nationalism is founded on exclusive cultural unity, where the basis of exclusion is most often ethnicity: ancestry, language, religion, race, or "cultural distinctiveness." Ethnic identities have also been much more common over the past 200 years.

In almost all of the examples from the late twentieth century, whether in Armenia, the former Yugoslavia, Quebec, or post-communist Eastern Europe, ethnic, rather than civic, nationalism has been used to construct new national or subnational collective identities.[25] The same has been true for Spain as well. For example, in the Basque Country, Basque nationalism has been based on a unique language and on the exclusive notions of ethnic and even racial superiority.[26] In Catalonia, Catalan nationalism has been based on a distinctive language and the concept of a shared historical and cultural past. Madrid, however, was different. In contrast to these other examples, the project in the capital was specifically designed to promote inclusion and openness.

In Madrid there was no insistence on religious particularism, on ethnic or racial distinctiveness, or on a shared cultural past. In part because of the lack of a common ethnicity, a distinctive language, and a reclaimable past, the creation of a new democratic identity in Madrid had to be as open as possible. In addition, Madrid's large immigrant population—with more than half of all residents born in other regions—and the capital's heterogeneous mix of urban inhabitants further created the need for an inclusive form of identity. Thus, rather than focusing on ethnic belonging, the project to transform Madrid was designed to promote a feeling of voluntary, civic attachment. More specifically, the project was based on the idea of creating equal and free citizens, who enjoyed membership in the community by virtue of their residence in the capital, irrespective of their ethnicity, place of birth, or traditional cultural practices. In this way the effort to create a new collective identity in Madrid relied more on the French-inspired ideal of political citizenship than on the exclusiveness of culture or ethnicity. But, of course, any new identity in the capital could not be tied strictly to the notion of "citizenship," as citizenship can only be guaranteed by the nation. Instead, Madrid's new sense of place stressed voluntary residence in the capital and the acceptance of a set of democratic values, such as active participation and peaceful coexistence. In addition, the program to transform the capital promoted social integration and a shared commitment to, and pride in, Madrid's new democratic institutions, which further connected residents to the place in which they lived. The result was a unique civic identity that was open to everyone who resided in the capital.

The desire to create a new civic identity that included all of Madrid's residents was made clear at the time by both the local and regional administrations. In a guide to the capital, published by the Ayuntamiento in 1982, Madrid is described as "one of the most hospitable cities that can be encountered," welcoming people from "every corner of the country."[27] According to the text, coming from another part of the country "does not impede someone from being as *madrileño* as someone whose roots can be traced back to the founding of the capital."[28] In this way, identification with the capital is not defined by birth or ethnicity, but by the voluntary decision to reside in Madrid. Inclusion within the regional identity of Madrid was thus a matter of residence: "[Madrid is] a human conglomerate for which being born in the capital is the least important part of being *madrileño*."[29] The emphasis on inclusion, rather than exclusion, is further seen through such assertions as: "[I]t is necessary to say that, once in Madrid, no one is an outsider."[30] Exactly the same sentiment is found in a book sponsored by the Comunidad of Madrid in 1984, *Madrid es más que Madrid*. Promoting the idea that the region of Madrid was open to everyone, the book explains: "It is not necessary to be a child of Madrid to be a *madrileño* . . . no one denies this title to those who arrived here from someplace else."[31]

In a special issue of the *Revista de Occidente* dedicated to Madrid in 1983, Joaquín Leguina directly addressed the issue of the identity of the Comunidad of Madrid. For the president of the Comunidad, the region represented, above all, "an open society and a melting pot [*crisol*]."[32] This same feeling was echoed by others in the regional administration. For example, in a text presented to the Assembly of Madrid in September 1983, the Consejero de Cultura y Deporte (Head of Sports and Culture) of the Comunidad of Madrid, José Luis García Alonso, explained that Madrid's identity was unique because it was the product of a variety of influences. He explained:

> [C]ultural identity can be understood as a process, as an objective, and in this case, it is possible to speak of an identity of Madrid, constituted, fundamentally, as a cultural synthesis, as a catalyst of a wide series of cultural values from very distinct origins.[33]

In other words, the capital's cultural and social diversity produced a unique identity that was more "universal" than "exclusionary."[34] According to García Alonso, this identity was to be fostered through "the promotion of the character of a melting pot of cultures (*crisol de culturas*)."[35]

In addition to including residents from diverse cultural and geographical backgrounds, a wide spectrum of political affiliations was also to be included in this new "open" Madrid. In his first official address as mayor, Tierno Galván announced: "[T]he *Ayuntamiento* is not a parliament. There is going to be respect for all of the political opinions that are going to make up the municipal corporation. We have to obtain a better Madrid, forgetting our political militancy."[36] Beyond political inclusiveness, even Madrid's most marginalized residents were to be included in the project to create an inclusive civic identity. When Tierno Galván visited the prison of Carabanchel in June 1985, he announced: "[E]ven though you are prisoners, you have not lost your status as residents of Madrid."[37] Along with prisoners, Madrid's traditionally marginalized gypsies also were welcomed as an important part of the capital's community.[38]

Age was not a factor either. Both Madrid's oldest and youngest residents were to be included in this new vision of Madrid. Hoping to incorporate Madrid's older residents into society, Tierno Galván wrote in 1982:

> It makes me profoundly sad to see buses filled with old people. I like to see the oldest people with the youngest, grandparents with children and with adults. It is not necessary to segregate the elderly . . . retirees should be an active class, they should intervene in society because their experience is very valuable.[39]

Young people were equally as valued because, more than any other segment of the population, they represented the capital's democratic future. Madrid's political elite, and especially Tierno Galván, appreciated their ability to directly contribute to the creation of a new Madrid: "We are surprised by the youth that understand one another, that help one another, that is united, [and] that is giving lessons to grown ups."[40] As a result, Madrid's youth were to be genuinely included in the project to redefine a new identity for the capital: "We don't deceive the youth, we don't teach them the road to success but the one of the ideal, of understanding, of unity and solidarity, and they will know to say to the dictators and to the plunderers that their mandate has ended because [Madrid's] young people are standing proud."[41] In sum, rather than basing inclusion on place of birth, ethnicity, political affiliation, or age, all madrileños were to be included within a new civic identity based primarily on the notion of voluntary residence, solidarity, and equal "citizenship."

The specific framework for this inclusive regional identity lay in the promotion of a series of civic values that could draw all residents into a common project. In fact, the promotion of inclusive and participatory civic values is one of the most effective means by which a cohesive democratic identity can be created. Nurturing civic pride, restoring civic trust, improving civic education, and fostering civic participation all function independently of cultural difference, language, age, class, place of birth, or political affiliation. In other words, the promotion of these four civic values was designed to allow all madrileños to "imagine" themselves as part of a new democratic community. And it was these four values that were at the heart of the ambitious project to transform Madrid.

1. PLANNING A CITY TO BE PROUD OF

As seen in the previous chapter, Madrid had lost much of its appeal and unique personality during the dictatorship. To overcome the past and improve the quality of life in the capital, the local administration began by deliberately working to restore equality between all residents by modernizing the capital and reequilibrating its services between the various districts. Modernization and revitalization did not mean starting entirely from scratch. Instead, the best parts of the city were to be preserved in order to build a better Madrid in the future. Most importantly, all of the efforts to physically transform Madrid were designed to help residents identify more closely with the capital and foster a communal spirit through what might be called "local patriotism." This desire to promote greater civic pride among all madrileños can be seen both in the theoretical plan to physically remake the capital and in the actual urban reforms that were implemented around Madrid between 1979 and 1986.

The effort to create a new theoretical framework for the physical transformation of Madrid began immediately in 1979 with the development of the *Plan Especial Villa de Madrid*. This provisional plan was then replaced the following year by a more comprehensive, yet still temporary, proposal.

Approved by the Ayuntamiento in 1980, the *Plan Especial* was first and foremost a preventative measure designed to cease the destruction of the city's historical structures and to halt some of the more egregious new construction projects. It shifted the focus from demolition and new construction to rehabilitation and renovation, especially in the city's center. Such protectionism was necessary because, rather incredibly, before 1972 there had been no specific ordinance that limited new construction in the central historic district of the city.[42] Up until that point it was just as easy to get a license to put up a new building project in Madrid's historic center as it was to construct a new building on the outskirts of the capital.[43] Even the 1972 ordinance was severely limited, preserving only a short list of "buildings of interest."[44] The *Plan Especial* of 1980 marked the first step toward recovery by defending the capital's unique and most valuable urban characteristics.

With a temporary plan in place and with official control of planning and urban development returned to the municipal administration on September 26, 1980, through the *Decreto-ley 11/80*, the way was cleared for the creation of a new long-term plan of renewal.[45] In November, a brand new office within the Ayuntamiento, the *Oficina del Plan General*, was created to formulate a new plan to formally replace Franco's plan of 1963.[46] After a lengthy process, which included significant public input discussed in the final section of this chapter, the *Plan General de Ordenación Urbana de Madrid* (General Plan for the Urban Organization of Madrid), or simply the *Plan General*, was finally approved by Madrid's City Council in 1985.

The *Plan General*

Moving beyond the temporary *Plan Especial*, the *Plan General* was designed to modernize and provide greater equality for the different areas of the city, and, in the words of the administration, "to mend the wounds produced by wild development, by uncontrolled speculation, [and] by a political leadership that counted the interests of its citizens as least important."[47] The result was nothing less than the complete renovation of the capital. In fact, Madrid had not seen such an ambitious plan since the time of Carlos III in the eighteenth century.[48] This comprehensive project was identified under the slogan "*Recuperar Madrid*" ("Revitalize Madrid"). Among other things, the *Plan General* called for the reorganization and rationalization of city services, the improvement of the capital's infrastructure, the building of new public facilities, and greater decentralization in all structural areas. However, the main goal of the *Plan General* transcended the mere physical recuperation of the capital. The plan's desire "to order and equip the city" served a more fundamental purpose: "the social recuperation of the city."[49] So even though the specifics of the plan called for physical changes to the capital, the real focus was the people. As such, any physical change was desired not for its simple aesthetic value or increased functionalism, but for how it would improve the lives of ordinary madrileños.

In the "Introduction" to the 1982 book promoting the *Plan General*, Tierno Galván underscored the desire to create this new Madrid: "[T]he city should be universal, heterogeneous, [and] equilibrated."[50] The mayor believed that all citizens deserved access to the same services, and, more importantly, they all deserved respect. To create a more equitable city and foster civic pride, the *Plan General* proposed four specific aims. First, in order to provide more affordable housing and guarantee the "right of the city" to all citizens, the plan sought the conservation and rehabilitation of usable preexisting housing units, instead of demolishing them to make way for commercial projects. It also allowed the construction of new housing units in specified areas where the need was particularly great.[51] In addition, the plan tried to protect industrial employment within its traditional areas of the capital and limit the takeover of the city's center by banks, business headquarters, and large department stores.[52] The idea was that the city's center was to be enjoyed by all citizens, and not monopolized by commercial interests.

Second, to socially reequilibrate the city, the plan called for better access to the city's center so that all segments of the population could take advantage of its services. The political and fiscal abandonment of many neighborhoods on the periphery, particularly those in the south, was also to come to an end. And Madrid's infrastructure would be improved so that all neighborhoods would be more closely connected to each other in order to create a less-centralized city.[53]

Third, the plan called for the establishment of an inexpensive and rapid public transportation system to improve the quality of life and make the capital more habitable for all residents.[54] This system would be designed to facilitate easier access to Madrid and decrease vehicular traffic. Along the same lines, urban spaces were to be used to promote a "communitarian daily life," and not used to support more traffic.[55] In addition, city services were to be decentralized and extended to all citizens, paying attention to the local character of each area.[56] The plan proposed the construction of recreation centers, medical clinics, libraries, and cultural centers particularly in the south of Madrid where 52 percent of the population resided, but where only 20 percent of the recreation centers were located, for example.[57]

Fourth, in order to revitalize the capital's cultural patrimony, historical monuments and buildings were to be conserved and restored. Green spaces were also to be preserved. In addition, the plan was "to create the conditions for the recuperation of the memory and traditions of the city, the reinforcement of its 'signs of identity,' and the development and enrichment of its 'personality' and its specific urban culture."[58] In many respects, this final aspect of the program was most significant. The *Plan General*'s goal was not just the physical rebuilding of the city; instead, it was the transformation of the capital's identity. For the local administration, the physical changes formed "the background for the recuperation of an identity that is only possible to achieve under democracy and popular participation."[59] And Madrid's political elite believed that for residents to assume more of an active role and participate in a new democratic society, they had to feel a connection to the place they lived: "[The Ayuntamiento] has desired to increase the sensitive relationship of the citizen with the space he or she inhabits."[60] This relationship would improve as the plan for physical revitalization carried Madrid down the road "towards modernization, progress, and equilibrium between different parts of the city."[61] More importantly, it was also a road toward "peaceful coexistence."[62] Thus, the official motivation behind urban renewal was not simply to brush off or fix up the capital's infrastructure and landmarks; rather, it was to give a "'*madrileñista*' feeling of ownership to the city" and create democratic citizens.[63] Symbolizing the large amount of resources devoted to this effort, the local administration spent more than $300 million just on the restoration of Madrid's landmarks and monuments.[64]

When the *Plan General* was definitively finalized and approved on March 7, 1985, the administration's vision for Madrid's democratic future was made even clearer. Unlike any of the capital's previous plans, including those from the nineteenth century, such as the *Plan Castro*, the finalized draft of the *Plan General* did not call for the overall expansion of city territory. Likewise, the solution for a better tomorrow would not be further development, which was thought to have spawned greater economic inequality. According to the finalized plan, "The future will be better, distinct, but not bigger."[65] Additionally, rather than reacting or responding to change after the fact, the new plan was also designed to be proactive. In the past Madrid's plans had simply been remedial so this was a new approach. In fact, it reversed the traditional method of managing the capital: development and then plan, rather than plan then development. In other words, it symbolized preparation for tomorrow, rather than only a response to yesterday. In looking toward the future, the plan would, for the first time, "leave opportunities open for later transformations, with land put aside to satisfy new demands that today only begin to show and that will appear, without a doubt, tomorrow."[66]

Living up to this promise, the finalized version of the plan offered more than just a vague vision of that future. It offered a "comprehensive project [*proyecto global*]" that established not only "the what and the where, but, above all, the how to do things from this comprehensive perspective."[67] In this way the plan was much more than an "abstract and theoretical territorial model."[68] Rather, it expressed a series of concrete and integrated proposals to reequilibrate Madrid's resources, improve the quality of life in all areas of the capital, and create an urban environment that all residents could be proud of. While including a wide range of initiatives, the finalized plan set forth five main structural components. First, there would be continued development of the Parque Lineal de Manzanares. Its purpose was to create a different kind of park that developed a variety of uses along distinct segments of the river Manzanares and that would "break the diametrical difference between the north and the south."[69] Second, the renovation of the area around the train station of Atocha was to be completed. This project included the expansion of the station and rail services, the elimination of the tangled web of traffic in front of the station, nicknamed "*scalextric*," the revitalization of commercial services, and a general improvement of the area to create a major urban focal point in the southern part of the city. Third, access to the capital from the south, specifically the southeast, was to be increased in order to provide traditionally underserved areas of the periphery better access to the resources of the capital. Fourth, new residential and commercial development in the eastern sector of the city was called for. As the only structural operation of expansion, this project was designed to increase affordable housing and regenerate that area of the periphery. Fifth, the north and west quadrants of the city were to be "meshed" together through the completion of Madrid's ring highway, the M-30.[70]

Of course, as with any large and complex public plan, not all of these objectives were carried out, or carried out in exactly the way they were originally designed. Nevertheless, the formal plan did represent the administration's desire to promote a new feeling of civic pride through the physical transformation of Madrid. Modernization, reequilibration, decentralization, and the revitalization of the valuable parts of the capital's past were some of the ways in which the official plan tried to improve the lives of ordinary madrileños and create a new sense of community. While the *Plan General* symbolized the theoretical framework to remake Madrid, a whole series of actual concrete changes were implemented in the capital between 1979 and 1986. These changes ranged from the renovation of Madrid's symbolic landmarks and its system of public transportation to the cleanup of the capital's environment.

Urban Revitalization: Landmarks, Buildings, and Monuments

Starting in 1979, the capital's landmarks and most important monuments were cleaned and restored, along with hundreds of paintings, sculptures, and porcelains in the city's art collection. The exhibit *"Madrid Restaura"* was held in May 1981, during the city festival of San Isidro, to show off the administration's restoration efforts to the public. The three most visible projects highlighted in the exhibit included the fountain of Cibeles, Teatro Español, and the Puerta de Alcalá. Other projects included the Fountain of Apollo, the Fountain of Neptune, the Puerta and Puente de Toledo, the Portada del Cuartel de Conde Duque, the Templo de Debod, the Monument to Daoíz y Velarde, and the Kings of the Plaza de Oriente. All of these monuments were restored in only the first two years of the administration, and further restorations were carried out under the administration's *Plan de Restauración Monumental.* By 1986, there were 27 large-scale urban restoration projects going on in Madrid, many with high symbolic value. Some of the major landmark projects included Puerta del Sol, Atocha, San Francisco el Grande, Avenida de la Ilustración, Cuartel de Conde Duque, and the Feria de Madrid.[71] While the preservation of these symbols of Madrid was valuable for its own sake, all of the revitalization programs were designed with the idea of increasing a feeling of common ownership and civic pride.

Writing at the time of the *"Madrid Restaura"* exhibit, Enrique Moral, the Concejal de Cultura (Councilor of Culture), described the kinds of monuments restored in the capital: "[P]ublic monuments of such deeply rooted and *madrileño* symbolism as the Fountain of Cibeles, the Puerta de Alcalá, and the monument to Alfonso XIII and more than 25 urban statues."[72] He also highlighted the importance of the monuments for Madrid's historical patrimony. For Moral, Madrid's monuments and landmarks, "which represent the tradition, the physiognomy, and the history of the people [*pueblo*], constituted a collective patrimony of inestimable value."[73] The restoration of the capital's monuments was so important that the chief architect in charge of the city's historic patrimony declared that the Ayuntamiento saw "the survival, protection, and development of the urban patrimony as one of the fundamental keys to the cultural identity of Madrid."[74] In the minds of the local political elite, the renovation of Madrid's monuments was directly related to the promotion of local pride and identification, and not to the image of the nation or to national identity.[75]

The local administration also tried to promote civic pride by preserving and restoring Madrid's historical buildings. While this first began in 1979, the greatest renovation effort came between 1983 and 1984. For example, the number of buildings selected for structural protection tripled from 250, in 1982, to 750, in 1983.[76] Some of the projects that promoted the most public interest included the reconstruction of the Teatro Español, the Centro Matutano, the Palacio de Reilly, the Ciudad de los Niños in the Casa de Campo, the renovation of the Matadero Municipal, the Parque Móvil, the Huerta de la Salud, and the Centro Municipal de Informática.[77] In addition to the projects in the city proper, efforts were also made to restore the urban areas around the capital. Again demonstrating an interest in the region as a whole, the local administration undertook projects to revitalize the *cascos viejos* (old town centers) of Fuencarral, Carabanchel Bajo, Caranbanchel Alto, Vicálvaro, Villa de Vallecas, and Hortaleza.[78]

After 1983, the regional government also began to restore the region's historical buildings, turning many into cultural centers.[79] One of the most important restoration projects was the renovation of the historically significant Las Cocheras de la Reina Madre in Aranjuez.[80] Other projects included the rehabilitation of the Casa del Duque de Rivas in Sevilla de Nueva, and the theaters of Navalcarnero, Colmenar de Oreja, and Chinchón.[81] According to Eduardo Mangada Samaín, the Consejero de Ordenación del Territorio, Medio Ambiente y Vivienda (Chief of Housing, Environment, and Development) for the Comunidad of Madrid, these projects were undertaken out of an understanding that "the betterment of public spaces is a necessary task for their revitalization."[82] And, in fact, the regional administration solicited a wide variety of proposals to "recuperate and regenerate" the region's urban and architectural patrimony between 1983 and 1986.[83]

However, not all of the urban renewal efforts were visible. In fact, many decisions were important for what was not produced. For example, between

1979 and 1983, the municipal administration did not permit the construction of the Torres de Valencia, the Torres de Colón, or a significant part of the large-scale commercial project destined for Azca.[84] In addition, 108 licenses for new construction projects were suspended in 1982 to make way for the *Plan General* and to end speculation and shoddy construction (*la chapuza*).[85] Such efforts were specifically aimed at ending the undemocratic "*banusadas*," large-scale commercial developments, which economically benefited only a select few at the expense of society as a whole.[86] By limiting the amount of commercial development in Madrid, the administration hoped to create an urban environment that more madrileños could identify with and be proud of.

Transportation

In order to make Madrid more livable and bring residents together, the local administration also tackled the capital's traffic and transportation problems. This was especially necessary because the use of public transport was lower in Madrid than in other European cities prior to 1979. For example, in London the percentage of commuter trips (between home and work) made by public transportation was 81 percent in 1970, and in Paris it was 75 percent. In Madrid, in 1983, only 60 percent of such trips utilized public transport.[87] The problem primarily stemmed from the previous regime. It left a radial system that favored the automobile over public transportation, leading even to the removal of Madrid's once famous *tranvías* (streetcars). Favoritism toward the automobile and enforced centralism also combined to produce a public transportation system that was inefficient, uncoordinated, and compartmentalized. For example, local trains did not connect with the metro system. And bus service was irregular and operated mainly between the center and the periphery, not between districts on the periphery. Another part of the problem was that the physical and economic expansion of Madrid in the 1960s and 1970s corresponded with the boom of automobile ownership in Spain, creating a situation in which over 800,000 cars clogged Madrid's streets every day.[88]

Rather than building more highways, new tunnels, and more elevated roads, which generated only further congestion in the 1970s (and again later in the 1990s), Tierno Galván's administration had a more democratic and communal philosophy: "[T]o promote public transportation and restrict private transportation [automobiles] in congested zones."[89] The first task was to rationalize and reorganize the entire public transportation system: rail and bus services were connected with metro stations, the Empresa Municipal de Transportes (EMT) was restructured, and additional metro lines were added. In addition, the administration built new underground parking structures and implemented the *Ordenación Regulada de Aparcamiento* (Control and Regulation of Parking) to ease traffic problems. Finally, automobiles were restricted from some areas of the capital, including from the Retiro, and many of the streets in the city's historic center were turned over to pedestrians. Each of these changes was designed to increase access to the capital and improve the quality of life of all residents, particularly those living on the periphery.

Cleaning up the Capital

Beyond the overhaul of Madrid's transportation system, the promotion of civic pride extended to improving Madrid's environment. Years of neglect under Franco left the region facing a mosquito and rat infestation, stagnant run-off in neighborhoods on the periphery, and the accumulation of 30 years of industrial discharge in the city's river. In addition, sanitation had become a major problem as public waste multiplied with the growth of a consumer society in the capital.[90]

Given the size of the mess, several steps had to be taken at the same time. To deal with the litter-filled sidewalks, literally thousands of trashcans were placed in the streets of the capital.[91] For the first time in Madrid's history, in conjunction with the Policía Municipal, abandoned vehicles were removed from the city's streets.[92] Also for the first time, medical waste was separated from regular domestic waste in order to lower the risk of contamination.[93] The capital's recycling program also first got started during this period, as glass collection began in selected neighborhoods.[94]

Particular attention was paid to Madrid's public spaces, with an emphasis on the cleaning and ordering of parks and plazas. In order to encourage residents to help in this process, a community outreach program was implemented that included a publicity campaign and weekly educational visits by school groups and neighborhood associations to one of the main waste collections center in Valdemingómez.[95] In addition, every façade in the city was systematically washed, district-by-district, in 1982.[96] It was as if the new administration wished to wash away the lingering dust of the Franco regime and invite Madrid's residents back on to the streets.

The capital's pollution problem was another area where the local administration tried to restore a feeling of pride. By 1979, Madrid's water and air qualities had deteriorated to historic lows. With practically no limits on air pollution under the Franco regime, Madrid's once famous deep blue skies had turned dark brown. Pollution from the capital also contaminated the region's rivers: the Henares, Jarama, Tajo, and, of course, Manzanares.[97] To fight the increasingly alarming episodes of air pollution, the worst coming in December 1979, the Ayuntamiento, in an agreement with the Ministerio de Obras Públicas y Urbanismo (Ministry of Public Works and Planning), instituted the *Plan de Saneamiento Atmosférico* (Atmospheric Cleaning Plan) in June 1981. The plan included increased vehicle inspection, inspection of all city furnaces, and the expansion of the system of automatic pollution detection and control.[98] In addition, the administration passed the *Ordenanza General de Protección del Medio Ambiente* (General Regulations for the Protection of the Environment) at the end of 1985. This measure further reduced parking and standing on Madrid's main thoroughfares,

allowed for the immobilization of vehicles that produced excessive omis-
sions, and restricted the use of some furnaces.[99]

Rather than limiting their efforts to the center of Madrid, the municipal
administration instituted additional programs to improve the environment in
all areas of the capital, and especially those on the periphery. For example, in
order to cleanup Madrid's waterways and to safeguard the capital's drinking
supply, *Plan Saneamiento Integral* (PSI, Integrated Sanitation Plan) was
begun in 1980. As the largest such project of its kind in all of Europe, the
PSI was designed to capture and filter all of Madrid's wastewater and run-
off.[100] In all, eight new wastewater collection and purification facilities were
built and a network of 200 km of wastewater pipes was laid in the ground.[101]
In addition to improving the overall quality of the city's water, the program
was specifically aimed at ending the contamination of drinking water in such
peripheral neighborhoods as Carabanchel, Villaverde, and Vallecas.[102]

This improvement of the quality of the capital's wastewater was critical to
another major effort to remake the capital: the cleaning and redevelopment of
Madrid's river. After decades of complete neglect, the Manzanares was unable
to support any kind of life, had become an eyesore, and even posed a health
danger to residents living nearby. In the mind of Tierno Galván, if Madrid was
going to be a place to be proud of, then it would need a great, new river. And
if greatness was not a possible aspiration for the diminutive river, then at least
it should not be a civic embarrassment and an ecological disaster.

The plan to restore the river involved the cleaning of the river and the creation of a new park along its banks, the Parque Lineal de Manzanares.[103] To
clean the 26 kilometers of the river, all of the capital's wastewater and runoff
had to be purified.[104] That was the job of the PSI. Once the river was drained
and cleaned, the banks of the river were turned into a unifying green corridor
that stretched from Monte del Pardo in the north to the Parque Manzanares-
Sur, adjacent to the district of Vallecas, in the south. In addition, the local
administration built docks for recreation, repopulated the river with fish (carp
and tench) and ducks, and created "spaces for urban agriculture" along the
banks of the river.[105] More than simply cleaning the river, the administration
hoped that the restoration of the Manzanares would provide residents living
in both the north and south with a unifying symbol of Madrid.

In addition to the new park along the Manzanares, the administration
worked to improve the quality of life in the capital by increasing the amount
of green space throughout Madrid. For example, in 1979, Madrid contained 324 parks and, at the end of 1982, the number had risen to 451. The
127 new parks represented almost 500 hectares of new green space for the
capital.[106] In fact, by 1986, more new green spaces were created in Madrid
than in any other city in the European community.[107] Improvements were
also made to the capital's existing parks. Parque del Retiro, Casa de Campo,
Parque del Oeste, and Parque de Fuente del Berro received enhancements,
including road improvements, restoration of hedges, improvements to the
irrigation systems, restoration of monuments, regulation of traffic, cleaning of ponds, and the construction of new fences.[108] There was also the

extension of the parks of Entrevías, Pradolongo, Villaverde, and the creation of the Museo Floral in the Parque de Osuna.[109] Finally, the *Programa de Utilización Intensiva de los Viveros Municipales* (Program for the Intensive Utilization of Municipal Nurseries), focusing on Puerta de Hierro, Bombilla, and Casa de Campo, increased the number of plants produced annually for the capital from 50,000 in 1979 to 240,000 in 1983.[110] And to reach as many areas of Madrid as possible, the *Fiesta Popular del Árbol* (The People's Tree Festival) was begun in 1981. Celebrated on December 16 each year, this tree planting campaign encouraged all residents to help make Madrid more green and hospitable.[111] Tierno Galván appeared so obsessed with replanting Madrid that Dutch tulip growers even named a new dark red variety after the old professor.[112] In all, more than 120,000 new trees were planted in Madrid by 1983.[113] Along with the administrations' other efforts to physically transform the region, the "greening" of Madrid helped transform the formerly gray and somber capital into a vibrant place that madrileños were increasingly proud to call their own.

2. Educating Madrid's Citizens

The physical transformation just described was complimented by explicit efforts to promote civic education and awareness. As with the other initiatives, these programs were also aimed at all of Madrid's residents, regardless of age, class, or where they lived in the capital. Because formal schooling was, for the most part, outside the purview of the local and regional administrations, Madrid's political elite focused less formal education and more on informal methods of civic education, from the promotion of community activities to the sponsorship of publications that described and celebrated the region of Madrid.

All of the educational programs worked off the same basic assumption: the better you know something, the more you appreciate it and identify with it. To increase these feelings of affiliation, efforts were made to inform madrileños about the various functions and services of Madrid's new local and regional democratic institutions, as well as the plans for urban renewal already in progress. Some of the initiatives also presented a specific image of Madrid that overlooked the capital's more recent conflictive history. Others tended to downplay Madrid's role in the nation and, instead, highlighted Madrid's regional uniqueness.

Of course, there were limits to these efforts, especially after the coercive and repressive experience of the Franco dictatorship. Tierno Galván, in particular, was aware of these limitations. Early in his administration, the mayor began a radio address on the subject of civic education by stressing the limits of the administration's interventionism:

> I believe that everyone knows that we have nothing to do with the subject of official education: that corresponds to the Ministry of Education or the universities, but not to us. We lay the floors, we clean up, we provide the ushers, but we can't intervene more than that.[114]

After this initial qualifier, Tierno Galván went on to express the need for greater civic awareness, commenting that being a madrileño was a "condition that we should not give away or hide."[115] Because of both a lack of jurisdiction over formal education and a desire not to repeat the blatant paternalism of the Franco regime, the promotion of civic awareness had to be done through other kinds of educational efforts. Along with the sponsorship of publications related to Madrid, discussed below, the democratic administrations began a number of new activities that were directed at the region's adults and children.

Informal Educational Activities

In order to promote greater public awareness among all residents, the local administration, under the Delegación de Relaciones Sociales y Vecinales (Delegation of Local and Social Relations), first began the program "*Conozcamos Madrid.*" This program had the objective of "providing citizens knowledge about the city, through organized visits to monuments, churches, parks and plazas, [and] historic buildings."[116] In 1982, in the month of May alone, more than 1,700 citizens participated in the program.[117] By 1986, more than 20,000 residents were participating in the program every year.[118] The program also promoted the investigation and popularization of the history of the capital's different districts through a series of books about the history of neighborhoods.[119]

A similar kind of civic awareness was also promoted through the creation of a new regional government office. In October 1984, the Oficina de Información, Iniciativas y Reclamaciones (Office of Information, Incentives, and Complaints) of the Comunidad of Madrid was created to "collect, process, and answer every consultation, complaint, or suggestion brought forth by residents."[120] The office was also charged with the task of "facilitating all types of information about the jurisdictions, functions, or locations of different departments [of the Comunidad] . . . in writing, in person, or by telephone."[121] In addition to allowing the regional government to respond to citizen suggestions and criticism, the office played the important role of educating the public about the new Comunidad.

Back on the municipal level, the Ayuntamiento of Madrid even created its own radio station in 1980. This officially sponsored FM radio station informed the residents about the formal activities of the local administration and about many of the issues that affected the capital more generally.[122] Throughout the early 1980s, Tierno Galván personally broadcasted a number of radio addresses that focused on such areas of administration as sanitation, education, health services, the environment, economics, public safety, urbanization, traffic, sports programs, and public festivals.[123] Thus, rather than simply entertaining the public, the municipal radio station was designed to educate madrileños about the place in which they lived.

In addition to these administrative efforts, Tierno Galván made a personal effort to increase civic education through the periodic dissemination of official *Bandos.* With a nod to a centuries-old tradition, these often ironic proclamations were written by the mayor himself and were specifically addressed to all of Madrid's residents. They were also widely disseminated to reach as many madrileños as possible and were plastered around the capital, read on the radio, and published in the newspaper *Villa de Madrid*.[124] More than simply obscure or pedantic proclamations, the *Bandos* were meant to inform, instruct, educate, and guide madrileños. So despite their Baroque style, the *Bandos* served a clear pedagogical mission: they informed Madrid's residents about the policies and programs of the new democratic administration. Stemming from the desire to improve Madrid's quality of life and thus promote a stronger feeling of connection with the capital, the mayor's declarations encouraged residents to conserve water, park in appropriate places, respect parks and gardens, enjoy the newly reinstated public festivals, plant more trees, and clean up after themselves.[125]

This last request, and its link to civic education in particular, was frequently stressed by the mayor. In fact, the very first *Bando* of July 31, 1979, urged citizens to take care of the capital's parks, streets, and gardens.[126] In the second *Bando* of October 10, 1979, the mayor went on to point out some of the problems and solutions to the capital's unclean state. A lack of respect was highlighted as the major cause: "[A] lack of mutual respect, in some sectors of *madrileño* people, is leaving the city ugly, sad, and dirty."[127] And greater civic responsibility was proposed as the solution: "[T]o increase the cleanliness of Madrid is the responsibility of everyone."[128] Four additional *Bandos* discussed the need for a clean and well-ordered city, dealing with such topics as handbills, graffiti, park and garden preservation, and proper parking.[129] Despite their sometimes archaic language and pedagogical function, the *Bandos* were well received and extremely popular with the residents. This popular reception probably had to do with Tierno Galván's unique ability to be ceremonial and down to earth, gentle and stern, and humorous and serious all at the same time.[130]

In addition to the efforts directed toward adults, the local and regional administrations paid particular attention to the capital's children as the future democratic citizens of Madrid. However, as mentioned above, Madrid's political elite understood that there was a difference between increasing a sense of civic awareness and the outright manipulation of the educational system. Writing in the *Villa de Madrid*, Tierno Galván explained to the residents of Madrid that "in no way can we alter or instigate changes in the educational system."[131] Nevertheless, the mayor, and the rest of his administration, wanted to promote an "active and direct education" to create better citizens today and in the future.[132] This was accomplished, in part, through after-school visits to city institutions in buses provided by the Ayuntamiento. These excursions visited the *Juntas del Distrito*, to see firsthand how neighborhood problems were solved; the municipal police stations, to meet the individuals who protected and provided order on the city's streets; the Laboratorio Municipal, to learn how the city's water and food supply were tested and kept safe; the Museo Municipal, to gain an appreciation for the city's history; municipal libraries, to find out what books were available; and district cultural centers, to experience firsthand some of the activities offered there (ceramics, dance, music, language classes, etc.).[133] In order for children to get to know the whole region of Madrid, Tierno Galván also explained in a radio address how the administration had organized trips in city vehicles "so that children can visit not only Madrid, but also the interesting places on the outskirts [of the capital]."[134]

Another important program directed at the capital's young people was "*Madrid para los Niños*" (Madrid for Children). This program was specifically created so that students in grades seven and eight could get to know the capital and its services better. It consisted of two parts: "One touristic and the other dedicated to getting to know municipal services and facilities."[135] Some of the program's specific topics included "the historical development of the city, the urban transportation system, and the provision of municipal community services."[136] By 1984, over 12,000 students, from 215 schools, had participated in the program.[137] In addition to this program, the administration organized visits to the Prado Museum, the Archeological Museum, the Museo Municipal, the Botanical Gardens, and to Madrid's zoo for almost 40,000 students by 1984.[138] Tierno Galván and others in the local administration believed that these efforts directed at children would ultimately help their parents identify with Madrid as well. It was hoped that civic awareness and knowledge of how the democratic administration functioned would be transferred from children to parents, with the understanding that "many times children serve as a link to instruct their parents."[139]

Representing an exception to the use of informal educational initiatives, the regional government of Madrid fostered a feeling of civic belonging through some actual school programs. The program "*Conoce tu ciudad*" (Know Your City) started in the 1981–1982 academic year and expanded by the Comunidad after 1983, represented an example of the kind of program that sought to increase secondary school students' knowledge of and identification with the region of Madrid. In fact, "*Conoce tu ciudad*" had two official objectives in this regard. The first was to increase "the understanding of the city as a social fact and the sensibility toward the formal economic, cultural, and social aspects that shape the urban reality."[140] The second was "to foment and facilitate knowledge of our actual territory of Madrid [*territorial madrileña*]."[141] And the program itself came in the form of a competition to create the best project about a locale within the Comunidad. The winning projects were collected and later published after 1983 by the Comunidad in a series of annual books.[142] Although it was sponsored by the Comunidad's Area de Urbanismo y Ordenación Territorial (Department of Planning and Development), the program was designed to do more than just foster an interest in urban structures and architecture; it promoted greater appreciation and pride for the region of Madrid as a whole. For example, the 1983–1984 program focused on such things as the capital's historical development, economic activities, architectural patrimony, and urban problems and solutions. Such questions as, "If you were mayor, what would you change?" increased the feelings of civic awareness and responsibility felt by the students.[143] Importantly, these new feelings were promoted among a large number of students, with 1,500 of the region's schools participating in the program in the 1983–1984 academic year.[144]

Officially Sponsored Publications

Complimenting the activities described above, informal civic education was also promoted through the official sponsorship of books, guides, investigations, surveys, and histories that focused specifically on Madrid.[145] These publications were designed to reawaken a genuine interest in local and regional affairs. Likewise, many of the works also highlighted and celebrated Madrid's unique character or attributes.

Mentioned previously, the book *Madrid es más que Madrid* represents one of the best examples of this type of description and promotion of the region of Madrid.[146] Published in conjunction with the Comunidad of Madrid in 1984, the full color, high-quality coffee-table style book includes photos of villagers and city dwellers, diverse landscapes, historic and artistic monuments, small towns, and urban city streets. As the title suggests, the book depicts Madrid as representing more than just the city itself. The region of Madrid is represented as a unique "land (*tierra*)," identified by its own people, food, landmarks, and history.[147] According to the text, the collection of these different attributes represents a unique "*Comunidad madrileña.*"[148] In addition, the region of Madrid is promoted as a distinguished place, defined in part by its many royal residences and landmarks: El Escorial, Aranjuez, El Pardo, and the large number of royal sites within the city. In other words, the region of Madrid is not represented as just any ordinary place. Instead, "the land of Madrid is a Royal Place."[149] The region of Madrid is also described as a single "geographical and cultural entity."[150] The authors argue that "the ski slopes of Navacerrada, the town square of Chinchón, the gardens of Aranjuez, or the Castile of Villaviciosa of Odón, to name just a few, are as *madrileño* as the Puerta del Sol."[151] The combination of the city and its surrounding region creates what is called "Madrid." Thus the capital is presented as indistinguishable from the region, and vice versa. More than simply describing Madrid, the book paints an extremely attractive image of the whole region that allowed all madrileños the possibility of identifying more closely with the broader region in which they lived.

This desire to describe and promote the region's unique characteristics can also be seen in such projects as *Pensar en Madrid*. In February 1984, a series of *jornadas* (conferences) were sponsored to investigate madrileño cultural activity, with regard to the plastic arts, theater, music, and architecture.[152] The conferences were open to the public and took place in various localities across the region: Alcalá de Henares, Aranjuez, El Escorial, Alcobendas, Manzanares, and Leganés. The conferences' proceedings and presentations were collected by the Comunidad and later published as the book *Pensar en Madrid* in order to promote greater knowledge of the region.[153]

Similarly, the municipal administration sponsored writing that described and celebrated Madrid. Each year the Asociación Madrileña de la Federación

Española de Periodistas y Escritores de Turismo (Madrid's Association of the Spanish Federation of Journalists and Writers of Tourism), in collaboration with Madrid's Patronato de Turismo (Board of Toursim), awarded a prize for the "best work of promotion" of the capital.[154] Many of these works, celebrating Madrid's gastronomy, architecture, history, parks, inhabitants, art, music, and nightlife, were collected in a book published by the Ayuntamiento in 1987.[155] All of these writings fostered a unique sense of place by highlighting what was perceived as noteworthy, special, and even noble about the capital.

However, not all of the capital's unique characteristics were equally highlighted. Two aspects of Madrid, in particular, were often ignored in these informal educational efforts. First, Madrid's conflictive history during the Second Republic and the civil war was frequently ignored. Second, Madrid's role as the capital of the Spanish nation-state was often downplayed. As a result, officially sponsored publications promoted a particular civic identity that overlooked the capital's divisive past and focused instead on Madrid as a distinct region.

For example, in 1983, in cooperation with Equipo Viajar, the local administration published a guidebook of the capital entitled *Madrid*. The guide was designed with the express purpose of allowing the reader "to visit and get to know in depth" the city of Madrid.[156] Like the examples cited above, the guidebook highlights Madrid's unique characteristics and describes in great detail the region's culture, history, and gastronomy. However, in the section detailing the historical and cultural background of the capital, the history of Madrid is only recounted up until the Spanish American War (1898).[157] In fact, there is no mention of the Second Republic, the civil war, or the Franco dictatorship. Given the considerable impact of the civil war on the capital, the omission of this event is especially obvious. The Madrid that readers were supposed to "get to know in depth" was simply not the polarized and conflictive Madrid of the pre– and post–civil war periods. A similar omission can be found in another guide to Madrid, *Conocer Madrid*, published a year earlier.[158] Even though it presents a more impressionistic view of the capital's past and present personality through a series of colorful essays, this guide again demonstrates the administration's wish to overlook the capital's conflictive past. Rather than mentioning the civil war or the period leading up to the conflict, the guide offers a variety of verbal "snapshots" of Madrid's less divisive history and culture, focusing on such themes as Madrid under the Hapsburgs, the writings of Galdós, and artwork in the capital.

This same desire to overlook Madrid's more recent conflictive past can also be seen in many of the histories of Madrid sponsored by the regional government. For example, Fernando Jimenez de Gregorio's book, *Madrid y su Comunidad*, partially sponsored by the Comunidad of Madrid, gives the history and even the prehistory of the region all the way back to 600,000 BC but ignores its recent history.[159] According to the author, "only by knowledge [of the Comunidad] can we value it, appreciate it, defend it."[160] However, even though the history of the region is traced all the way back to prehistoric times, the narrative of Madrid's modern history ends at the year 1833.[161] Here again, the region's more recent history is simply left out. Other similar histories sponsored by the regional administration included *Madrid y los Borbones en el siglo XVIII: la construcción de una ciudad y su territorio* (1984), *Madrid en la sociedad del siglo XIX* (1986), and *Madrid: una historia en Comunidad* (1987).[162] Favoring the capital's less-divisive distant past, the regional administration also published a number of facsimiles of old "histories" of Madrid. These books promoted the idea of Madrid as a unique region with a long and distinguished history, while leaving the tumultuous twentieth century aside.[163] Such newly reissued editions included *Crónica de la provincia de Madrid: Madrid 1865* (1983) and *Madrid, Audiencia, Provincia, Intendencia, Vicaría, Partido y Villa 1848* (1986).[164]

In addition to the desire to forget Madrid's conflictive past, there was also an effort to distance the capital from the previous authoritarian regime by minimizing Madrid's role as the capital of the nation. For example, the authors of the guide mentioned above, *Conocer Madrid*, deliberately try to distance Madrid from its previous position as the center of Franco's Spain:

> [Madrid's position as capital of Spain] is today for Madrid more of a burden than an advantage. The mayor of Madrid, Professor Tierno Galván, often says that if the fanatical centralism of the past was detrimental to all Spaniards, it was especially so for the citizens of Madrid, having suffered more for having been closer.[165]

Contrary to what might be expected, here Madrid's position as the capital of Spain is not portrayed as an advantage, but rather as a disadvantage. Furthermore, the residents of Madrid are described as the first victims of Francoism. Put another way, its role as the national capital of the Spanish state is not what makes Madrid important or unique. Instead, the region of Madrid is valued throughout the guide for its own unique characteristics and personality. The promotion of civic education and civic awareness in this case clearly served to distance the capital from its conflictive past and demonstrate that Madrid could have an identity that was separate from it role as the national capital of Spain.

3. Restoring Faith in Public Institutions

The project to create a new civic identity in Madrid also included an effort to increase the public's confidence and trust in public institutions. Under Franco, the local government was known for its isolation, inefficiency, and centralization. Moreover, like in other large cities across Spain, the rapid demographic, social, and economic changes that occurred under the dictatorship were not accompanied by corresponding changes in the institutional structure of the capital's administration.[166] As a result, there was little confidence in public institutions prior to 1979. In order to create a new sense of trust between residents and Madrid's newly created democratic institutions, the local administration hoped to transform the capital's municipal government from a bureaucratic tangle into a kind of "public defender" for all citizens of Madrid.[167] This greater confidence and trust in Madrid's democratic institutions would, in turn, increase the likelihood of madrileños identifying more closely with the capital. To accomplish this task, the administration both put its own house in order and increased its transparency to residents in all areas of the capital, regardless of their socioeconomic or political position.

Reform Within

Internal reform of the administration was launched under the slogan: "*Poner la casa en orden* [Putting the house in order]."[168] Specifically, the goal was to

> infuse the internal life of the Institution [the municipal government] with the necessary democratic spirit, to control the excessive bureaucracy of the administration, to promote neighborhood participation in municipal matters . . . and to make possible cooperation between politicians and government workers that "permits an efficient combined effort."[169]

Echoing many of the other efforts to create a new civic identity in Madrid, the renovation of the capital's administration focused on two objectives. The first was the emphasis on "collective necessities and not the interests of individuals."[170] So while the previous administration was unresponsive and catered to the desires of a few, the new government would look after the needs of the majority of the population. The second objective was to create a democratic administration that was responsible to all citizens, and one that was actively supported by the majority of those who lived and worked in Madrid. In the words of the mayor, the goal was to "convert obscurity into transparency and the lack of knowledge into information."[171]

One of the fundamental steps toward democratization and decentralization was the reorganization of the administration's 18,000 permanent staff members into 11 new areas of administration.[172] In contrast to the previous system, each and every individual was assigned to a specific department and charged with a particular task.[173] Efforts were also made to "normalize promotions, create child daycare facilities, and abolish sexual discrimination."[174] Likewise, the administration reformed its outdated legal structure, including the *Ley de Régimen Local* (Local Rule Law) and the *Estatuto de la Función Pública* (Public Duty Statute).

To promote responsiveness within the local government and greater public faith in the actual workings of the administration, many city functions were automated or mechanized, including expenditures, record keeping, and administrative requests.[175] By the mid-1980s there was even a computer network that linked the various districts to each other and to the capital's new central computer: Ordenador Central del Centro Municipal de Informática (CEMI).[176] Decision-making was also delegated to various departments, rather than centralized in the mayor's office. This decentralization stemmed from a desire to democratize the local administration and, in part, from the recognition that "a city the size of Madrid is simply not manageable from a central body."[177]

In order to satisfy the needs of residents living in all areas of the capital, the reordering of many municipal services was also necessary, including the reorganization of the Delegación de Hacienda, Rentas y Patrimonio (Office of Finance, Taxation, and Patrimony), the restructuring of the Policía Municipal and of the Departamento de Saneamiento (Sanitation Department), the partial reorganization of the Intervención Municipal, and the reform of the Instituto Municipal de Educación.[178] In addition to the restructuring of existing organizations, new municipal entities outside the direct control of the Ayuntamiento were created, such as the Patronato del Recinto de la Feria del Campo, the Patronato Municipal de Turismo, the Instituto Municipal de Deportes, and the Centro Municipal de Informática. Each of these new institutions represented the desire to promote greater decentralization and the delegation of responsibility. And, more importantly, this shift away from centralization was meant to foster greater civic confidence in Madrid's new democratic institutions.

The administration's efforts to promote greater faith in the new democratic Ayuntamiento extended to the realm of public finance as well. Demonstrating a large degree of fiscal responsibility, Tierno Galván's administration balanced the city's books for the first time in recent history. In 1979, the new administration began with an $81 million budget deficit. By 1983 the budget was balanced, and in 1984 the city enjoyed a $1.9 million surplus.[179] This goal was achieved through controlled spending, greater efficiency, and the rationalization of all segments of the administration, and not through a large increase in taxes.[180] A rationalized and fiscally responsible Ayuntamiento provided an ideal image of a local democratic administration that residents could more easily trust and identify with.

Although not directly related to administrative reform, another step toward greater civic confidence was the changing of more than two dozen street and plaza names in Madrid.[181] Beginning in June 1980, the local administration restored most of the streets renamed by Franco to traditional names, ones that did not have a connection to the civil war or the capital's conflictive past. With regard to the question of changing street names, Tierno Galván asked the citizens of Madrid during a radio address: "Why have warlike testimonials that recall past times that are not going to return, and why not put back the names that traditionally existed?"[182] According to the mayor, traditional names "give confidence."[183] Echoing the commitment to forgetting the capital's divisive past discussed in the previous section, Tierno Galván announced, "We are ready for the civil war to erase itself from the [capital's] consciousness and have it remain only with the intelligentsia, as a historical memory."[184] The administration offered evidence to back up the claim that changing the capital's street names had more to do with promoting civic confidence in Madrid's public institutions than with political revenge: "The proof for this is that all of the names that were returned were from before the Second Republic: El Paseo de Calvo Sotelo returned to Recoletos, García Morato to Santa Engracia, Víctor Pradera to Mendizábal, Onésimo Redondo to San Vicente . . . and alike for 27 streets."[185] The specific choice of traditional street names was meant to demonstrate that the new democratic administration "only means the best for Madrid and for peace between *madrileños*."[186]

However, probably the most important effort to increase civic trust came through the reform of Madrid's police force. To begin with, the fundamental role of the city's police was reversed. Under Franco, the police worked not for the protection of the citizens, but for the protection of the central government. The result was citizen fear and insecurity. The new philosophy of the police department was to increase public confidence by putting the residents of Madrid first, with the number one priority being the "preoccupation with the safety of the citizen."[187] To this end, a series of new objectives were laid out for the police force: "[I]ncrease efficiency, rationalize service, increase communication with citizens, establish preventative measures, impart a solid humane training [to officers], and decentralize policing activities."[188] All of these objectives were implemented in order to increase confidence in the formerly repressive police force and to overcome the general feeling of insecurity felt by many citizens.

Veteran police officers were retrained through "*cursos de adaptación*" (adaptation courses) and the training modules at the capital's police academy were revamped.[189] The overall size of the force was also increased by 24 percent, from 3,417 to 4,230 members, between 1979 and 1983.[190] A community outreach program and public information campaigns were also started. Such campaigns included "The Municipal Police Coexists with You," "Every One for Everyone," "Child Security," and "Help Us Save You."[191] Symbolizing a desire for greater responsiveness to the public's needs, a 911-like central telephone number "*092 Policía Municipal*" was created in 1980, the first of its kind in Spain.[192] Most importantly, neighborhood policing was instituted to reach all areas of the capital, and all segments of the population. So instead of a single centralized force, "neighborhood police" were stationed in each and every district of the city.[193] Rather than only traveling to an area of the capital when the necessity arose, for the first time police officers would get to know their respective neighborhoods and its residents, fostering greater communication, confidence, respect, and trust.

Improving Administrative Openness and Transparency

The project to foster public confidence, and thereby increase a feeling of connection to Madrid, also included efforts to increase administrative transparency and openness. While Article 69 of the 1985 Basic Law on local government states, "[T]he local corporations shall provide the fullest information about their activities and facilitate the involvement of all citizens in local life," this desire was expressed from the very begin of Tierno Galván's administration.[194] In 1979, in his inaugural address, the mayor announced that he wanted to create an "open and transparent *Ayuntamiento*" that would be "of everyone and for everyone."[195] This desire for openness and transparency was most clearly seen through better channels of communication between the Ayuntamiento and Madrid's residents. These new channels incorporated both print and broadcast media, ranging from the personal *Bandos* of the mayor to radio addresses and a new newspaper. The administration also literally "opened its doors" to the press, promoting frequent contact between journalists and various departments of the municipal government.[196]

After getting off to a rather slow start, with the mayor even admitting in a 1982 interview that "we have thought more about what we were doing, than about reporting what we were doing," improving the channels of communication become a constant preoccupation of the administration after 1982.[197] In that year, along with opening the *Plan General* to public comment, discussed further in the next section, the administration launched one of its most ambitious projects to promote civic confidence: the creation of the biweekly newspaper, *Villa de Madrid*.

In the words of Tierno Galván, this broadsheet style publication was created "to increase the knowledge on the part of residents of the municipalities' activities and results."[198] The paper was available through free subscription, at metro kiosks, and at the Juntas de Distrito, and reached a circulation of 150,000 by the mid-1980s.[199] Although exclusively funded by the Ayuntamiento, the publication was not simply a mouthpiece for the administration; rather it was "conceived as a means of diffusion and not as an instrument of propaganda."[200] In fact, in an effort to promote confidence across the political spectrum, it frequently included articles by the opposition figures from both the left and the right. Notably, the opposition leader, and future mayor of Madrid during the 1990s, José María Álvarez del Manzano, was a frequent contributor during this period.[201] Articles by Adolfo Pastor, representative of Spain's Communist Party, also frequently appeared in the publication.

The administration continually stressed the fact that the *Villa de Madrid* was not merely an instrument of propaganda. Instead, it presented the newspaper as a publication designed to promote greater faith in local government by opening up formerly closed and centralized public institutions, from the Delegación de Hacienda, Rentas y Patrimonio to the Departamento de Saneamiento. In 1982, Tierno Galván announced that the paper was published "in a spirit of absolute sincerity and honesty that in no way seeks to distort either the facts or their interpretations to the benefit of any particular interest."[202] In January 1986, the publication reiterated its position: "[T]he pages of our periodical are open to anyone that has something to say about our city, its problems and its possible solutions and, of course, and with more reason, they are open to the members of the opposition party, who . . . makes regular use of our offer."[203]

While the *Villa de Madrid* was more than a mouthpiece for the administration, Tierno Galván did use the publication to communicate personally and openly with the public, writing a column to the citizens of Madrid in every issue. In each column he discussed the capital's problems, relayed important information about the Ayuntamiento's agenda, and sometimes even praised and scolded Madrid's residents. Many of the articles were several thousand words long and were always directed at describing the workings of the Ayuntamiento and, ultimately, at improving the lives of madrileños. It was a commitment to the public that the mayor took very seriously—even writing a column less than 24 hours before entering the Ruber Clinic for cancer surgery in February 1985.[204]

4. Promoting Citizen Participation

In addition to encouraging madrileño pride, promoting civic education, and restoring public confidence, the local and regional governments also hoped to create a new environment of greater civic participation in Madrid. In contrast, under the Franco regime, public activity had been replaced with a culture of disengagement and passivity. The residents of Madrid were more subjects than citizens and the capital's streets were a place of mistrust and suspicion, where the possibility of police patrols and the fear of informants was a constant feature. The goal of the new democratic administrations was to erase the habit of disengagement and create a community where active participation was the norm. However, civic participation meant more than political participation, either formally or informally, and this was especially true in the context of a consensus-driven transition to democracy. Instead, it meant a broad engagement with all aspect of public life in the capital.

The desire to foster a new feeling of civic belonging through participation was most clearly expressed by the mayor himself. Tierno Galván sought to promote civic participation because he believed "with passivity we are not going to resolve anything."[205] Active participation was the only way to guarantee that the capital would be a democratic place created by all residents, and for all residents. According to the mayor, the capital was for everyone, not just for specific individuals or classes, and everyone needed to participate to keep it that way:

> Madrid is for everyone and Madrid is of everyone . . . we should not understand that the park is "our" park, nor should we understand that the street is "our" street. This is a mistake and a grave mistake. It is a park for everyone, it is a street for everyone, it is a garden for everyone and everyone should take care of it, cultivate it.[206]

To achieve this kind of feeling of identification with Madrid, it was necessary to break down the previous regime's binary model of government that had divided the capital between those who ruled and those who obeyed. And Tierno Galván's administration provided a new model to do this: "[W]e should discuss [the city] between everyone as protagonists and not simply as those who dictate the norm or as those who obey the norm, but elevate everyone to the level of protagonist within the collaboration."[207] In this civic and democratic model, collaboration would replace mandates, and everyone would be free to participate in the capital's future on an equal footing.

Out of the desire to create a new inclusive collective identity specifically centered on Madrid, all of the programs during this period focused participation on local and regional, rather than on national, affairs. These programs can be divided between efforts to increase "formal" participation in the official institutions of government and efforts to increase "informal" participation. Formal participation included the revitalization of neighborhood governance, especially Madrid's Juntas del Distrito, and the inclusion of the public in the creation of the *Plan General*, the official long-term development plan for Madrid. Informal participation was developed largely through the public's return to the capital's streets.

Formal Participation

Beginning in 1979, the two central principles of the democratic administration's program to promote formal civic participation were the increase of "citizen participation in the life of the *Ayuntamiento* and the decentralization of municipal responsibilities."[208] In order to simultaneously increase decentralization and civic participation, the administration distributed responsibility and resources to the district level. The goal was "to create channels of citizen participation starting from the districts and neighborhoods."[209] This process formally began in 1980 with the creation of the *Normas de Participación Ciudadana* (Citizen Participation Norms). Building on Article 23 of the 1978 Constitution—"Citizens have the right to participate in public matters, directly or through the means of representatives, freely elected in periodic elections by universal suffrage"—the new legislation sought to reform the existing Juntas del Distrito as a means of developing and channeling civic participation.[210] The Juntas were originally established by the *Ley Especial para el Municipio* (Special Law for Municipalities) on July 11, 1963. Under Franco, however, their scope was rather narrow, limited mainly to official ceremonial purposes and minor functions.[211] The new *Normas de Participación Ciudadana* were designed to facilitate "the exercise of the right of citizens to participate and to force a decentralization process in the *Juntas del Distrito*."[212]

In conjunction with reforming the Juntas, the administration created dozens of *Consejos de Distrito* (District Councils).[213] As an intermediary between the municipal government and neighborhood associations, civic and cultural entities, and individual citizens, the *Consejos de Distrito* were concerned with areas such as healthcare, urbanization, and sanitation. Working together with the Juntas, they also began organizing events in the various neighborhoods to foster participation, such as the Ciclo de Cultura, the Semana Popular del Árbol, and the Escuela de Verano.[214] New public seminars were also held on topics such as healthcare, the environment, education, and urban planning.

In 1981, the Juntas' responsibilities were expanded to include executive functions, the maintenance of public roads, supervision of consumption and supplies (*consumo y abastos*), and the promotion of civic participation.[215] Four years later, in 1985, additional powers were added that promoted further citizen participation, including authority over district markets, the programming and administration of district cultural centers, Casas de la Juventud, sports centers, health clinics, and senior centers, and control over minor public construction and restoration.[216] By this point, the Juntas had transformed, in the words of Tierno Galván, into "practically a second Ayuntamiento."[217] Competencies had expanded so that, by the end of 1986, the Juntas controlled 22 percent of the overall city budget.[218]

During this period, the Ayuntamiento also sponsored another series of *jornadas*, or conferences, to promote formal civic participation. In the words of Tierno Galván, the *jornadas* were held for citizens "to discuss, to participate, [and] to collaborate" with the administration.[219] In addition, he called for a level of participation that was "permanently active and collaborative in order to augment the positive qualities of the democracy."[220] In November 1980, the first *Jornadas sobre Participación Ciudadana* was held in Madrid. With over 400 participants and representatives from all 18 Juntas de Distrito, the conference provided feedback that was incorporated into the final *Normas Reguladoras de la Participación Ciudadana*, approved by the city government in March 1982.[221] In December 1982, the second *Jornadas sobre Participación Ciudadana* was held to provide a further opportunity for civic participation and for citizen feedback. As with the first *Jornadas*, various citizen groups presented detailed reports outlining their concerns and suggestions on topics such as healthcare, sanitation, culture, and education.[222] By the middle of the decade, these *jornadas* were expanded to the district level as well. For example, in January 1986, the *Junta Municipal de Centro* celebrated its first *Jornadas de Participación Ciudadana*.[223] These efforts symbolized the local administration's desire to further promote a feeling of civic participation and engagement among residents living in all of Madrid's different districts.

The other important way of increasing formal civic participation and local democratic affiliation was the public's involvement in planning Madrid's future. In 1982, a preview to the *Plan General* was made available for public consideration and comment. Tierno Galván and the administration specifically opened the *Plan General* to the participation of everyone so that when residents saw the newly revitalized capital in the future they would identify with it and to be able to say: "I also gave my opinion, aware of what was going on, I exercised my critical function, a critical duty, the most important because criticism is the method of giving an opinion that transforms and recreates."[224]

In order to achieve this goal, the administration sought the public's input and went to extraordinary lengths to distribute information about the plan. A massive public information campaign was launched at this time to "make accessible and intelligible the information about the preview of the new *Plan General* and to motivate citizens so that they intervene in the planning of the city's future."[225] Efforts to inform the public about the *Plan General* included a press campaign, dozens of public seminars, the publication of books and brochures, public opinion surveys, and multiple public expositions at the Cuartel de Conde Duque.

In addition to more traditional print ads, radio spots, and billboards, the media campaign to promote broad public involvement included the song *"Pongamos que hablo de Madrid"* in two versions: *"suave"* and *"rock duro."*[226] The "easy" version was performed by the very popular Joaquín Sabina and the "hard rock" version was sung by Antoñito Flores.[227] And, in addition to the informational spots on the radio, a radio program on Radio-Cadena was also produced in order to promote a public debate about the *Plan General* between residents, professionals, and local officials. Focusing not just on the center but also on the various districts around the capital, 12 different roundtable programs were aired to discuss the plan.[228]

The media campaign in all of its different forms also stressed the main democratic objectives of the plan with such slogans as "To recuperate the open Madrid," "To recuperate the Madrid of everyone," and "To recuperate the accessible Madrid."[229] And the campaign neatly summarized some of its most important themes: "utilizing what exists," "conserving the monuments," "cleaning the environment," "protecting the center," "equipping the periphery," "defending employment," and "everyone participating."[230] In all of the methods of communication, the administration made it clear that the participation of everyone was needed to accomplish the goal of creating an open and democratic Madrid: "The fundamental objective of the *public information* is to promote *citizen participation* in the elaboration of the plan [italics in the original]."[231]

Beyond the media campaign, official informational books and brochures were published about the *Plan General* in order to promote greater public involvement. And, as usual, these resources were distributed to all segments of the population. Some of the most detailed information about the administration's plan to remake the capital came in the high-quality book, *Recuperar Madrid*. More than 24,200 of these full-color books were sold at a cost of only $2.70, and an additional 18,500 were distributed to various public institutions, private organizations, schools, and libraries. A folder of information, summarizing the preview of the *Plan General*, was also made available for free to all citizens. A total of 250,000 copies were distributed. In addition, there was the production, and free distribution, of a brochure for each of the capital's districts, explaining the impact of the *Plan General* in each area. More than 90,000 district folders were distributed through the Juntas. Finally, a new map of Madrid, *Plano Madrid*, and a guidebook to Madrid, mentioned above, *Conocer Madrid*, were published as part of the campaign to spark public interest and foster identification with the process.[232]

Probably the single most important effort to promote public debate and participation were the Ayuntamiento's expositions at the Conde Duque. The first exposition opened on March 16, 1982, and detailed the *Plan General* with graphics, models, and documentation. The basic message of the exposition was to offer "the *Plan* to the citizens of Madrid for their information, consideration, and free comment."[233] The exposition was scheduled to close at the end of May but was extended twice due to public demand, first to the end of June and finally to the end of July.[234] In all, more than 56,000 people visited the exposition.[235] At the exposition, everyone was invited to respond with their corrections, observations, and suggestions on a survey provided at the end of the exhibit. The survey was also made available in each district at the offices of the Juntas del Distrito.[236]

In conjunction with the exposition at the Conde Duque, six major public debates were held in 1982 to promote participation and encourage citizen feedback. The six debates covered a variety of topics related to the plan and the capital's future: "The Politics of Transportation in Madrid" (April 1982), "The City and Economic Crisis" (May 1982), "The Preview of the *Plan General* of Madrid" (June 1982), "The Recuperation of the Manzanares River and Its Surroundings" (June 1982), "Madrid's Citizen Movement and the Plan General" (June 1982), and "The Social Problems of Madrid and the Preview of the *Plan General*" (June 1982).[237] In addition to the central exposition at the Cuartel de Conde Duque and the six major debates, 18 smaller exhibits were held in each of the districts to provide more detailed information pertaining to the respective areas, and to promote and collect citizen suggestions in Madrid's peripheral districts.[238] Finally, in addition to all of the above, 75 public hearings were held around the capital in 1982 to debate the *Plan*, with many of them taking place in the most marginal southern and eastern districts of the city, where the discussion was often the most lively.[239]

The administration undertook all of these efforts "so that the citizens are able to *inform themselves of the contents and objectives of the Plan and partici-pate* with their opinions and suggestions in its definitive writing [italics in the original]."[240] There was a difference, however, between informing the public and "selling" the *Plan* as a ready-made product. The administration's goal was "to inform citizens during the process of developing the *Plan* and not 'to sell the *Plan*' (*vender el* Plan)."[241] In fact, the first campaign proposal to promote the *Plan* was rejected by the municipal Oficina del Plan because it tried to "sell" the plan rather than authentically including the public.[242]

Likewise, the administration understood civic participation not as "an obligatory phase of a legal prerequisite, but a permanent activity that influ-enced, influences, and will influence [the plan's] conception, elaboration, and its future management."[243] Increased participation around the plan was designed "to inform, to make aware, to interest, and to mobilize the whole of the population."[244] In other words, increased civic participation would lead to a form of democratic mobilization. Interest groups were encouraged to participate in this process as well. So debate and participation was not just to come from individual citizens but from neighborhood organizations, business groups, labor unions, and political parties, religious organizations, and professional schools, such as the Colegio de Arquitectos, the Escuela de Arquitectura, the Colegio de Abogados, and the Cámara de Comercio.[245]

In fact, some 7,300 suggestions, proposal, criticisms, and alternatives were presented by organizations and individuals during the comment period.[246]

Citizen involvement and participation did not stop there. After several of the suggestions were incorporated into the project, the *Plan General* was again turned over to the citizens of Madrid for another public review in 1983. A second exposition was held in June and July 1983, after the tentative approval of the plan on April 6, 1983. Like the year before, the official exposition and comment period was extended, this time from July 31 to September 30, due to popular demand.[247] This time, however, the comment period was more formal, allowing individuals and organizations to make official claims (*alegaciones*). During this period, the administration received more than 3,000 separate claims[248]

The administration's desire to promote the public's involvement in the planning of Madrid's democratic future extended beyond the solicitation of feedback. While a detailed description of the public's response to the *Plan General* is outside the scope of this work, there is evidence to suggest that the local administration took public participation and comment seriously, resulting in concrete changes to the plan. According to the 1985 finalized version of the *Plan General*, public participation prompted the inclusion of such things as the bypass for the Carretera de Andalucia in the southern part of the city, the removal of the plan to link Madrid and the Barajas airport by train, and the extension of the metro into more neighborhoods on the periphery, including Vicálvaro, Peñagrande, and Hortaleza.[249] The incorporation of these changes symbolized the administration's desire to bring all segments of the population into the process of planning the capital's future and to produce a democratic plan that was "found on the principle that the city is made *by* its citizens and *for* its citizens [italics in the original]."[250]

Informal Participation

At the same time, there was also a strong interest in promoting more than just formal forms of civic participation; the local and regional administrations wanted to promote spontaneous and informal participation by returning residents to the city's once deserted streets. After the experience of the closed and repressive dictatorship, bringing the citizens of Madrid out into the public was seen as a crucial way of promoting democratic *convivencia*, or coexistence. Thus, rather than representing a public nuisance or civil disorder, the idea of returning residents to the streets symbolized a real feeling of community. Writing in 1982, Tierno Galván underscored the deep meaning of street life in Madrid: "In the city is where one enjoys oneself, where one is sad, in the streets of the city is where your life has its most profound emotions, its most clear realizations."[251] The local administration believed that returning residents to the streets was one of the surest ways to distance Madrid from its undemocratic past and transform the capital, and madrileños themselves.

In his inaugural address in 1979, Tierno Galván announced, "[I]t is necessary to return trust to the street."[252] According to the mayor, the recent lack of trust, combined with urban disorder, had negative consequences for the capital's inhabitants: "*[M]adrileños* whose happiness has been narrowing, because the urban structure, disordered and chaotic at times, display a sadness that dries up even a smile."[253] In order to return ordinary madrileños to the city's streets and create a new sense of place in Madrid, both the local and regional administrations implemented a variety of specific programs to promote informal participation. Discussed in detail in the next chapter, open-air theater and movies, footraces, the revival of both large-scale and neighborhood festivals, outdoor sporting events, and free concerts were part of the process of cultural mobilization that called madrileños out of their homes and into the street. But, of course, residents could not be forced to participate in these or in any other activities; the local and regional administrations needed to create an environment that fostered spontaneous participation.

The cleaning and revitalization of Madrid's public spaces, parks, gardens, and plazas was part of this task. With the passage of the *Ordenanza sobre Publicidad Exterior* (Outdoor Advertising Ordinance), pedestrians were also rescued from the constant assault of advertising in public spaces. Likewise, the democratic administrations wanted people to replace automobiles on Madrid's streets. Some of the capital's streets were freed from traffic and pedestrianized, particularly those in the city's center. This effort can be best seen in two important reorganization projects. Many of the streets around the centrally located Puerta del Sol were pedestrianized and traffic was relegated to the southern portion of the plaza. In addition, the aforementioned jumble of underpasses and overpasses, or the *scalextric*, of the Plaza de Atocha was replaced by a tunnel in order to create a more pedestrian friendly zone around Madrid's southern train station. In conjunction with these two major projects, fifty underground parking structures for residents were built between 1979 and 1985 to remove automobiles from Madrid's streets and make the capital more pedestrian friendly.[254] Other efforts to curb the use of the automobile included the *Programa de Limitación del Tráfico* and personal appeals by the mayor himself. Four different *Bandos* encouraged madrileños to park in appropriate places and to drive less frequently and more reasonably, especially during the usually chaotic holiday season.[255]

In addition to these broader initiatives, the Ayuntamiento also sponsored specific activities and events in order to foster a desire for informal participation, including the *Muro de la Paz* (Peace Mural) in the Plaza of Carmen, installed in November 1982, and the revitalization of Madrid's annual marathon. Popular participation was further promoted through the annual *Fiesta de la Bicicleta*, started in 1979. The festival was officially supported by the Ayuntamiento and the mayor personally inaugurated and fired the starting gun, as he did for the annual marathon and for all of the capital's athletic events. Even though it may now be hard to conceive of the capital not dominated by the automobile, the *Fiesta de la Bicicleta* was one of the most popular festivals throughout the first half of the 1980s. In 1980, 100,000 participants celebrated the second *Fiesta de la Biciceleta* and more than 200,000 madrileños participated in the fifth *Fiesta de la Bicicleta* in October 1983.[256] Tierno Galván believed that the high degree of participation in the bicycle festival represented a "protest for a city that is more accessible and tranquil."[257]

One of the events that best exemplified the administration's sponsorship of massive popular participation was Plácido Domingo's free concert in the summer of 1982. Using the free concerts in New York's Central Park as a model, more than 200,000 people attended the performance on the campus of the Ciudad Universitaria de Madrid on July 9, 1982.[258] This concert, along with all of the other officially sponsored initiatives and activities, symbolized Tierno Galván's belief that informal participation was one of the keys to identifying with a new democratic Madrid: "The joy of being is the joy of participating, one who does not participate does not exist."[259]

CONCLUSION

The dramatic transformation of the capital between 1979 and 1986 did not happen by accident. Rather, it was the result of purposeful efforts by Madrid's political elite. Both the local and regional administrations understood that Madrid's identity could be altered and revitalized, or even destroyed if neglected for too long. With this in mind, they consciously implemented a broad plan to create a new inclusive civic identity for the region. Speaking at a conference held in 1984 to "study the present and future of *madrileño* culture," Tierno Galván revealed his understanding of the constructed nature of Madrid's collective identity.[260] At the conference's closing, the mayor explained that up until recently

> the city had been losing its personality, the word "identity" is now used, the identity of Madrid was getting lost, dissolving, and it remained more as a reference on an identity card or more as an official designation then as something that was deeply linked to the people that dwell or had been born or that lived together peacefully in the city of Madrid.[261]

Although not explicitly mentioned, the "dissolving" of Madrid's unique identity was blamed on the Franco regime: "During many long years" there was the notion in all of Spain that Madrid "was not only the seat of government but the center of power and that part of the errors of power came from the city, that the city itself was like the physical space of the errors."[262] The wide-ranging program described in this chapter was the deliberate attempt to remake Madrid and break the association between the capital and Franco's "errors of power." As we have seen, Madrid's political elite used the transformation of the capital to instill civic pride, to educate its citizens, to restore public confidence, and to promote active participation. Together, these changes were meant to forge a common sense of place that included all madrileños. In this way, each of the different aspects of Madrid's transformation—from the restoration of historic buildings to the ending of real estate speculation, from the cleaning of the Manzanares to the creation of thousands of acres of new green spaces, from regulating parking to improving air quality, from the reform of the police force to the construction of new sports centers—served to foster civic affiliations and create a democratic regional identity that was based on voluntary residence and equal citizenship, rather than on ethnicity or place of birth. The following chapter looks at how culture, and cultural mobilization in particular, helped solidify these new attachments to the capital.

CHAPTER 4

CULTURAL MOBILIZATION AND THE
CIVIC IDENTITY PROJECT IN THE CAPITAL

Under Franco, madrileños were mostly cultural "subjects," often forced to receive what they were given with little or no alternative. They could only listen, watch, and accept. They were spectators at the movies and in the theater, silent listeners at concerts and to the radio, and passive receivers of state-controlled television, censored books, and magazines. To overcome this legacy of passivity, and for the new democracy to ultimately succeed, active and engaged "actors" were needed. In addition, all madrileños needed to be able to live together in peace. Madrid's political elite believed that within the context of Spain's top-down transition to democracy, cultural mobilization—as opposed to political mobilization—was the key to changing madrileños' thoughts and behaviors after decades of repression and inactivity. So in conjunction with the promotion of a series of civic values (discussed in the last chapter), culture and cultural activities were used to redefine the capital and promote a new collective identity for Madrid.

Cultural activity in the capital was not, however, about "bread and circuses." In other words, it was not an effort on the part of the local political elite to simply win votes, pacify the masses, entertain the public, or to battle the so-called *desencanto*.[1] Nor was cultural change designed to form an exclusivist "ethnic" identity. Rather, the project was about the residents of Madrid identifying themselves as active democratic citizens after the experience of the dictatorship. To accomplish this task, Madrid's political elite promoted local and regional cultural symbols and implemented a program of broad cultural mobilization in order to reinforce the creation of an inclusive civic identity that centered on Madrid. Put another way, new forms of cultural activity were designed to create a united citizenry that identified itself as open, active, and democratic. At the same time, it was also a form of identification that was linked directly to the capital.

The first part of this chapter explores the relationship between cultural mobilization in Madrid and the creation of this new civic identity. This identity, along with breaking the connection to the dictatorial past, defined a unique set of attributes for what it meant to be a democratic madrileño. A specific connection to Madrid, active participation, and peaceful coexistence were the three most important new "signs of identity." The second part of the chapter then goes on to specifically show how the democratic administrations increased cultural mobilization, which was consciously directed at all madrileños, by expanding Madrid's cultural infrastructure—including the construction of new museums, libraries, recreation centers, and archives—and by promoting new cultural activities, such as art expositions, sports programs, and public festivals.

PART I: CULTURAL MOBILIZATION AND CIVIC IDENTITY IN MADRID

As discussed in the previous chapter, a kind of broad "cultural revolution" was seen as preferable to potentially divisive political mobilization in the capital. Therefore, new ways of thinking and acting, and a corresponding change of identity, would not be achieved through the polarizing rhetoric of formal politics, but instead through a more peaceful and unifying cultural transformation. In other words, cultural mobilization promised to produce a fundamental evolution of daily customs, without the need to invoke the language or rituals of formal politics. This reliance on the cultural over the political also meant that change in the capital would largely be perceived as apolitical or nonpartisan. Consequently, cultural mobilization could happen across the political spectrum, including for those on the right. In this way, all madrileños were to benefit equally from the project to culturally transform Madrid.

The addition of this "cultural element" within the project to define a new civic identity should not be seen as a contradiction. Despite the tendency to label nationalisms (and regionalisms) as either "civic" or "ethnic," the two are often intertwined in practice. In fact, most projects of the late twentieth century display both civic-political as well as ethno-cultural characteristics.[2] In the words of Brian Jenkins and Spyros Sofos, the description of "nationalism as 'Janus-faced' is indeed appropriate here . . . the ambiguity of nationalism does not so much lay in the existence of both . . . 'open' and 'closed' variants; it is the potential coexistence of both elements within every nationalist movement and ideology."[3] And, in this regard, the case of Madrid was no exception.

But the project in Madrid was unique in a different way, in that it specifically used culture to promote *more* inclusion than exclusion. So whereas culture is usually tied closely to an ethnic identity, in this case it was linked to a democratic civic identity. This is quite unusual. As the rest of this chapter describes, broad cultural participation was designed to weave democratic values and an inclusive sense of madrileño identity into the fabric of society.

In other words, the promotion of specific forms of cultural mobilization was used to reinforce the ideals of openness and inclusiveness. Furthermore, after 1983, Madrid's political elite increasingly promoted a kind of official cultural identity, based on the movida madrileña, that reinforced this new civic identity. The next chapter shows how the modern symbols of the movida were adopted and officially promoted in order to further distance the capital from its authoritarian past and redefine Madrid as an open, democratic, and proud region. Both the use of cultural mobilization and the promotion of an official cultural identity based on the movida demonstrate that "culture" does not have to be exclusivist or ethnocentric with regards to the formation of a new collective identity.

In a "Madrileño Vein"

While the movida madrileña eventually became a central part of the project to create a new kind of cultural identity for Madrid after 1983, the effort to culturally transform and redefine Madrid began much earlier. In fact, from the very beginning of the new democratic municipal administration there was an effort to promote a variety of different manifestations of madrileño culture in order to distance the capital from the Franco regime. This separation was designed to allow madrileños to form new democratic affiliations not with the nation but specifically with Madrid itself.

The desire to culturally mobilize the capital in a particularly "madrileño vein" actually extended to before the first democratic local election. In an interview in May 1979, Tierno Galván expressed a desire to replace "hermetical or purely whimsical" forms of culture with a culture that was "more open, more shared, more general, and more madrileño."[4] The reference to "hermetical" and "whimsical" referred to Madrid's culture under the dictatorship. The new democratic administration considered culture under the Franco regime to have been artificially split into elite culture and a patronizing culture of evasion. On the one hand, Franco's cultural program was understood as elitist and mainly for the few, as it favored knowledge, instruction, and individualism over practice, spontaneity, and collectivity. Access to this pious and ornamental high culture was limited, for the most part, to those with superior schooling and economic means. On the other hand, the creation and imposition of an official "Spanishness," including the promotion of soccer and bullfighting, was seen as a kind of mass culture of evasion that served to distract the public and overwhelm local cultural traditions.

In contrast to the past, Tierno Galván's administration wished to foster a new revitalized popular culture that focused specifically on Madrid: "A culture that is not based on elitist activities, but picking up the best of this city at the crossroads, develops cultural activity in its broadest sense."[5] The idea of a popular culture in this case should not be confused with the concept of mass culture, as in American consumer "pop" culture. Instead of representing a homogenized consumer-driven mass culture, it represented a plural culture, by and for the people of Madrid. Also, it was to be a culture free from ideological, economic, political, and religious motivations; instead, it was to represent all segments of the community. To create this "authentic 'cultural revitalization,'" the administration invested resources "in order to elevate the cultural level of all citizens, to modernize the culture of the city, to improve the facilities and the state of preservation of cultural patrimony in this area."[6] The idea was not to bring the level of culture down to all citizens, but to elevate the cultural level of everyone. In short, Tierno Galván's administration believed in creating a new feeling of belonging through both the promotion and democratization of Madrid's culture, and not through its massification.

After 1983, the new regional government of Madrid reinforced and enlarged this project throughout the entire region. Overall, the goal was the same as the one within the city: to foster a cultural program that would promote equality, make culture more accessible to everyone, foster a common identity, and, ultimately, democratize madrileños. While the creation of a new regional flag, hymn, official publications (*Alfoz* and *Agenda Cultural*), and even a television channel was important for promoting regional identity in Madrid, the most significant effort came from this broader cultural program. Similar to the local administration, the regional administration fostered a new civic identity based specifically on madrileño culture, and not on a national culture or on the culture of the surrounding regions of Castilla.

Active Participation

In addition to being based specifically on madrileño culture, cultural mobilization also linked active citizen participation to Madrid's new civic identity. Both the local and regional administrations understood that getting residents engaged and interested in participating was necessary for securing the transition to democracy. In the words of the Concejal de Cultura, Enrique Moral, success was only possible "through the participation and collaboration . . . of neighborhood organizations, cultural associations, parents of students associations, and youth groups of all kinds."[7] In order to accomplish this task, a broad program was implemented to promote cultural activities "at an affordable price for all sectors of the society."[8]

The local administration's official project to promote this kind of active participation was summed up in a detailed series of objectives:

> The restoration of culture through the increase of cultural offerings in the most disadvantaged districts, the definitive abandonment of state-controlled and paternalistic cultural practices that characterized the preceding decades [the Franco regime], the support and promotion of cultural initiatives by residents, groups, and entities of all types, and the construction of the necessary cultural facilities.[9]

In addition to these new cultural facilities and programs, there was also the promotion of the freedoms of expression, creation, and imagination.

And Tierno Galván himself was in the street almost every day, promoting these freedoms with his intellectual prestige, his symbolic position as mayor, and his personal charisma. All of these efforts were designed to create a common sense of democratic belonging through free and active cultural participation.

Peaceful Coexistence

The third aspect of cultural mobilization in the capital was the notion of peaceful, or democratic, coexistence. Specifically, the habits of inclusion and tolerance were created by bringing all madrileños together, guaranteeing equal access to cultural opportunities, and supporting free expression. For Tierno Galván, engagement in cultural activities represented acts of "profound coexistence, of general satisfaction, in which the individual comes into contact with everyone else, and, from this encounter, leaves fortified."[10] This process of bringing everyone together was aided by the fact that Madrid's political elite was willing to embrace cultural difference and that official public sponsorship was available for a wide variety of activities.

For example, it was under Tierno Galván's administration that the first modern mosque was commissioned and designed in Madrid. The high-profile project was located in the northeast quadrant of the city, just outside the ring highway M-30. Showing its support for the project, the Ayuntamiento originally sold the parcel of land for the new mosque for a single *peseta*.[11] Many of the officially sponsored expositions held during this period also reflected the administration's tolerance and openness to change. In October 1983, for example, artists from Israel, Switzerland, Venezuela, France, Argentina, France, Hungry, Germany, and China were brought together in Madrid to exhibit their work at "*La experimentación en el arte*." Tierno Galván served as a member of the organizing committee and inaugurated the exposition, explaining that the exhibit demonstrated "what it is possible to do with relation to a past that strongly demands something new (*novedad*), understanding that experimentation always implies modesty, faith in what it creates and at the same time the will to correct and innovate."[12] Although describing the exposition, Tierno Galván could have been describing Madrid's own transformation. He went on to explain: "[O]ur time is one of birth and not renaissance."[13] In this sense, the promotion of openness and peaceful coexistence led to a new kind of place to live, and not to any sort of a return to the past.

PART II: EXPANDING CULTURAL MOBILIZATION IN THE CAPITAL, 1979–1986

With the idea of creating this "new place to live," both the local and regional administrations enacted a comprehensive and ambitious program to culturally mobilize Madrid between 1979 and 1986. These efforts can be divided into two different categories: first, Madrid's political elite worked to improve the region's cultural infrastructure to the benefit of all residents; second, new cultural activities were officially sponsored that would lead to greater "informal" public participation across the capital.

Infrastructure

In order to create the cultural infrastructure necessary to fully mobilize the residents of Madrid, the democratic administrations built new museums, libraries, cultural centers, and exhibit halls. As just described, Madrid's political elite hoped these structural improvements would promote greater equality and unity among all residents and open up opportunities for increased cultural participation. In other words, it was hoped that an expanded cultural infrastructure would lay the foundation for a democratic identity based on the values of active participation and peaceful coexistence. And, like the rest of the project, these new institutions fostered a particularly madrileño sense of identity, and not "Spanishness" or a national identity, by emphasizing the unique symbols and characteristics of Madrid.

The development of Madrid's infrastructure was significant for another reason as well. It was specifically designed to create lasting change in the capital. Ramón Serra, the head of cultural programming within the Ayuntamiento, said in 1985 that the goal of the local and regional administrations was to "create new infrastructure, infrastructure that would remain in place even if there was a change of political leadership."[14] Thus, the promotion of cultural mobilization through the development of new public institutions was not seen as a series of temporary measures to win votes or entertain residents; instead it was about creating a permanent democratic identity for all madrileños regardless of which political party might be in power.

One of the best examples of this kind of change was the restoration of the Museo Municipal. Beginning shortly after the 1979 elections, the museum was first restored and then reopened to the public in May 1980, after remaining closed for much of the dictatorship.[15] Like much of the capital's historical and cultural patrimony, the Museo Municipal had been neglected by the Franco regime out of a desire to impose an official national identity on the capital. Under the dictatorship, virtually no new items were added to the collection, leaving, in the words of the museum's director, "a void almost impossible to fill."[16] Upgrades needed to reopen the museum included even such basic necessities as air-conditioning, a security system, and a sprinkler system.[17]

After its official reopening, the Museo Municipal held a number of expositions that directly promoted and celebrated madrileño culture, including "Madrid's Ceramic Makers," "The Classic Gardens of Madrid," and "Cartography in Madrid."[18] In addition, the museum acquired 740 new pieces between 1979 and 1983, purchasing "works with madrileño themes or by artists native to the city."[19] In addition to the new acquisitions, there was also the complete restoration of more than 50 madrileño paintings from the sixteenth to twentieth centuries and the restoration of almost 100 porcelains and woodcuts.[20] The museum also began the publication of the magazine *Gaceta* in order to promote both the new institution and madrileño culture.[21]

The Museo Municipal was not the only public institution to lay the foundation for greater cultural participation in the capital. Both a new municipal periodicals library (*hemeroteca*) and an archive were installed in one of the capital's largest historical buildings, the Cuartel de Conde Duque. After serving as the center for the municipal police during the Franco regime (and with its north section in complete ruins), the municipal administration transformed the Conde Duque into one of Madrid's most important cultural centers. The building's notable Baroque portal by Pedro de Ribera was restored and its large patios were redesigned to host a wide range of cultural activities, including festivals, musicals, and concerts to conferences, expositions, and theatrical performances.

Inside the building, the new *hemeroteca* was installed in fire resistant and humidity controlled rooms in the basement. Not only were the facilities much improved, but the library was also moved into a space that could accommodate its 250,000 volumes, whereas the collection was practically unusable before due to a lack of space.[22] A program was also instituted to microfilm and modernize the collection. Similarly, Madrid's archival material, the Archivo de la Villa, was reorganized and moved to the building as well. Instead of being dispersed in different locations across Madrid, the documents chronicling the capital's history were collected, cleaned, disinfected, and installed in 16 kilometers of new shelving.[23] In addition to the *hemeroteca* and the archive, the city's central municipal library was also moved to the Conde Duque in 1986, creating by far the greatest concentration of municipal historical documentation in the capital. Such cultural investment, and the symbolic transformation of the Conde Duque from a police station into a cultural center, clearly demonstrated the administration's desire for not only cultural promotion, but also "the conservation of the memory, the history, and the documents of Madrid."[24] It was exactly his kind of conservation and promotion of Madrid's cultural patrimony that helped foster a particularly madrileño sense of identity in the capital.

In some areas, the development of Madrid's cultural infrastructure had to begin practically from scratch. This was the case for the rest of Madrid's public library system. To serve a city of 3.5 million people, only four libraries were left over from the Franco period.[25] Making matters worse, the four existing libraries were in a poor state of repair. In what must stand as the most bizarre example, the library in the district of Tetuán was only accessible through a police commissary, which made it necessary to pass between detainees to use the library services.[26] Throughout the system, Madrid's collection of books suffered from neglect and censorship during the dictatorship. First editions of Lope de Vega, Arias Montano, Arensola, and Góngora, among others, had been damaged by misuse or neglect.[27] In addition, many books were confiscated immediately following the civil war, and those that remained were not always made available to the public.[28]

To remedy the situation, the *Delegación de Cultura* estimated that 100 libraries were needed for a city the size of Madrid.[29] To begin the process of recovery and to promote greater public access, the local administration installed four new libraries and 15 lending kiosks, with many of these located in public parks and plazas, between 1979 and 1983.[30] Keeping the objectives of reequilibration and decentralization in mind, almost all of these new facilities were located on the periphery of the city. Later, after 1983, the administration opened five new libraries, most in districts that lacked any kind of library services up until that point. Those districts included Buenavista, Arganzuela, Portazgo, and Charmartín.[31] In addition to increasing the number of facilities, the spectrum and quantity of books were increased as well. It was not, however, the administration's desire to stack the shelves full of Socialist or Leftist books. Instead, Tierno Galván's administration wanted to fill the libraries with a wide variety of books: "[W]e are not going to flood them with Marxist books nor are we going to flood them with conservative books."[32] The selection of books would be guided by "good sense" and a desire for "equilibrium."[33]

In addition to museums, archives, and libraries, Tierno Galván's administration also built cultural centers. Active participation and collective encounters were fostered at these new institutions through musical performances, theatre, poetry recitals, conferences, and classes for dance, music, pottery, and ballet.[34] To make sure these opportunities were accessible to all citizens, the administration opened five new cultural centers between 1983 and 1984, in Vallecas, Carabanchel, Arganzuela, Chamartín, and Fuencarral.[35] The large Aula Municipal was also created in the center of Madrid for lectures, conferences, and public courses on such topics as journalism, art, and computer science.[36] All of these opportunities led to greater cultural activity and public discourse. From December 1983 to November 1984, the Aula Municipal put on more than 180 acts, with 103 sponsored exclusively by the Ayuntamiento, and the rest in collaboration with other organizations.[37]

After 1983, the new regional government worked to foster the development of Madrid's cultural infrastructure as well. In addition to fulfilling the basic needs of the newly created regional administration, the creation of new archives, museums, theatres, exhibit halls, and libraries was designed to allow greater cultural mobilization across the entire region. Beginning with the desire to promote the collection of archival material, the regional administration created the *Plan Regional para Archivos Municipales* (Regional Plan for Municipal Archives).[38] This program standardized and preserved archival material throughout the region. There was also a new plan to create a network of regional museums, beginning with the opening of the Museum Buitrago de Lozoya in March 1985 and the Casa Natal de Cervantes in Alcalá de Henares in July 1985.[39] The following year a regional architectural museum was opened in Alcalá de Henares. Each of these examples opened up new possibilities for cultural activity and participation outside the city of Madrid.

In addition to this network of museums, the Comunidad created a series of theatres and exhibit halls. After four years of construction and renovation, there were 19 new locations both in the city and around the region by 1987.[40] And just like on the municipal level, the other important area of structural improvement was the library system. In only two years, between the middle of 1983 and 1985, four major new libraries were opened in Galapagar, Colmenorejo, Las Rozas, and Torrelodones.[41] The groundwork was also laid for a large new central library for the region: Biblioteca Regional de la Comunidad. Overall, the number of regional libraries increased from 74 in 1983 to 102 by 1987.[42] Likewise, the total number of volumes increased by more than 90 percent in the same period, from 270,000 in 1983 to 514,200 in 1987.[43] Such improvements to the library system dramatically increased cultural participation throughout Madrid, with patronage increasing from 216,000 books checked out in 1983 to 536,500 in 1987—a 147.9 percent increase.[44]

Cultural Activities

Along with the efforts to expand Madrid's cultural infrastructure, the local and regional administrations promoted a wide range of new cultural activities and initiatives, including expositions, theatre, youth programs, sports programs, and popular festivals. All of these projects, and especially the revitalization of Madrid's public festivals, emphasized the kind of "informal" public participation discussed in the previous chapter. These new initiatives also promoted a new collective identity that was linked specifically to the region and the culture of Madrid.

From the very beginning of the new local administration, public expositions were used to promote cultural activity in the capital. Starting in 1979, literally hundreds of expositions, conferences, and exhibits were sponsored at the Centro Cultural de la Villa, the new Centro Cultural del Conde Duque, and the reopened Museo Municipal. A small sampling of the exhibits included "*Arte al aire libre*," "*Exposición del Barroco Iberoamericano*," "*Muestra de Cine experimental*," "*Exposición conmemorativa del XXXV Aniversario de la Declaración de los Derechos Humanos*," "*Exposición de obras de Tom Philips*," and "*Imágenes de Madrid*."[45] Between only 1980 and 1983, more than 750,000 people turned out to visit exhibits sponsored by the capital's three main cultural institutions mentioned above.[46] Many of these expositions, such as the exhibit "*Imágenes de Madrid*," specifically highlighted madrileño culture.

Likewise, the regional administration sponsored expositions that contributed "to the knowledge of the diverse social and cultural aspects of the history and the present state of Madrid."[47] Between 1983 and 1987, 25 major regional expositions were dedicated to "*madrileño* themes."[48] Following a trend discussed in the last chapter, many of these expositions also overlooked Madrid's more conflictive recent history. Examples of such expositions included "*Madrid y los Borbones en el Siglo XVIII*," "*Madrid en el Renacimiento*," "*Arqueologia Madrileña*," "*Planimetria de Madrid*," and "*Dibujar Madrid: Análisis y propuestas gráficas sobre arquitectura madrileña*."[49] Despite the fact that some of the expositions tended to neglect Madrid's twentieth-century history, they all reinforced the idea of a distinctively madrileño culture in the nation's capital.[50]

Along with the promotion of artistic expositions, theatre was another area where Madrid's' political elite worked to promote cultural mobilization. In fact, by most accounts, the considerable efforts made by the democratic Ayuntamiento resolved the "theatre crisis" that had developed during the Franco period. Faced with declining spectatorship, crumbling infrastructure, and discouraged theatre companies (due to censorship and a lack of funding), the new administration began a comprehensive program to revitalize existing institutions and revive public interest and participation. For example, the prestigious Teatro Español was reopened after a complete renovation on April 16, 1980. It opened with a grand production of *La Dama de Alejandría*, based on the work of Calderón de la Barca.[51] Similar classics, such as the works of Shakespeare and plays from Spain's Golden Age, were performed to increasing popularity throughout the early 1980s.

This kind of official support for theatre was found at other venues as well. In the Centro Cultural de la Villa, 18 works were staged in 1980 alone, including *El Alcalde de Zalaméa* and *Tragicomedia del Serenísimo Príncipe Don Carlos*.[52] In addition, *Teatro de Verano* (Summer Theatre) was started in 1979 to fill the theatrical, and more general cultural, gap during the months of July and August. As with the administration's other initiatives, this open-air program quickly became popular and expanded rapidly, with both the number of venues and attendance increasing significantly between 1979 and 1986. In 1979, five works staged in four different open-air venues were performed 127 times with a total audience of 30,000 spectators. By 1982, 11 works presented in seven locations were performed 388 times with more than 150,000 people in attendance.[53] In addition, many of these events picked up on the local historical and cultural traditions of Madrid.

Eventually the *Teatro de Verano* was turned into *Los Veranos de la Villa* (Summers in the City), and came to include a wide variety of cultural activities designed to spark the interest and participation of all residents: theatre, dance, ballet, concerts, and films. The acts were also held at increasingly more diverse locations around the capital to promote equality of access. Such new locations included Teatro Monumental, Parque del Retiro, Templo de Debod, Plaza Mayor, Almudena, Cuartel del Conde Duque, and the Plaza de las Ventas (Madrid's main bullfighting arena).[54] By 1986, the size of the program had become truly staggering. More than 300,000 people attended a program that included 13 theatre companies offering more than 150 performances, five ballet and dance companies with more than 30 performances, 184 movies screened in the Retiro, and more than 400 acts comprising 1,000 artists.[55]

On top of all the other theatrical activity, the *Teatro al Aire Libre* (Outdoor Theatre) typically produced five additional shows each summer and presented them "in the streets and plazas to an elevated level of participation."[56] Broad participation was encouraged through the sale of inexpensive tickets and the selection of popular plays. Again displaying an aversion to politically divisive programs, the works were usually chosen from between the Golden Age and the early nineteenth century, including such examples as the popular *La Fiesta de los Austria* from the seventeenth century.[57]

In addition to catering to adults, the local and regional administrations also directed their cultural efforts toward Madrid's young adults. In fact, probably for the first time in the capital's history, the municipal administration put a special emphasis on Madrid's youth by promoting special workshops, conferences, and expositions.[58] The administration also opened a new information center and a number of *casas de juventud* (youth centers) across the capital and funded such activities as art classes, outdoor concerts, and recreation programs.

These efforts to include Madrid's young adults in the cultural mobilization project were particularly significant because of the relative youthfulness of Madrid's population. As a result of a baby boom in the 1960s, just over half of Madrid's population was under 30 years old in 1981, and only 10 percent of the population was over the age of 65.[59] In all, there were more than 1.1 million people between the ages of 15 and 30 living in the region of Madrid in 1981.[60]

Tierno Galván, in particular, understood the importance of Madrid's young people, as they represented the capital's democratic future. Symbolizing his faith in the capital's youth, the mayor frequently praised their virtues: "We have as adults the vain idea that the youth of our generation were better, but the youth of today is honest, united, and virtuous." In addition, the mayor believed, "The young people are filled with ideals, are filled with will, with strength; they are possessed by a feeling of generosity and understanding, and we should support the youth."[61]

Support for Madrid's youth came through the official "development of youth culture, [and] the promotion of associationalism."[62] However, the capital's political elite also recognized that young people were often reluctant to participate in official or formal forms of associationalism, so efforts were made to promote spontaneous and "informal" forms of participation.[63] Both the local and regional administrations sponsored such things as rock-and-roll concerts and contests, including the *Concurso de Rock Villa de Madrid* (Madrid's Battle of the Bands); a magazine dedicated to comics and graphic novels, *Madriz*; and the creation of a Centro de Información for young people.[64] Another activity designed to engage the capital's youth and promote young artists was the creation of the *Salón de Pintura Joven* (Exhibitions of Youth Painting) of Madrid in 1984. By 1986, more than 400 young artists exhibited almost 800 works of art in an exposition attended by 10,000 visitors.[65] Also in 1984, the *Semana de la Juventud* (Youth Week) was created to promote participation in a wide spectrum of cultural events throughout Madrid. In the 1986 program, more than 100,000 young people participated in activities ranging from theatre, poetry, film, and artisan workshops.[66] Although not specifically a cultural activity, the Universidad de Educación a Distancia (UNED) was expanded by the municipal administration in 1980. This expansion made it possible for 11,000 additional students to enroll in classes in the 1982–1983 academic year alone, most of them from four neighborhoods on the periphery of Madrid: Concepción, Atocha, Tetuán, and Móstoles.[67]

Sports and recreation also figured in the local administration's program of cultural mobilization. According to the administration, within the area of culture, "the promotion of popular sports and mass participation is one of the greatest objectives of the Ayuntamiento of Madrid."[68] In 1984, after only three years of development, Madrid's new *Instituto Municipal de Deportes* (Municipal Institute of Sports) was the largest such organization in Spain and the third largest in Europe.[69] The 26 new municipal recreation centers spread out across the capital allowed local participation and instruction in activities ranging from water polo to rhythmic dance. The administration also paid particular attention to the recreation needs of children, the physically disabled, and senior citizens. For example, in 1983 alone, more than 30,000 children were taught to swim at municipal swimming pools.[70] To increase mass participation, the municipal administration began a large club-sports program: *Juegos Deportivos Municipales* (Municipal Sports Activities). Started in 1981, the program's purpose was "to develop the practice of sports and in order to allow all kinds of clubs, associations, and mere groups of friends the possibility of practicing some kind of sport in an inexpensive and simple way."[71] This program, which brought different kinds of people together and clearly symbolized the ideal of peaceful coexistence, proved very popular among Madrid's residents. In fact, the number of participants quadrupled between 1981 and 1984, increasing from 5,000 to 200,000 members.[72] This kind of mass participation stood in stark contrast to the Franco period, when sports activities were controlled by exclusive *federaciones deportivas* (sports federations).

The Return of Madrid's Festivals

Probably the most important initiative taken to culturally mobilize the capital and create a new civic identity was the revival of Madrid's festivals. The only hint of official festival activity that remained after the dictatorship was the Christmas parade and the fiesta of *San Isidro*. Under Madrid's new democratic government, the capital went from having literally no major festivals in 1979 to claiming some of the most popular festivals in Europe by 1986. In 1980, the local administration reinstated *Carnaval* and officially sponsored *San Isidro* and various other city fiestas. Many of these were the first such celebrations since the Second Republic. While activities first began in 1980, the real revival came in 1981 with more than 1.5 million people celebrating *San Isidro* that year.[73] Between 1979 and 1986, more than a dozen festivals were either reinstated or newly created by the local and regional administrations, with some quickly achieving international recognition.

Like the rest of the programs to culturally mobilize Madrid, these festivals served three main purposes: to increase "informal" public participation, to promote a sense of peaceful coexistence, and to tie those two democratic values specifically to the capital. The Concejal de Cultura, Enrique Moral, again explained that the festivals were designed to "bring culture to the streets and make sure that each madrileño got excited and actively participated."[74] However, the administration could not unilaterally create public interest and ensure a festival's success. Instead, the success of these new festivals depended on voluntary participation. In the official program for *San Isidro* 1985, Tierno Galván announced, "It is not enough for the *Ayuntamiento* to propose one thing or another, but it is necessary for social spontaneity to contribute to the efforts of the public institutions. For that reason we request the participation and collaboration of everyone."[75]

Thus for Madrid's political elite participation and collaboration meant *active* public engagement. Writing in the *Villa de Madrid*, Tierno Galván explained to residents:

> We don't want the festivals only to be observed, pure spectacle, but rather enjoyed because the people [of Madrid] participate. For that reason, we look for music of participation, dancing, and we intend that no one remains marginalized from the protagonism of the fiesta.[76]

In order to include all segments of the population, Madrid's festivals offered a diverse range of activities that brought together madrileños from all walks of life. When asked about the administration's role in this regard, Tierno Galván responded:

> Well, we did a lot because the people were without orientation, without order, without direction [*sentido*]. And we gave them order, we gave them orientation, we gave them direction because we organized great fiestas. In this aspect we contributed powerfully. But it is an aspect that, although powerful, is secondary. What is important is popular participation.[77]

According to the mayor, it was the citizens of Madrid that, through their active participation, produced the vital change "not only in daily life but also in the public life, in the cultural life."[78] It was exactly this kind of change that helped create a new democratic identity in the capital.

Writing in the *Villa de Madrid*, Tierno Galván explained, "We want the festivals of Madrid to form a part of our attempt to make the city a living lesson, a permanent pedagogy."[79] The purpose was not however to increase the appreciation for fine art or opera; instead the objective was to transform madrileños in a way that would allow them to identify themselves as democratic citizens. According to Tierno Galván, the festivals taught civic awareness, democratic coexistence, and a host of other important values. For example, the festival of *San Isidro* demonstrated honesty, devotion, and industriousness, all virtues that would help transform madrileños. Tierno Galván believed: "From its own mythic history . . . from the very symbol of *San Isidro*, historical and legendary figure, linked to industriousness, to devotion, to honesty, to the chores of the peasant, and, at the same time, linked also to relaxation and the celebration of the town . . . from all of this symbolism, our festivities are educational"⁸⁰

Festivals were also educational in a way that enriched the culture of the capital. For the mayor, "not having fiestas erases many other things: the traditions of the neighborhoods, accents, expressions, and peculiar manners; practically converts existence into gray."⁸¹ From this perspective, the recuperation of Madrid's festivals would help revitalize the unique characteristics of the capital's identity. At the same time, it also demonstrated that a unique madrileño culture did not have to succumb to a mass consumer society. In the words of the administration: "Madrid regained its festivals and madrileños demonstrated that this city could live without necessarily being yoked to the automobile and the television."⁸² Finally, the revival of the capital's festivals helped show that Madrid could assume a more "confident" identity and overcome its authoritarian past. With the help of Madrid's festivals, the fear and insecurity left over from the Franco regime was replaced with "happiness and confidence."⁸³ And returning the festivals helped madrileños "lose the fear of the street, and of the night."⁸⁴ Of the many different festivals that served to culturally mobilize the capital and promote a new democratic identity, *Carnaval, Navidad,* the *Festival de Otoño,* and *San Isidro* were some of the most important.

On February 27, 1981, only four days after the attempted coup of 23-F, Madrid's residents celebrated *Carnaval* for the first time in more than 40 years. For the administration, the celebration symbolized the "defeat of fear by happiness [*alegria*]."⁸⁵ Held at different locations around Madrid, "but, above all, in the streets," *Carnaval* included parades, live music and dancing, fireworks, and joke competitions.⁸⁶ As a result, thousands of madrileños from all walks of life peacefully came together on Madrid's streets just days after the potentially disastrous coup. The reinstatement of *Carnaval* also promoted a particularly madrileño notion of culture with its revival of local traditions. For example, the *Entierro de la Sardina*—a tradition that had been maintained for decades by only a few dozen citizens—was again popularly celebrated on March 3 with dancing and music.⁸⁷ And like many of Madrid's other festivals, the popularity of *Carnaval* grew sharply over the early 1980s. For example, in 1983, more than 100 floats and processions with thousands of participants were part of the celebration, whereas, in 1981, there had been only 12 floats and smaller processions.⁸⁸

The celebration of *Navidad,* or the Festival of Christmas, was also expanded by the democratic administration in the years following 1979. While the cavalcade of the three kings was the only officially sponsored event under the dictatorship, the new local administration quickly expanded the festivities to ensure that "Madrid was a joyful city, that the collective space of the city would be full of activities that amused and enriched the citizens, with special attention paid to young people."⁸⁹ To better include Madrid's children, the festivities of *Navidad* were enlarged to include activities such as the Week of Children's Theatre, choral and nativity scene competitions, puppet shows, *zarzuelas* at the Centro Cultural de la Villa, a circus, and the Artisan Festival. All of these different activities were officially supported and promoted by the Ayuntamiento.[90]

As he did with all of Madrid's festivals, Tierno Galván took a personal interest in developing and promoting the *Fiestas de Navidad*. In a 1981 radio address, he explained the importance of the festival's universal symbolism, and in particular the story of the three kings:

> They are three kings from distinct parts of the world, they signify the whole planet; one of them, moreover, has a different skin color to better represent the universal. And they go, following a star, to offer a tribute to the innocent.[91]

For Tierno Galván, the story of the three kings represented the qualities of equality, diversity, and universality. These were exactly the kinds of democratic values that the administration wished to impart to the residents of Madrid. To better spread this message and decentralize the festival of *Navidad*, the administration commissioned additional sets of kings for the capital's celebration. Thus, rather than only have a single set of three kings in the center of Madrid, kings were dispatched to every district, even to those "where there is poor lighting, where the streets are narrow, and where the conditions of life are more difficult," so all Madrid's children could experience the gift of the Magi and the democratic message of Tierno Galván's administration.[92]

The diffusion of the local administration's program of cultural mobilization included the revival of neighborhood festivals as well. Like the other activities, these neighborhood festivals were purposely democratized and decentralized across Madrid. According to Enrique Moral, the festivals were to be organized by local residents, "by themselves, in a way totally free and spontaneous."[93] Tierno Galván also stressed the importance of reviving the neighborhood fiestas for Madrid's efforts toward cultural mobilization: "[I]n the place of having lifeless and drowsy neighborhoods, we are reviving them and the residents are making their own fiestas, often using money from their own wallets."[94] In fact, local residents, working with the democratic administration, revived dozens of neighborhood festivals all across the capital, including the fiestas of *San Antón, la Paloma, el Carmen, el Pilar, la Melonera, la Bomba* (*San Cayetano*), *San Antonio de la Florida*, and *San Lorenzo*.[95]

Complimenting these neighborhood festivals, the regional government created its own festival for the entire region in 1984. As a celebration of music, dance, and theatre, the *Festival de Otoño* (Fall Festival) was designed to get residents back on the streets and bring an "elevated level . . . of cultural expression to the entire region of Madrid."[96] While many of the events focused specifically on madrileño culture, the *Festival de Otoño* also tried to expand the culture of Madrid. According to the director of the festival, Pilar de Yzaguirre, the goal was "to seek the participation of the public" and "to open Madrid to all [cultural] trends and to every continent."[97] To open Madrid to the rest of the world, the festival often emphasized international acts, bringing in the Symphonic Orchestra of Vienna, the Orchestra of Paris, Leonard Bernstein, ballet from the Grand Théâtre of Geneva, and traditional music from Japan.[98] And to encourage the involvement of everyone, the acts were held both in the city and around the region. For example, in 1984, there were 31 acts held in the capital itself and 47 in the rest of the region, in such places as Torrelodones, Leganés, Alcalá de Henares, El Escorial, Chinchón, Móstoles, and Getafe.[99] However, compared to such festivals as *San Isidro*, attendance at the *Festival de Otoño* was relatively more modest in the beginning, with only 200,000 people participating in 1984.[100]

In addition to this new region-wide festival, the capital was also given a new "fiesta" day to celebrate and commemorate the region of Madrid. Again demonstrating a desire to overlook Madrid's more recent conflictive history, the second of May was chosen in 1984 as the region's official holiday. According to a spokesperson for the Comunidad, the second of May represented the "date of Independence of the *Comunidad* of Madrid."[101] The date symbolized both independence and regional pride because it celebrated the popular uprising against the French in 1808 in the district of Móstoles. In addition, Madrid's new holiday was to represent "an optimistic commemoration, in contrast to other historical celebrations that are usually negative or painful for the population to remember them."[102] In order to help promote this new holiday, the regional government sponsored concerts, exhibits, and parades annually on May 2. Like the administration's other cultural initiatives, this self-consciously "optimistic" holiday helped change the way madrileños thought about each other and the place in which they lived.

While all of Madrid's festivals were designed to culturally mobilize the capital and foster a particularly madrileño sense of identity, the fiesta of *San Isidro* was probably the most important in this regard. In an effort to repress Madrid's unique cultural identity, the Franco regime downplayed the capital's most important festival for almost forty years.[103] It was as if the former regime wanted to remove any symbol that would give Madrid a cultural uniqueness and differentiate it from the Spanish "nation." As a result, by 1975, *San Isidro* was little more than a distant memory for most madrileños.

Under the new democratic administration, the residents of Madrid were actively encouraged to come together and honor their patron saint. As mentioned above, the main revival occurred in 1981 with more that 1.5 million residents turning out. To realize as much popular participation as possible, all of the acts were officially subsidized and they were "diversified in order to reach the sensibilities of every generation."[104] In 1982, for example, more than 200 diverse acts were offered for the enjoyment of residents of all ages.[105] Except for a few performances in the Palacio de los Deportes, all of the acts were free and open to all madrileños.

When the time came to decide exactly where the celebrations of *San Isidro* would be held, the administration chose "the space corresponding to the Madrid of the nineteenth century."[106] This decision to celebrate *San Isidro* in the center of the capital was done with a clear purpose: "Although the policy of the *Ayuntamiento* is in every way, and including with regards to culture, decentralization, it was thought in this case the citizens of the periphery should take as their own the center of the city."[107] Thus, for ten days during the festival, the city's center, symbolizing "official" Madrid, would be turned over to all residents. Enrique Moral summed up this desire: "[W]e want the center of Madrid to be a fiesta where the people go during those days not to go shopping, or pay a ticket, or resolve paperwork, but to enjoy themselves."[108]

While simple enjoyment and bringing everyone together on Madrid's streets were important goals, *San Isidro* also specifically promoted madrileño culture. Rather than focusing on national symbols, the festivities centered on the music, food, and culture of Madrid. For example, as part of the official *San Isidro* 1984 celebration, 25 films about Madrid were featured.[109] The film series, inaugurated by Tierno Galván, showcased films related to Madrid, or that represented Madrid's cultural traditions. During the opening presentation, the historian Julio Pérez Perucha pointed out the sometimes difficult task of distinguishing "films of Madrid (*cine madrileño*)" from Spanish cinema in general. According to Pérez Perucha, this difficulty existed for Madrid even though it was not the case for other parts of the country: "[I]n the case of the cinemas of other nationalities [or regions] of this territory that we call Spain, it appears relatively easy to decide what types of movies originate from a certain nationality and not from another."[110] For Pérez Perucha, the case of Madrid was problematic because of the common association of the capital with Spain's "national" cinema.[111] Despite the perceived difficulties of recognizing them as such, the festival presented more than two dozen films that showed off a "traditional *madrileño* character."[112] And, in general, the festivals of *San Isidro* consistently emphasized the cultural symbols of Madrid, not national symbols.

While some aspects of traditional madrileño culture were part of the festivals of *San Isidro*, modern cultural symbols increasingly played an important role after 1983. As discussed in detail in the next chapter, the music, art, and general aesthetic of the movida madrileña were incorporated both into *San Isidro* and into the administration's broader program of cultural mobilization between 1984 and 1986. Despite this shift toward modern cultural symbols, all of Madrid's new cultural initiatives, and especially the capital's newly reinstated festivals, promoted a particularly madrileño sense of identity. It was a new sense of place that stressed active participation, peaceful coexistence, and the unique characteristics of Madrid in order to distance the capital from its undemocratic past and create a new feeling of belonging.

CONCLUSION

It is widely acknowledged that in the other regions of Spain the development of a regional consciousness, or identity, was tied directly to the promotion of regional culture. Juan Pablo Fusi reminds us:

> In each of the autonomous communities there has been a proliferation of local historical studies, a political program to recuperate lost or almost lost local traditions, support for the maintenance of its historical patrimony, the organization of cultural acts—conferences, expositions, seminars, and congresses—, financial support for new artists, independent theatre groups and alike, [and] attempts to promote university studies and impel cultural popularization.[113]

Even though it is not typically recognized, this exact promotion of regional culture happened in the capital as well. However, rather than using culture to create a collective identity based on exclusion (as in the other regions of Spain), the regional and municipal democratic administrations of Madrid used culture to reinforce the creation of a new inclusive civic identity. Regardless of age, political affiliation, economic status, language, or place of birth, all madrileños were encouraged to come together and actively participate in a wide variety of cultural activities that related specifically to the capital. Madrid's political elite believed that this cultural mobilization—emphasizing active participation and peaceful coexistence—would form the foundation of a new democratic identity. In other words, cultural mobilization in Madrid was designed to weave democratic values and an inclusive sense of madrileño identity into the fabric of society. Cultural participation also provided a viable path to democratic consolidation in an environment where formal political mobilization was not possible.

However, Madrid's political elite did not rely solely on a program of broad cultural promotion to redefine madrileños. Instead, increasingly after 1983, the local and regional administrations focused cultural mobilization and a kind of official cultural identity specifically on the modern symbols of the movida madrileña. As the next chapter shows, the movida's modern symbols were far more effective at redefining Madrid as an open, democratic, and proud region, than were traditional cultural symbols recovered from the capital's tainted past.

CHAPTER 5

JUST A "TEARDROP IN THE RAIN"?
THE MOVIDA MADRILEÑA AND A NEW
DEMOCRATIC REGIONAL IDENTITY

While the programs described in the previous chapter encouraged all madrileños to come together and actively participate in a wide range of cultural activities, Madrid's political elite increasingly focused cultural mobilization on the very "modern" symbols of the movida madrileña.[1] Thus, in contrast to many of the other regionalist projects in Spain during this period, Madrid's political elite did not rely on the capital's traditional customs or cultural heritage (*lo castizo*) to promote a new post-Francoist democratic identity. The focus simply was not on such symbols as Madrid's traditional dance, the *chotis*, or dress, or forms of artistic expression, such as *zarzuela*. Rather, the official projection of Madrid through cultural symbols was based on the capital's culturally vibrant present, and especially on the new movida madrileña. In the words of the president of the Comunidad of Madrid, Joaquín Leguina, it was to be based on the "*contra-castizo*." The creation of this new and modern cultural image of Madrid was meant—like the rest of the project—to engage all madrileños, regardless of economic status, political affiliation, or original place of birth.

While the local and regional administrations used the movida madrileña to help create a new identity for Madrid after 1983, it is important to recognize that the capital's political elite did not fabricate the movida. Instead, the movement developed largely spontaneously between 1975 and 1983. Only after the specific characteristics of the movida had fully developed did the administrations take an interest in the movement between 1984 and 1986. When it was clear the movida represented an inclusive, participatory, optimistic, and modern culture, the mayor and the other political elite appropriated the movement in order to further distance Madrid from its authoritarian past and transform madrileños into active democratic citizens. The movida was thus an important part of the "cultural revolution" (discussed in Chapter 3) to change the underlying values and habits of madrileño society. In other words, the local and regional administrations specifically promoted the movida's modern symbols in order to create a new dynamic cultural image of the capital, which in turn reinforced Madrid's distinct regional democratic identity.

Among other things, the movida symbolized greater tolerance toward homosexuality, an embrace of youth and youth culture, the liberalization of sexual norms, the popularization of culture, the inclusion of traditionally marginalized groups, and a significant degree of pride and optimism with regard to Madrid's future. Such an open and universal projection of madrileño culture was meant to close the gaps caused by differences in class, age, political affiliation, and place of birth. Also included in the movida's symbolic meaning were the freedoms of creation, imagination, and participation. In addition, the embrace of the movida's modern culture also made Madrid unique in the Spanish context in the mid-1980s, as no other region in Spain had opened itself to modernity, or at least to modern cultural currents, in quite the same way. Seen from this perspective, the promotion of a modern cultural image of the capital clearly differentiated the region of Madrid from other parts of the country.

After first reviewing the ways in which the movida madrileña has typically been understood up until this point, the majority of this chapter will show how the development and eventual appropriation of the movement took place in Madrid between 1975 and 1986. Part I explains what the movida was and where it originally came from. Part II describes why the movida was so attractive to Enrique Tierno Galván and Madrid's other political elite. Part III explores how the local and regional governments co-opted and instrumentalized the movement after 1983. The goal throughout the chapter is to highlight the connections between the movida madrileña and the larger project to define a new post-Francoist democratic sense of place for the newly designated region of Madrid.

As a "spontaneous" cultural movement encompassing film, the plastic arts, music, and a roaring nightlife, most observers have described the movida as a brightly burning, but ultimately unimportant, youth movement or counterculture that had no lasting political or cultural impact either on the capital or on the country. As a result, since the 1980s, academics, writers, and journalists, both inside and outside of Spain, have ignored or marginalized the movida madrileña. Apart from the colourful and provocative films of Pedro Almodóvar, the movida has attracted little attention from Hispanists working outside of Spain.[2] Inside the country, the movida had been neglected completely until very recently, dismissed as an ineffectual and ephemeral blip on the cultural radar during the post-Francoist period.[3] In fact, there is not a single monograph in any language on the movida madrileña.[4] The movida has also been left out of major historical and cultural examinations of the period. To cite one of several possible examples, in Santos Juliá's review of Spanish political and cultural history between 1975 and 1996, the movida madrileña is not specifically mentioned at all.[5]

In the small body of literature that does exist about the movida, three main interpretive trends can be identified. It is important to note that all three of these trends place the movida in either a broader national or international context, rather than focusing specifically on the movement's relationship to the capital itself. The first sees the movida as one part of a nationwide cultural renaissance that swept Spain after the end of the dictatorship. The second trend views the movement as a kind of belated counterculture. And the third trend understands the movida within the context of national and international youth culture. While each of these trends explains certain aspects of the movida madrileña, none of the perspectives are specifically rooted in the historical context of Madrid. As a result, all three of the academic positions emphasize the movida's apolitical nature and none see a direct connection between the movement and the project to transform the capital into a new democratic region.[6]

As for the lasting or overall significance of the movida madrileña, all three of the positions just outlined conclude that there was little. Practically no one sees the *movida* as having much long-term political or cultural significance. As far as political importance, the movida was understood as apolitical to begin with, so there has been little question of long-term political significance. On the cultural front, most agree it was a movement that burned too brightly for its own good, leaving behind almost nothing of value and making little impact on madrileño society. The spread of AIDS, increased drugs use, and co-option by the mass media are the usual reasons cited for the movida's swift and permanent demise. In the popular oral history of the movida, *Solo se vive una vez: esplendor y ruina de la movida madrileña*, the editor, José Luis Gallero concludes: "[W]hat has endured is the going out for drinks and conversation habit."[7] Mark Allinson, on the other hand, sees only the work of Pedro Almodóvar as having any lasting cultural significance: "What survives of the defunct *movida madrileña*, the only real candidate for mythical status, is Pedro Almodóvar."[8] Teresa Vilarós holds even a dimmer view. Vilarós laments the lack of any lasting cultural legacy and insists that apart from memorabilia nothing remains of the movida: "[W]hat is left of the '*movida*' is fodder for collectors."[9] Similarly, in one of the few articles devoted exclusively to the movida, Peter Scales concludes that the movida, as a transitory and ephemeral movement based on fleeting audiovisual media, was ultimately just "a teardrop in the rain."[10]

In addition to the three academic positions, critics and commentators on both the left and the right have also discounted the importance of the movida in the capital's development after 1978. As a result, they have failed to see any relationship between the movement and regionalism in Madrid. Generally speaking, both sides of the political spectrum have perceived the movida as apolitical, trivial, banal, and frivolous. The left has looked down on both the form and the content of the movement, and on the way in which it was popularly received. The flashy, brash, and popular character of the movida clashed with the high cultural standards set by many of those on the left. Cultural critics, such as José Carlos Mainer, have often been—in the same breath—both critical and exasperated by those who participated in the movida and by what the movement produced: "[T]hey design useless objects, impossible decorations and impossible clothes that, nevertheless, sell in all of Europe."[11] For Mainer, the movida's cultural products were bought and sold despite their obvious uselessness. In addition, many of the "*progres*" of the left decried the movida's apparent lack of "values" and believed that the movement was a distraction from formal political participation. The founder of *El País*, Juan Luis Cebrián, has described the movement as a "cultural sub-product" advocating a reversal of values, which eventually leads to a kind of cultural fascism.[12] For Cebrián, and many others, the movida's "very individualistic, very hedonistic, [and] very outwardly annoying" character did little to further the left's progressive political and cultural mission.[13]

In contrast to the left, the right was more inclined to see the movida madrileña as political, but as ineffectively so. The movement was generally viewed as a blatant attempt by the new democratic administrations to construct an artificial culture exactly to their own specifications. Conservatives such as Ricardo de la Cierva criticized the Socialists, and the left in general, for purposely intervening in matters of culture, and for intervening in a way that produced a "red" culture for the masses.[14] It was also believed that this populist culture was promoted to the detriment of more formal and "authentic" artistic traditions. Specifically, the right accused the left of inventing a kind of "light" culture to serve their specific political goals and to win elections. In 1991, the long-time city councilman, and new mayor of Madrid, José María Álvarez del Manzano summed up the right's general understanding of the movida:

> It was something ethereal, political propaganda, leaving not a single trace behind. I do not remember a single book, a single painting, a single album; the "*movida*" left nothing. It was an invention, and therefore it vanished.[15]

For conservatives such as Álvarez del Manzano the movida was simply an artificial invention of the left. It produced nothing, represented no one, and left no cultural or political legacy. For the right, it was as if the movida never occurred at all.

While almost all observers have insisted on describing the movida as a sometimes flashy, but ultimately unimportant, youth or counterculture movement that had no lasting impact, the movida can better be understood by placing it within the particular political and cultural context of the capital itself. This is not to say, however, that the three academic positions outlined above are untrue. In fact, all three provide an important layer of meaning: the movida was part of a broader cultural renaissance; it did have certain similarities to cultural movements of the past; it was influenced by the culture of Madrid's youth; and it did largely manifest itself as formally apolitical. But, within the specific historical context of Madrid in the 1980s, the movida madrileña also played a significant role in the transformation of the capital after the experience of the dictatorship. In fact, as mentioned above, the institutionalization and official promotion of the colourful, and at times chaotic, movement proved to be an essential piece of the program to create a new sense of place based on inclusion and greater cultural participation. While the refurbishment of Madrid's infrastructure and the restoration of its crumbling monuments constituted a major part of the program to promote this new identity in Madrid, the movida madrileña increasingly shaped the forms of cultural mobilization in the capital and provided the foundation for a new official cultural image, or cultural identity. Together, these two separate aspects—the physical and the symbolic—formed a more complete regional identity project. In this sense, and despite its apparently apolitical nature, the movida was broadly political in that it played an essential part in the formation of the capital's new democratic regional identity.

PART I: SPONTANEOUS DEVELOPMENT, 1975–1983

Although it is difficult to fix the date of the exact birth of the movida, the years 1975 and 1976 were vital for the development of the movement. After the death of Franco in November 1975, increased freedom of expression and fresh influences from abroad combined to create a new environment of cultural curiosity and creativity in the capital. And the new forms of cultural and artistic expression that especially began to appear in the summer of 1976 under Adolfo Suárez's UCD center-right government were the result of the confluence of several additional factors: less censorship, relative economic prosperity, high hopes accompanying the new democracy, and pent up cultural demand. Despite the fact that few people in Spain knew how to play an electric guitar in the 1970s, rock-and-roll and pop music quickly became two of the most common means of expressing these hopes and new-found freedoms.[16] Among other cultural trends, a mostly underground rock-and-roll movement, known as the "rollo," was started in Valencia, Barcelona, Seville, Santander, and Madrid.[17] The movement grew out of the first rock festivals held in Burgos and León in the mid-1970s. Popular music, however, was not the only way Spaniards chose to express themselves after the dictatorship. It seemed as though everyone wanted to try their hand at writing, painting, comics, or photography during this period. In 1977 the music critic and promoter Jesús Ordovás commented on this increase of new cultural activity: "On every corner of every city you find a guy or a girl putting together their own magazine, their own comic, their own song, be it on toilet paper, on a vinyl record, or on a stone."[18]

By the end of the 1970s, the rock-and-roll rollo had faded and was being replaced by the nueva ola, or "new wave." Inspired in part by the punk and new-wave bands from England and, to a lesser extent, the United States, new musical groups, sporting head-turning haircuts, sprang up in Catalonia, the Basque country, Valencia, and León. Loquillo and Los Trogloditas came from Barcelona, Siniestro Total from Vigo, Los Ilegales from Gijón, and PP Tan Sólo from Elche. But, it was in Madrid that these new cultural trends, which first formed the rollo and later the nueva ola, developed into something more—something that would ultimately turn Madrid into what many madrileños believed was "the cultural capital of the world."

Before the movida madrileña developed into a mass phenomenon that captured the attention of Madrid's mayor, the international press, and even the French Minister of Culture, Jack Lang, the movement first began as a loose collection of marginal cultural currents.[19] And, in contrast to the massive official support it would later receive, the movida started largely as a spontaneous movement. In the late 1970s, no one was in charge and there were no official objectives, no manifestos. The movement developed through a diverse mix of bohemian artists, punk rockers, and pop music devotees. It also got help from Madrid's youth in the rundown neighborhoods of the city's center—Lavapies, Malasaña, and Chueca—and in the much neglected districts on the periphery. From the beginning, the combination of newly found freedoms, youthful enthusiasm, and diverse artistic interests quickly intersected to form a budding cultural movement that became recognized for its vitality and spontaneity.

The appearance of new mainstream outlets for differing opinions, such as *El País* and *Diario 16*, the arrival of British and American rock and pop bands, and the development of a number of "alternative" magazines, such as *Star* and *Ozomo*, all helped to inspire the creation of new publications and musical groups specifically in Madrid. Young madrileños began expressing themselves freely through such self-published magazines as *Bazofia*, *Cascorro Factory*, and many others, most of which are now forgotten. At the time, the popularity of these early magazines was so great that the creation of a small coordinating publication was needed: *Premamá* (*Prensa Marginal Madrileña*). Soon specialty magazines focusing on popular music joined in the development and diffusion of the movement. Early magazines devoted to pop and rock music included *Star*, *Vibraciones*, and the very popular *Disco Exprés*.[20] These were followed later by *Rock Espezial*, *Rock de Lux*, and *Ruta 66* in the early 1980s.[21] Music fans also began publishing their own magazines, or fanzines. Dedicated to specific bands, musical genres, or even neighborhoods within Madrid, these spontaneously produced magazines were created out of the sheer affection for the music and were often distributed free of charge. Early examples included *96 Lágrimas*, *La Pluma Electra*, and *Lollipop*, followed later by *Degalité*, *Ediciones Moulinsart*, and *Banana Split*.[22] Finally, inspired by Robert Crumb and graphic novels from California, young madrileño artists, such as El Hortelano, Ceesepe, and Javier de Juan, produced expressive and often outlandish comics that reflected the growing vibrancy of the period.[23]

At the same time this publishing activity was under way, new musical groups were being formed by eager young musicians, many with little formal training. The group Burning, whose first record was appropriately entitled *Madrid*, and Kaka de Luxe, led by the future movida icon Alaska, first started playing in clubs in Madrid in 1977.[24] Other early groups included Aviador Dro and Tos. From these initial precursors, literally hundreds of bands eventually came to form a spectrum of musical styles in the years to come from "heavy" rock to jazz rock and everything in between.[25] Some of the most famous names from this period included Barón Rojo, Ramoncín, Zombies, Radio Futura, Nacha Pop, and Paraiso.[26]

With these new musical developments came the emergence of a seemingly infinite number of new bars, concert halls, and nightclubs. The Pentagrama in 1978, the Vía Láctea in 1979, and the Marquee in 1980 were three of the early pioneers.[27] Other well-known locations came to include El Sol, El Jardín, Carolina, Morasol, Universal, and, the most famous of all, Rock-ola.[28] In addition to bars and clubs, new groups also played in small theaters and concert halls, such as Martín, Alfil, and Barceló. Soon new recording opportunities came to the aid of this developing music scene. Independent record labels, including Discos Radiactivos Organizados (DRO), Tres Cipreses, Grabaciones Accidentales, Spansuls Records, Goldstein, Victoria, Dos Rombos, and Nuevos Medios, allowed an increasing number of madrileño bands to access the rapidly growing market.[29]

Broadcasting also played a decisive role in the early propagation of the movement that later came to be called the "movida." First local stations, such as Onda 2 de Madrid and Radio 3, and later national FM radio stations provided a continual outlet for the new records being produced in Madrid. Before 1982, Onda 2 achieved popularity with its musical programs hosted and produced by Jesús Ordovás, Rafael Abitbol, Mario Armero, and Gonzalo Garrido.[30] Some of the most popular shows included "Dinamita," "Revolver," and "Dominó." Radio 3 also made a splash with its shows "Esto no es Hawaii," "Diario Pop," and "Tiempo de Universidad."[31] The station also featured other programs related to the movida and the urban culture of Madrid "that discussed literature, linguistics, photography, art, architecture, urbanism, philosophy, and environmentalism."[32] In addition to radio, television programming on Spanish national television, TVE, also featured the musical and cultural currents of Madrid. Early shows dedicated to popular music included "Popgrama," "Aplauso," and, from Barcelona, "Musical Express."[33] The most important early program, however, was Paloma Chamorro's "Imágenes." While primarily a space for the plastic arts, the show also featured popular musical groups from Madrid, such as Radio Futura. Later television programs that featured the capital's popular music scene included "Pista Libre," "Caja de ritmos," and "Popque."

Mixed in with the writers and musicians was a collection of aspiring artists with interests ranging from film and photography to painting and fashion design. In the area of film, Pedro Almodóvar was without a doubt the director most closely associated with the movida. Released in 1980, Almodóvar's *Luci, Pepi, Bom y otras chicas del montón* was the first film to represent the music, artists, and general cultural aesthetic of the movida. Almodóvar went on to create three other films about Madrid during this period: *Laberinto de Pasiones* (1982), *Entre tinieblas* (1983), and *Que he hecho yo para merecer esto?* (1985). Other filmmakers connected to Madrid in the 1980s included

Fernando Trueba, Fernando Colomo, and Félix Rotaeta.[34] Some of the most significant works from the period included Trueba's *Ópera Prima*, Óscar Ladoire *A Contratiempo*, and Manuel Gutiérrez Aragón *Maravillas*.

Photography, which first began to be taken seriously during this time, played an important role in the early development of the movida as well. In addition to producing album covers and posters, photographers such as Alberto García-Alix, Pablo Pérez-Mínguez, Gorka Dúo, Juan Ramón Yuste, and Miguel Trillo captured the images of the movida that were then circulated through both magazines and galleries, increasing the visibility and popularity of the movida.[35] Bárbara Allende, better known as Ouka-Lele, also helped increase the visibility of photography with her highly stylized painted photographs. As for painters, Guillermo Pérez Villalta, Alfonso Albacete, Fernando Vicente, Sigfrido Martín Begue, and the homosexual partners known as Las Costus created the images that symbolized the creativity and diversity of the movement. In turn, newly opened art galleries, such as Buades, Moriarty, Estampa, Vijande, and Sen, hosted and promoted the works of these new photographers and painters.

While photographers and painters were busy expressing themselves on paper and canvas, young designers were converting Madrid into *the* center of fashion and design. For the first time, streets such as Almirante and Argensola in the center of Madrid displayed cutting-edge fashion, the likes of which could have only previously been found in Barcelona or outside of Spain. The new designers responsible for this change, such as Adolfo Domínguez, Sybilla, Ágatha Ruiz de la Prada, Jesús del Pozo, and Manuel Piña, were extremely young and energetic, and brought to Madrid fresh new ideas from a variety of backgrounds.[36] Both Ágatha Ruiz de la Prada and Sybilla were only 20 years old when they presented their first fashion shows in Madrid in 1980 and 1983, respectively. Adolfo Domínguez got his start at the end of the 1970s, presenting his first collection at Ibermoda in 1979.[37]

This explosion of cultural activity in the areas of fashion, music, photography, film, and the plastic arts was due, in part, to close and overlapping associations within the movement, and by what can only be described as "synergy." New magazines promoted new bands. Graphic artists and cartoonists designed album covers. Singers wrote for music magazines. Rock bands performed at gallery openings and magazine launches. In short, everyone lent a hand with everyone else's projects and enjoyed the same in return. Likewise, it was not uncommon for the same individual to wear many hats, participating in a range of activities: from writing for a magazine to hosting a radio show or playing in a band.[38] The same held true for the sites of the movement. Music venues, such as Rock-ola, held fashion shows, art expositions, and theatrical productions. In short, it was a highly interconnected cultural scene with different disciplines and venues reinforcing and supporting each other. The result was a world where the cultural elite all knew one another, gathered at the same bars and cafes, attended the same concerts and gallery openings, and passed through the Rastro, Madrid's flea market, on Sunday mornings. By the early 1980s, however, this original nucleus began to expand at an ever faster rate due to greater mass media attention and due to broader changes within the capital.

The year 1981, in particular, represented a turning point for the movida. When, on February 23, Colonel Antonio Tejero burst into parliament shouting, "No one move! [*Que no se mueva nadie!*]," it was already too late. Of course inside the building no one was moving, especially after the ceiling was riddled with bullets. Outside the parliament building, however, was a different story. New forms of social and cultural "movement" had already spread around the capital. The coup's resounding failure the next day only succeeded in giving more confidence to those who desired to take Madrid in a new direction.

In fact, after the failed coup in February 1981, Madrid was a more secure and hopeful place. A stronger feeling of freedom and tolerance, and less fear that the authoritarian days of Franco could return could be sensed in the capital. Buoyed by massive displays of popular support and the successful recuperation of *Carnaval* less than a month after the attempted coup, cultural participation expanded all across Madrid.[39] For example, on May 23, 1981, the students of the School of Architecture of the Universidad de Complutense, with little money and no administrative support, organized the "*Concierto de Primavera*" on the campus of Ciudad Universitaria. More than 15,000 people attended the eight-hour festival, which concluded without a single major incident.[40] Groups at the concert included Alaska y los Pegamoides, Los Secretos, Nacha Pop, Los Modelos, and Mamá.

Also in 1981, after focusing heavily on politics for nearly six years, the mainstream mass media started paying more attention to the cultural phenomenon of the movida madrileña. Under the direction of José Manuel Costa, the cultural section of *El País* began devoting more space to rock and pop music. At *Diario 16* (now *El Mundo*), José Antonio Maillo focused a great deal of attention on the city's growing cultural scene. In fact, *Diario 16* published the first front-page story covering a movida rock concert in September 1980.[41] Interest in Madrid's new cultural gyrations also came from some surprising places. Julián Ruiz wrote about concerts and rock music for the sports daily *Marca*.[42] Testifying to the movement's initial lack of political affiliation, the right wing paper, *El Alcázar*, in its Sunday editions, even covered the capital's popular music scene under the direction of José Manuel Cuellar.

At the same time, Madrid's local bands could be increasingly heard on national radio stations, such as RNE (*Radio Nacional de España*), thus greatly increasing the diffusion of the movement.[43] It was later in 1981 that many of the concerts held at the city's local clubs, including those at Rock-ola, which also opened that year, were broadcast live or rebroadcast on the radio.[44] Concerts became so popular that many were even broadcast on television. Marking an unprecedented level of interest in popular music, the year 1981 set an all-time record for total music sales, with $138 million spent on music nationwide.[45] The following year, even a new international art fair was started in the capital. After a last minute decision to change the location from Barcelona to Madrid, ARCO brought further attention to the capital's increasingly prestigious cultural scene.[46]

If 1981 represented the consolidation of the movida, then the period after 1983 represented its full popularization. It was at this point that the "official organs" of the movida appeared: *La Luna de Madrid, Madrid Me Mata, Madriz,* and, later, *Sur-Exprés.*[47] More influential than profitable, these magazines were the citadels of culture that promoted the movida's writers, designers, musicians, and artists. Launched in November 1983, *La Luna de Madrid* was the most important of these publications. There was not an artist related to the movida who did not appear on the pages of what became the most emblematic monthly magazine of the movida.[48]

In the realm of music, 1983 saw the creation of numerous free radio or pirate radio stations eager to spread the sounds of the movida. Examples included Onda Sur, Radio Luna, La Voz de la Inexperiencia, Onda Verde, Radio Fortaleza, and Radio Rara. Madrid's bands also benefited from the creation of a new commercial radio station. Dedicated almost exclusively to the music and culture surrounding the movida, Radio El País got started with the help of the newspaper by the same name. The station's new programs, such as "Tribus Urbanas" and "Lo que yo te diga," successfully linked together the music, culture, and urban language of the movida in a professional and widely popular format.

With a title that referenced Spain's sixteenth century "Golden Age," the television program *La Edad de Oro* also débuted in 1983. Hosted by Paloma Chamorro, the former creator and host of *Imágenes,* the program featured many of the movida's most important musical groups.[49] The one-and-a-half to three-hour live show quickly became a favorite of both performers and music fans.

With its own television program, radio stations, and magazines, the movida soon reached a fevered pitch that incorporated mass participation. Hundreds of thousands of people actively participated in the movida on a daily basis, attending concerts, expositions, and film openings, and clogging the city's streets at all hours of the night. For many madrileños, the world seemed to revolve around new paintings, songs, movies, and clubs, rather than around the former gray and lifeless administrative world of the capital. There was a feeling of euphoria and of optimism, a feeling that the world had somehow changed. For a time, it seemed anything was possible. It was at this point that Madrid's local political elite began to take notice of the movement known as the movida madrileña.[50]

PART II: FROM THE MADRID OF THE DICTATORSHIP TO THE MADRID OF THE MOVIDA

While it is clear that the Ayuntamiento played no direct part in inventing the movida, it is important to recognize that the administration did indirectly aid the movement's development by creating a climate of tolerance, openness, and free expression between 1979 and 1983. In this sense, Madrid's political elite did not originally create the movida, but rather opened the space for the movement to develop through its desire to culturally transform Madrid. In other words, the Ayuntamiento's emphasis on cultural promotion and participation created the space for new cultural trends—common in other parts of the country after the dictatorship—to become something greater in Madrid.

As described in the previous chapter, Madrid's municipal administration did more than simply tolerate free expression; it actively promoted and sponsored a wide spectrum of cultural initiatives designed to increase participation and instill a sense of pride in the residents of Madrid. Tolerance and openness to experimentation were the hallmarks of this program. For instance, in addition to the previously cited examples, the work of Robert Mapplethorpe was shown openly in Madrid during this period and, after 10 years of prohibition, Andy Warhol's films *Flesh* and *Trash* were shown at the cinema Bellas Artes in 1979.[51] Warhol himself even made an extended trip to the capital in 1983. Theatres featuring x-rated adult movies were also legalized in April 1983.[52] In one of the most obvious examples of the political elite's tolerance, the mayor of Madrid, on January 28, 1984, stood before more than 15,000 people gathered in the Palacio de los Deportes for the opening of Radio 3's 24-hour rock festival and offered the following advice: "Rockers: whoever is not high, get high and watch out (*Rockeros: el que no esté colocado, que se coloque y al loro*)."[53] Tierno Galván's hip sounding message of openness and tolerance was received not only by those present in the stadium, but was also transmitted live on the radio and viewed by an estimated 10 million spectators on national television. It was also reported verbatim in Spain's major newspapers the following day.[54] Mary Nash has observed that the statement "was perhaps the most unequivocal exhortation to have fun ever to issue from someone in authority."[55] This exhortation by Madrid's most prominent public official, and its dissemination by the mass media, was understood as a "blessing for tolerance" and was typical of the process that created the environment for new forms of cultural activity to flourish within the capital in the early 1980s.[56] This early indirect support, however, should not be confused with the local and regional administrations' later official adoption of the movida after 1983.

CHARACTERISTICS AND MOTIVATIONS

It was only after the movida had fully matured and enjoyed widespread popularity that the political elite took a particular interest in the movement because of its enormous potential. In addition to taking advantage of its energy and creativity, cooption and institutionalization of the movement occurred because the movida's modern symbols and characteristics were simply more effective at defining Madrid as an open and democratic region than were the traditional cultural symbols recovered from Madrid's past. Put another way, the movida madrileña happened to offer a distinct set of characteristics that neatly coincided with the project to create an inclusive civic identity in Madrid. Specifically, the movida represented an inclusive, participatory, optimistic, and modern culture that could be used to distance the capital from the Franco dictatorship and differentiate the region of Madrid from other parts of the country.

First, the local municipal administration, and later the new regional government, was attracted to the movida because it represented a plural and democratic movement that embraced a wide spectrum of styles and groups. In this way, and in contrast to many contemporary cultural movements, the movida tended toward inclusion rather than exclusion. Support for such an inclusive or "open" movement further reinforced the notion of peaceful coexistence, or *convivencia*, within the capital.

First, there was no single dominant group or style. Nor was there a leader or manifesto. Instead, the movida was made up of a diverse number of overlapping groups: mods, rockers, punks, post-punks, and heavys (*jevis*). Likewise, the movement was comprised of a diverse range of musical styles: Oviformia, Aviador Dro, Terapia Humana, and CSI played techno music; the group Arco Iris dedicated itself to jazz rock; Alaska y Los Pegamoides dominated the new wave scene; Derribos Arias catered to the crossover "pop-rock" audience; and Tritón, Barón Rojo, Obús, and Goliath belted out *rock duro*.

All of these groups and cultural currents mixed together in the capital's bars, cafes, galleries, and nightclubs, creating a vibrant blend of styles and ideas, and symbolizing the notion of coexistence. At the usual movida locales, there were no doormen to decide who was stylish enough to enter. All groups were free to participate. In 1987, Fabio de Miguel recalled the scene in Madrid's most famous hot spot earlier in the decade: "To be in Rock-ola was like being in Noah's ark, the mix of rockers, rockabillys, mods, punks, technos, and new romantics, everyone packed together and very pleased, it was something biblical."[57]

Although leaning heavily toward the under-40 generation, this "ark" of the movida was inclusive with regard to age and class. Despite various attempts to characterize it as such, the movement was not comprised only of disaffected teenagers. Instead, the movida represented diverse age groups. Although Alaska was only 17 years old in 1980, many participants, such as Jesús Ordovás, Paloma Chamorro, Pablo Pérez-Mínguez, Moncho Alpuente, Diego Manrique, and Pedro Almodóvar, were in their late 20s and early 30s. In addition, madrileños of all ages increasingly participated in the vibrant nightlife and general cultural scene related to the movida. Just as different age groups participated in the movida, different social classes also came together within the movement. Commenting on this phenomenon, the journalist Alfredo Villaverde wrote in 1987: "[It was a movement] that intended no one remained excluded from it."[58] Rock-ola was especially known for its mixture of different social classes, from lower-class *macarras* to upper-class *pijos*. A broad cross-section of society also frequented the Bar Universal, usually presided over by the poet Leopoldo Panero. The movida's cultural elite was also comprised of a mix of classes. Carlos Berlanga came from a prominent family, while Alaska was from a middle-class family in

Mexico.[59] Pedro Almodóvar hailed from even more humble beginnings in La Mancha. The second editor of *La Luna de Madrid*, José Tono Martínez, summed up the movement's lack of class distinctions in 1987: "We are not very classist (*clasista*)."[60]

This feeling of universal inclusion was typified by the popular movida radio station, Radio 3. With regard to the music, the station offered programming that was "open, free, and without prejudice."[61] The director of Radio 3 from 1982–1986, Pablo García, recalls the diversity and inclusiveness of all of the programming

> whose contents about literature, linguistics, photography, art, architecture, and urbanism, philosophy, environmentalism, and sociology were incorporated and debated in a new style and with the participation of the listeners without major hindrances imposed by the direction of the station.[62]

Rather than simply being motivated by the bottom line, the station's programming was free to try to embrace all groups, including those considered marginalized at the time: "homosexuals, objectors, ecologists, immigrants, and prisoners."[63]

Representing a distinct break from the Franco regime, the movida also embodied greater coexistence through its inclusion of alternative lifestyles. Within the movida, gays and lesbians proclaimed their sexual orientation openly for the first time. In fact, with Chueca—the city's traditional gay neighbourhood—as one of the centers of the movida, Madrid's queer scene played a prominent role within the movement. Gabriel Giorgi has already described the importance gay life had in the formation of the cultural movement and in making Madrid a modern, open, and democratic city.[64] In particular, the success and visibility of Fabio McNamara, Pedro Almodóvar, and the couple known as Las Costus represented greater acceptance of homosexuality. Bibi Andersen was even able to achieve great popularity as a transsexual. Years later, the writer and poet José María Parreño commented on the role of homosexuals in the movida: "[Homosexuals] played quite an emblematic role. In part, it was an index of liberty and tolerance . . . there was such a number of homosexuals in the world of painting and literature that they began to function as a group of power."[65] The editor of *La Luna de Madrid*, Borja Casani, also recalled the importance of homosexuals in the movement: "Homosexuals produced the first great liberation. That is totally evident. They were the first to liberate themselves out of all Spaniards. They were 15,000 kilometres ahead of everyone else."[66] Due in part to the movida, one of Franco's strictest taboos was even in vogue to a certain degree. After reading the book *Gay Rock* by Eduardo Haro Ibars, Alaska told her mother, "I want to be a boy so I can be queer."[67]

Finally, the movida symbolized inclusion and greater coexistence because it incorporated the diverse styles and personalities of a cultural elite that, like the majority of the population of Madrid, originally came from some place else.[68] For example, Alaska was born in Mexico, Alberto García-Alix and Kiki D'Aki in León, Pedro Almodóvar in Castilla-La Mancha, Jesús Ordovas in La Coruña, El Hortelano in Valencia, José Tono Martínez in Guatemala, Enrique Costus and Miguel Trillo in Cádiz, Juan Costus in Palma de Mallorca, Adolfo Domínguez in Galicia, and Rafael Abitbol in Tangiers.[69] These artists, writers, and musicians came to Madrid from other regions of Spain, bringing with them their own unique set of customs and forms of expression. It was the combination of these diverse characteristics that made the movida and Madrid both unique and inclusive at the same time. The popular movida singer Nacho "Nacha Pop" García Vega conveyed this feeling particularly well in 1987: "It is like a guesthouse or a five star hotel. Everyone is a visitor or a child of those born elsewhere and this is the best thing. No one is more from Madrid than anyone else, nor less [from Madrid]. Even though they just arrived."[70] Everyone had an equal claim to the capital, and an equal opportunity to create an image of Madrid based on his or her own needs and desires. As a result, the movida did not emphasize traditional madrileño customs; instead, the cultural activity of the movement included a broad range of interests and themes. It was exactly this diversity and openness that made the movida attractive to Madrid's heterogeneous population, and to its political elite. The movement's inclusiveness of form and expression was particularly attractive to the political elite that hailed from various parts of the country as well: the mayor spent his youth in Soria, the mayor's first lieutenant was from Jaén, the Concejal de Cultura was from Valencia, and the president of the Comunidad of Madrid was from Santander. The movida's openness and inclusion of a wide range of people and ideas made it ideal to employ in the official project to distance Madrid from its authoritarian past and reinforce the creation of a democratic civic identity based on peaceful coexistence.

Second, the local administration supported the movida because it exemplified the idea of active and popular participation. The movida was not about sitting idly around in cafes and bars. It was about participation and movement—thus the term "movida." In addition, although there was a core cultural elite within the movement, the movida was a public phenomenon open to everyone. Moreover, the main sites of participation were Madrid's streets, plazas, festivals, bars, galleries, and cafes. For the most part, activity did not take place in private homes, in private clubs, or behind closed doors. Some of the main public spaces of the movida included the Plaza del Dos de Mayo, the Rastro, and the open-air bars (terrazas) along the Paseo de la Castellana. This focus on public places closely coincided with Tierno Galván's desire to return residents to the streets of Madrid. In this way, the movement further helped create a new kind of place to live where the streets and plazas were a prolongation of one's own home.

In general, social exchange and participation were also fostered by the movida's decentralization and lack of hierarchy. While Malasaña may be the neighbourhood most closely associated with the movida, the movement was not centralized in any one location; instead it was spread out across the capital. In addition to the heavy rock played out on the periphery neighbourhoods, there were at least four major zones of the movida. In Argüelles, in the northwest region of the city, the bars and clubs frequented by university students were clustered around the calle Princesa. Extending from the Plaza Santa Ana to the Paseo del Prado, the area of Huertas was preferred by the most politically progressive, *los progres*. The area of Orense, located around the commercial center of Azca, was the most upscale center of the movida, featuring shops and bars frequented by upper-class *pijos*. Finally, Malasaña and Chueca, located just north of the Gran Vía, were home to some of the most active and raucous scenes of the movida. There were also hangouts, such as La Bobia, around the Rastro, in the southern part of the city, and various other hot spots scattered across Madrid, such as the Club Carolina in Cuatro Caminos.[71] This decentralization increased accessibility and participation in the movement. At the same time, the movida's own media outlets further increased popular participation in the movement. The numerous radio programs, the television show, *La Edad de Oro,* and magazines, such as *La Luna de Madrid* and *Madrid Me Mata,* all helped popularize the movida beyond an exclusive cultural elite.

Within the popularized movement, the simple role of spectator was not satisfactory. Activity and creativity were the norm. No one wanted to be limited to just viewing paintings, sculptures, or photographs; many wanted to become a painter, sculpture, or photographer. It was no longer enough simply to go to the movies; making movies or videos became the goal. In the same way, movida bands did not play for money or fame in the beginning. They played for pure and simple amusement, or simply because they could.[72] The movida also symbolized the belief that there was something more to life than simply economic production and consumption. Years later, one of the members of Los Secretos, Álvaro Urquijo, recalled: "We did not think about making money. It was pure affection [for the music] and if you triumphed it was almost a fluke."[73]

With its embrace of "everything's OK (*todo vale*)," the movida also opened the way for new forms of participation, representing the idea that everything had value, especially those things that had been labelled "popular" or "ordinary." For example, it was at this time that the "popular" art form of photography became accepted and even fashionable. The movida photographer Pablo Pérez-Mínguez spread the idea that "everything can be photographed."[74] Photographers such as Pérez-Mínguez, Alberto García-Alix, and Miguel Trillo increasingly took pictures of everyday objects and ordinary people. Pérez-Mínguez claimed at the time, "I think that photography is the easiest and most popular art in history."[75] The popular nature of photography—and of the movida in general—helped break the association of artists and cultural production with elitism. It was no longer important, or even necessary, to have a big studio or fancy photographic equipment to be a photographer. Anyone could participate and take photos. This kind of liberty and lack of cultural elitism was typical of the movida. Anyone could pick up a camera, microphone, or paint brush and participate. As a result, a popular feeling of active participation was created around the movement.

This participation, however, favoured cultural activity over other forms of engagement, specifically over formal political activity. Without question, the movida failed to align with the traditional political positions of the transition and post-transition periods. Although representing greater cultural mobilization, the movida reflected a joyous and sometimes self-indulgent rejection of political conservatism on the right and of social conformity on the left. As mentioned above, it supported neither the "traditional" left of Felipe González and Juan Luis Cebrián nor conservatives such as Manuel Fraga and José María Álvarez del Manzano. As a result, formal political mobilization was not a significant part of the movement. In fact, the movida's apparently apolitical nature has often been pointed to as evidence of its triviality and unimportance.[76] However, in an environment where Madrid's political elite wished to have sharp political positions forgotten, the movida's emphasis on cultural participation perfectly coincided with the desire to avoid political mobilization, which might have led to polarization and social unrest. Likewise, the themes of violence and political revolution were largely absent from the discourse surrounding the movida, thus making it more acceptable to Madrid's political elite. Fun and sometimes frivolity based on active participation, peaceful coexistence, and artistic creativity became, for all practical purposes, a political posture in and of itself. While this position displeased many on both the traditional left and right, it completely fit with Tierno Galván's desire to create a new participatory and inclusive madrileño identity in the capital.

Third, in addition to the movement's inclusive and participatory aspects, the local and regional administrations also wished to take advantage of the confidence and pride associated with the movida. Despite its later spread to other parts of the country, the movement was firmly rooted in Madrid. And, in general, the participants of the movida had a great deal of enthusiasm and pride for their work, for each other's projects, and for Madrid in general. As the movement tended toward artistic creation and production, rather than destruction, self-loathing, and cynicism, the movida also reflected a significant degree of optimism and vitality.[77] Most importantly, and in contrast to the traditional image of "Spanishness" promoted by the Franco regime, the movement offered cultural symbols that focused specifically on Madrid.

Without calling directly on traditional customs from the past, much of the movida was inspired by various aspects of the capital. Madrid's flea market, el Rastro, lent a certain bric-a-brac aesthetic to the movement. Heavy rock influences came from the peripheral districts of Vallecas and Legazpi. As mentioned above, Chueca, at that time a run-down neighbourhood in the city's centre, contributed a distinctively gay influence. Likewise, the cultural production of movida artists proudly features symbols of the capital. For example, Ouka-Lele produced painted photographs of Madrid's most famous fountain, Cibeles. Pablo Pérez-Mínguez took pictures of the Gran Vía that put the old boulevard in a stunning new light. The musical group Burning recorded an album entitled *Madrid*. The titles of the movement's most emblematic magazines made reference to the capital: *La Luna de Madrid* and *Madrid Me Mata*. And the films of Pedro Almodóvar prominently featured the capital itself. Even the name of the movement, the "movida madrileña," specifically highlighted the locality of Madrid.[78] Furthermore, the musical groups of the movida sang strictly in Spanish, during a time when English songs were widely popular. For the municipal and regional administrations, the movida appeared to embrace many "authentic" characteristics of Madrid.

Those madrileños associated with the movida were also very proud of Madrid and confident of its new culture. For example, journalists related to the movement were fond of comparing the Madrid of the movida to Florence during the Renaissance.[79] Many madrileños even came to believe that Madrid had been transformed by the movida into the new "cultural capital of the world." The journalist Moncho Alpuente first suggested in January 1984 that Madrid, with its diverse collection of poets, musicians, expositions, and fashion designers, would in fact become the capital of the world that year, at least on a cultural level.[80] This idea of Madrid as the cultural capital of the world quickly became widespread within the movement. In a letter to the editor of *La Luna de Madrid*, two readers of the magazine plainly observed: "Madrid is at a moment in which we don't doubt to classify it the 'Capital of the world' as Paris, London, or New York had been in their day."[81] The same readers wanted "to buy up many copies of *La Luna* and send them to their friends in New York, London, etc. in order to say 'You see? Now don't you wish you had a city like ours?'"[82] Even the head of the Centro Cultural de la Villa, Antonio Gómez Rufo, believed the movida "made this city the cultural capital of Europe."[83] By the middle of 1984, there was the firm belief that, with the help of the movida, Madrid had been transformed into some kind of new cultural mecca.

It is less important whether or not Madrid was actually the cultural capital of the world at that moment. What is more important is that many madrileños, especially those who participated in the movida, believed that it was. As a result, for the first time in many years, Madrid symbolized cultural vibrancy, rather than political repression. In addition to inclusion and participation, the movement's specific connection to Madrid inspired pride, new feelings of affiliation, and optimism toward the future. In this way, the movida represented a new way of perceiving the capital and a new way of life that many residents—of course, not all—could be proud of. The political elite recognized the importance of this pride and chose to assimilate the movida into the project to distance the capital from its repressive past and create an inclusive cultural identity based specifically on the symbols of Madrid.

Fourth and finally, Madrid's political elite wished to adopt the movida because it represented a "modern" culture that was in line with, or even ahead of, the rest of Europe. In fact, the dramatically different style, music, fashion, and artistic production of the movida made both intellectuals and the popular press at the time call the movement something completely new.[84] The movida appeared to be so different from what had come before that it was labelled "postmodern." With constant references to such French postmodern philosophers as Jean-François Lyotard and Jean Baudrillard,

Spanish journalists, writers, professors, and even politicians argued that the development of the movida symbolized Spain's, or at least Madrid's, entry into the postmodern age.[85] According to the French academic, Bernard Bessière: "No other concept pertaining to the social sciences had such a resonance among Spanish intellectuals, in the course of the past decade [1980s], as that of 'post-modernity.'"[86] Despite its popularity, not everyone agreed with this designation, resulting in a debate between "modernists" and "postmodernists."[87] This debate, which in the end came down to little more than semantics, had the important effect of associating the movida with the cultural and intellectual cutting edge and of increasing its visibility even further.[88] Regardless of whether the movement was a modern or postmodern phenomenon, the movida clearly represented something novel and contemporary in the eyes of the new democratic administrations. Most importantly for them, the movement was obviously not a part of the culture of the Franco regime. In this way, the modern image of the movida symbolized a decisive break from the past.

Almost everything about the movement was the opposite of the Franco regime: new vs. old, open vs. closed, night vs. day, promiscuity vs. chastity, color vs. greyness, and popular vs. elite. The movida's nocturnal cultural activity seemed to replace the emphasis on administrative and functionary daylight activity of the former regime. Likewise, experimentation took the place of traditional ways of doing things, as the movida represented a fascination for what was new and untried. Instead of the clean, pressed uniforms of the Franco period, the young fashion designers of the movida assured that "the wrinkle is beautiful."[89] The movida also brought with it brand-new artistic forms, including the first major efforts in Spain in the areas of installation art and video as artistic forms. And, overall, the popular nature of the movida contrasted sharply with what was often perceived as the cultural elitism of the former regime. The forms, symbols, and style of the movida all appeared as something new to Madrid's political elite. As a result, the movement provided both an important aesthetic break from the authoritarian past, and the symbols to create a distinctively new image of madrileño culture.

For Madrid's political elite interested in transforming the capital, the movida also represented a high level of modernization, at least in terms of culture. The types of modern music and art that were being produced in the capital at this time were comparable to those in England and the United States. Moreover, movida artists had their own unique look and musical sound. In other words, they were not mere copies of their Anglo-Saxon counterparts. Participants in the movement were even called "*los modernos*," and the movida was claimed to have a "look *moderno*." This modern "look" was also aided by the fact that the movida centered, in part, on the region's youth, and on the idea of "youth." Without question, the movida was, to a certain degree, a youth movement, as many of the participants were "*jóvenes*" under the age of 30.[90] Just as importantly, however, the movida also represented the characteristics that were associated with youth in general: freedom, spontaneity, and curiosity. These were the same modern "values" that were increasingly becoming esteemed in the rest of the West at the same time.

Finally, the origins and inspirations of the movida were located not in the past, but in the present. While many observers have linked the movida to the 1960s counterculture movement in the United States and to the "swinging sixties" in London, the movida was actually related to more contemporary cultural currents. The international punk scene and the contemporary new-wave phenomenon, originally from Manchester, were two of the most important early influences. Other inspirations included glam rock (typified by David Bowie, Gary Glitter, and Alvin Stardust), the work of Andy Warhol, and "alternative" publications from California.[91] Movida musicians, in particular, were inspired by a diverse mix of contemporary musical influences: the Sex Pistols, the Ramones, Siouxsie and the Banshees, the Clash, and Lou Reed. These links to modern cultural currents made the movida more attractive to an administration wishing to redefine Madrid as a uniquely open and tolerant region than were those symbols retrieved from the past.

PART III: OFFICIAL ADOPTION AND INSTITUTIONALIZATION, 1984–1986

By the mid-1980s, Madrid's mayor, more than anyone else in the administration, recognized the movida's ability to transform the capital. For Tierno Galván, the movement represented a collaborative effort to renovate and revitalize Madrid through popular participation, openness, and spontaneity. In March 1986, Tierno Galván's replacement, Juan Barranco, quoted the old professor's understanding of the transformative process associated with the movida:

> The "*movida*" signifies participation . . . a collaboration between cultural organizations, the administration, and the people. We have passed from rigid and institutional forms to a largely spontaneous culture, which created itself through democracy and municipal efforts. In this sense, we have remade Madrid.[92]

In order to "remake" Madrid in this way, the symbols of the movida had been deliberately incorporated into the official program to transform the capital. Specifically, the local and regional administrations based greater cultural mobilization and the official projection of madrileño culture on the symbols of the movida madrileña. As a result, the movement became fully institutionalized—and further popularized—between 1984 and 1986.

Institutionalization of the movida on the municipal level came in a variety of forms: financial support for publications and popular music directly related to the movida, sponsorship of expositions, declarations of support by Tierno Galván, and the inclusion of movida bands and personalities into institutional celebrations such as the festival of *San Isidro* and *Navidades*. Generally speaking, appropriation of the movement started at the end of

1983 and culminated with the official exhibit "Madrid, Madrid, Madrid" held at the Centro Cultural de la Villa, in the summer of 1984. After that point, the administration fully adopted the movida as the official cultural identity of Madrid until the death of Tierno Galván in January 1986.

The first major public acknowledgement of the importance of the movida came in February 1984. At a weeklong conference dedicated to the culture of Madrid, Tierno Galván for the first time, publicly linked the importance of the movida to the recovery of madrileño identity. Echoing many of the journalists of the movida, Tierno Galván announced at the closing of the conference, "In many aspects, today Madrid is the cultural capital of Europe."[93] He then went on to give credit for this achievement to Madrid's youth and to the movida:

[Young people] speak of the *movida' madrileña*, but already surpassing the scope of what is strictly juvenile [*juvenile*], the *movida madrileña* is a general fact that embraces more than folkloric amusements or displays of joy that come each year during the conventional dates [of celebration], or acts of collective revelry on the street, the *movida madrileña* also refers to being the capital of the plastic arts. In summary, this thing that is called "the *movida*" has become generalized.[94]

For Tierno Galván, the movida represented more than just a youth culture or a subculture; it was a movement that permeated a large portion of society. Just as importantly, the movida was largely responsible for Madrid's growing cultural prestige and the pride associated with that transformation. This recognition and admiration for the movida translated directly into greater institutional support for the movement.

The year 1984 saw a sharp increase in public support for both publications and music related to the movida. In January 1984, the Ayuntamiento of Madrid launched its own movida-inspired comic magazine, *Madriz*.[95] Guided by the concepts of "liberty, imagination, and a lot of quality [*cantidad de calidad*]," *Madriz* provided a platform for the young graphic artist, writers, and cartoonists of Madrid.[96] One of the most obvious expressions of the local administration's support for the movida came in the first issue of *Madriz*. In an editorial signed by the Ayuntamiento of Madrid, the capital's new cultural atmosphere was celebrated: "There has emerged an urban culture with a vitality, a force, and certain peculiarities that happen in few places in the world."[97] Specifically it was a culture characterized by "free, generous, and open coexistence."[98] The Ayuntamiento went on to directly credit the movida for the creation of this new cultural milieu:

The *movida madrileña*—with its musicians, its artists, its poets, its painters, its *enrollado* crowd, with all of their new values—is an authentic cultural revolution. The future is loaded with promises. The city is becoming more free, imagination takes over the street—because the street belongs to everyone— and advances irresistible over what is dead and the old expired "glories" of official culture.[99]

In a very short time, this official publication, which openly supported and celebrated the culture of the movida, achieved both widespread popularity and critical success in Madrid. The artists Ana Juan and Fernando Vicente were finalists for the Icaro prize for the most promising young artist for their work in the magazine. Ana Juan also won the competition for the best magazine cover presented by the *Salon Internacional del Comic y la Ilustración de Barcelona* for issue number four of *Madriz*.[100] In addition, *Madriz*'s popularity in the capital inspired imitations both at home and abroad. Backed by institutional support, the Andalusian town of Granada saw the creation of *Granada de Papel*, while *Trama Futura* was started in Valencia. In France, imitators included *Chic, Zulú,* and *Metal Hurtlant*.[101]

Madriz was not the only movida related publication to receive support from the local administration. It was widely believed that the Ayuntamiento of Madrid, through the Concejalía de Cultura, helped start another one of the magazines most closely connected to the movement: *Madrid Me Mata.* Launched in the summer of 1984, *Madrid Me Mata* was the creation of the institutionally well-connected Óscar Marimé.[102] Along with the famous *La Luna de Madrid, Madrid Me Mata* was one of the quintessential publications of the movida. Filled with a mix of photographs, illustrations, interviews, and heterodox texts, the publication became required reading for those interested in the capital's rapidly expanding cultural scene.[103]

While it remains unclear whether or not *Madrid Me Mata* was launched with the direct help of the administration, it is for certain that the magazine, along with *La Luna de Madrid*, was subsidized by both the Ayuntamiento and the Comunidad of Madrid through advertising. Several full-page ads promoting Madrid and its new regional status appeared in the magazines between 1984 and 1986, often on the back cover.[104] Institutional support for these magazines was significant because they represented the most successful and emblematic publications of the movida. These were the magazines that directly promoted the artists, filmmakers, and musicians of the movida. Moreover, they were quite successful in this task. In fact, the French Minister of culture, Jack Lang, known for his strong support of "national" cultural activities, sent a small delegation to Madrid to study the success of such magazines as *Madriz* and *La Luna de Madrid*.[105] The difference, however, was that the publications backed by the municipal and regional administrations of Madrid promoted a specifically madrileño culture identity, and not a national identity.

Similarly, the administration sponsored the music that represented Madrid's unique urban culture. In 1984, the Ayuntamiento of Madrid put out its own recording of movida music, invited a large number of movida bands to play at *San Isidro* that year, and held a huge rock festival, showcasing local groups.[106] In February 1984, the Ayuntamiento organized a party at the club Morasol in order to present its own record of the winners from the sixth *Concurso Rock Villa de Madrid*.[107] The same year, more than 300 groups competed in the seventh *Concurso Rock Villa de Madrid*. There were so many participants that it took the entire month of May to showcase all the bands.[108] The event achieved such popularity because winning the *Concurso de Rock* could propel a band to national and even international fame, as many winners went on to sign major record deals, including Alaska, Zombies, Gran Wyoming, Obús, La Frontera, Derribos Arias, and Mercedes Ferrer.[109] The administration's support of the *Concursos de Rock* literally gave hundreds of madrileño bands their start.[110]

The administration's official embrace of the movida was also evident in the celebrations of *San Isidro* that year. The program for 1984 focused on the capital's youth and, in part, on the movida. Many of the activities were directed toward young people because, according to Tierno Galván, in addition to representing the future, they "are the most *madrileño.*"[111] Writing about the city's festival that year, Tierno Galván maintained: "The fiestas form part of what we call the cultural *movida* of Madrid."[112] Accordingly, *San Isidro* featured a number of movida bands that year: Ramoncín, La Mode, Alaska, Loquillo, Nacha Pop, Gabinete Caligari, Golpes Bajos, and Radio Futura. As usual, the mayor lent his personal support to the festival in 1984, attending on average six acts per day during each of the nine days of celebration.[113] At the end of the festival largely devoted to the movida and the culture of the capital's youth, Tierno Galván declared: "Madrid is turning into the capital of *fiestas* of Europe."[114]

While sponsorship of publications and music served the administration's agenda of promoting the movida, the most important linkage between the official cultural identity of Madrid and the movement came in June 1984 with the exhibit "Madrid, Madrid, Madrid" held at the Centro Cultural de la Villa.[115] The exposition, inaugurated by Tierno Galván on June 25, recounted the history of Madrid from 1975 to 1984. However, instead of offering a generic history of the capital, the exposition described how the capital had transformed from the Madrid of Franco to the Madrid of the movida. As a result, the movement was directly tied to the official history and cultural identity of Madrid.

The large exposition, which was on display all summer, was organized by the Comunidad and Ayuntamiento of Madrid with a $176,000 budget.[116] It consisted of more than 2,000 objects, which were meant to represent the capital's social and cultural transformation from 1975–1984. Objects included a marijuana plant, a curtain from the cinema Capital, books by Francisco Umbral, fashion creations from Paco Casado and Adolfo Domínguez, sculpture, paintings by Ricardo Villalta, posters, photos, music videos, press clippings, and scale models.[117]

However, the exposition did more than just feature the inanimate symbols of the movida, it celebrated both the personalities and the style of the movement. Typifying this dominating presence, the inaugural celebration for the exhibit was filled with movida notables: Ceesepe, Pedro Almodóvar, Fabio de Miguel, Ágatha Ruiz de la Prada, Ana Currá, and others. There were so many movida personalities that Pedro Almodóvar exclaimed during the opening, "In this exposition I feel like I am in a private party, filled with private knick-knacks (*chismes*)."[118]

The exposition's objective, according to Rafael Peñalver, a representative from the Centro Cultural de la Villa, consisted of "bringing together what makes Madrid one of the capitals of the world of art."[119] It was clear to all who attended the exposition that the capital's political elite believed it was specifically the movida that made Madrid one of the "capitals of the art world."

Embracing the diversity and seemingly chaotic nature of the movida, Tierno Galván even inaugurated the exhibit with the words: "Blessed be chaos [*bendito sea el caos*] because it is the mark of liberty."[120] On the tenth anniversary of Tierno Galván's death, Enrique Moral, recalled how the mayor had shouted those words and the effect they had on the audience:

> Tierno invited everyone, including ambassadors from every country and army generals [to the exposition]. After passing through the exposition he climbed up on a platform and spoke. His speech was a dissertation about the value of chaos in the shape of the universe. When he finished he called on everyone present to shout *viva el caos* [long live chaos]. He said, "I believe that after these words the only thing left is to shout *viva el caos* together." It was a singular moment, all of those military men looked at each other while shouting *viva el caos*.[121]

After the official linkage between the movida madrileña and the cultural identity of Madrid was made through the exhibit that summer, the local administration continued to increase its association with the movement and promoted even greater cultural activity around the movida. In fact, through the next year and a half, it became almost impossible to distinguish where the popular movement of the movida left off and where the administration's official sponsorship began.[122] For example, in 1984, the group Radio Futura premièred their second album, *La ley del desierto / la ley del mar*, in Madrid's Centro Cultural de la Villa, with official backing.[123] It was also in 1984 that Pedro Almodóvar announced that he wanted to make a movie with Tierno Galván "in which he would be shown exactly how he is."[124] In other words, there was no need for the mayor to act or play a different role. He would fit perfectly into Almodóvar's silver-screen world of the movida exactly as he was.

With regard to the political elite, many personally showed their support for the movida. In addition to sporting the fashion creations of movida designers (with the exception of Tierno Galván, of course), politicians increasingly posed for photos with movida singers and artists.[125] The mayor even granted a one-on-one interview with Alaska for the magazine *Primera Linea de la Actualidad* at the end of 1985.[126] Different institutions within the Ayuntamiento also directly took advantage of the movida. In 1985, the youth program *Fin de Semana*, organized by the Concejalía de la Juventud of the Ayuntamiento of Madrid, featured the movida acts of Kiko Veneno, Semen Up, and Hombres G, in addition to more traditional offerings (*jazz hispano* and *flamenco joven*).[127] And under the direction of Antonio Gómez Rufo, the Centro Cultural de la Villa promoted a variety of musical and cultural events related to the movida.[128] The movement was even a part of Madrid's official Christmas celebrations in 1985. At the opening of the festival of *Navidades*, Alaska delivered the annual Christmas address to the citizens of Madrid from a balcony on the city hall.[129] While Alaska's holiday address from the seat of municipal power clearly demonstrated official support for the movida, the best example of the institutionalization of the movement came earlier that year with the huge celebration of *San Isidro* in 1985.

In fact, the official cultural identity of Madrid during *San Isidro* 1985 was almost exclusively the image of the movida madrileña. Simply put, the public festival was an officially sponsored movida event. The banner headline on the front page of the newspaper *Villa de Madrid* read, "Nine Days of the *Movida*."[130] Not surprisingly, the vast majority of the festival's musical acts were groups from the movida. Alaska y Dinarama headlined the festival, while Radio Futura and La Frontera closed the celebration on the final day. Other movida bands that performed during the nine-day festival included Coyotes, Gran Wyoming, Mecano, Nikis, Barón Rojo, Burning, Orquesta Mondragón, Siniestro Total, Desperados, Gabinete Caligari, Los Elegantes, and Glutamato Ye-Ye.[131] Tierno Galván officially opened the festival, dedicated to Madrid's patron saint, with a call for total participation: "Everyone on to the streets [*todos a la calle*]!"[132] Madrileños apparently heeded the mayor's call, as the celebrations that year were the most popular ever in the festival's history. More than two million citizens turned out to participate in the hundreds of different activities dominated by the music and culture of the movida.[133]

For Tierno Galván, the festival symbolized Madrid's definitive transformation. And it was a transformation made possible, in large part, by the movida madrileña. In the official program to *San Isidro* 1985, filled with the photographs and biographies of movida rockers and pop stars, Tierno Galván wrote, "Madrid has converted itself into the darling [*encanto*] of Europe."[134] According to the mayor, Madrid achieved its position as the "darling of Europe" through "peace, joyfulness, the satisfaction of being *madrileño*, and the spirit of coexistence."[135] The overwhelming presence of the movida at this official celebration clearly linked the movement with this transformation. Moreover, Tierno Galván was very proud of this peaceful cultural transformation and wanted to share the capital with the rest of Europe: "[W]e have invited and we will invite all of the young people from Europe to come to Madrid."[136] In other words, literally everyone was invited to participate in Madrid's transformation into an open and democratic society.

COMUNIDAD OF MADRID AND THE MOVIDA

In addition to the Ayuntamiento's efforts, the Comunidad of Madrid also promoted the movida, although to a lesser extent. Created only in the middle of 1983, the Comunidad of Madrid was not fully active in the cultural sphere until 1984. In addition, the Comunidad also had much of its attention directed toward improving the cultural infrastructure of the region: building libraries, cultural centers, theaters, and exposition halls, and collecting archival material.

With regard to the promotion of an official cultural identity for Madrid, the new regional government desired to promote an identity based on the image of an inclusive "melting pot" (*crisol*), where all cultures were mixed and blended together. In a text presented to the Assembly of Madrid in September 1983, the Consejero de Cultura y Deporte of the Comunidad of Madrid, José Luis García Alonso, explained that "cultural identity can be understood as a process, as an objective, and in this case, it is possible to speak of an identity of Madrid, constituted, fundamentally, as a cultural synthesis, as a catalyst of a wide series of cultural values from very distinct origins."[137] Specifically, cultural synthesis in Madrid produced an identity that was "universal" rather than "exclusionary."[138] According to García Alonso, this cultural identity was to be developed through "the promotion of the character of a melting pot of cultures [*crisol de culturas*]."[139] As a result, the cultural activity of the Comunidad was quite diverse. Thus, in addition to focusing on the movida, Madrid's regional government stressed the promotion of an open and cosmopolitan culture that incorporated international currents as well. For instance, more international acts, and fewer movida bands, performed during the Comunidad's annual *Festival de Otoño* between 1984 and 1986 than at the festivals of *San Isidro* during the same period.[140]

However, as a vibrant symbol of an inclusive and modern culture, Madrid's regional government did openly promote and support the movida madrileña. For the president of the Comunidad, Joaquín Leguina, official support for the movement helped to reinforce a "*contra-castizo*"—or open and unconnected to the past—cultural identity for the region of Madrid.[141] And like the Ayuntamiento, the regional administration promoted the movida through a variety of different means. For example, the Comunidad of Madrid helped sponsor the most important exhibit related to the movida, "Madrid, Madrid, Madrid," in the summer of 1984.[142] Also mentioned above, the Comunidad placed full-page advertisements in *La Luna de Madrid*, providing valuable financial support for a magazine dedicated almost exclusively to the culture of the movida. These full-page ads, promoting the creation of the new Comunidad of Madrid, implicitly linked the new culture of the movida with the creation of the new region of Madrid. In addition to this advertising support, it was also widely rumored, but never confirmed, that *La Luna de Madrid* received direct financial subsidies from the Comunidad.[143] Finally, although not representing direct support for the movement, the Comunidad's official magazine, *Alfoz*, also published a number of in-depth stories specifically highlighting the movida madrileña.[144]

In the realm of broadcasting, the Comunidad of Madrid started its own radio station, Onda Madrid, that linked the region's official cultural identity to the movement. Like many of the radio stations in Madrid at this time, the Comunidad's new station did more than just play music. It was a form of cultural animation, offering cultural programming, calendars of events, interviews, and most importantly, a dialogue about the changes taking place in the region of Madrid.[145] From its inception in 1984, much of the programming of this new station was dedicated specifically to the culture and music of the movida. Programs such as "Hecho en Madrid" focused on the capital's cultural scene, while "Party Pop" featured new madrileño musical groups.

While the new Comunidad may not have embraced the movida to exactly the same degree as the Ayuntamiento, regional governmental support for the movement was nonetheless clearly evident between the middle of 1984 and the beginning of 1986. As discussed further in Chapter 7, the regional administration actually took a greater interest in the movida after the end of Tierno Galván's administration, sending "movida cultural delegations" to Vigo, in the north of Spain, at the end of 1986, and all the way to Italy in 1987.

CONCLUSION

Rather than simply representing one vivid aspect of a wider cultural phenomenon, or another example of Spain's fundamental backwardness, the movida madrileña formed an integral part of the project to transform Madrid after the experience of the dictatorship. But, as we have seen, the movement was not fabricated outright by Madrid's political elite. It was first created by a privileged cultural elite, made up of photographers, writers, fashion designers, artists, and musicians, who freely expressed themselves in an environment of tolerance and openness between 1979 and 1983. This new environment was created in part by the Ayuntamiento's support of cultural diversity and civic participation, and by its insistence on returning the streets of the capital to the citizens of Madrid. In this sense, Madrid's political elite did not originally create the movida, but rather opened the space for it to develop through its desire to culturally transform the capital. In this new space the movida flourished and eventually became adopted first by the municipal administration after 1983, and then later by the new regional government. Again, it was co-opted and institutionalized because it offered another way for the local administrations to distance the capital from the past and to create a new democratic identity for all madrileños.

Thus, similar to other regions in Spain after 1975, Madrid's local political elite promoted specific cultural symbols and forms in order to reinforce a new regional identity project. But, because of the specific context in which it was created, Madrid's official "*contra-castizo*" cultural identity demonstrated a couple of important differences compared to other similar projects. First, the official projection of Madrid through cultural symbols was consciously constructed on the present, and not on the past, as is usually the case. In other words, the goal was not to rediscover "authentic folk traditions" or to revive traditional symbols and customs, as in Catalonia, the Basque Country, and Galicia. Instead, the project to promote a new cultural identity in Madrid was an attempt to express regional differentiation through contemporary or modern culture. This embrace of a modern western culture was also what separated the capital from the rest of Spain, as no other region had identified itself with modernity to quite the same degree. In this way, Madrid's regional identity was based on a culturally vigorous present, and not on a real or imagined past. So in contrast to most nationalist and regionalist projects at the end of the twentieth century, the case of Madrid suggests that a shared cultural past does not have to be called upon to construct a new collective identity in the present.

Second, whereas "culture" is usually tied to narrowly defined ethnic affiliations, here again culture—and the movida madrileña, in particular—was linked to an open or universal identity in the capital. In this way, the project in Madrid was unique because it reinforced an inclusive "civic" rather than an exclusive "ethnic" regional identity. Due in part to such factors as the region's diverse and largely immigrant population, Madrid's political elite consciously chose to base greater cultural mobilization and the pursuit of a "*crisol de culturas*" specifically on the modern and inclusive symbols of the movida. The amalgamation of cultural influences brought to Madrid by the principal actors of the movida created a set of symbols associated with the capital that were particularly non-ethnic. The result was a more tolerant and more pluralistic cultural phenomenon. The promotion of an official cultural image of Madrid based on this inclusive and tolerant movement demonstrates that, unlike the examples from Eastern Europe or the Basque Country, culture does not have to be exclusivist or ethnocentric with regard to the formation of a new national or regional identity.

Seen in this light, the remaking of Madrid goes far beyond changes in musical tastes and cultural preferences in the capital. It was instead about a break from the past and a shift toward democratic behavior and attitudes that helped secure Spain's formal political transition to democracy. Likewise, official institutional support for the movida madrileña was less about making Madrid modern—it already was—and more about using a unique set of cultural symbols to give all madrileños a new sense of pride and a new democratic sense of place. In this way the transformation of Madrid in the 1980s was not simply about the formation of a youth subculture, or evidence of the capital's laggardness; rather, it was part of a complicated process of reinventing a democratic Spain and democratic Spaniards after the demise of the dictatorship.

CHAPTER 6

NOT YOUR SAME OLD MADRID:
THE CHANGING FACE OF THE
CAPITAL, 1979–1986

As the three preceding chapters illustrate, the local and regional administrations of Madrid undertook an ambitious project to broadly transform the capital between 1979 and 1986 and create a new democratic sense of place based on a shared commitment to Madrid. But did the project really produce a change in individual and collective habits as it was designed to do? Or was it a program that remained mostly in the imaginations of Madrid's political elite? In other words, how successful was the project to change the actual attitudes and behaviors of all madrileños after the experience of the dictatorship?

To address this issue, this chapter provides answers to such fundamental questions as: To what degree were residents of Madrid culturally mobilized? Did the movida madrileña make up a significant part of the cultural identity of most residents? Were the democratic values of active participation and peaceful coexistence absorbed by most madrileños, regardless of age, class, or political affiliation? And, was there a significant level of regional identification in the capital? While Madrid clearly did not become the utopian community that Tierno Galván and the other local political elite had hoped for, there is evidence to suggest that the goal of changing society's underlying values—with the hope of solidifying the transition to democracy and bringing greater peace, liberty, and equality to the capital—was at least partially achieved.

Using evidence from both the press and from sociological surveys, this chapter demonstrates that between 1979 and 1986 Madrid really did transform in a way that supports the claim for the formation of a new democratic regional identity. It does this by describing some of the ways the behaviors and attitudes of madrileños actually changed during this period. Specifically, the chapter details the changes related to four different aspects of the official project to create an inclusive democratic identity in the capital. The first section shows an increase in the level of cultural mobilization in Madrid, and also how that cultural activity was shaped by the assimilation of the movida madrileña. The second section describes the development of a new feeling of democratic coexistence in the capital and the degree to which ordinary residents of Madrid felt included in the official project to transform the capital. The third section illustrates the growing feeling of pride felt by madrileños for the place in which they lived over the first half of the 1980s. The fourth section then explores the development of a new regional sense of place in Madrid within the context of preexisting neighborhood and national identifications. While no project designed to create a new imagined community turns out exactly the way it was envisioned, the program conceived and implemented by the local and regional administrations did help produce a significant transformation in Madrid between 1979 and 1986.[1] As they adopted new ways of thinking and behaving, madrileños transformed from passive subjects of the dictatorship to active democratic citizens that identified with each other and with Madrid in a new and positive way.

I. Increased Cultural Mobilization

While Madrid may not have turned into the true "cultural capital of the world" by the mid-1980s, as some had a tendency to claim, there are several indications that the level of cultural mobilization in the capital significantly increased between 1979 and 1986. Most obviously, Madrid's formerly silent and empty streets became completely transformed by Tierno Galván's death in January 1986. Literally hundreds of thousands of madrileños actively participated in a variety of cultural activities on a daily basis: attending concerts, expositions, album releases, public festivals, and jamming Madrid's streets at all hours of the day and night. Due in large part to this activity, Madrid passed from being a place marginalized from world cultural currents during the Franco regime to one of the centers of those currents in the mid-1980s.

As early as 1983, the combination of infrastructure improvements and new cultural initiatives created a kind of self-perpetuating cultural effervescence in the capital. According to the writer and journalist Luis Carandell, there was so much going on that journalists covering the capital's cultural scene had to "go out to two acts per day, at least: presentations of new books, of new magazines, of musical groups."[2] And, at the end of 1983, two French publications, *Liberation* and *Actuel*, both proclaimed that Madrid was one of the most entertaining and creative cities anywhere.[3] In other words, Madrid had become *the* new place to be, increasingly attracting artists and musicians from around the world.

The enthusiasm for cultural activity was so great that the capital became one of the most important centers of art expositions in the world, even rivaling Paris and New York for a while. The art critic Rosa Olivares later described the situation in the mid-1980s: "In Madrid one could see better and more expositions than in Paris, London, and even New York. The result was definitive: Madrid had transformed itself, and in its own right, into one of the artistic metropolises of the world."[4] To a large degree, cultural demand or participation was the motor that drove this transformation. For example, between 1979 and 1983, the number of visitors at the Museo de Arte Contemporáneo increased by 525 percent from 73,744 to 387,548 visitors. Visits to the Prado increased by 61 percent, from 1,101,538 to 1,780,074. Even the Museo Arqueológico saw a 74 percent increase in the number of visitors, from 139,066 to 241,755.[5] Residents also attended thousands of art exhibits at Madrid's countless private art galleries and at larger publicly funded institutions: Museo Municipal, Centro Cultural de la Villa, Conde Duque, and the Círculo de Bellas Artes.[6] John Hooper has described this new cultural activity from his firsthand experience:

> When I visited Madrid a year later [in 1984], I was struck by an atmosphere that I had never encountered before—that of a city gripped by art fever. Every-where I went in cafes, bars, and restaurants, there were posters advertising exhibitions and on all sides friends and acquaintances had a story to tell of how they had to queue for hours to get into this or that exhibition.[7]

By the end of the decade, this "art fever" supported 232 galleries and exposition halls in Madrid, more than any other metropolitan area in the country.[8] It was because of this cultural demand and Madrid's new reputation as a cultural mecca that helped Swiss Baron Heinrich von Thyssen decide to locate one of the world's finest private art collections in the capital, eventu-ally creating the Thyssen-Bornemisza Museum in 1992.

Writing in 1985, Tierno Galván likewise acknowledged the capital's over-whelming growth of cultural activity: "Today in Madrid one can pass the whole day without spending a penny, [going] from exposition to exposition, as much sculpture and painting as drawings and every other art form, as well as historical expositions."[9] According to the mayor, Madrid had become "one of the most prestigious cities in Europe and one of the cities most talked about in Europe or even America, now that its cultural activity is the highest that is produced in Europe."[10] Madrid was literally a place overflowing with culture. It was exactly this cultural effervescence that had so impressed the author of the *Rolling Stone Magazine* article quoted at the beginning of this book.[11]

While there was a broad increase in cultural mobilization over the first part of the decade, the movida madrileña increasingly came to define that activity in the two years before Tierno Galván's death in 1986. As the political elite officially adopted and promoted the inclusive, participatory, optimistic, and modern symbols of the movida, the movement came both to shape the forms of cultural activity that were developing in the capital and to provide a dis-tinctively modern cultural identity for madrileños. Although it is difficult to prove the degree to which ordinary madrileños adopted the movida as part of their cultural identity, there is evidence to show that the movement was widely embraced by the residents and that it helped define cultural activity in the capital. This widespread assimilation can be seen both in the acceptance of the movida into mainstream madrileño culture and in the large numbers of residents who directly participated in the movement.

In contrast to the movement's humble beginnings, it seemed as though the movida was everywhere by the mid-1980s: featured at popular festivals, on the radio, in the mainstream press, and on television. The region's embrace of the modern cultural trends was so great that artists, intellectuals, journalists, and politicians from Europe and the United States looked to Madrid as the very center of modernity, or "postmodernity" as it was called then. At the same time, Madrid's new cultural scene became widely acknowledged in Spain as the most important in the country, beating out even Barcelona. It was not until the end of the decade that other Spanish cities, such as Barcelona, Valencia, and Seville, began to catch up with the capital.[12] Referring to Madrid's profound transformation in the decade following the death of Franco, the former editor of *La Luna de Madrid*, Borja Casani, argued in 1987: "Here not only has there been an exemplary transition to democracy, but also there was produced simultaneously an authentic cultural revolution."[13] As the movement moved from the margins to the center of madrileño society, movida artists and musicians also began receiving a number of important honors, further symbolizing their popularity and mainstream status. By the end of 1985, the movida madrileña appeared to be as closely related to the culture of Madrid as the Puerta de Alcalá, the Prado Museum, or the football team, Real Madrid.

With regard to music, the movida provided the unofficial "soundtrack" for Madrid in the years between 1984 and 1986. Musicians such as Alaska and Carlos Berlanga dominated Madrid's popular music scene as they sold hundreds of thousands of records, performed at massive public concerts and music festivals, and became the objects of popular adoration. Musical icons also frequently appeared on Spanish television (TVE) and were constantly featured in a variety of different magazines. In addition, movida bands such as Radio Futura, Gabinete Caligari, and Siniestro Total topped the music charts in 1985 and even performed on the country's most popular radio program, SER's *Los 40 principales* (The Top 40). Finally, demonstrating the movement's further acceptance and legitimacy, music contracts were no longer handled by independent record labels. Instead, major record labels, such as CBS España, headquartered in Madrid, took over many of the recording contracts of the movida musical groups.[14]

The magazines dedicated to the movida, such as *La Luna de Madrid*, *Madriz*, and *Madrid Me Mata*, also achieved a mainstream presence during this period. The officially sponsored *Madriz* reached a respectable circulation of 15,000 copies per month in April 1984.[15] At the same time, *La Luna de Madrid* came to be referred to as the "B. O. E.," or the *Boletín Oficial del Estado*. Echoing this view, in a letter to the editor describing *La Luna de Madrid*'s popular acceptance in the capital, Arturo Arnalte argued, "*La Luna* is more representative of the official culture [of Madrid] than the *Revista de Occidente*."[16]

The movement's popularity was reflected in the mainstream press as well. Carlos Ferrando was writing about the movida music scene in *Diario 16* almost everyday between 1984 and 1985. When the same newspaper held a party in Madrid to celebrate its three-thousandth edition, two musicians from movida bands, Poch of Derribos Arias and Iñaki of Glutamato Ye-Ye, were invited to serve as masters of ceremony.[17] Over at *El País*, major stories related to the movida also became more commonplace. For example, the newspaper's popular Sunday magazine insert, *El País Semanal*, dedicated its cover to the "Urban Tribes" of the movida in December 1984.[18] And, in January 1985, the movida photographer/painter Bárbara Allende (Ouka-Lele) was interviewed on the back cover of Spain's most popular daily newspaper.[19] It was also in 1985 that articles about Madrid's seemingly miraculous transformation began appearing in the international press. The capital's cultural makeover was touted in *Time*, *Newsweek*, *Le Monde*, *Le Nouvel Observateur*, and *National Geographic*. *Le Soir* even published an extensive four-part story on the "new" Madrid and the popularity of the movida madrileña.

The movement received other forms of recognition that demonstrated its acceptance into mainstream madrileño culture. In 1985, the movida painter, Guillermo Pérez Villalta received the *Premio Naciónal de Artes Plásticas*; it was the first time it went to a young artist. The year before, Alaska received the National Prize for Makeup (*Premio Nacional de Maquillaje*) from the *Asociación de Alta Perfumería y Estética*.[20] It was also in 1984 that the diva of the movida became part of the children's television program *La Bola de Cristal*. Later, in 1985, Alaska was granted a series of interviews with well-known politicians and celebrities, including Manuel Fraga, Marcelino Camacho, Antonio Garrigues Walker, Camilo José Cela, and Enrique Tierno Galván, for the magazine *Primera Linea de la Actualidad*.[21] In the ultimate sign of mainstream legitimacy, Alaska was offered the chance to have a line of dolls, "Barbie Alaska," created in her image in 1985.[22] Even though many of these forms of official recognition were associated with national institutions, they represent a significant level of acceptance for the movida in the capital because most of these institutions were headquartered in, and focused on, Madrid.

In addition to the evidence demonstrating its acceptance into mainstream madrileño culture, widespread assimilation of the movida can be seen in the large numbers of residents that directly participated in the movement on a daily basis. As the movida was no longer confined to select bars, clubs, and galleries, thousands of madrileños actively participated in activities ranging from film debuts and book releases to late-night barhopping and open-air concerts. The single best example of this mass participation came in 1985 with the official "movida" San Isidro—discussed in the previous chapter. During the nine-day celebration, more than 2 million people turned out to participate in hundreds of concerts and cultural events related directly to the movida madrileña.[23]

Of course, however, it must be remembered that not everyone openly embraced or identified with the movida to the same degree. As discussed further in Chapter 8, many on the right, in particular, objected to both the form and apparent content of the movement. Based on 1986 political party affiliations, perhaps it could be estimated that the 11 percent of madrileños who affiliated themselves with the conservative AP would have directly opposed the movida.[24]

Nevertheless, although it is hard to make a direct connection to the movida, there is additional sociological evidence from this period that suggests the presence of massive cultural participation and engagement in the capital. Surveys produced by the Ministry of Culture and the Comunidad of Madrid demonstrate that, even though cultural activity increased across Spain between 1979 and 1985, the region of Madrid had the highest levels of cultural demand and participation anywhere in the country. Furthermore, there are data to suggest an increase in cultural activity that could be specifically associated with the movida madrileña.

In a study carried out by the Ministry of Culture in 1985, the region of Madrid was determined to be by far the greatest "consumer of culture" in Spain.[25] In fact, with respect to 15 different cultural activities surveyed, madrileños were the most active out of all Spaniards, and had the highest level of cultural consumption.[26] The activities included such things as visiting museums, going to the theater, attending concerts, playing sports, dancing, and playing a musical instrument. In addition, Madrid was the only region to be above the national average in all 15 of the cultural activities.

The Ministry of Culture's study also concluded that cultural activity in the region of Madrid was also the most diverse.[27] On average, madrileños engaged in 7.07 different types of cultural activities (i.e., going to the movies, visiting museums, playing instruments, attending a concert, etc.) during a three-month period, compared to the national average of 5.85.[28] Overall, 67.8 percent of the residents of Madrid were classified as either very active or active by the study. In contrast, the national average was 16 points lower, at 51.8 percent.[29] Additionally, madrileños themselves believed that the level of cultural activity in the capital had increased during this period. In a public opinion poll from September 1986, 81 percent of the residents of Madrid thought there were far more cultural activities in Madrid than there were a few years earlier.[30]

Another study by the Comunidad of Madrid in the mid-1980s also demonstrated very high levels of cultural mobilization in the capital.[31] And, in addition to measuring actual participation, the Comunidad's study also considered "potential demand," or the *desire* to engage in a given cultural activity. In 1985, for example, almost three-quarters (73.8%) of the population of Madrid either actively visited museums and expositions or wanted to do so. In addition, more than two-thirds (64.3%) of all madrileños either actively visited historic monuments and buildings or wished to. Finally, 41.6 percent of residents actively attended, or wanted to attend, conferences and colloquies.[32]

The study also showed a relatively high level of cultural activity in Madrid associated with public institutions. For example, 38.6 percent of madrileños reported visiting a publicly funded cultural center at least once, with 28.9 percent attending regularly or occasionally. Similarly, 45.8 percent of madrileños had visited a public library at least once, with 31.2 percent visiting regularly or occasionally.[33] With regard to Madrid's youth, 41.6 percent reported visiting a youth center (*centro de juveniles*) at least once, with more than a quarter of the population (25.6%) visiting regularly or occasionally.[34]

But, as discussed in Chapter 5, participation in the movida symbolized much more than simply attending concerts or passively viewing paintings, sculptures, and photographs. The movement signified *active* cultural production and creativity. In other words, the role of spectator was not sufficient. While it is hard to draw a direct connection to the movement, the same 1985 survey by the Comunidad of Madrid reported high levels of cultural activity that closely coincided with four different types of activities commonly associated with the movida madrileña. First, almost half (46.1%) of all the residents of Madrid either played or wanted to play a musical instrument. Second, just under 40 percent of madrileños either practiced an artistic "*afición*" (painting, sculpture, etc.) or wanted to practice such an activity. Third, 45 percent of madrileños either practiced or wanted to practice photography. Fourth, and probably most remarkably, 25 percent of the population either actively made movies or videos, or wanted to do so.[35] Again while it is difficult to prove the degree to which ordinary madrileños actually assumed the movida madrileña as part of their cultural identity, such evidence of direct participation in activities related to the movement, coupled with its mainstream acceptance, demonstrates the large degree to which cultural mobilization was defined or shaped by the movida in the mid-1980s. At the same time, it also seems to suggest at least a partial acceptance of the movida's democratic symbols and values by the residents of Madrid.

II. GREATER DEMOCRATIC COEXISTENCE

While there is evidence to support the notion that madrileños were actively participating in the capital, did this new participatory culture create an ethos of *convivencia*, or democratic coexistence, after years of repressive dictatorship? In other words, did this participation promote a functioning democracy? Madrid's political elite had hoped that the broad parameters of urban and cultural renewal would transcend political differences and incorporate all madrileños into a common project. Here again there is evidence to suggest that the connections they sought to make were at least partially accepted by many in the capital.

Overall, it appears as though most residents understood Madrid's transformation as apolitical. Rather than as a kind of deliberate "Socialist revolution," both the programs themselves and the actual changes that occurred in the capital were most often seen as a kind of "natural" or "inevitable" process that came along with the transition to democracy. Because of this perception, there was less resistance to the various aspects of the program and, as a result, more residents were positively affected by the project, regardless of their political affiliation. In fact, even though there was clearly partisanship and political dis-agreement in Madrid between 1979 and 1986, several of the main aspects of the project to create a common democratic sense of place in the capital were not highly politicized, including urban renewal, cultural mobilization, and many of the activities surrounding the movida madrileña.

It was precisely the breath of the plan, which touched almost everyone, that helped create broad support and acceptance. As described in Chapter 3, change extended from environmental cleanup and cultural renewal to urban restoration and the formation of more responsive public institutions. In addi-tion, while not everyone directly supported the Socialist administrations, the project to promote social cohesion and a feeling of democratic coexistence was not limited to or directed at a small percentage of the population. Instead, it was purposely designed to appeal to and affect all madrileños. Changes such as the restoration of a public monument, cleaner drinking water, the reinstatement of a banned festival, and the cleaning of a neighborhood park transcended differences of class, age, or political affiliation. In other words, the program was meant to make all residents feel part of a common project, and as such contributed to a new sense of democratic coexistence.

Any evaluation of the success of this effort cannot be based on formal political support for either the local or regional administration, as the main purpose of the program was not to eradicate the political opposition, or even to erase all political difference in the capital. Nor was the project designed to divide Madrid into pro-left and pro-right blocks. Instead, the program was intended to have a positive affect on everyone. As the goal was to affect the underlying values and behaviors of all madrileños in a way that would foster participation and a sense of community within the new democratic system, broader indicators of social unity and democratic *convivencia* have to be considered.

One of the most significant indications of greater peaceful coexistence in the capital was the decline of political violence. Simply put, fewer madrileños were killing one another on account of political and social divisions by the middle of the decade. Between 1978 and 1980, there were 88 political kill-ings by the left and the right across the country, with many of these murders taking place in the capital.[36] To cite one of many examples, an assault on the bar San Bao by a group of rightwing ultras left one person dead in December 1980.[37] After 1981, there was little political violence and far fewer political disturbances in the capital.[38]

Along with the decline of political violence, there was also little division between residents with regard to political self-position by the middle of the decade. When asked to identify their political position on a scale of 1 to 10, where 1 represented the extreme left and 10 the extreme right, only 13 percent of madrileños put themselves on either the extreme left (1–2) or the extreme right (9–10) in 1986.[39] And 55 percent of respondents consid-ered themselves to be in the center (5–6) or on the left (3–4). In other words, rather than at either extreme, the majority of madrileños located themselves at the center-left of the political spectrum (see Table 6.1). With the majority

Table 6.1 Political self-position of madrileños (1986)[40]

Political Position	Percentage
Extreme Left (1 + 2)	10
Left (3 + 4)	34
Center (5 + 6)	21
Right (7 + 8)	8
Extreme Right (9 + 10)	3
Don't know	8
No response	16

1 represents the extreme left and 10 represents the extreme right.

of the population grouped together on the political spectrum, there is little evidence to show that the developments in Madrid over the first half of the 1980s produced political polarization or social division.

The clearest example of democratic coexistence in Madrid, however, was seen at the time of Tierno Galván's death. After a year-long struggle with cancer, the first democratically elected mayor of Madrid since the Second Republic died on January 20, 1986. With his death came an explosion of popular emotion and support from all segments of the population, which was unprecedented in the modern history of Madrid.

The day after the funeral, the newspaper *El País* summarized the connection between the popular outpouring of emotion for Tierno Galván and the creation of a more open and hospitable environment in Madrid:

> The gratefulness of *madrileños* for the recuperation of their identity, after the prolonged period in which the capital of glory and the breakwater [*rompeolas*] of all of the Spains was transformed into the symbol of political oppression and bureaucratic centralism, played a significant part in that overflowing expression of grief. The proposal to convert Madrid into an open city [*ciudad abierta*] and its support given to the cultural and youthful *movida* was only one part of the labor carried out by the *Ayuntamiento* presided by Tierno during almost 6 [*sic*] years. The plans to clean the city's water, the recuperation of the city's center, the attention paid to the neighborhoods on the periphery, the construction of parks and auditoriums, [and] the defense of the Retiro have made more inhabitable that horrible monster of cement that the real estate speculation of the dictatorship bequeathed to the subsequent generation. With Tierno, *madrileños* recuperated their city, the streets of their city; yesterday they poured out onto these same streets in order to offer a final homage of gratefulness.[41]

In fact, more than one million madrileños came together on that day to pay their last respects to the old professor.[42] In what stood by itself as a massive symbol of civic participation, close to one-third of the city's population filled the streets out of a desire to honor the individual most closely associated with the project to transform Madrid. In addition, tens of thousands of madrileños from all walks of life solemnly stood in line for more than six hours to personally say their final farewells to Tierno Galván at a small chapel set up inside the City Hall.[43]

When specifically asked why they had waited in line so long to pay their last respects, a cross-section of residents proudly responded in a variety of ways that showed their solidarity for Tierno Galván and that directly connected the mayor to the changes that had occurred in Madrid between 1979 and 1986:

- A woman from the upper-class neighborhood of Retiro responded, "The answer is simple. Because there has never been anyone like him. He was a person that gave us a lesson in life, on how to live and comport oneself in this world, a political, a moral, and an ethical lesson, a lesson about democracy, about citizenship."[44]
- A man in his sixties cried, "He did a lot that man. Over in Moratäláz, where we live, he built parks and everything. He was always very good, very good."[45]
- A teenage boy insisted, "He did a lot for Madrid, he revived the festivals that were dead."[46] When asked about politics, the same boy responded: "As a politician? Well, politics doesn't interest me a lot, what interested us about Tierno was the person."[47]
- Another man explained, "Listen, I am not a Socialist, nor a Communist. The only party I am a member of is Madrid's electrical union, but I am here because what this man has done deserves a tribute. In the plaza of the old *Ayuntamiento* of Carabanchel, where there was garbage, he gave us benches and even a kiosk to borrow magazines."[48]
- A young woman dressed in punk clothing (*chica punki*) said, "He was a person that, in spite of being quite old, could seem very dynamic, very fun-loving [*marchoso*], doing everything possible for Madrid."[49] Another young person next to her summed up the close relationship between the mayor and Madrid's diverse population: "We liked him because he got along very well with young people, he spoke very normally and everyone understood him. And he understood everyone."[50]

In addition to expressing a feeling of gratitude and appreciation, each of these statements also linked the changes that occurred in Madrid between 1979 and 1986—from the cleanup of parks to the "lessons" about democracy—either directly or indirectly to the mayor. Put another way, for madrileños, Tierno Galván symbolized or embodied the transformation of the capital during this period. Thus, the massive and diverse display of support for the old professor at the time of his death represented the considerable degree to which ordinary residents felt a common connection to the new Madrid.

In addition to this popular display of support, similar sentiments of solidarity and unity were formally expressed by politicians on both the left and right. Despite the differences between Tierno Galván and the national PSOE, the Socialist president of Spain Felipe González awarded the *Gran Cruz de*

Carlos III to the old professor for changing Madrid into "a city with a universal pulse, a free spirit, and an open sensibility."[51] On the opposite end of the political spectrum, the leader of the political opposition in Madrid, José María Álvarez del Manzano, wrote of Tierno Galván at the time of his death: "No one can deny, nor have we ever tried to deny it, the popularity of the mayor that leaves us. He knew how to reach everyone in madrileño society in a direct way."[52]

This broad display of solidarity was also shown for the mayor in the period leading up to his death. When hospitalized in February 1985 for cancer surgery, Tierno Galván received thousands of letters and telegrams from all segments of society: "inmates, soldiers, governors, heads of state, lawyers, journalists, bankers, athletes."[53] Later, at the end of 1985, he was even voted the most popular person in the Comunidad of Madrid by the listeners of Radio Nacional de España.[54] When Tierno Galván was hospitalized in January 1986, shortly before his death, the mayor again received flowers, cards, children's drawings, and even carafes of "miracle water" from hundreds of residents.[55] And, for months after his death, the *Ayuntamiento* continued to receive telegrams, drawings, poems, and homages from residents, expressing their grief and solidarity.[56] In fact, letters and poems were still being dedicated to the mayor more than a year after his death.[57]

On top of these expressions of public support, Tierno Galván, as a symbol of Madrid's transformation, received a number of official acknowledgments from a variety of different institutions after his death. For example, the City Council of Madrid unanimously bestowed its highest civic honor—the *Medalla de Honor de la Villa*—on the mayor for his exceptional service to the residents of the capital.[58] And the *Federación Regional de Asociaciones de Vecinos* opened a bank account in order to finance a monument to Tierno Galván.[59] Even all of Madrid's public and private schools and universities, including the Complutense, Politécnica, and Autónoma, were closed in his honor. For two days after his death, newspapers across the political spectrum ran front-page stories featuring the mayor's accomplishments in Madrid. And, in the following weeks, a large number of homages to Tierno Galván's contribution to the capital were held at both left- and right-leaning institutions across Madrid, including *Club Internacional de Prensa*, *Tertulia Madrileña de Avapiés*, *Comunidad Autónoma de Madrid*, *Cámara de Comercio e Industria*, *Sociedad General de Autores*, *Real Madrid Club de Fútbol*, *Sociedad Cervantina*, *Instituto de Estudios Madrileños*, *Fundación Villa y Corte*, *Asociación de Productores de Espectáculos Teatrales*, *Club Siglo XXI*, and *Peña los Marcianos*.[60]

José Antonio Vizcaíno has more recently summed up the degree to which Tierno Galván was accepted by all of Madrid's residents:

[He was] the mayor from this last century that entered most deeply into the heart of *madrileños*, without any doubt among the young people . . . [and] also among the conservative classes, without distinction of age, sex, or [political] predisposition.[61]

Such a claim for unity and solidarity is substantiated not only by the broad display of support at the time of Tierno Galván's death, but also by public opinion surveys conducted in the mid-1980s. In fact, even though only approximately half of the population supported Tierno Galván's administration in the 1983 municipal elections, the responses to several different surveys from this period demonstrate a lack of sharp separation between residents and suggest a feeling of democratic coexistence in the capital.[62] Specifically, there is evidence to suggest that there was both widespread support for many of the programs initiated by Madrid's political elite and little division between madrileños with regard to political position.

As for the level of acceptance of the administration's project, a survey carried out by the *Centro de Investigaciónes Sociológicas* (CIS) at the end of February 1986 showed that the overwhelming majority of the population supported the efforts to transform Madrid. In fact, 87 percent of the residents of the region of Madrid believed that the municipal administration's program between 1979 and 1986 had been favorable for Madrid in general.

When asked more specifically about Tierno Galván and his policies, madrileños responded with a similarly high level of unity. In fact, neither the specific figure of the mayor, nor his administration's policies, sharply divided the residents of Madrid. Specifically, more than 93 percent of the region's population responded that they liked Tierno Galván and 78 percent said they liked his policies in general.[63] In addition, when asked for which political party they would vote if municipal elections were held that day, only 47 percent of madrileños would have likely voted for the PSOE, Tierno Galván's own party.[64] The figure was even lower with regard to regional elections; only 44 percent of madrileños would have most likely voted for the PSOE if regional elections had been held that day.[65] And, in fact, the PSOE only received 36.7 percent of the vote in the next municipal elections of 1987. Clearly, then, approval for Tierno Galván and the program to transform the capital transcended party affiliations: the mayor had very high approval ratings (around 90 percent), but less than 50 percent of the population was committed to the PSOE.

Beyond this general feeling of inclusion related to the program, there is evidence to suggest that three of the fundamental aspects of the project to create a new democratic identity in the capital were also widely accepted by the residents of Madrid. These different aspects included the efforts directed at urban renewal, the promotion of cultural mobilization, and the development of the movida madrileña.

First, with regard to the capital's physical transformation, even though not all madrileños politically supported Tierno Galván's administration, the vast majority of the population was satisfied with the most important and visible urban renewal projects undertaken by the *Ayuntamiento* between 1979 and 1986. For example, another survey commissioned by CIS in September 1986 found that almost 90 percent of the residents of Madrid were satisfied with the program most closely associated with the local government's urban renewal plan: the cleaning of the river Manzanares. Similarly, more than 80 percent of madrileños were happy with three other key aspects of

Madrid's physical transformation: the revitalization of capital's historic center, the cleaning of the façades of historic buildings, and the pedestrianization of city streets. Overall, at least three-quarters of the population were satisfied with all the surveyed official programs designed to physically transform Madrid.[66]

Second, the program of cultural mobilization was not a highly polarizing or divisive issue in the capital either. Similar to the attitudes toward urban renewal, the vast majority of residents approved of the local and regional administrations' efforts to culturally mobilize the capital. In the same survey from September 1986, 75 percent of madrileños believed the *Ayuntamiento* had done a lot (*mucho*) or quite a lot (*bastante*) to put cultural activities within the reach of everyone.[67] Even more significantly, 80 percent of madrileños believed that the most important and symbolic cultural mobilization initiative—the sponsorship of popular festivals—was very important or quite important for the life of the city.[68] Although the percentage is smaller, the majority of residents of the region of Madrid also specifically approved of the Comunidad's effort to promote cultural mobilization. In another CIS survey from 1986, 64 percent of madrileños believed the regional government of Madrid did a lot or quite a lot for culture.[69]

While not included in the public opinion surveys from the period, it can be inferred that attitudes toward the movida madrileña did not produce sharp divisions in the capital either. As discussed in Chapter 5, the phenomenon of the movida madrileña was largely understood as apolitical by most madrileños. In fact, there was greater acceptance of the movida because, even though some on the right understood the movement simply as an artificial culture of the left, it was usually seen as something that offered new and exciting cultural possibilities, rather than as something related to formal politics. Due to the fact that the cultural activity surrounding the movida—along with many of the other aspects of the official project to transform Madrid—was not perceived as explicitly political, there was less resistance to change across the political spectrum.

III. A NEW "*MADRILEÑISMO*"

However, simply promoting greater participation and coexistence was not enough to create a new democratic sense of place among the capital's residents. The purpose of the political elite's project was also to link the promotion of active participation and a feeling of peaceful coexistence specifically to the region of Madrid. While it is not easy to judge exactly how ordinary madrileños felt about Madrid during this period, there is evidence to suggest that residents were increasingly proud of the place in which they lived. The development of such feelings also suggests that madrileños were identifying more closely with Madrid as a geographical region and with each other. This change can be seen both in statements attesting to a kind of newfound pride among madrileños and in several sociological studies from the period.

As early as August 1982, a certain *madrileñismo*, or pride for Madrid, was starting to be recognized in the capital. An editorial in *El País* noted how Madrid had recently become a "happy and confident city" and that "*madrileños* had recuperated some enthusiasm for the fact of being [madrileños]."[70] In contrast, only a few years earlier, the same newspaper had declared Spain, and Madrid in particular, the most "boring" and "unenthusiastic" place in Europe.[71]

Gradually, between 1983 and 1986, such expressions of madrileño pride became more and more common. In January 1983, Miguel Gato, in the *Villa de Madrid*, observed that Madrid was "recuperating a kind of *madrileñismo* whose existence was only just a memory."[72] In November of the same year, the editors of *La Luna de Madrid*, Borja Casani and José Tono Martínez, explained where some of that pride was coming from: "Madrid can now be proud of being a city that has fought to integrate within itself all of the old social and esthetic taboos."[73] Pedro Almodóvar also described the growing feeling of attachment to the capital in the second issue of *La Luna de Madrid*:

> Those who lived in this city never had roots, a local feeling never existed . . . one lived in Madrid as one could live in any other place. No one cared enough to defend Madrid, no one identified with the city at all. All that was done here was seen as a mere accident.[74]

However, that lack of identification with the city had recently changed: "Now a *madrileño* culture is spoken of, which is defended and confronts others. It is frequently said (including myself) that in Madrid there are ideas, that Europe has turned its gaze here. There is now a certain pride of living in the place that you inhabit."[75]

Even the president of Spain's Constitutional Supreme Court (*Tribunal Constitucional*), Manuel García-Pelayo, recognized Madrid's change of character at a conference of *Tribunales Constitucionales Europeos* in 1984: "[Madrid] was in the past a symbol of centralism, but is now a symbol of Spanish change [*cambio español*]."[76] While highlighting the region's independence, pride, and originality, he observed that, unlike capitals in other countries, the Comunidad of Madrid was not "a federal district with direct dependence on the government of the nation."[77] Instead, the region of Madrid had developed a level of independence and uniqueness since the end of the dictatorship.

Of course, there was also a great deal of enthusiasm among the municipal and regional political elite for Madrid's newfound pride and self-confidence. Antonio Gómez Rufo, then the director of the *Aula Municipal de Cultura*, proudly urged the capital forward in 1984: "Paris and Barcelona are depressed [*estan de copa caida*]; Milan and Amsterdam are beginning to yawn; London is down for the count . . . It is Madrid's moment, and it can not be wasted."[78] Such an obvious statement of regional chauvinism reflected the growing sense of identification with and pride for Madrid among the capital's political elite.

Even the mayor commented on the growing sentiment of madrileño pride in 1984. Speaking at the closing of a conference devoted to the study of madrileño culture, Tierno Galván observed:

> It appears that [Madrid] is regaining its personality, its physiognomy, and its unitary spirit (*ánimo unitario*), as it is said, its "identity," and now the common reference to Madrid is an affectionate reference and implies the connotation of one's own place, in which one lives with the satisfaction.[79]

While increasing steadily over the first part of the decade, the level of pride and satisfaction with living in the capital reached its peak in the period between 1985 and 1986. On the occasion of Tierno Galván's entry into the hospital for surgery, in February 1985, an editorial in *El País* highlighted some of the important changes that had taken place in the capital under the mayor's administration: "Since 1979, Madrid is now a more habitable and less gloomy [*hosca*], a more cultured and better managed, a more welcoming and less loud-mouthed [*gritona*], a more happy and less centralist city."[80] Madrid, in other words, had become "a place to be proud of."[81] Likewise, later in 1985, Moncho Alpuente observed that, with the changes that had taken place in Madrid since the death of Franco, "it was inevitable that . . . *madrileños* have begun to like themselves."[82]

While the examples above highlight the growing feeling of pride and self-confidence among the residents of Madrid, evidence for the development of a new kind of *madrileñismo* was probably again best illustrated by the declarations surrounding the mayor's death at the beginning of 1986. Furthermore, many of these statements directly linked the administration of Tierno Galván with the growing feeling of pride for Madrid. For example, in one of the many letters sent to *Villa de Madrid* immediately following the mayor's death, Manuel Ariza described the great impact Tierno Galván's administration had on all madrileños, and especially on young people like himself:

> With young people he always maintained a personal and transparent relationship, he understood well that we neither believe in the closed politics [of the right] nor in the change promised by those other Socialists. He believed in utopias and fought for them. He knew how to create in us a feeling of *madrileñismo*, a new identity far removed from centralists' triumphalism, teaching us to care for and enjoy the city (not the capital) . . . He never promised us anything. He never denied us anything. He struggled and suffered for liberty, a liberty that now the usual politicians [*governantes de turno*] want to hide and then give to us as a gift wrapped in colored paper.[83]

Young madrileños were not the only ones to recognize the connection between Tierno Galván and the recuperation of a sense of pride for Madrid. The mayor of Barcelona Pasqual Maragall remarked, "Tierno Galván was a great patriot who knew how to create madrileño patriotism, a feeling very important for a city."[84] The opera singer Plácido Domingo commented, "[W]ith him, Madrid regained its traditions and is now one of the most joyful and beautiful cities in the world."[85] The actor Paco Rabal observed, "Now Madrid is a city more cultured, less provincial, more lucid, and more clean."[86] Moncho Alpuente later summed up the profound change in the attitude of madrileños toward themselves and toward Madrid that occurred under the administration of Tierno Galván: "It was the first time in many years that the people looked at themselves in the mirror, just like the city itself, and said to themselves: 'well we are not so bad; we are not so ugly; this is not so bad; we are not to blame.'"[87]

This notion of a new *madrileñismo* is also backed up by evidence found in sociological surveys from the period. Although it is difficult to make a direct connection to the local and regional administration's official policies, the surveys demonstrate a significant increase in the feeling of pride for Madrid among residents since the formal transition to democracy. Specifically, there is evidence to suggest a greater association with Madrid, greater territorial affiliation, and an increase in regional pride among residents.

In the CIS survey from September 1986, when asked if they identified more or less closely with Madrid than in the past, 52 percent of madrileños felt more identification with Madrid, while only 9 percent felt it less.

In addition to this increase in identification with Madrid, the results of a separate study from 1986 also expressed a distinct feeling of pride and territorial affiliation. When university students in Madrid were asked to select adjectives that described madrileños, 37.5 percent of respondents picked the word "proud" and 25 percent chose the term "lovers of their land."[88] Significantly, the adjective most frequently chosen by Madrid's university students was "open."[89] Each of these three responses directly corresponded to the political elite's objective of creating an open and proud common sense of place in Madrid. In fact, all of the top five most frequently selected adjectives—"open," "cocky" (*chulo*), "hospitable," "happy," and "proud"—specifically related to the kind of imagined community the local and regional administrations hoped to promote in the capital (see Table 6.2).

Finally, there is evidence to suggest that madrileños in general were very satisfied with living in the Comunidad of Madrid. In a 1986 survey covering the entire region, 86 percent of madrileños reported being very satisfied or quite satisfied with living in Madrid.[91] Similarly, the residents of the region of Madrid had an appraisal of the general social and political evolution since 1975 that was higher than the national average.[92] In fact, the appraisal of the situation in Madrid was higher than in Andalusia, Catalonia, or the Basque Country (see Table 6.3). In other words, madrileños were generally happy with how their lives had changed since the end of the dictatorship.

By the time of Tierno Galván's death in 1986, life in the capital was far removed from how it had been under the dictatorship. Extending beyond a mere physical transformation, an important emotional and psychological change had taken place in Madrid. In part because of the local and regional administrations' efforts to forge a new democratic community in the capital, madrileños no longer believed they lived in the shadow of authoritarianism, oppression, and centralization. Instead, they were once again proud of where

Table 6.2 Adjectives most frequently used by university students in Madrid to describe madrileños (1986)[90]

Adjectives	Percentage
Open	**57**
Cocky (*chulo*)	**52**
Hospitable	**51.5**
Happy	**38**
Proud	**37.5**
Practical	34.5
Fun-loving (*juerguistas*)	34
Lively	33
Accommodating	31.5
Kind	29
Polite (*educados*)	27
Lovers of their land	**25**
Changeable (*cambiantes*)	23
Boastful (*fanfarrones*)	19.5
Individualistic	18.5

Table 6.3 Appraisal of the social and political evolution since 1975 (1986)[93]

Region	
Galicia	3.55
Madrid	**3.46**
National Average	3.41
Andalusia	3.39
Catalonia	3.36
Basque Country	3.32

1 = much worse and 5 = much better.

they lived, proud of their culture, and proud of how the capital had changed. In addition, as active participation and peaceful coexistence replaced passivity and mistrust, the residents of Madrid assumed the values and habits that helped transform them into new democratic citizens. In short, madrileños had come to identify with the region of Madrid and with each other in a new and positive way.

VI. Madrid's Regional Identity in Context

In contrast to the tendency by almost everyone—scholars, journalists, and politicians—to associate Madrid with a kind of vague national identity or a monolithic Spanishness, this growing feeling of regional identification in the capital points to a more complex reality. This is not to say regionalism replaced national identity, or any other preexisting form of affiliation in the capital. Instead, as explained in Chapter 1, regionalism became one axis of a multiple set of overlapping geographical identities. Thus, a new regional sense of place made up one part of a multiple identity that included both community and national affiliations. In other words, the residents of Madrid came to identify with at least three distinct layers of geographical identity in the early 1980s.

On the most basic level, it is commonly understood that neighborhood affiliations were still found on the community or the district level. For example, residents identified with upper-class neighborhoods, like Salamanca; working-class neighborhoods, like Embajadores; bedroom communities, like Alcobendas and Pozuelo; and peripheral districts, like Vallecas. The idea of "Madrid," however, symbolized something larger.

While many of the changes described in the first three sections of this chapter—greater cultural mobilization shaped by the movida madrileña, a growing feeling of peaceful coexistence, and increased pride for Madrid—occurred within the city of Madrid, the effort to create a new inclusive democratic sense of place resulted in the creation of something more than just a municipal identity. Due in part to the city's domination of the region, and in part to the formal development of the system of autonomous communities, the city and the region blended more easily together. Specifically, the creation of a ready-made framework of regional government after 1983, along with the designation of Madrid as an official region, made it possible to form a more inclusive madrileño sense of place that was broader than a local or municipal identity.

In addition to being based on the notion of voluntary citizenship and reinforced by the democratic values of active participation and peaceful coexistence, this new regional identity also embodied an urban identity. Although the Comunidad of Madrid included rural communities, more than 90 percent of the population lived within the urban metropolitan area.[94] As a result, identification was shaped, in large measure, by the city of Madrid, but by the activities of modern urban life understood most broadly. The bedroom neighborhoods on the periphery, the areas of work and recreation in the city's center, and the places of relaxation and excursion in the capital's hinterland, all made up the complex urban, social, and cultural structure that was "Madrid." Thus, living in a bedroom community, attending a popular festival in the center of the city, barhopping from neighborhood to neighborhood, visiting a museum in Alcalá de Henares, borrowing a book from a new lending kiosk, or passing the long weekend in the *sierra* all made up part of the unique madrileño experience.

The development of this new sense of place in Madrid also succeeded in part because of its very nature. As a civic identity that emphasized tolerance and inclusion, it was adaptable to more people from a variety of backgrounds. This fact was especially important in a region where more than 50 percent of the population had been born elsewhere. After leaving smaller and more traditional homes, newcomers were faced with the task of assimilating themselves into the metropolis of Madrid. These first- and second-generation immigrants were madrileños, but lacked the ties to a consolidated collective identity. The project by Madrid's local political elite offered an agreeable urban, democratic, and inclusive option for Madrid's diverse population.

With half of Madrid's population also under the age of 30, these same characteristics were particularly attractive to the region's youth.[95] Born in the baby boom of the 1960s, Madrid's young people had not suffered the experience of the civil war, its aftermath, or the full repression of the dictatorship. Nor had they experienced May 1968. This was the "beardless" generation stuck between the "*progres*" on one side and the "bunker" on the other. In other words, Madrid's youth represented neither "old" Marxists of the left nor reactionary conservatives of the right. They were instead the adolescents of the consensus-driven transition to democracy. A new sense of place that not only allowed, but also promoted, modern cultural trends, free expression, and mass participation represented an alternative that was more attractive than any form of identification based solely on the traditional politics of either the left or the right.

Additionally, because of the large number of immigrants and the young age of the population, there was also less of a solid bourgeois identity to overcome in Madrid. Moreover, the bourgeois identity that did exist in the capital was discredited through its previous connection to the Franco regime. At least during the first half of the 1980s, business interests were tarnished by links to Franco's system of patronage and favoritism, while middle class functionaries were unavoidably associated with the former regime's bureaucratic centralism. As a result, a new regional identity in Madrid did not have to compete against a powerful or institutionally established bourgeois identity.

Finally, and perhaps most importantly, the larger context in which the project was carried out favored the creation of new forms of identification in Madrid. The end of the dictatorship and the new possibilities that came with the transition to democracy, coupled with the social changes that accompanied the dual processes of urbanization and modernization that began in the 1960s, opened a space for new democratic identities to be formed in the capital and across Spain. Within this context, a new democratic sense of place based on the "modern" aspects of Madrid's culture was the perfect fit for madrileños who were tired of being associated with centralism, oppression, and the authoritarian past. Of course, this was a sense of place that not everyone identified with to the same degree, as feelings of identity are never uniform. Nonetheless, as an urban island—squeezed in-between two rural Castillas—the imagined community of Madrid represented something more than just a city or a capital. It symbolized a region that could claim its own unique features, its own history, its own regional festivals, its own regional cultural institutions, and its own active and inclusive way of life. It also represented a place where residents were encouraged to feel "madrileño," and not simply Spanish.

However, the formation of this new regional identity did not deny, or contradict, the existence of national affiliations in the capital—the third layer of identity. As the literal physical and political center of Spain, it was impossible to refute Madrid's connection to "the national." Nor did Madrid's local political elite try to create an identity that was exclusively regional. In an interview with José María Baviano shortly before his death, Tierno Galván admitted the importance of nationalist sympathies: "I confess to you that I am a nationalist, not a blind nationalist that transforms nationalism into prejudice and falls into fanaticism, but a nationalist that defends one's nation, and, unfortunately, there are not very many of those."[96] The mayor also frequently called for Spain's neutrality and exit from NATO on account of national pride.[97] Furthermore, there was no reason to deny national affiliations, as local, regional, and national identities are not mutually exclusive.

Speaking in January 1986 at the homage to Tierno Galván in the Club Siglo XXI, Madrid's new mayor, Juan Barranco, acknowledged the multiple layers of identity in the region of Madrid:

> The three realities [realidades], national, regional, and local, that converge in the urban territory of Madrid can articulate themselves, without great difficulty, above all if there exists a harmony of purpose and a common will of progress in liberty. National, regional, and neighborhood [vicinal] consciousnesses articulate themselves, in the bosom of the city, in rational and natural harmony.[98]

Even among Madrid's political elite, there was the recognition that neighborhood, regional, and even national affiliations could exist all at the same time. In Madrid, the coexistence of multiple identities meant that residents felt a simultaneous affiliation to the nation of Spain, the region of Madrid, and the neighborhood or district in which they lived. While it is difficult to gauge exactly how ordinary madrileños identified with these three different layers in the mid-980s, public opinion evidence from the period demonstrates both a significant degree of regional affiliation and the presence of at least a "dual identity" in the Comunidad of Madrid.

First with regard to the creation of a new regional identity, a survey conducted in 1987 directly highlights a higher level of regionalist sentiment in Madrid than in the past. In contrast to *declining* regionalist political aspirations (defined as popular demand for greater autonomy) in the Basque Country, Galicia, and Valencia between 1979 and 1987, regionalist aspirations in Madrid actually *increased* during this same period.[99] In addition, although the highest regional sentiments in 1987 were found in the Basque Country and Catalonia, regionalist feelings in Madrid were within the same range as three other autonomous communities with widely acknowledged regional identities: Valencia, Galicia, and Andalusia (see Table 6.4).

Along with this indication of increased regional identification, there is also evidence that shows that feelings of national affiliation were no higher in Madrid than in many other regions of the country. Put another way, Madrid exhibited no special identification with the nation. In another CIS survey conducted in 1987, 93 percent of madrileños described themselves as very proud or quite proud of being Spanish.[101] While this percentage is

Table 6.4 Evolution of regionalist political aspirations, 1979–1987[100]

Region	1979	1987	Change
Basque Country	1.70	1.42	−0.28
Catalonia	1.16	1.31	+0.15
Valencia	1.07	0.93	−0.14
Madrid	**0.67**	**0.86**	**+0.19**
Castilla León	0.62	0.84	+0.22
Galicia	0.92	0.83	−0.09
Andalusia	0.78	0.83	+0.05

Centralist attitudes are valued 0 and regionalist attitudes are valued 2.

Table 6.5 The feeling of pride for national identity (1987)[101]

Region	Very or quite proud	Little or not at all proud	Don't Know/ No response
Asturias/Cantabria	98	2	–
Castilla La Mancha/ Extremadura	97	2	1
Castilla León	97	2	1
Galicia	97	3	–
Valencia/Murcia	96	3	1
Andalusia/Canarias	94	6	–
Madrid	93	5	2
Catalonia/Baleares	87	10	3
Aragon/Navarra/Rioja	86	14	–
Basque Country	53	37	10

very high, the Comunidad of Madrid did *not* display the highest levels of national pride within Spain during this period. In fact, the vast majority of regions registered a slightly higher feeling of pride for a national identity than did Madrid. Specifically, feelings of national identity were higher in Asturias, Cantabria, Castilla-La Mancha, Extremadura, Castilla-León, Galicia, Valencia, Murcia, Andalusia, and the Canary Islands than in the region of Madrid (see Table 6.5).[102] Thus, by 1987, the region of Madrid simultaneously exhibited evidence of growing regional affiliations and a level of national identification that was lower than most of the other regions in Spain. Despite this evidence suggesting a more complex form of geographical identity within the capital, Madrid has mistakenly remained the region most closely associated with nationalism and Spanish national identity since the 1980s.

The best evidence for this false assumption was that no one thought to ask the standard "dual identity" question in the region of Madrid during the 1980s. Despite the fact that this question had been asked in practically every other region in Spain since the late 1970s, it was not until 1990 that sociologists asked madrileños: "In general, do you feel more *madrileño* than Spanish, as *madrileño* as Spanish, or more Spanish than *madrileño*?" Before this time, sociologists appear to have thought that everyone in Madrid simply felt "Spanish."[104]

As it turned out, only 26.1 percent of madrileños felt exclusively "Spanish" when the question was finally asked in 1990. The majority of the residents of Madrid, in fact exactly two thirds (66.6%), expressed some form of dual identity: either more Spanish than madrileño, as Spanish as madrileño, or more madrileño than Spanish (see Table 6.6).[105] According to this evidence, in 1990, the region of Madrid was no different than any other region of Spain in terms of identity. Exactly like the majority of the residents in the other regions of Spain, most madrileños felt some degree of overlapping feelings of identification, rather than any kind of singular identity.

Although it is impossible to determine the exact levels of national and regional affiliation in Madrid around the time of Tierno Galván's death because of a lack of data, evidence from the years 1990 to 1995 seems to suggest that the levels of regional identification may have been even higher, and the levels of national identification even lower, in the mid-1980s. Again, see Table 6.6. From 1990 to 1995, there was a distinct decrease in regional identification (from 4.4 to 1.6 percent exclusively madrileño), while at the same time there was almost a doubling of national identification (from 26.1 to 49.7 percent exclusively Spanish), and this is not at all surprising given the changes during the second half of the 1980s described in the next chapter. Followed into the past, those two trends suggest higher regionalism and lower nationalism in the region of Madrid in the mid-to-late 1980s. However, since the actual numbers from the mid-980s are not available, the data from the year 1990 must be used for further analysis.

When Madrid is compared more closely to other regions, the case for a "multiple identity" that incorporated a significant degree of regional identification becomes clearer and the argument for Madrid's monolithic "Spanishness" becomes even more tenuous. This case can be made in two ways. First, several regions exhibited higher levels of national affiliation than Madrid. And, second, the level of regional identification in the capital was comparable to several autonomous communities with widely acknowledged regional identities.

Table 6.6 National and regional identification, region of Madrid, 1990–1995[106]

Madrid	Only Spanish	More Spanish than madrileño	As madrileño as Spanish	More madrileño than Spanish	Only madrileño	Don't know/No response
1990	26.1	19.3	40.8	6.5	4.4	2.8
1991	32.9	9.1	48	5.6	2.7	1.7
1992	33.6	4.2	52.9	5.3	2.9	1.2
1993	31.7	8.2	47.7	8.8	2.1	1.5
1994	46.4	7.1	37.1	6.4	1.5	1.5
1995	49.7	4.9	36.7	5.3	1.6	1.8

With regard to national affiliation, in four separate regions a greater percentage of the population identified themselves as "exclusively Spanish" than in Madrid (see Table 6.7).[107] Those regions included Castilla-La Mancha, Extremadura, the Balearic Islands, and Valencia. Likewise, Madrid fell into a group of four regions where only roughly 45 percent of residents identified themselves as predominately Spanish (either only Spanish or more Spanish than regional): Valencia (46.6%), the Balearic Islands (45.6), Castilla-León (45.1%), Murcia (46.2), and Madrid (45.4). Based on this comparison, the level of national affiliation in the region of Madrid was clearly not unique or extraordinary during this period.

In terms of regional identity, 71 percent of the residents of Madrid expressed some level of regional identification (either exclusively regional, more regional than national, or as regional as national, or more Spanish than regional). In other words, almost three quarters of the population reported some level of affiliation to the region of Madrid. In addition, more than half (51.7%) of all madrileños expressed a level of regional identification that was *equal* to or *greater* than their level of national identification (either exclusively regional, more regional than national, or as regional as national). This figure for Madrid was comparable to Valencia (53.1%) and not that distant from the regions of Andalusia (65.9%) and Catalonia (65.7%), three regions with generally recognized regional identities. Based on this evidence, it is clear that, despite the many assertions to the contrary, there was a form of identity in the Comunidad of Madrid that was more complicated than a monolithic

Table 6.7   National and regional identification, 1990[108]

	Only Spanish	More Spanish than regional	As regional as Spanish	More regional than Spanish	Only regional	Don't know/No response
Castilla-La Mancha	38.8	15.6	31.3	7.5	6.1	0.7
Extremudura	35.6	2.3	28.7	19.5	10.3	3.4
Baleares	33.8	11.8	26.5	19.1	5.9	2.9
Valencia	30	14.6	39.1	11.4	2.6	2.3
Madrid	**26.1**	**19.3**	**40.8**	**6.5**	**4.4**	**2.8**
Castilla-León	24.9	20.2	25.6	15.9	0.9	2.6
Cataluña	22.3	9.5	36.4	23	6.3	2.5
Andalusia	20.3	11.3	44.6	13.4	7.9	2.6
Murcia	16.7	29.5	37.2	12.8	1.3	2.6
Asturias	16.4	3.6	40	29.1	8.2	2.7
Aragón	14.3	6.7	58	14.3	6.9	–
Canarias	13.6	2.1	37.1	16.4	27.9	2.9
País Vasco	8	4.5	23.6	32.2	24.6	7
Navarra	7.5	1.9	45.3	22.6	22.6	–
Cantabria	7.3	10.9	72.7	7.3	–	1.8
Galicia	4.9	14.1	38.4	21.7	19.4	1.5
La Rioja	3.7	11.1	74.1	3.7	7.4	–

"Spanishness." In fact, relatively strong regional affiliations had come to coexist with national and neighborhood affiliations in the capital during the 1980s.

CONCLUSION

Although it is difficult to directly connect the local administrations' official efforts to the actual changes that occurred in the capital after 1978, Madrid in the 1980s was clearly no longer the same place it had been under the dictatorship. Madrid had changed so much, in fact, that the Queen of Sweden announced on a visit to the capital in 1983—her first since 1970—that she "found Madrid a complete stranger [*desconocido*]."[109] Precisely while the Queen was away, the capital had become a more active, inclusive, and democratic community. Attitudes and behaviors clearly had changed. Cultural mobilization was replacing demobilization, and the movida madrileña was beginning to leave a definite mark on the capital. In addition, the residents of Madrid were also learning to be more proud of and to identify more closely with the place in which they lived. In an interview first granted in 1982 to the Spanish national television (TVE) program *Informe Semanal*, and rebroadcast on January 25, 1986, six days after his death, Tierno Galván explained:

> Before it was more important to be from a town in Andalusia, or Castile, or from the Basque Country than to be from Madrid. There one had roots and here one had nothing more than universality [*universalidad*], which in the end was little, or nothing. Madrid has recuperated its roots and now *madrileños* feel proud to say that they are from Madrid, wherever they come from.[110]

The creation of this new form of democratic identity based on the region of Madrid did not, however, exclude other forms of identification in the capital. As just described, regional affiliations made up just one part of a multiple identity that included a connection to local communities, or neighborhoods, and to the nation. And these identifications were not equal, nor were they static. In fact, the death of Tierno Galván in January 1986 brought an end to the official project to create a unique madrileño identity and with it the eventual decline of regional sentiment within the capital. The following chapter examines how the project to create a new form of democratic regional identity in Madrid was forced to come to an end as the space that had allowed for its articulation was closed. After 1986, the national PSOE was able to consolidate power on both the national and local level, and readopt Madrid as the capital of a "Europeanized" Spain. As a result, the notion of Madrid as a mobilized and independent region had to be left aside by the end of the decade.

CHAPTER 7

NOT YOUR SAME "NEW" MADRID: THE END OF THE REGIONAL IDENTITY PROJECT AND CHANGING FORMS OF IDENTIFICATION IN THE CAPITAL, 1986–1992

On the cold January day that Tierno Galván was laid to rest, the broad expression of popular support and gratitude for the figure most closely associated with Madrid's transformation was also accompanied by a promise never to forget him. This pledge was made by both citizens from all walks of life and Spain's political elite. After the horse-drawn carriage carrying the body of the mayor made its way through an ocean of placards reading, "We will not forget you, professor," the official coach eventually arrived at the cemetery of La Almudena, where a host of dignitaries, including even President Felipe González, promised "never to forget" Tierno Galván's contributions to the capital.[1] The actions of the residents of Madrid that day also showed a strong desire to remember how Madrid had changed since the end of the dictatorship. Along the route of the funeral procession,

> lined up on the pavement, intermingling ideologies and beliefs, ages and professions, bags under their eyes, grasping roses and carnations, photographs pulled from newspapers, banners waving in the air with the image of Don Enrique drawn in pencil, *madrileños* waited stoically [*a pie firme*] for their mayor . . . From the jackets and overcoats the black letters of the stickers shouted "*Hasta Siempre*."[2]

In addition to the thousands of madrileños who turned out with their little stickers pledging "For Always," the day of the funeral saw a full-page advertisement sponsored by the Ayuntamiento of Madrid in the newspaper *ABC* that exclaimed the same simple words: "*Hasta Siempre*."[3] However, despite the multitude of pledges to never forget the old professor and the many lessons he imparted to Madrid, both the memory of Tierno Galván and his project to create a new form of democratic regional identity in the capital, along with the movida madrileña, quickly slipped into oblivion after 1986.

In fact, while the memory of "the Dictator has slid into oblivion in the space of one generation," as Sebastian Balfour has observed, it took only half a decade for the memory of the old professor to completely vanish into the past.[4] By the end of the 1980s, it was almost as if the changes that had occurred under Tierno Galván's administration never happened. In the place of a socially equitable and culturally mobilized region, Madrid had become the neoliberal, consumer focused, and demobilized capital of a Europeanized Spain. This reversal did not occur because Tierno Galván's project was wiped out by the political opposition, as the center-right was not able to reclaim the Ayuntamiento of Madrid until 1989. Rather, this change largely occurred because of decisions made by Tierno Galván's very own party, the PSOE.

While it is unlikely that the frenzy for the movida madrileña could have continued unabated forever, the primary cause for the demise of a unique madrileño sense of place was a change of priorities in the capital. Specifically, new restrictions and demands on Madrid from the national level caused the space for a unique regional identity in the capital to close. After 1986, the national PSOE, led by Felipe González and Alfonso Guerra, increasingly reappropriated and redefined the image of the capital in its bid for European integration. For the national leadership of the PSOE, Spain's integration into the rest of Europe was seen as the surest method of solving Spain's mounting economic difficulties and of overcoming the country's national identity "problem" bequeathed by the experience of the dictatorship. In addition, even though there was a degree of continuity within the regional government, no one replaced the independent spirit of Tierno Galván within Madrid's Ayuntamiento. Instead, the capital's new young mayor, Juan Barranco, increasingly relied on the national administration for support after the death of his mentor. As a result of these factors, the space for an independent regional identity was permanently closed in Madrid. So by the end of the decade, there was no chance for any alternative democratic future for Madrid, especially one where social equality was valued as highly as the free market, where citizen participation was promoted rather than seen as an inconvenience or at worse a threat to the political order, and where regional and national pride were free to coexist without being supplanted by the imperatives of Europeanization.

The following chapter describes how that space was closed and tries to measure the impact that closure had on the forms of identification in the capital. The first part of the chapter examines how the political ideology of the national PSOE, based primarily on a centralized vision of European integration and economic neo-liberalism, became a more dominant force in the capital. The second part of the chapter then tries to gauge the effect of that shift on the residents of Madrid. Specifically, it looks at the disappearance of the more participatory form of democratic identity in Madrid and at the emergence of new forms of local and supranational affiliation as the regionalist project came to an end in the capital after 1986. Yet, despite these changes and the ultimate failure of Madrid's regional identity project, a certain feeling of pride for the capital was still evident at the end of the decade. And, more importantly, Madrid's connection to its authoritarian past had been broken once and for all.

PART I: THE SPACE CLOSES (1986–1991)

Just as the opening of a political and institutional space between 1979 and 1986 allowed for the creation of a new democratic regional identity in the capital, the closure of that space after 1986 brought about the end of the project to redefine Madrid as a unique region. Rather than happening from both above and below, as in the period before 1986, the closing of this space after the death of the old professor primarily occurred from above. Specifically, the national PSOE was able to consolidate its political program on both the local and national level, and reappropriate Madrid as the capital of a Europeanized Spain. At the same time, the local and regional administrations of Madrid moved closer to the political ideology of the national PSOE over the second half of the decade. Madrid's young new mayor, in particular, increasingly turned to the national leaders from his own generation for guidance and political backing after the death of his mentor and predecessor. As a result, the political ideology of the national PSOE became the dominant force in Madrid after 1986, forcing out a unique regional identity in the capital.

THE NATIONAL LEVEL

After its electoral victory of 1982, the national PSOE increasingly chose a less-participatory, less-independent, and less-mobilized path for the country. It was essentially a neoliberal path based on closer ties to Europe, free market economics, and the hope for greater material prosperity.[5] Creating this new image of Spain based on European convergence and economic well-being was more acceptable to more people in more areas of the country, but it was also more conservative and more state centered. The emphasis on order and prosperity also came at the expense of social equality and popular mobilization. As discussed in Chapter 3, the result was a more formal model of democracy that stressed political parties and the election of representatives, rather than direct participation. This decision to embrace economic growth and stability over greater mobilization and democratization firmly placed Spain on the road toward liberal democracy, and away from a more participatory form of democracy by the middle of the decade.[6]

While the implementation of neoliberal fiscal and monetary policies began as early as 1982 in order to promote economic development, decrease unemployment, and broaden the party's electoral appeal, the national PSOE increasingly sought a particular vision of Europeanization in the second half of the 1980s.[7] This vision of Europeanization favored unity, stability, national economic growth, and Cold War security with the West. But even though the idea of European integration had been closely connected to "democracy" since the time of the dictatorship, Europeanization in the late 1980s did not necessarily mean greater democratization for Madrid, or for the country as a whole.

Speaking before Congress in the spring of 1992, González argued for the fundamental importance of joining the rest of Europe: "For a country like ours, historically isolated, no effort should be spared to board this train. Our well-being and our stability depend on our success in adapting to the construction of Europe."[8] In fact, the national leadership of the PSOE believed that "their generational responsibility was above all the Europeanization of Spain."[9] But why exactly did the national PSOE place such an emphasis on the notion of European integration? As far back as the Franco regime, the idea of Europe was an important point of reference and an aspiration for the left. It was an idea intimately tied to the recovery of social liberties and a democratic form of government. After the death of Franco, "democrats in Spain looked longingly north towards a Europe which to them embodied all the ideals which they were denied."[10] However, in the 1980s, the national leadership of the PSOE looked to Europe for three specific reasons: (1) for political and international legitimacy, (2) for help in solving the country's economic problems, and (3) as a means of resolving Spain's national identity "problem."

To begin with, entry into the community of European nations promised to confer political respectability on the PSOE and on the country in general. It was hoped that inclusion into such institutions as the European Community (EC) would legitimize the new democracy and symbolize the country's "normalization" after the experience of the dictatorship.[11] Likewise, it was also believed that after years of relative isolation European integration would bestow new international acceptance on Spain. In fact, during the general elections of 1989, González even claimed that through the process of European integration, the country had gained "an international prestige greater than at any time since Charles V in the sixteenth century."[12] In other words, bringing Spain into the European fold was seen as one of the surest ways of turning the country into a legitimate player on the world stage.

Spain's Socialist leaders had even more pragmatic reasons for looking to Europe. Faced with rising unemployment, which peaked at over 22 percent in 1986,[13] González sought greater European integration in the belief that it would foster international confidence and financial investment in Spain, and give the country access to modern technology. This was especially true since Spain's entry into the EC would also come with a multiyear transition period that would allow the country access to a huge European market, while enjoying protections and subsidies.

Equally as important, Europeanization also eased Spain's anxieties and insecurities with regard to the past. The decision to join the rest of Europe would verify that Spain was no longer "different" in the way the Franco regime had tried to define the country. In this way, official entry into the community of European nations was an important means of distancing Spain from its recent dictatorial past. If Spaniards became Europeans, there was no way they could still be the same Spaniards of the dictatorship. In other words, entry into the EC was the ultimate denial of any claim to Spain's essential difference. The country simply could not be different, in the way the Franco regime had tried to define it, if Spain was fully integrated into the community of European nations.

Connected with the need to overcome the past, embracing European integration and a new European supranational identity provided a solution to Spain's national identity "problem," offering a way of uniting a country increasingly divided by regional differences. Economic prosperity and higher levels of consumption, predicated on European integration, were goals that all Spaniards could relate to, as the desire for high disposable incomes and parity with Spain's European neighbors was not limited to specific regions or social classes. Within this context, economic self-interest, either on an individual or regional level, served to unify and stabilize the nation as a whole. Convergence with the rest of Europe also offered a common point of pride. The country as a whole gained from Spain's increasing prestige on the international stage, for example, with González's election to the Presidency of the EC in 1989, and from the real, and sometimes imagined, economic benefits that came as a result of joining the European club. In this way, the growth of a supranational identity based on European integration provided a kind of unifying collective identity for the country as a whole. Or, put another way, Europeanization served as a form of nationalism.

Although not often recognized as such, the PSOE did in fact adopt an increasingly nationalist stance in the 1980s. Shortly after the general elections in 1982, Felipe González "stated that those foreign media who had labeled the Socialists as 'young Spanish nationalists' were right in pointing it out since 'I believe that it is necessary to recover Spain's national sentiment,' by appealing to the Republican tradition of liberal nationalism prior to 1931."[14] This focus on national unity was clearly demonstrated, for example, by the PSOE's attempt to restrict the transfer of responsibilities to the autonomous communities after 1982. And the desire to catch up with Europe, to increase international prestige, and to promote nation-wide economic prosperity were all clearly nationalist goals. The means used to achieve these ends, however, increasingly took the form of a very nonnationalistic-looking program, namely the entry into a supranational framework of political and economic alliances with the rest of Europe. Nonetheless, a new European identity offered the possibility of unifying Spain at a time when all forms of official national identity were perceived as illegitimate and when regional differences were increasingly dividing the country. Thus, a supranational identity provided the national leadership of the PSOE a means to both overcome the past and create a new form of democratic identity for Spaniards in the posttransition period.

Entry into the European club, however, did not come without its sacrifices. Both in Spain and in the rest of Europe, it was understood that security interests were inseparable from economic interests in building a united Europe.

Thus, continued NATO membership was essential for negotiating Spain's entry into the EC. Recognition of this fact led to the PSOE's abrupt reversal on the NATO referendum. In fact, González ultimately staked the fate of his government on Spain's continued membership in the alliance. Speaking on behalf of the central administration, Javier Solana threatened to dissolve the Congress in 1986 if Spain was forced to withdraw from NATO: "The decision to dissolve parliament is a final decision . . . if the people consider that national interests are better defended outside of the Alliance [NATO], the government will act as a consequence."[15] After a massive publicity campaign, and the application of a significant degree of political pressure, the country voted to remain part of the alliance in March 1986.[16]

European integration also required strict economic policies. In particular, pursuing economic convergence through a neoliberal program was seen as a necessary precondition to active participation in European affairs. So in an effort that was ultimately designed to meet stringent European Economic Community (EEC) requirements, the PSOE moved further down the road toward a classic neoliberal economic program: fiscal austerity, reform of the welfare system, and even a significant degree of privatization.[17] More than simply meeting a set of legislated requirements, it was hoped such a program would improve the fitness of the Spanish economy in the second half of the 1980s—by reducing inflation and increasing productivity—and thus prepare Spain to meet the competitive challenge from other EC countries in the future. However, the articulation of a fiscal and monetary policy that so obviously contradicted the tenets of Socialism brought criticism of the party from a variety of sources. It even caused the opposition, in this case the future mayor of Madrid, Álvarez del Manzano, to comment, "The PSOE has no ideology, only pragmatism."[18] Due to the fundamental desire to pursue the path of European integration, pragmatism won the day over utopic idealism within Spain's Socialist party after 1986.

The contrast between this pragmatism and the regional identity project in Madrid was too clear to be ignored. Tierno Galván's project was especially problematic because Madrid symbolized the capital of the country and, to many both inside and outside the country, all of Spain. Endless cultural engagements and staying out all night contradicted Spain's new image as the serious and industrious member of the EC. Likewise, a regional identity founded on the hope for a Socialist utopia, on a relative lack of interest in economic activities, and on the desire for neutrality sharply conflicted with the central administration's plan for a Spain modeled on the rest of Europe, especially given the neoliberal climate at the time. In short, the particular type of democratic model that Madrid's new regional identity and the movida madrileña represented had to be replaced by the national PSOE after Tierno Galván's death in 1986.

Ironically, the national PSOE also took a much greater interest in Madrid after 1986 precisely because of the way the capital had changed under Tierno Galván's administration. On account of Madrid's both real and symbolic shifts away from centralism toward democracy, there was more of a propensity on the part of the national leadership of the PSOE to invest in the capital and, likewise, to have Madrid reflect the image and the ideology of the party. In other words, the desire to readopt Madrid as the capital of a Europeanized Spain depended on the transformation the city had undergone in the first half of the 1980s. As previously mentioned, the foreign press, in particular, promoted Madrid as the image of the "new Spain" to the rest of the world.[19] And at home, Spanish writers and journalists hailed Madrid as "one of the most interesting cities in Europe."[20] Put another way, rather than representing a political liability, Madrid had been transformed into a political asset by 1986. In fact, Madrid's transformation into a vibrant and internationally prestigious center for arts and culture temporarily offered the PSOE a valuable new political tool, especially at a time when the national PSOE's political dominance was increasingly challenged by the rise of other regionalisms across the country.

While the PSOE was interested in Madrid's new-found prestige, it was not so welcoming of a unique regional identity in the capital, and was especially not supportive of one that conflicted with its less mobilized neoliberal agenda. Within the context of the national PSOE's program of economic development and European integration, Madrid was now called upon to play a new role in the second half of the decade. Specifically, it was to become the *capital* of a pluralist European nation. As a result, Madrid would no longer be one region trying to differentiate a distinct sense of place among many other regions. Instead, as the capital of a "nation of nations," Madrid would be, by definition, different than the other regions of Spain. In other words, this new role caused Madrid to again become the exception. This change also symbolized a return to a more centralized and vertical model of administration, rather than a horizontal model of equal democratic regions. Because of this readoption as the capital of Spain, any plans for a separate path or a unique regional identity for Madrid had to be permanently put aside.

The movida madrileña, too, had to be left behind. Despite the movement's apparent vitality only a year earlier, the movida madrileña showed definite signs of coming to an end by the close of 1986. The sudden demise of the movement caused many former participants in subsequent years to wring their hands and to wonder what it all meant and why it ended so suddenly.[21] Some argued that people burned out, particularly from drug and alcohol abuse, or that they simply moved on. Others believed that the movida sold out, citing most frequently the commercial successes of Pedro Almodóvar, Adolfo Domínguez, and Alaska. While each of these reasons is partially true, the movida madrileña primarily came to an end because, like the broader project to create a new regional identity based on cultural mobilization, official support was withdrawn from the movement after the death of the mayor and because of changing priorities in the capital after 1986. Getting people to work and "convergence" with Spain's European neighbors became the main preoccupations in the capital. In 1990, the writer and former singer for such groups as Kaka de Luxe and Paraíso, Fernando "El Zurdo" Márquez, summed up what happened to the movida after 1986: "It was a movement of people with new ideas. What happened was that the PSOE fell on top of it, as it later fell on so many other things."[22]

Beginning as early as 1986, the policies of the national administration, and of the Ministry of Culture, in particular, helped to redefine Madrid as the capital of a Europeanized Spain and ignored any connection between the capital and the movida madrileña. And, in general, the promotion of culture was seen by the national PSOE as a way of stimulating the country's sagging economy. With unemployment reaching historic levels, and peaking right before the general elections in 1986, even the Minister of Culture saw the need to put culture to work for economic growth in Madrid and elsewhere in the second half of the decade. Speaking before the Congress in September 1986, Javier Solana stressed the "economic implications" of culture and underscored the importance of culture in Spain's "economic life."[23] He went on to speak of the importance of supporting the country's "cultural industries" as a means of increasing Spain's prestige in the world, competing economically on the world market, increasing employment, and stimulating economic growth within Spain.[24]

Because of the economic importance of culture, Solana stated, "the state could not, and cannot, remain passive with regards to assisting cultural creation."[25] However, the Minister of Culture argued for "supporting cultural industries and businesses in the private sector" rather than aiding individual artists, writers, or musicians.[26] Specifically, Solana recommended increased subsidies for theatre, film, and publishing.[27] Not coincidentally, these were the three industries, especially film and publishing, which had the greatest potential for mass penetration and, as a result, the greatest possibility for economic growth and profit. Supporting Spain's cultural industries was also particularly important for increasing employment. According to Solana, "Film and books, video and records, theatre and communication technologies employ every day more professionals and workers."[28] In other words, culture, defined as an industry, was to serve the purpose of creating jobs.

Thus, in contrast to Tierno Galván's use of cultural mobilization, there was no clear intention of promoting democratic participation and coexistence behind the Ministry of Culture's support for cultural activity after 1986. Instead, cultural creation was simply promoted for its apparently "apolitical" economic benefits. Solana himself assured the assembled Congress: "Our approach is going to be aesthetic and ideological neutrality."[29] This new approach to culture on the national level was a sharp departure from the period prior to 1986, as the Minister of Culture had mentioned nothing about the economic implications of culture in his previous address to the Congress three years earlier in December 1983.[30]

In conjunction with the desire to stimulate the economy, the national administration also pursued a cultural program that tried to achieve the goal of incorporating Madrid, and Spain as a whole, into the rest of Europe. And, at the same time, there was also a tendency to minimize the expression of Madrid's new regional identity. For instance, outside of Spain, artists from the movida madrileña were not featured in the Ministry of Culture's large exhibit *L'Imagination Nouvelle. Les Anées 70–80* held in Paris in 1987. Even though it focused specifically on contemporary art from the 1970s and 1980s, this exposition in Paris neglected all references to the movida. In fact, only one of the ten artists came from Madrid—Guillermo Pérez Villalta. Ironically, many of the artists featured in the exhibit showcasing contemporary Spanish art actually resided in Paris: Miguel Barceló, José Manuel Broto, Miguel Ángel Campano, and José María Sicilia.[31] Other artists came from such regions as Valencia (Miguel Navarro) and Catalonia (Susan Solamo). And, like the exposition held in Paris a year earlier, the movida did not make up part of the large 1988 exposition of Spanish contemporary art in Chicago either.[32] In general, the expositions sponsored by the Ministry of Culture after 1986 featured artists from Spain's various regions and Spanish artists who lived in different parts of Europe, but not artists that were connected to Madrid's regional cultural scene.

Similar to the situation abroad, the objective at home was to minimize the expression of a unique regional identity and readopt the image of Madrid as the symbolic capital of Spain. Thus, even though there was assistance for regional cultural activities in other areas of Spain, there was no support for a unique regional identity or for the movida madrileña specifically in the capital between 1986 and 1991.[33] In other words, while the national PSOE, in general, and the Ministry of Culture, in particular, accepted a more plural vision of Spain and of Spanish culture in the second half of the decade, there was no sign that a separate madrileño regional identity would be accepted as a part of the official vision of Spain after 1986. The national PSOE did, however, exert more control over and take a greater interest in the capital during this period.

Beginning in the mid-1980s, the central administration, often through the Ministry of Culture, devoted greater attention to the capital and started funding large *national* projects in Madrid. In addition to the creation of the Compañia Nacional de Teatro Clásico in Madrid in 1986, the national PSOE backed such projects as the renovation of the Museo Arqueológico Nacional, the further amplification of the Reina Sofia (after its initial lackluster inauguration in 1986), the enlargement of the Prado Museum, the renovation of the Teatro Real, and, most notably, the inauguration of the new Auditorio Nacional in 1988. Besides these new or renovated cultural spaces, other new institutions and organizations were also created by the national administration in the second half of the decade and included the Joven Orquestra Nacional, the Compañia de Teatro Clásico, the Ballet Clásico y Español, and the Centro de Nuevas Tendencias Teatrales. Additionally, the Ministry of Culture's program took on more of an international perspective. Thus, in addition to such expositions as "La fotografía Española hasta 1900" and "Fotografía Iberoamericana," the Ministry of Culture brought the work of a number of important foreign artists to the capital for the first time, including Man Ray, Walker Evans, and Wernar Bischof.[34] The central administration also took a renewed interest in ARCO, Madrid's international art fair, bringing some 218 galleries from around the world to the capital in 1990.[35]

The level of interest shown for Madrid by the PSOE reached such a point by the end of the decade that the administration was openly accused of favoritism. In 1989, much to the embarrassment of the national administration, a study sponsored by the regional government of Catalonia reported that 53 percent of the cultural funding for all of the country's autonomous communities went to Madrid. According to the study, the amount of cultural investment "increased by almost 35% in recent years."[36] In addition, the study reported that the region of Madrid was receiving by far the greatest level of cultural investment per capita from the Ministry of Culture than any other of the 16 regions.[37] But, of course, the national administration's goal was not to simply devote more attention to Madrid. Again, the goal was to reinforce the image of Madrid as the symbolic capital of a country committed to Europeanization and economic prosperity.

This desire by the national leadership of the PSOE to appropriate and redefine the image of the capital was probably most clearly demonstrated in the bid to nominate Madrid as the Cultural Capital of Europe.[38] In the mid-1980s, a number of different cities around Spain sought the nomination to European culture capital for the year 1992, including Madrid, Granada, Córdoba, and Salamanca. However, the central administration explicitly backed Madrid's campaign for the nomination, first initiated by the Ayuntamiento in January 1987.[39] The national administration chose to support Madrid's candidacy to Cultural Capital of Europe because, as described further in the next section, the Ayuntamiento's initial nomination had more to do with incorporating Madrid into the rest of Europe than with promoting local pride or a unique madrileño identity. Thanks, in part, to the national administration's backing, Madrid was officially selected as the Cultural Capital by the EC in 1988. National support for Madrid, however, did not stop there. At the official announcement in 1988 of Madrid's election as the Cultural Capital of Europe for 1992, Javier Solana promised that Madrid would be "endowed with all the necessary resources" from the central administration to ensure a successful event.[40]

In a year when all eyes would be turned to Barcelona's Olympic Games and to Seville's Expo-92, Madrid's nomination as the Cultural Capital of Europe in 1992 provided the national PSOE with a way of reasserting the capital's importance.[41] In other words, it was a way of making sure that the image of "Spain," and the national administration, was not overshadowed by the country's various regions, namely by the events in Catalonia and in Andalusia. Specifically, Madrid was to be recognized as the capital of Spain, and not as a distinct region.

So rather than presenting Madrid as an example of one of Spain's many regions, the nomination campaign presented Madrid as a "sensitive" national capital with an "understanding attitude toward the recuperation of the identities of the regions."[42] In this way, Madrid's uniqueness as the capital of the state of Spain was emphasized over its status as a unique autonomous region with its own specific attributes. Similarly, the campaign presented Madrid as "a projection of national character" and frequently referenced its "position as the political capital" of Spain.[43] The campaign also specifically stressed Madrid's "long tradition as the capital of the state [of Spain]."[44]

In conjunction with the efforts to highlight Madrid's position as the national capital of Spain, the campaign also specifically emphasized the national institutions of Madrid, such as the Prado Museum, the Reina Sofía, the National Archeology Museum, the Museo Nacional de Artes Decorativas, and the Museo Nacional de Ciencias Naturales. Other national sites highlighted by the campaign included the Royal Palace, the Teatro Real, and the Catedral de la Almudena.

In contrast to the attention paid to Madrid's national institutions, very little effort was made to highlight its regional or local culture. This was espe cially true with regard to cultural activities related to the movida madrileña. In fact, when the director general of the program, Pablo López de Osaba, was asked during an interview in 1991 if the movida left anything behind, he responded: "I believe it left nothing."[45] Along with no specific references to the movida madrileña, the most significant mention of Madrid's own culture came in the form of a proposal to build a new City Museum (*Museo de la Ciudad*) in time for the celebrations in 1992. As a completely new institution, the museum offered the possibility of presenting a totally new image of the capital, thus alleviating the need to rely on any image of Madrid defined in the past. In other words, with the creation of a new museum, promotion of Madrid as the "capital" did not have to include the recognition of the movida or the symbols of the distinct regional identity created prior to 1986.

In contrast to these efforts to deny the expression of a unique madrileño regional identity and to reappropriate the image of Madrid as the capital of Spain, the national PSOE was far more accommodating of regional identities with regard to the two other major events of 1992. Even though Felipe González and the other national leaders of the PSOE favored "the strong internal unity of Spain" and occasionally even restricted the transfer of responsibilities to the autonomous communities in the period after 1982,[46] regional identities were allowed to express themselves and were even promoted to a degree during the Barcelona Olympic Games and Sevilla's Expo-92.

In his sociological study of the 1992 Olympic Games, John Hargreaves has shown how regional and national identities coexisted and even complimented one another in the staging of the Barcelona Games.[47] In contrast to the promotion of Madrid as the capital of a "nation of nations," the national PSOE did not try to appropriate or "Españolize" the Barcelona Olympics. Nor did the national political leadership repress the expression of Catalan identity in relation to the 1992 Olympics. Instead a collaborative effort between national, regional, and local authorities secured the success of the Barcelona Games, reinforcing Catalan prestige and autonomy in the process.

Specifically, Hargreaves's work shows how the national leadership actually accepted the fact that Barcelona and Catalonia, along with its center-right regionalist party (CiU), would be the main beneficiaries of the 1992 Olympics.[48] In fact, he argues that the national leadership allowed the Games to be a "heavily Catalanized occasion."[49] Furthermore, rather than simply allowing the opportunity for the Games to become Catalanized, the central government "diverted the required resources and responded positively to Catalan pressures for concession."[50] As a result, the preparation and eventual execution of the Games were collaborative processes in which Catalan and national political leadership worked together to the benefit of everyone. Even though "Catalan identity had been more enhanced than Spanish identity" by the end of the event, Hargreaves concludes that the Barcelona Games strengthened Catalan identity and autonomy without diminishing the prestige of Spain.[51]

Similar to the circumstances surrounding the Olympic Games in Barcelona, Richard Maddox's anthropological work on Seville's Expo-92 likewise demonstrates the national PSOE's acceptance and even support for multiple regional identities within the context of the post-transition Spanish state.[52] In fact, one of Maddox's central arguments is that the national leadership of the PSOE consciously presented a modern, optimistic, and plural image of Spain at the 1992 world's fair in Seville in order to show that the country was "ready to assume its responsibility as a full partner in the European Union."[53] From this perspective, the Expo-92 offered "an opportunity to define Spain's basic identity in terms of the country's aspirations to join the ranks of the most advanced nations of Western Europe."[54]

Specifically, Maddox describes how the country presented itself "as a microcosm of European pluralism, an entity composed of many particular ethnic and regional cultures, each with its own distinctive character."[55] In addition, Spain was offered as "the model of a new kind of complex, post-nationalist, liberal polity that is cosmopolitan in its ties, commitments, and openness to its neighbors and the rest of the world and is free, internally diverse, and tolerant."[56] In other words, the basic goal of the Expo-92 "was to project an image of Spain as composed of diverse but equal regions freely and harmoniously participating in the development of a confederal state and the 'new Europe.'"[57] As a result, local, regional, and national identities were simultaneously promoted and strengthened to varying degrees.

While Spain's 17 regional identities were generally promoted at Seville's Expo-92, Andalusian regional identity received special attention. For example, several special events at the Expo honored the host region and Andalusia's own regional pavilion was allowed to be four times the size (approximately 8,000 square meters) of the 16 other regional pavilions.[58] In contrast, however, the autonomous region of Madrid did not receive such favorable attention. Madrid's pavilion at the Expo, for example, is described as "undistinguished" and unpopular among "the critics and public alike."[59] Maddox also notes that Madrid's "poor showing in the regional sphere . . . was in obvious disproportion to its real politicoeconomic power and cultural influence."[60] Despite the varying representation of regional identities, Maddox maintains that a multitude of local and regional identities were presented in a positive way that reinforced the notion of national unity and pride.[61]

So even though the main goal of the three major events of 1992 was to present Spain as an open, plural, and fully European country, not all regions and regional identities were treated equally by the national administration. According to Maddox, "holding the state-sponsored and state-funded events in Catalonia and Andalusia would serve both to satisfy regional pride and to impede demands for greater autonomy by tying the governments and private sectors of these two key regions to Madrid [to the national PSOE] in a mutually beneficial and cooperative way."[62] However, as described above, this was not true when it came to the promotion of regionalism in the capital, and particularly with regard to Madrid's nomination as the Cultural Capital of Europe. Thus, when compared to the two other major events of 1992, Madrid's position as the exception comes more clearly into focus. In contrast to collaborative efforts that produced enhanced regional and local identities in Barcelona and in Seville, there was far less tolerance on the part of the national PSOE for the expression of a separate regional identity in the capital. In short, after 1986, madrileño regionalism was squelched in a way that did not happen in Catalonia or Andalusia.

The Local and Regional Level

At the same time the national leadership of the PSOE started paying more attention to the capital, the local and regional administrations were also moving closer to the political ideology (i.e., pragmatism, economic neoliberalism, and European integration) of the national PSOE during the second half of the decade. Convergence from this direction further closed the space for a unique regional identity in Madrid. When Juan Barranco succeeded the old professor in January 1986, he became the youngest mayor in the history of Madrid, at only 38 years old. Without the years of self-imposed exile and philosophical meditation, and without the benefit of a kind of personality cult behind him, Barranco was less individualistic and more of a team player than his predecessor. The premature death of his mentor and his relative inexperience also led the young mayor to seek out guidance and support. Within this context, the national leadership of the PSOE provided a logical choice. The choice was probably influenced by the generational connection between Barranco and the national leaders as well. As a result, Felipe González became much more of a political boss to Barranco than he had been to the old professor.

While the relationship between the two leaders cannot be described as close or affectionate, the young mayor received frequent support from González, especially during the municipal elections of 1987.[63] And, with the loss of the absolute majority that year, Barranco was forced to rely even more on the PSOE for support after 1987. At the same time, the national leadership also had to pay more attention to Madrid because of Barranco's increasingly unstable political position. After winning only a simple majority in the municipal elections of 1987, Barranco offered to form a coalition with both the center CDS (Centro Democratico Social) and the left IU (Izquierda

Unida); both parties, however, declined. As a result, Barranco's administration was forced to constantly negotiate with all sides, creating political instability and a certain degree of administrative paralysis. Despite the support from the central administration, in less than two years Barranco's worst fear came true. In the middle of 1989, the CDS and the newly constituted Partido Popular (formerly the AP) joined forces to pass a motion of censure that removed Barranco from office.[64]

Before Barranco was ousted in 1989, his administration did little to support Tierno Galván's original project of fostering a new form of democratic regional identity in Madrid. Compared to the old professor, Barranco had more modest goals for Madrid and was less confident in the Ayuntamiento's ability to effect a change on the capital. In an interview shortly after taking office, Barranco explained:

> I believe that from the *Ayuntamiento* in general, and logically from this one also, we can only do modest things, quite modest things; that is to say, from the *Ayuntamientos* there have never been made nor can they make great revolutions, neither can they solve in a resounding way the most serious problems that the society has.[65]

Due in part to these lower expectations, Barranco's administration was guided more by inertia than by anything else. Thus, rather than starting any new urban initiatives or implementing any grand new agenda, Barranco's administration mostly finished up the urban renewal projects previously started by Tierno Galván's administration. In the period after 1986, projects such as the renovation of the Atocha train station, the revitalization of the Puerta del Sol, the renovation of the plaza Carlos V, and the construction of the park eventually named for Tierno Galván, where the new planetarium was located, were all finally completed. But, on the whole, the memory of Tierno Galván's utopian ideals quickly faded from the local political elite's imagination after 1986. For instance, despite the many proposals and promises at the time of Tierno Galván's death, a foundation was never established to collect and study his work.[66]

In addition to Barranco's less ambitious goals, there was another important difference between the two administrations. In contrast to Tierno Galván's rare collaboration with the private sector, the new mayor spoke often of "private institutions" and "private initiatives."[67] The Barranco administration even took the first steps toward the privatization of public services, such as sanitation, park services, public works, and even cultural programming.[68] Not surprisingly the privatization of municipal services prompted the concern of labor unions, and stood in sharp contrast to Tierno Galván's reluctance to look to the private sector or to the market in order to solve Madrid's problems. At the time, a member of the Ayuntamiento confessed: "Enrique Tierno was reluctant to have this relationship with private initiative, but a gradual change is happening."[69] While this gradual change was affecting certain areas of the administration, more significant change was occurring in others, especially in the spheres of business and culture.

Mirroring the priorities of the national leadership of the PSOE, Barranco's administration increasingly emphasized economic growth and business development at the expense of other concerns. Thus, instead of fostering a kind of participatory democracy based on cultural mobilization, as Tierno Galván had done, Barranco's efforts were directed toward economically transforming the capital. To accomplish this task, the new mayor wanted to take advantage of all of Madrid's unique characteristics, including the capital's cultural reputation. Echoing Solana's 1986 speech before the *Cortes*, Barranco explained:

> Traditionally, Madrid has been a city of services, but it is, of course, a center of decision making, increasing its capacity for economic attraction. Continually it is concentrating activities in what is known as the tertiary sector, increasing as such the production and distribution of information and in the so-called leisure industry.[70]

To better promote all of the capital's unique economic attributes, the organization Promadrid was founded in 1987. Through the cooperation of the Ayuntamiento of Madrid, the Comunidad of Madrid, and the private sector, Promadrid was formed precisely in order to promote economic activity in the region and to "sell the image and the brand [*la marca*] of Madrid."[71] According to Barranco, the objective of Promadrid was "the attraction of investments that generated wealth and employment [to Madrid]."[72]

Economic development was also personally promoted by the mayor. For example, in January 1988, Barranco held a conference with 200 of France's most important business executives during a trip to Paris to promote foreign investment in Madrid.[73] During the trip to the French capital, the mayor was to "sell the image of Madrid as an economic and special head of a market of 50 million [*sic*] people, an axis of communication, an international industrial and financial center of distribution and exchange, and as a city with an ample range of cultural and recreational activities."[74] Although mentioning Madrid's cultural activities, Barranco's focus in Paris was on promoting economic development: the capital's vibrant culture was just one more reason to invest in Madrid.

Similarly, one of the few large projects initiated under Barranco's administration was related not to the capital's cultural infrastructure, but to promoting economic growth. Completed in 1990, the Campo de las Naciones provided Madrid with a new complex of convention halls and luxury hotels that was designed to attract business meetings and conventions from around Europe and beyond.

By the end of the 1980s, the efforts to promote economic activity started to show signs of paying off. In 1988, Madrid became the fifth most important city in the world for conventions and congresses, behind Paris, London, Brussels and Geneva.[75] Unsatisfied with even this position, the local administration hoped to propel Madrid to the third position by 1992.[76] In short, economic growth and business development had become the primary concerns of the Barranco administration by the end of the decade.

Along with this new emphasis on business, there was also a change of direction in terms of culture. Starting in 1986, the climate of cultural openness, tolerance, and equality that was so characteristic of Tierno Galván's administration came to an end in Madrid. In general, Barranco's administration was more interested in the revival of traditional madrileño culture and European cultural integration than in new cultural currents based specifically in the capital.[77] As a result, the official image of Madrid was no longer tied to the symbols of the movida madrileña in the second half of the decade. Instead, it was an image that increasingly represented Madrid as a more traditional and pro-business capital of a Europeanized Spain.

Even before taking office, Barranco expressed a desire to return to more traditional expressions of madrileño culture, such as Madrid's traditional dance, *el chotis*. In early January 1986, he suggested: "Perhaps in our city there is an abandonment of traditions that are typically *madrileño*."[78] Barranco also lamented the fact that, compared to other cities in Spain and around the world, Madrid had "not conserved its unique musical traditions."[79]

Soon after taking office, the new mayor underscored his desire to revive Madrid's cultural past. During his homage to Tierno Galván at the Club Siglo XXI on January 29, 1986, Barranco described his wish to look to Madrid's past in order to build its identity in the future: "The Madrid of the future should be a Madrid faithful to itself and respectful of the best marks that the past has left in creating its physiognomy and personality."[80] Likewise, he stressed the need for the new local administration to be "sensitive to the recuperation of tradition."[81] In contrast to Tierno Galván's propensity to focus on the present and the future, Barranco argued that "the Madrid of the left has to be an expert in the traditional and attentive to preservation."[82]

In addition to favoring more traditional forms of madrileño culture, Barranco's administration also promoted a cultural program that emphasized European cultural integration. This effort was most clearly demonstrated in the bid to nominate Madrid as the Cultural Capital of Europe, mentioned above. For the local administration, the nomination had more to do with incorporating Madrid into the rest of Europe than with promoting local pride or a unique regional cultural identity. Speaking at the time the decision was made to initiate the process, the mayor's first lieutenant, Emilio García Horcajo, explained:

> To be selected for a celebration of this kind assumes an event of the highest magnitude for any city. For Madrid, this designation would presume the recognition, on the part of the members of the EC, of the important role that it plays within the group of European capitals, at the same time it would set down the foundations for greater coordination and cooperation in cultural matters in the future.[83]

Likewise, Barranco petitioned for Madrid's nomination not to promote a distinctive regional identity but to ensure "that our capital does not remain at the margins of the major axes [of Europe] that are delineated for the next decade."[84] In other words, the nomination meant ensuring a future position for Madrid within the growing EC.

More than simply highlighting the capital, the nomination of Madrid as the Cultural Capital of Europe was also meant, in part, to bring prestige to Spain as a new member of the EC. Barranco believed that Madrid's nomination as the Cultural Capital of Europe would "obtain the maximum benefit for all of Spain and for Europe from the unbeatable conditions that will come in 1992 [in Madrid]."[85] Not surprisingly, the actual campaign to promote Madrid's nomination downplayed a unique regional cultural identity and highlighted the capital's traditions and long-time connection to Europe: "Madrid represents the present day spirit of Europe: a rich, vital, and innovative culture seated in the foundations of a solid past and long tradition."[86]

Echoing the position of the national PSOE, the Ayuntamiento of Madrid stressed the fact that European-wide cultural events, such as the nomination of an annual European Cultural Capital, were some of the most effective ways to promote "the construction of the idea of supranationality."[87] In this way, the purpose of Madrid's candidature was to further incorporate Madrid, and Spain as a whole, into Europe and to increase the overall prestige of the EC: "Madrid offers, therefore, to the European community and to the Spanish government in this special occasion of 1992, all of its patrimony and cultural vitality in order to magnify the image of Europe in the world."[88]

The local administration's change of cultural priorities was clearly reflected in its attitude toward the movida madrileña as well. Unlike Tierno Galván, Barranco did not assign any special importance to the movida, or to the movement's relationship to the transformation of Madrid. According to the writer and former singer for Paraíso, Fernando "El Zurdo" Márquez, "It can not be forgotten that the decline of the *movida* began when Tierno died . . . now we live in an anti-utopia."[89] When specifically asked in 1988 if the movida madrileña still existed, Barranco responded, "I have never known very well what that is. For me it is the creative cultural capacity that was reinforced with the arrival of democracy."[90] Reflecting this lack of enthusiasm, the Ayuntamiento stopped funding activities directly related to the movida madrileña and the symbols of the movement were no longer promoted as the official projection of madrileño culture after 1986.

In fact, as early as May 1986, the movida madrileña had lost much of its official visibility. For example, in stark contrast to the movida-dominated *San Isidro* of 1985, the movement was noticeably absent from the celebrations in 1986. The opening *pregón* for *San Isidro*-86, for example, made no mention of the movida and, instead of movida bands headlining the Festival, the major performances included international stars like The Kinks from England and James Brown from the United States, and nationally known singer–song writers associated with the political left: Joan Manual Serrat, Ana Belén, and Victor Manuel.[91] While some groups related to the movida did play at the Festival, including Obús, Orquesta Mondragón, and Ramoncín, they were billed as representatives of national popular music, and not specifically representing madrileño music or culture.[92]

Also in clear contrast to the festivities held the two previous years, *San Isidro*-86 incorporated more traditional expressions of Spanish and madrileño culture. There were classical music recitals in the Teatro Real, a homage to the *chotis* in the Centro Cultural Conde Duque, and a return of the very traditional *gigantes y cabezudos* in the Plaza Mayor.[93] Likewise, Madrid's other local festivals took on more traditional and *castizo* accents in 1986, especially La Verbena de la Paloma held in the middle of August that year.

Later in 1986, the Ayuntamiento of Madrid halted its very popular rock music competitions, which had previously propelled many movida bands to stardom. The local administration also cancelled a movida concert for the first time in June 1986. Commando 9mm was not allowed to play in El Campo de Gas after winning Madrid's Concurso de Rock award only a few years earlier.[94] The concert was also to include the groups Kortatu and TDK. The year ended on the same non-movida note. In contrast to Alaska's Christmas address the year before, no reference was made to the movida madrileña in the capital's 1986 holiday *pregón*.[95]

The year 1987 saw an even greater shift away from the movida. In February 1987, after the publication of 33 issues, the municipal administration withdrew its support for one of the magazines most closely associated with the movement, *Madriz*.[96] At the time of its closure, Federico del Barrio, one of the magazine's contributors, maintained that *Madriz* had been "an example of the struggle for independence."[97] In other words, the closure of the magazine was understood as a move away from artistic freedom. Without the local administration's support, Madrid's artists would have to rely more on the demands of the market and on commercial projects driven by profit.

Along with less support for artistic freedom, there was also less freedom on Madrid's airwaves and on the city's streets. In 1987, the capital's pirate radio stations, often associated with the movida, were shut down by the local administration. These closures were prompted by complaints from the owners of legitimate radio stations and by the need to conform to European standards of broadcasting.[98] In the summer of that same year, the Ayuntamiento also closed down 13 *terrazas*, or open-air street bars, which had been some of the most representative locations of the movida.[99] At the end of the year, Barranco's administration even closed down one of the last venues in Madrid that still featured musical performances related to the movida. Despite its attempts to comply with all official regulations, the Sala Universal was closed by the city without explanation in November 1987.[100] In contrast to the "anything-goes" and freewheeling days of the early 1980s, the management had made every possible effort to keep the venue open: "We made all kinds of renovations, even to the floor, we spent a ton of money. We put on concerts at 8:00 pm so that they will finish by 10:00 pm, and the disc jockey had orders not to exceed the authorized decibels; and we even had that level verified."[101]

The shift away from the movida continued in the Festival of *San Isidro* that year. In general, jazz and American pop music dominated *San Isidro*-87, as it did in subsequent years. Tina Turner and Genesis headlined the festival in 1987, while groups related to the movida were overlooked altogether.[102] In 1988, Frank Zappa and Van Morrison were featured as the main performers.[103] The following year marked the first time that spending on the festival declined. In 1989, the Ayuntamiento of Madrid spent only $1.1 million on the Festival of *San Isidro*, 30 percent less than the year before.[104] The celebrations in 1989 also saw a further increase of "folkloric" presentations, with performances by Lola Flores, Paquita Rico, Lola Sevilla, and Marifé de Triana.[105]

All of these changes represented not only the end of institutional support for the movida madrileña, but also the end of the project to associate the movement with the official image of Madrid. As described above, the local administration was interested in presenting a more "practical" image of Madrid. Probably the best example of this shift was seen in 1987 at an officially sponsored exposition that promoted the capital and its recent history. In contrast to the 1984 exhibit "Madrid, Madrid, Madrid," the 1987 exposition "Vivir en Madrid" had nothing to do with the movida madrileña or with the capital's vibrant cultural scene. Opened in the Centro Cultural de Conde Duque in March 1987, the exposition lacked any reference to the films, photographs, artwork, or general cultural aesthetic of the movida. Instead, the exposition focused on the capital's economic development and on the improvements made to Madrid's infrastructure. It also highlighted the local administration's efforts to solve the problems related to traffic, unemployment, and drug addiction.[106] In contrast to the exhibit in 1984, the official image of Madrid in 1987 was one of hopeful prosperity and economic stability, and not one of cultural mobilization promoted through an embrace of "chaos." In other words, the movida was clearly no longer representative of the capital's official cultural identity by 1987.

In a move that had significance far beyond support for the movida, and that directly contradicted Tierno Galván's desire for a more participatory form of regional identity, Barranco's administration actually placed formal limits on citizen participation and mobilization in the capital. Although protected by Article 21 of the Constitution, the Ayuntamiento of Madrid approved a motion to limit the right to demonstrate in Madrid at the end of 1987. Prompted in part by the central government, the Ayuntamiento of Madrid passed the measure in order to limit what it considered to be the disruption unleashed by public demonstrations on the capital's traffic and economy.[107] Even Barranco himself complained to the press about the detrimental impact of demonstrations on the capital's economy.[108] Over the objections of the IU and the country's trade unions (UGT and CCOO), the motion was passed in November 1987 to restrict the routes, the times, and the dates for demonstrations within the capital.[109] Despite several challenges, the national government upheld the motion in May 1988.[110] Such measures symbolized the degree to which the Ayuntamiento's was willing to privilege economic growth and stability over greater popular mobilization in the capital after 1986.

The evolution in priorities that defined the municipal administration in the late 1980s happened more slowly within the regional administration, but by the end of the decade the two paths increasingly converged. For a short time after 1986, the political leadership of the Comunidad of Madrid remained more independent from the national PSOE and, as a result, was more faithful to the project of creating a new regional identity in Madrid. In fact, rather than working more closely with the central administration, Joaquín Leguina was frequently critical of "the new neo-liberalism inside the PSOE."[111] Likewise, he criticized his own party for not allowing any authentic debate between "the neo-liberals and the radicals" within the Socialist party.[112] However, the Comunidad's support for the movida, and for the associated regional identity based on cultural mobilization, waned toward the end of the decade as Madrid's regional government became more preoccupied with economic priorities and with "encouraging Madrid to establish itself as an area for high-technology industries."[113]

The regional identity project did, however, live on for a short time after 1986 through such efforts as the Comunidad of Madrid's cultural "exchange" programs, which most often only worked in one direction. For example, in September 1986, a specially chartered train with more than 100 members of the movida madrileña traveled from Madrid to Vigo in order to promote "the cultural avant-garde of both cities."[114] While the event was supposed to increase the cultural prestige of both Madrid and Vigo, the officially sponsored expedition to Galicia primarily served to promote the movida as the official image of the region of Madrid.

The cultural delegation from Madrid was led by the president of the Comunidad of Madrid himself, Joaquín Leguina, and included such movida celebrities as Ouka-Lele, Pedro Almodóvar, Alaska, Agata Ruiz de la Prada, Ceesepe, Alberto García-Alix, El Hortelano, Carlos Berlanga, and Ana Curra. While traditional madrileño stew (*cocido madrileño*) was brought from the restaurant La Bola to Vigo, the encounter overwhelmingly emphasized the "modern" symbols of Madrid.[115] The celebration of contemporary madrileño culture in Vigo included concerts by movida bands and expositions that showcased cutting-edge fashion, photography, sculpture, and painting from Madrid.[116] Even though the trip to Vigo was meant to represent the first half of a cultural exchange, no cultural delegation from Vigo ever made it to Madrid.[117] As a result, the cultural exchange with Vigo served only promote the cultural symbols of the movida as the official image of Madrid both inside and outside of the capital.

A month after the events in Vigo, in October 1986, fifty participants of the movida also traveled to the Italian cities of Turin, Rome, and Milan to, in the words of Jaime Lissavetzky, the Consejero de Cultura of the Comunidad of Madrid, "permit a part of the *movida madrileña* to come closer to the Italian public."[118] Similar to the program in Vigo, the expositions in Italy— one of Europe's most important centers for art and design—showcased the work of the movement's artists and designers. Thus, in addition to linking the movida to the official image of Madrid, the trip to Italy also served the more practical purpose of providing a larger market for the creators associated with the movida madrileña. Similar cultural expeditions were also originally planned to France and Germany, although they never took place.[119]

In 1987, the Comunidad of Madrid continued to make some efforts to associate itself with the movida specifically within the region of Madrid. In conjunction with the *Fiestas del 2 de Mayo*, the regional government sponsored an exposition by the two movida painters known as Los Costus. Referring to the movida, Virgilio Cano de Lope, the Consejero de Gobernación de la Comunidad de Madrid, explained that the exposition was designed "to promote the young plastic arts [in Madrid]."[120] The exhibit, entitled *El Valle de los Caídos, 1980–1987*, featured quasi-religious portraits that offered homage to the movida madrileña. In the portraits, colorful portrayals of movida celebrities were juxtaposed with Franco's gray and somber memorial to the Spanish Civil War, the Valley of the Fallen. The officially sponsored exposition included portraits of Alaska, Paco Navarro, and other movida notables.

Also in 1987, the regional administration published a coffee table–style book depicting the Comunidad of Madrid: *Madrid Hoy*.[121] In the "Introduction" to the large book, Joaquín Leguina explains that the work "provides a more complete and comprehensive vision of our *Comunidad*."[122] Unmistakably, this was a vision dominated by the movida madrileña. While the book is comprised of a series of essays by artists and intellectuals about the region of Madrid, the majority of the 93 essays represent contributions specifically from movida personalities that focus mainly on *"anti-castizo"* aspects of Madrid. Contributors include Alaska, Moncho Alpuente, Ceesepe, Enrique Costus, Juan Costus, Gorka Duo, Fanny de Miguel, El Hortelano, Borja Casani, Nacha Pop, Ouka-Lele, Ramoncin, and Fernando "El Zurdo" Marquez. In addition, these contributions stand side-by-side with essays written by such "mainstream" figures as the cartoonist Maximo and the singer–song writer Joaquín Sabina. Therefore, there was no differentiation between movida and non-movida culture by the regional administration. In other words, the movida madrileña was still presented as an integral part of the Comunidad's official image of Madrid during this period.

However, in the late 1980s, the Comunidad of Madrid began to show signs of turning away from cultural mobilization and toward the business of business. This shift away from culture and toward economics was first witnessed at the end of 1987. In the fall of 1987, the budget, the length, and the number of acts for the Comunidad's *Festival de Otoño* were reduced for the first time. According to José María González Sinde, the Comunidad's manager of the Centro de Estudio y Actividades Culturales, "the festival had become a little overwhelming."[123] Overall, funding for the *Festival de Otoño* decreased 20 percent in 1987, from $2.7 million to $2.1 million.[124] After 1987, fewer performers were hired, fewer works were performed, and the budget for the festival continued to shrink.[125]

Separate from the *Festival de Otoño*, general spending on cultural activities also declined for the first time in 1987 in the region of Madrid, after increasing steadily since the Comunidad's inception in 1983. For example, support for music decreased by 74.2 percent in 1987, dropping from $685,000 to $177,000. Funding for theatrical productions was cut by 26 percent, from $354,000 to $261,000. The Comunidad's total spending on culture decreased by almost 30 percent, from 3.9 million in 1986 to $2.7 million in 1987.[126] It would not be until 1992, with the celebrations surrounding the Cultural Capital of Europe, that expenditures on culture returned to their 1986 peaks.[127] However, by 1992, this renewed cultural spending would have different political and cultural goals.

Another blow to the region's culture came with the cancellation of the Comunidad's official cultural magazine, *Agenda Cultural*. After serving as a guide to the region's cultural events since 1983, the magazine was terminated without explanation at the end of 1987. While not meeting the same fate as *Agenda Cultural*, the Comunidad's other official magazine, *Alfoz*, experienced a profound metamorphosis. After 1987, the magazine gradually shifted from being culturally and community-based to being largely business oriented. Thus, rather than featuring articles on art or social issues, the magazine increasingly presented special issues on business. For example, in 1992, the magazine offered nine articles on research and design in Madrid in a special issue entitled "Ciencia y Tecnología: I + D una apuesta compleja."[128] At the same time, Madrid's regional public radio station, Onda Madrid, also moved away from cultural programming that often featured the movida and toward a more conventional format directed at a more "heterogeneous and adult" audience.[129]

The Comunidad of Madrid's own specific interest in promoting business also showed up on the pages of *Alfoz*. In 1991, a full-page ad in the magazine announced the inauguration of a new helicopter service between the business park of Las Rozas, on the outskirts of the capital, and Madrid's international airport. The service, sponsored by the Consejería de Política Territorial of the Comunidad of Madrid, promised access to Barajas International Airport in "less than 15 minutes."[130] Such a substantial undertaking designed to promote national and international business investment in the region of Madrid symbolized just how far the regional government had moved toward a new conception of the capital based on economic development and financial prosperity rather than on culture.

So, in sharp contrast to the first half of the 1980s, there was a close alignment by the end of the decade between the three levels of government in Madrid. And, as just described, this was especially true between the Ayuntamiento of Madrid and the central government. As the national PSOE's political agenda of economic development and European integration came to dominate on the local, regional, and national level, there was little room left for the articulation or expression of a separate identity in the capital.

PART II: CHANGING FORMS OF IDENTIFICATION
IN THE CAPITAL, 1986–1991

But how much did the lives of ordinary residents actually change during this period? Simply put, between 1986 and 1991, Madrid changed almost as much as it had between 1979 and 1986. First and foremost, Madrid became more of a capital and less of a region with its own unique identity. The general atmosphere of the capital was also different. In 1989, the editor of *Alfoz*, Javier Echenagusia, summed up the change in the capital over the course of the decade:

> The decade of the 1980s began in Madrid with the consecration of the *movida*, the appropriation of public spaces by the people, and with a large number of projects with more or less of a precise shape. Everyone, more or less, felt satisfied to be a *madrileño* whether or not they were originally from the capital [*con o sin papeles*]. All of that sought protection in a man with the necessary instincts to put himself in front of the manifestation and give it wings: Enrique Tierno."[131]

By the end of the decade, however, things were no longer the same:

> At the other end of the decade the city is half closed [*se entorna*], appears much less inhabitable, and with a much shakier creative pulse. There is more passivity than revelry. More of a hurry to make money than to create.[132]

More recently, a former participant in the movida similarly remarked: "Before Madrid was more clean, less violent, more luminous and a more enjoyable city: even to the point where the people were different."[133] And, for José Manuel Costa, a writer for *El País*, everything was also different in the capital by the beginning of the 1990s: "The 'feeling of urgency' has passed a long time ago. Everything is normal and foreseeable [*previsible*]. And, therefore, rather boring."[134] Things had changed so dramatically largely because the enthusiasm and optimism surrounding the capital's vibrant cultural scene came to an end as a preoccupation with business and making money replaced the passion for culture. And, just as significantly, madrileños, like Spaniards in general, increasingly put their hopes in European integration. Although it is difficult to quantify such qualitative changes, there is a range of evidence from the press and sociological data that supports these general conclusions.

But, again, how exactly were these changes reflected in madrileño society? First, the residents of Madrid increasingly defined themselves through passive economic consumption rather than active cultural participation. Second, madrileños began to identify more closely with the rest of Europe and displayed signs of developing a supranational identity. These new forms of identification replaced the unique regional identity that had developed in the first half of the 1980s and, at the same time, permanently laid to rest Tierno Galván's dream of creating an alternative form of participatory democracy in Madrid.

From Culture to Economics

First and most notably, over the course of the 1980s, emphasis in the capital turned from cultural activities to economic activities. While institutional support for the movida madrileña was drying up after 1986, bankers and entrepreneurs increasingly replaced artists as society's new celebrities and role models. At the same time, a revived economy brought new hopes for wealth and material prosperity. As a result of these changes, the communitarian spirit that surrounded broad cultural participation in the first half of the decade was traded for the more individualistic and neoliberal goal of personal economic consumption. In other words, the accumulation and expenditure of private wealth took the place of active civic engagement in the capital.[135]

In conjunction with the national PSOE's emphasis on prosperity, this shift from culture to economics also occurred on account of Spain's improving economic conditions. After 1986, the country experienced a "typical post EC-entry boom."[136] Aided by new foreign investment, the economy expanded, company profits surged, and average per capita income increased. In fact, specifically between 1986 and 1991, the Spanish economy experienced the fastest growth rates of any member in the EC.[137] Spain's entry into the EC also came with a seven-year transition period that allowed the country access to the EC's 340 million consumer market, while enjoying protections and subsidies. In such favorable conditions, inflation fell as productivity rose, and a budget deficit became a surplus.[138] In addition, Spain reaped substantial economic gain from several EC structural funds, which benefited the country's infrastructure in particular.[139] Overall, the country experienced an annual growth rate of 4 percent until 1991.[140]

Bankers and investors in particular took a renewed interest in the capital on account of its revived economy and because of its new connections to other European financial centers. Madrid's improving economic fortunes were most clearly symbolized by its lower unemployment. By 1988, unemployment had decreased in Spain in general, but even more so in the region of Madrid. For example, at the end of 1987, the rate of unemployment in the capital was three-and-a-half points lower than the national average, which was 17.5 percent.[141] In contrast, at the end of 1985, the official level of unemployment in Madrid was 23.5 percent for the active population, one-and-a-half points above the national average.[142] Such substantial improvements helped fuel a new sense of economic optimism and redirected the capital's attention toward the business of making money.

In fact, improved economic conditions and renewed confidence led to a kind of business frenzy in the capital. Just as culture had become fashionable in the early 1980s, business and economics became all the rage in the second half of the decade. Bankers, lawyers, accountants, and property developers made vast fortunes, often based on speculation alone. In the process, these new successes came to symbolize the possibility of getting rich quickly and effortlessly.

The embrace of the almighty "*peseta*" was accompanied by a change of attitudes and behaviors as well. After 1986, the capital passed from "punk" to "yuppie," as everyone aspired to be a financier instead of an artist. The public's imagination was particularly captured by "*los butiful,*" jet setters who traveled freely within the highest social, political, and economic circles of Spanish society. According to the journalist Elizabeth Nash, material success and fame made "flashy young entrepreneurs like Javier de la Rosa and Mario Conde the new fashionable role models and darlings of a nation."[143]

Such newly rich bankers, entrepreneurs, and middle-class yuppies became the object of media attention and popular admiration, with their extravagant lifestyles frequently showing up in the country's society and gossip magazines (*revistas del corazón*). Writing about changing behaviors in madrileño society, the sociologist Amando de Miguel observed in 1989:

> Now, the famous, the celebrities, are for the most part bankers, businessmen, speculators, and professionals of great prestige. Their "heroic feats" [*hazanas*] consist simply of enriching themselves rapidly . . . the best example could be Mario Conde, the young president of the largest bank in the country. His elegant and worldly image has become the ideal for many young people.[144]

Despite the fact that Spain's new prosperity benefited mainly the rich and upper middle class, while leaving most of the working class behind, the superstardom of Mario Conde, and others like him, sustained the get-rich-quick fever that prevailed in the capital until the financial bubble finally burst after 1992.[145]

The new enthusiasm for business and making money also changed feelings toward wealth and money. In general, the display and enjoyment of wealth became more fashionable and conspicuous consumption became less of a sign of bad taste in the second half of the decade. John Hooper has described the change that occurred in the 1980s:

> In Spain, social attitudes towards money underwent a revolution. A nation whose historic poverty had led it to build an entire value system around non-materialistic virtues—dignity, austerity, and sobriety—all of a sudden flung itself into the business of earning and spending money with, it seemed, scarcely a backward glance.[146]

Writing in 1989, Amando de Miguel likewise observed: "There is a surprising fact in Spanish society in the past few years: the hidden social importance of money, of material success."[147] This material success, however, only counted if it could be displayed, and displayed well. Simply spending money was not enough; it was "necessary to consume the best brands."[148] As a result, luxury consumption became increasingly valued for its own sake over the course of the second half of the decade.

The greater emphasis on consumption, coupled with higher levels of disposable income, fully solidified a mass consumer culture in Madrid and in the country's major urban areas. Economic growth also meant that more people had full-time jobs, and less time to devote to cultural enterprises. Faced with the future prospect of having to compete toe-to-toe with the other members of the EEC, residents of the capital found it increasingly important to be at work at 8:00 a.m. The prevailing get-rich-quick attitude also directed energy away from cultural engagements and toward activities that offered a higher probability of material success. In other words, a kind of cultural "normalization" took place in Madrid after 1986. The capital continued to host a relatively high number of art expositions, musical performances, and cultural celebrations, but the frenzy and optimism surrounding such events faded away.

In 1990, the long time rock critic Patricia Godes neatly summed up the cultural change in the capital: "What was euphoria and optimism ten years ago is now boredom and fraud [estafa]."[149] By the end of the decade, madrileños were simply less "moved" by cultural activities. For example, residents had little interest in Madrid's designation as the Cultural Capital of Europe. In June of 1989, only 66 percent of madrileños knew that Madrid would be the Cultural Capital of Europe in 1992.[150] The official magazine of the Comunidad of Madrid, Alfoz, even commented on the lack of public interest in a special report on the proposed celebration: "The foremost impression is the surprise for the limited attention that is given by madrileño society to this engagement."[151]

There was also far less interest in cultural activities associated with the movida madrileña. The second half of the decade saw the demise of the two magazines most closely related to the movement: Madrid Me Mata and La Luna de Madrid. These former cultural icons were replaced by new magazines that focused far less on the specific culture and personality of the capital. Not coincidentally, the new magazines from this period no longer featured the name "Madrid" in their titles and one, in fact, even specifically referenced Europe: Sur Express, El Pascante, and El Europeo. Similarly, the capital's major newspapers increasingly devoted less space to the movement and Madrid's radio stations shifted their focus away from the music of the movida after 1986.

Rather than offering programming that featured the movida, commercial radio stations assumed more conventional and profitable national formats after 1986. For example, Radio España converted into a Top 40 station. And, Radio El País, the regionally centered radio station that had directed its attention toward a younger audience in Madrid, transformed into a news radio format (Radio Minuto) with a national audience.[152] In addition, one of the original supporters of the movida, Radio 3, shifted its attention to more "adult" programming. The flight away from content related to the movida madrileña was such that, by 1989, there was not "a single station with features and programs dedicated to a 'youth' audience."[153]

Accompanying this sharp decline of the movement, there was also a shift in the meaning of the term "movida." Rather than referring to a new and vibrant cultural movement, in the second half of the 1980s the word increasingly became associated with what can only be described as "kitsch".[154]

In fact, even by 1987, the cultural aesthetic of the movida madrileña was not taken very seriously at all. In a book entitled, *Yuppies, jetset, la movida y otras especies*, Carmen de Posadas reduces the movida to caricature and pure commercialization. According to this tongue-in-cheek book on social climbing, "the only thing that really matters is selling and becoming famous."[155] And with chapters covering such topics as "Plagiarism is art [*El plagio es arte*]," "The 'musts' of the movida [*Los 'Must' de la movida*]," and "Mission impossible: how to be original [*Misión imposible: cómo ser original*]," the book repeatedly stresses that "what's important is to create something for commercial success. In a word: to sell."[156] For others, the movida had likewise become simply a marketing tool: "[All that is left to do is] to convert '*la movida*' into a model of an automobile."[157] Despite this significant shift in meaning, the term movida suffered an even further degradation of meaning after the end of the decade.

By the early 1990s, the word was almost completely separated from the notion of "culture" and was instead most closely associated with the phenomenon of youth alcohol consumption and "hanging out," or *el botellón*. This understanding of the term movida was later summed up by a professor of sociology, Julio Iglesias de Ussel, at a conference dedicated to social problems created by the so-called movida in Andalusia. According to Iglesias de Ussel, the movida consisted of "music, alcohol, night life, noise, drugs, large concentrations of young people, and the occupation of the street."[158] As a decidedly negative term, it made clear reference to youth discontent, angst, alcoholism, violence, unrest, and apathy (rather than participation).

In addition to the changes directly associated with the movida, participation at officially sponsored cultural events also declined in the region of Madrid during this period. For the first time since the festival's inception, attendance at the *Festival de Otoño* dropped in 1990.[159] Whereas attendance reached well over 100,000 people in 1986, only 88,000 residents attended the festival in 1990.[160] Interest in theatre suffered an even more severe decline. In 1984, Madrid counted 39 theaters and the capital's "stage life was comparable with that of London or Paris and much livelier than, say Rome's."[161] By 1993, however, the number of theaters in Madrid had dropped threefold to only 13.[162]

The number and quality of art expositions declined as well. In 1991, the well-known art critic Rosa Olivares described what the cultural scene was like in the capital in the mid-1980s: "In Madrid one could see more and better expositions than in Paris, London, or even New York. Madrid had converted itself, by its own right, into one of the artistic metropolises of the world."[163] By the beginning of the 1990s, however, the capital no longer held the promise of remaining one of the artistic capitals of the world:

> Madrid has left behind its great promise and has converted into just another point on the European axis. This is something much more worthy than what we had hoped for in the 1960s and 1970s, but after the fever of the 1980s it is difficult to say that this is not a disaster.[164]

Overall, there were fewer cultural activities in the capital and much of the enthusiasm for staying out all night had worn off. Less official support, a pre-occupation with more "practical" matters, and greater economic optimism all led to lower levels of cultural participation. Ironically, as Jesús Ordovás pointed out in 1989, this was all occurring at exactly the time Madrid was to become the official Cultural Capital of Europe in 1992:

> Public institutions are becoming less interested all the time in the organization of contests, festivals, and fairs. The *Concurso de Rock Villa of Madrid* has disap-peared in between the disorganization and the loss of imagination of those in charge. The programming of fiestas and events dedicated to the people have been cut down to a minimum. Private initiative has taken the reins: to live in Madrid is more expensive each day and more difficult. The *terrazas* have been limited to small luxury palaces on Castellana Boulevard. The bars that open up are each day more selective, exclusive, and refined [*exquisito*]. The pirate radio stations have been silenced by government order. The independent record com-panies have disappeared. The multinationals and the ones that have merged now control the market. Magazines are not being published and *Madriz*, *La Luna de Madrid*, *Madrid Me Mata*, and *Sur Expres* have disappeared from the news-stand . . . The view is not very encouraging, precisely when Madrid is about to become the Cultural Capital of Europe.[165]

THE EUROPEAN CONNECTION

In addition to this shift from culture to economics, the second half of the 1980s also saw a move toward greater identification with the rest of Europe. More specifically, global economic and cultural forces, coupled with the national PSOE's desire to promote European integration, caused the focus in Madrid to shift from the local and the regional to the national and the international. As a result, the identity of madrileños, and Spain's identity as a nation, increasingly became based on inclusion into the political and eco-nomic superstructures of Europe over the second half of the 1980s. The best evidence for this can be found in opinion polls from the period.

However, it must first be noted that European integration did not auto-matically exclude the articulation of a regional identity or other forms of identification in the capital. In fact, the notion of "Europe of the regions" was used as an effective strategy to promote regional identity in other parts of Spain, most successfully in Catalonia. The difference was that, in Madrid, the promotion of supranational affiliations was not part of a project to dis-tance the region from the national administration or from a national identity. Rather, just the opposite was true. Because European integration was part of an effort by the national PSOE to specifically reappropriate Madrid as the capital of Spain, supranationalism was used more as a replacement than as a compliment to regionalism in Madrid. While it is difficult to draw a direct connection to the motivations and policies of the PSOE, there are a number of indications that madrileños came to identify more closely with Europe than did residents from other regions of Spain by the end of the 1980s.

In general, there was a gradual shift in the public's attitude toward the idea of European integration over the course of the decade. Despite the initial reluctance, best symbolized by the anti-NATO campaign in the early 1980s, Spaniards came to fully support the idea of European integration by the end of the decade. In fact, they eventually became some of the strongest supporters of the process in all of Europe. In a 1989 survey sponsored by *El País* and the British paper, *The Independent*, more than half of all Spaniards believed that the country had experienced positive changes since Spain's official introduction into the EC in 1986. This percentage of favorable responses toward integration into the EC was the highest of any European country. In other words, Spaniards were more favorable of European integration than any other population in Europe. The most important benefits of integration cited by Spaniards included a greater selection of goods and services—again demonstrating the growing importance of consumption—and the possibility of having greater influence on the construction of the EC.[166] The study concluded that the Spanish "declared themselves convinced Europeanists [*se manifiestan europeístas convencidos*]."[167]

With regard to Madrid, there is evidence to suggest that the enthusiasm for becoming more European was equally as great, if not greater, than in the rest of the country. In fact, the region of Madrid reported the highest level of satisfaction for European integration out of any region in Spain. In 1987, a larger percentage of Madrid's population (68%) believed that the evolution of things had improved since Spain's integration into the EC compared to any other region of the country.[168] In addition, fewer madrileños believed things had gotten worse compared to the residents of other regions. Only 21 percent of madrileños believed things had gotten worse since integration into the EC at the beginning of 1986, compared to the national average of 30 percent (see Table 7.1).[169]

Similarly, a greater percentage of Madrid's population (58%), when compared to other regions of Spain, believed that Spain's entry into the EC in

Table 7.1 Opinion about the evolution of things in Spain since the integration into the EC (1987)

Region	Better	Worse	The same/ no answer
Madrid	68	21	11
Catalonia/Balearic Islands	62	26	12
Castilla La Mancha/Extremadura	60	28	12
Andalusia/Canary Islands	57	27	16
Castilla-León	56	35	9
Aragón/Navarra/Rioja	56	27	17
Galicia	52	39	9
Asturias/Cantabria	46	31	23
Valencia/Murcia	45	39	16
Basque Country	44	34	22
National Average	56	30	14

Table 7.2   Opinion about the integration of Spain into the EC (1987)

Region	A good thing	A bad thing	Neither good nor bad and no response
Madrid	58	10	32
Aragón/Navarra/Rioja	55	14	31
Catalonia/Balearic Islands	53	11	36
Basque Country	51	17	32
Castilla La Mancha/Extremadura	50	11	39
Andalusia/Canary Islands	49	14	37
Castilla-León	47	15	38
Galicia	42	17	41
Valencia/Murcia	41	15	44
Asturias/Cantabria	40	15	45
National Average	49	13	38

1986 was a good thing. At the same time, only 10 percent of madrileños believed it was a bad thing.[170] Across the country as a whole, 49 percent of Spaniards thought integration was a good thing, while 13 percent thought it was a bad thing (see Table 7.2).[171]

While there is no empirical data available specifically for Madrid, enthusiasm for its becoming more closely associated with Europe steadily climbed through the late 1980s in Spain and peaked at the beginning of the 1990s.[172] Specifically, the approval for Spain's integration into the EC reached a high-water mark in 1991, before dropping in 1992 with the difficulties surrounding the ratification of the Maastricht Treaty in France and Denmark.[173] In 1991, 62 percent of Spaniards believed that Spain's entry into the EC five years earlier had proved beneficial, a 13 point increase from the year 1987.[174] In one of the most comprehensive studies of Spanish attitudes toward European integration, the sociologist Inmaculada Szmolka concludes: "In comparison to the [other] citizens of the [European] community, Spaniards trust the EU more, exhibit a more positive attitude, and perceive more benefits from our participation in the Community of Europe."[175] This exceptionally positive attitude stemmed from the fact that Spaniards had become convinced over the course of the 1980s that the fate of the country was tied to the rest of Europe. And, madrileños, in particular, were most favorable to European integration because they had come to believe that they had the most to gain.

In the capital, the favorable attitude toward the EC and European integration symbolized the desire to identify more closely with the rest of Europe or, in other words, to be more European.[176] In his guide to the institutions of modern Spain, Michael Newton summarizes this close attachment to Europe:

> The European Union is now an increasingly relevant and important part of national life: whether it be in the public or private sector, in industry or education, in communications or sport, in tourism or the arts, the European dimension has become an inescapable reality.[177]

As described in the first part of this chapter, to identify oneself as a "European" meant respectability, legitimacy, a further break from the past, and, most importantly, the hope for a more economically prosperous future. In addition, it also symbolized how the goals of the local and national PSOE were at least partially accepted by the residents of Madrid. In 1992, when Spaniards were asked what words they most related with Europe, the three highest responses included "democracy," "free market," and "prosperity."[178] Not coincidentally, these were exactly the same three objectives the national PSOE wished to achieve through its specific vision of Europeanization.

CHANGING FORMS OF IDENTIFICATION WITH MADRID

While it is difficult to demonstrate how the two main developments just discussed—the shift from active cultural engagement to passive economic consumption and the closer associations with Europe—directly replaced the unique democratic regional identity that had developed in the first half of the 1980s, there is evidence to suggest that regional identification did diminish in Madrid after 1986. There is also some indication that, as the newly readopted capital of Spain, national affiliations increased in Madrid as well. Nonetheless, despite these changing forms of identification, the residents of the capital continued to retain a certain sense of madrileño pride throughout the end of the decade. In short, the changes over the entire course of the 1980s permanently broke the negative connotations that were formerly associated with the capital and produced the Madrid of today (i.e., a city defined by both its cultural and economic activity).

By returning to the public opinion surveys discussed in the previous chapter (Chapter 6), we can see both a distinct decrease in regional identification and a clear increase in national identification in the years between 1990 and 1995.[179] In fact, the percentage of madrileños that identified themselves as predominately madrileño (either only madrileño or more madrileño than Spanish) dropped by a third from 10.9 percent to 6.9 percent during this period. At the same time, the level of national identification nearly doubled in Madrid, from approximately a quarter (26.1%) of the population to almost half (49.7%) of the population identifying itself as only Spanish (see Table 6.6).[180] In other words, madrileños were identifying less with the region of Madrid and more with Spain by the end of this period. Thus, it would appear as though the political, economic, and cultural changes that had occurred in the capital after 1986 promoted national and supranational affiliations at the expense of regional affiliations by the beginning of the 1990s.

However, even though changing forms of identification broke down the unique democratic regional identity that had coalesced over the first half of the decade, not all forms of regional identification completely disappeared from the capital. As the feeling of affiliation for Madrid became divorced both from the movida madrileña and from the project to create a new regional identity based on cultural mobilization, identification with Madrid became more generalized and found expression through a variety of outlets.

In other words, madrileños continued to feel pride for the place in which they lived, but they expressed it in different ways.

In 1987, for example, there was an effort to support madrileño culture through the establishment of a *Casa Regional de Madrid* in the capital.[181] Modeled on other "regional houses of culture" already located in the capital—such as the *Casa Regional de Valencia*—the new institution would, in the words of one of its supporters, "consolidate all that characterizes the Villa of Madrid."[182] It was hoped that this new institution would help build a "profound *madrileñismo*."[183] It was also during the second half of the 1980s that the red and white bumper sticker of the flag of the Comunidad of Madrid started showing up on the back of cars in the capital, demonstrating an unmistakable sign of regional affiliation.

A kind of regional pride was also expressed through a surge of popular support for traditional madrileño, or *castizo*, culture at the end of the decade. In fact, several local associations worked to promote Madrid's regional customs and increase the visibility of *castizo* culture. Organizations such as the *Asociación los Castizos*, the *Asociación de Madrid al Cielo*, and the *Fundación Amigos de Madrid* proudly promoted *castizo* culture around the capital and lobbied the Ayuntamiento of Madrid for the inclusion of more traditional dances and cultural programs in public festivals such as *San Isidro*.[184] While this promotion of traditional madrileño culture represented a denial of Tierno Galván's project to build a new regional identity based on a culturally vibrant present, such actions demonstrated new forms of affiliation with Madrid and a new sense of pride for its regional customs. In some ways this was quite remarkable. It could be argued that the revival of traditional madrileño culture during this period was only made possible by the break from the authoritarian past that first occurred in the capital between 1979 and 1986.

In addition to these other new expressions of regional sentiment, Madrid also saw the birth of its very own regional political party in 1988. While usually offering unmistakable evidence of regionalism, Madrid's official new political party did not represent such a significant increase in regional affiliation in the capital. Instead, the creation of the *Partido Regionalista Independiente Madrileño* (PRIM) had more to do with political maneuvering than with a groundswell of regionalism in Madrid.[185]

While serving on the Regional Assembly of Madrid, Nicolás Piñeiro formed the PRIM in May 1988 after splitting with the conservative AP on account of internal disagreements with the party's leadership. The PRIM's only significant role in the region's politics came the following year, in May 1989, when Piñeiro's abstention during the vote of censure, brought by the CDS/PP coalition, allowed Joaquín Leguina to keep his seat as president of the Comunidad of Madrid.[186] Despite this one important swing vote, the party had little part to play in setting the Assembly's agenda and received practically no popular support from the citizens of Madrid. At the party's first regional elections in 1991, the PRIM resoundingly lost its only Assembly seat, the one originally held by Piñeiro since his departure from the AP back in 1988. Voter turnout for the PRIM was so low, in fact, that there was no mention of the party in any of the major election analyses produced at the time.[187] After the party's crushing defeat in 1991, the PRIM continued to present itself at Madrid's regional elections, but neither found greater support nor won back its lost seat on Madrid's Regional Assembly.[188]

Despite the changing shape of regional affiliations and the lack of support for a new regional political party (and the increased sense of connection to the nation and to Europe), a feeling of pride for Madrid was still evident at the end of the decade. In 1989, Javier Domingo, the former director of *Servicios de Cultura*, for first the Ayuntamiento and later for the Comunidad of Madrid, summed up the sense of pride experienced by those living in the capital. Recalling first the lack of pride madrileños felt prior to 1979, he said:

> I remember in my college days . . . that when someone asked us where we were from, where we were born, many of my classmates responded that they were from La Coruña, Barcelona, or Seville, and proclaimed it with pride. Others, almost blushing and in a low voice, acknowledge that we were from Madrid, almost as if we had to ask for forgiveness for having been born there. Those from Galicia spoke to us of their countryside, of the fruit of their land, including their Ribeiro wine. The Catalans told how grand Barcelona was, to the point of even boasting of their sausage. They all had their signs of identification [*señas de identidad*]. The rest of us, those born in Madrid, seemed like we had forgotten history, as if we had fallen from the sky and landed in this land where those from the outside had come to redeem us. They all had great things to tell, everyone except us.[189]

That, however, was all in the past. Over the course of the 1980s,

> we found the pride of being *madrileños* and something more; those Gallegos, Catalans, and Andaluces now feel proud that their children are *madrileños* and of you ask them where they are from they respond "from Madrid," despite being born in Seville or Lugo, as if that had been an accident.[190]

Despite the fact that most madrileños let go of Tierno Galván's specific dream of creating a more democratic society based on inclusion, equality, and cultural participation, residents of the capital maintained a certain sense of pride after 1986. Madrileños were proud of the capital's international prestige, proud of their culture, proud of their growing economic successes, and proud of finally taking a seat at the European table. Even though supranational affiliations may have increased and regional affiliations may have declined—or found different forms of expression—the self-doubt and the old associations to centralism and repression were gone forever by the end of the decade.

CONCLUSION

Compared to the development of multiple and overlapping identities in other regions of Spain, Madrid represented something of an exception after 1986.

Like Spaniards in general, madrileños came to assume multiple geographical identities in the post-Francoist period. However, regional affiliations were not allowed to develop as fully in the capital as in other areas of the country. Despite the development of a new democratic regional identity in the first half of the 1980s, the space for such a distinctive identity was closed in the second half of the decade as Madrid was reappropriated as the capital of a European "nation of nations." In the place of a unified regional identity project, the national PSOE, with the help of the Barranco administration, promoted the development of supranational affiliations and a neoliberal economic program that turned madrileños more into residents of the capital of a Europeanized Spain than into members of a unique regional community.

The PSOE's emphasis on prosperity, predicated largely on European integration, specifically privileged economic pursuits over other forms of activity in the capital. In this way, economic consumption came to replace cultural mobilization after 1986, both as the official goal and in daily practice. As a result, in the second half of the decade madrileños increasingly relied on consumption and European affiliations—rather than on cultural mobilization and a specific connection to Madrid—to define themselves. And, as madrileños relied less on active cultural engagement and more on passive material consumption to define themselves, the active form of democratic identity that initially developed during the first half of the 1980s was replaced by more passive forms of identification by the 1990s. While the combination of these changes may have definitively broken Madrid's tie to its authoritarian past, they also permanently laid to rest Tierno Galván's dream of a more participatory model of democratic consolidation.

C H A P T E R 8

Spain's Democratic Consolidation and Madrid as an Alternative National Model

Spain's position in the West now appears completely natural—simply a forgone conclusion. However, the years after Franco's death were filled with uncertainty, ambiguity, and risk. It should not be forgotten that the transition to democracy, and Spain's future democratic course, was not set in stone in 1975, or even in 1979. While the country's national leadership ultimately chose the path to full European integration and neoliberalism in the 1980s, Tierno Galván's project in Madrid represented an alternative social, political, and cultural path to democratic consolidation at a time when the country's final destination was not yet clear.

In the Madrid of the early 1980s there was the belief, or possibly the illusion, that a kind of Socialist utopia was still possible and that ideas and ideology could still change the world. History (or the belief in something other than neoliberal democracy and capitalism) had not yet come to an end.[1] Tierno Galván's program in the capital represented a form of Spanish Socialism that had not yet converted into pure pragmatism. And there was still the possibility of a more participatory democratic system that was not strictly based on political expediency and on the "imperatives" of the market. It is difficult to say if such an alternative path, applied more broadly to the rest of Spain, could have proven successful. Nonetheless, Tierno Galván's program for Madrid represented a possible alternative both for the country and for Spanish Socialists, neither of which exited from the formal transition to democracy with a preordained destiny.

This chapter explores the possibility that Madrid's experience in the first half of the 1980s could have served as a model for the rest of the country. The first part of the chapter examines how, even though the movida madrileña and the development of a more participatory form of democratic regional identity were specifically linked to the capital, the project in Madrid symbolized a model for greater civic engagement, social equality, and popular participation that could have been emulated elsewhere in the country. In other words, the example of Madrid's "civic" identity could have offered a possible alternative to Spain's eventual centralized and demobilized path to democratic consolidation. The second part of the chapter then tries to explain why a new civic collective identity, based on the model of Madrid, never made the transfer to the national level. Specifically, it discusses the resistance from other regions that were articulating their own ethnic or exclusive identities and from the national leadership of the PSOE, whose tendency toward European convergence favored stability and centralization over greater mobilization and decentralization. In addition, the second part of the chapter also looks at the opposition from both the left and the right to any kind of "national" civic identity associated with the movida madrileña. Despite the fact that it was never adopted on the national level, the existence of an alternative project in Madrid highlights the fact that there was more than one possible path to Spain's democratic consolidation in the 1980s. More specifically, it shows that demobilization and centralization were not necessarily prerequisites for social consensus and democratic stability after the end of the dictatorship.

PART 1: MADRID AS AN ALTERNATIVE MODEL

As pointed out in Chapter 2, Tierno Galván originally aspired to become the new democratic president of Spain after the end of the dictatorship. From this perspective, the project in Madrid can be seen not as a specific illustration of regionalism, but as a small-scale example of what might have been attempted on the national level. As described throughout the preceding chapters, Tierno Galván and Madrid's other political elite dreamed of changing society's underlying values and attitudes by creating new forms of participation and by fostering a sense of democratic coexistence. Throughout the capital, active cultural participation was intended to instill democratic habits and a feeling of civic engagement. The ultimate goal was a change in individual and collective habits that would solidify the transition to democracy and lead to greater peace, liberty, and equality for everyone.

Put another way, the transformation of the capital between 1979 and 1986 symbolized a path not toward neoliberal democracy, but toward a more participatory form of social democracy. In addition, cultural mobilization offered an alternative to political polarization, on the one hand, and a demobilized consumer society, on the other. In contrast to the democratic model that eventually prevailed in Spain, the example of Madrid represented a more radical or progressive spirit of democracy in which inclusion replaced exclusion, engagement replaced disengagement, equality replaced inequality, collectivism replaced individualism, and decentralization replaced centralization.

However, Tierno Galván's project in Madrid did not represent the kind of "citizen" or direct democracy that some had hoped for before 1975.[2]

Despite its embrace of greater popular participation and increased democratization, the model of Madrid did not symbolize a completely decentralized vision of Spanish democracy. Nor, of course, did it promote new participatory forms of direct democracy or emphasize formal political participation. Instead, the project in Madrid was a state-centered alternative, specifically designed to foster popular mobilization and civic engagement within the limitations of Spain's elite-driven transition to democracy. At the same time, unlike the program of the national PSOE, it was not committed at all costs to "capitalism's modernizing agenda."[3] In other words, Madrid's political elite was not interested in tempering democratic mobilization with the exigencies of economic development. Ultimately, then, the example of Madrid represented a path in between the radical democracy of the citizen movement and the form of demobilized representative democracy that was ultimately decided upon by the national PSOE in the second half of the 1980s.

From this point of view, the application of Madrid's "in-between path" on the national level may have offered the political stability or "normalization" that many scholars believe is necessary for the successful consolidation of democracy after a transition from authoritarian rule, but without resulting in the complete demobilization of society or upsetting the "culture of accommodation" that made the transition possible in the first place.[4] In particular, cultural mobilization could have provided the means to greater popular participation across the country as a whole, while specifically avoiding political polarization and social division. And, within such an environment, there was a greater possibility that "popular participation in social movements and civic forums" could be sustained.[5] This type of model was thus more likely to guarantee the consensus-driven transition to democracy and, at the same time, satisfy those "who argue that a functioning democracy must go beyond the institutional framework to incorporate meaningful popular participation."[6]

Additionally, while the system of autonomous communities created the outline for a new political framework, Tierno Galván's project—applied to the national level—would have also provided a positive form of identity that bridged the gaps between the "national" and the "regional." Rather than split between these binaries, an inclusive national identity based on the model of Madrid would have valued expressions of regional culture and, at the same time, would have provided the basis for social cohesion and interterritorial solidarity. In other words, it would have filled out the political framework of the autonomous communities with a unifying and inclusive democratic sense of place.

This new sense of belonging would have been founded on the acceptance of a set of civic and democratic values, namely active participation and peaceful coexistence. It would also have been based on a shared commitment to, and pride in, Spain's new democratic institutions. By reinforcing a common civic consciousness, citizens in all parts of the country would have had an alternative to exclusive, discriminatory, and inward-looking ethnic regionalisms. In this alternative world, regionalism would have been linked specifically to democratic participation, and not just to exclusivist cultural values or cultural distinctiveness. And, at the same time, each region of Spain would have gotten more than just political competencies. Cultural expression would accompany political autonomy in every region—not only in the three historical communities—without threatening the territorial integrity of Spain. In short, an alternative form of civic nationalism modeled after the example of Madrid would have provided a basis for solidarity and equality among all of the country's regions.

In some ways, this form of national identification would have been similar to Jürgen Habermas's idea of "constitutional patriotism," as it is based on an allegiance to universalist democratic principles contained in the constitution.[7] However, Tierno Galvan's project called for more than simply an unemotional attachment to Spain's constitution. The emphasis on cultural mobilization created a shared sense of place and time that transcended abstract ideals. In addition, the reliance on modern cultural symbols, denoted by the embrace of the movida madrileña, expanded the focus of collective loyalties beyond political institutions and the 1978 Constitution. Despite employing culture to promote a sense of democratic affiliation, a new national project of this sort would have been based, nonetheless, on promoting a feeling of voluntary civic attachment.

In sum, the adoption of a participatory and inclusive form of civic identity on the national level could have helped unify, mobilize, and democratize Spain, just as it unified, mobilized, and democratized the capital. While not representing a singular national identity, a new national civic identity, centered in part on the acceptance of democratic values and on greater cultural mobilization, could have helped create a unified collective identity characterized by openness, tolerance, civic engagement, and greater social equality for the country as a whole.

With regard to the viability of such a project, this new civic identity might have been a workable basis for a collective identity on the national level for exactly the same reasons that it succeeded in the capital. It represented an inclusive, democratic, modern, flexible, and largely nonpartisan sense of community, based not on a shared cultural past, but on the acceptance of a set of civic and democratic values. These specific characteristics would have made it more adaptable in more locations. In addition, the viability of such a national project was enhanced by two other factors as well. First, the national PSOE's close proximity to the original project in Madrid made the theoretical adoption of such a civic identity more possible. Second, this form of national collective identity differed greatly from previous attempts to unify Spain under a single coercive national identity.

In contrast to the programs during the Second Republic and the Franco regime that were designed to impose a national identity on the rest of the country separate from Madrid, an effort in the 1980s to foster a national collective identity based on the promotion of democratic values and cultural mobilization would not have represented the forced "Castilianization" of the rest of Spain.[8] Theoretically, a civic identity based on cultural openness, active participation, and peaceful coexistence would have been more acceptable for regionalists and nationalists because it did not insist on the primacy of Castilian culture.[9] But, of course, despite these possibilities, such an inclusive civic identity never made the transfer from Madrid to either the national level or to other individual regions around the country.

Part 2: Resistance to a National Civic Identity

Madrid's civic identity based on cultural mobilization and the acceptance of democratic values was never transformed into a broader collective identity because of resistance from three major sources. First, almost all of the regions in Spain during this period were articulating their own respective regional ethnic identity projects based largely on a real or imagined past—and in Galicia, Catalonia, and the Basque Country on a unique linguistic tradition. Second, as described in the previous chapter, the national PSOE chose to follow the path of European integration and economic development at the expense of greater mobilization and social equality. Third, there were groups on both the left and the right that would have opposed any form of national identity associated with the movida madrileña.

On the regional level, a new national civic identity represented a twofold threat. First, a collective identity based on tolerance and inclusion conflicted with emerging regional ethnic identities based on language, ethnicity, or a shared cultural past. This was especially true in the three "historic nationalities." Second, the experience of Franco's official state-sponsored nationalism caused any identity project coming from Madrid to be perceived as an imposed "identity of the center" and thus as a threat. Moreover, as described in Chapter 1, both Spanish nationalism and Spanish national identity in general had acquired authoritarian connotations through their association with the former dictatorship. In other words, all forms of nationalism were tainted by the Franco regime's legacy. As a result, even a democratically based national civic identity faced resistance from other parts of Spain.

In fact, although the movida madrileña only represented part of the project in Madrid, there was real resistance to the cultural movement in other areas of the country during the 1980s. In regions from Andalusia to Galicia, cultural activity associated with the movida was either ignored or co-opted by the respective regional identity projects. Particularly in areas with a strong regionalist or nationalistic movement, there was no room for any alternative form of identity based on inclusion or on the cultural symbols of the movida madrileña. And, again, anything coming from the former seat of the dictatorship was viewed with suspicion or even hostility by the rest of Spain.

For example, at a conference held by the PCE in 1985 to debate the politics of culture, the Catalan writer Ignasi Riera expressed the fear that the capital was trying to impose a kind of unified and homogeneous Madrid-based cultural identity on Catalonia and on the rest of the country, just as Franco had done: "The policies of the Ministry of Culture should worry us . . . with the Tierno-Leguina-Solana combination, agreeing on the '*re-madrileñización*' of the state with that invention of the *movida*, the prospects are not clear."[10]

Critics such as Riera were far more interested in increasing the amount of funding from the national administration than in receiving any kind of new cultural or civic identity from Madrid. Furthermore, it was feared that any imposition of cultural symbols from the center would overwhelm the "multiplicity of voices, shades, and accents of *the* Spains."[11]

Such fears, of course, were unfounded. While Madrid's project served as a possible model for the rest of Spain, it was never imposed on the country as a whole. As described in Chapter 2, despite the fact that the capital was the home to three levels of Socialist administration (municipal, regional, and national), the national government and Madrid's local political elite were not united behind a plan to carry out the "*remadrileñización*" of the rest of Spain, or even to remake Madrid. In fact, between 1979 and 1986, division and disagreement characterized the relationship between Tierno Galván and the national PSOE, thus making any kind of unified program impossible. More importantly, the old professor had no desire to forcibly impose a kind of madrileño identity on the rest of the country. Instead, he hoped that the capital would serve as a democratic exemplar for the rest of Spain. Writing at the end of 1985, Madrid's mayor explained:

> We were the first to open the doors of the city to the new and fresh air, which permitted the sweeping away of the sad air and heavy and asphyxiating atmosphere of the years of the dictatorship . . . [but] we have no pretensions to defeat anyone, nor do we put ourselves in a position of competition, we do what we have to do, if the rest of the cities follow us that would be good and beneficial for everyone.[12]

In addition, this sentiment was echoed by others in Tierno Galván's administration. Referring to the appearance of other "movidas" around the country, Antonio Gómez Rufo, the head of the Centro Cultural de la Villa, maintained in 1986 that "Madrid now contemplates with satisfaction that culture grows and develops in other places without entering into competition with them or trying to control them, or overcome them, or, much less, humiliate or denigrate them."[13] But, despite the fact that there was never any intention of forcing the *re-madrileñización* of Spain, any project centered in Madrid was perceived as a threat by other regions. In short, both the legacy of Francoism and the simultaneous articulation of a series of exclusive regionalist projects created resistance in other areas of Spain to a national civic identity originating from the capital.

In addition to this resistance on the regional level, there was resistance on the national level to such an identity as well. In the period after 1986, the possibility of Madrid serving as a model for the rest of the country became even less likely because of the national PSOE's pursuit of Europeanization and because of its reappropriation of Madrid as the capital of Spain. Although there was greater cooperation between Barranco's municipal administration and the national administration after Tierno Galván's death, thus making a common project more possible, the national leadership of the PSOE had no interest in promoting a new collective identity centered on greater popular mobilization and on the movida madrileña—either in the capital or elsewhere in the country. Even though the example of Madrid symbolized a tolerant, democratic, and inclusive sense of community, a comparable civic identity never made the transfer to the national level because the project conflicted with the goals of the national PSOE.

As described in the previous chapter, the national leadership favored centralization, economic stability, and European convergence over a more participatory form of democracy based, in part, on greater mobilization. Thus, the national PSOE failed to adopt Madrid as a model for use on the national level for the same reasons it failed to promote the project specifically in the capital. Tierno Galván's utopian goals of peace (through Spain's neutrality), popular participation, social equality for everyone, and cultural "reeducation," which would lead to mutual self-respect and peaceful coexistence, were simply not compatible with the PSOE's neoliberal agenda after 1986.

Finally, resistance to any kind of new national civic identity associated with the movida madrileña also could be found on both the right and the left. As first described in Chapter 5, a small but vocal group on the right viewed the movida as a deliberate attempt by the Socialist administrations of Madrid to construct an artificial cultural identity exactly to their liking. They accused Madrid's local and regional administrations of promoting a "state-controlled (*dirigida*)" culture that squandered the city's budget on financing comic books, rock concerts, drug- and sex-filled parties, and excessively large public festivals in order to win popular support. For example, in September 1982, Fernando Martín Vicente, a city council member representing the UCD, argued that neighborhood festivals and popular celebrations were nothing more than "cheap demagoguery."[14] In other words, the right believed that the left had invented specific cultural currents and tendencies to serve their political goals and to win elections.

It was also believed that the Socialist administrations promoted this populist culture to the detriment of quality. Specifically, the right accused the movida madrileña of being a kind of a media-dominated "light" culture—a culture not based on solid artistic traditions or precedents.[15] Nor did the right like the idea that anything could be considered art (*todo se considera arte*) and that everything was seen as legitimate (*todo vale*). The demystification of art and culture was simply not appreciated by many on the traditional right.

Not surprisingly, in right-leaning media outlets, such as *ABC* and *El Alcázar*, the movida madrileña was largely ignored or marginalized during this period. This was especially true after 1983 when the local and regional administrations of Madrid began openly supporting the movement. In general, there was very little coverage of the concerts, festivals, magazine launches, or film premièrs related to the movida. For example, *ABC* completely ignored all of the cultural manifestations surrounding the "movida" in *San Isidro* of 1985, except for the bullfights.[16] By the end of 1985, however, open condemnations of the movida became more frequent in the conservative press. The movement was most often condemned as a "false culture" promoted exclusively by the Socialist administrations in Madrid.[17]

Writing in response to an issue of the *Comunidad*'s official magazine, *Alfoz*, dedicated to the movida madrileña, Pilar Bidagor Altuna argued in 1985 that the movement was a "special" culture that reflected a small minority of the city's youth.[18] As such, the movida was not worthy of broader support: "The most surprising thing about this phenomenon is that the administration foments this 'special culture,' called the '*movida*.'"[19] For Bidagor Altuna, and for some others on the right, the special culture of the movida represented a degenerate subculture and a throwback to "the 1960s in England."[20] Similarly, the municipal administration's magazine, *Madriz*, which featured Madrid's young cartoonists and graphic artists, was labeled "repugnant rubbish (*porquería repugnante*)" by the Grupo Popular in April 1984.[21]

Likewise, as the head of the political opposition in Madrid, José María Álvarez del Manzano frequently accused Madrid's local and regional administrations of fostering a pseudo culture and of promoting cultural activities that were little more than state-controlled propaganda. In January 1986, he openly called for the end of the municipal administration's so-called politicization of cultural activities. Referring to Tierno Galván's dominance within the area of culture, Álvarez del Manzano appealed for a culture in Madrid "*sin apellidos*," meaning without last names or ownership: "It is not necessary to call culture anything, but simply culture . . . it should not be necessary that artists or their works have a certain political projection."[22] While Tierno Galván and Madrid's other Socialist political elite understood the movida as a representation of liberty, openness, free expression, and active participation, many on the right were more inclined to see it as an artificial culture promoted strictly for the political benefit of the left. Logically, those on the right would not have been keen to see the development of any kind of collective identity related to the movida madrileña applied more broadly to the rest of Spain.

Some intellectuals on the left were critical of the movida as well. Those who criticized the movement generally saw it as trivial, apolitical, and frivolous. Similar to the right, a few on the left also accused Madrid's Socialist political elite of promoting the "vulgarization" of culture and of supporting the cultural politics of mere "spectacle."[23] In other words, it was thought that many of the cultural events and products related to the movida madrileña lacked any real substance or useful meaning.

For example, Juan Luis Cebrián believed that the movida was all flash and no substance and that all the movement was destined to leave behind was "a couple of bars and a few witty anecdotes [*algunos chascarrillos*]."[24] Others offered an even more extensive critique. Juan Pablo Fusi argued that the movida's universalized social consumption of culture represented

a certain trivialization, turning cultural themes into fashion and spectacle; a devaluing of true [*verdadera*] culture, by the uncritical and de-hierarchical

acceptance of every type of pseudo-cultural initiative; a certain impoverish-
ment, in short, because that universalization was not, many times, without
stupid mimicry, collective conformity [*gregarismo*] and vain superficiality.[25]

Some on the left thus understood the movida as part of a cultural process
that obscured or destroyed traditional customs, celebrated only a homogenized cosmopolitan culture, and ultimately produced uniformity, synchro-
nization, and massification in all large urban centers regardless of geography
or local peculiarity.

Additionally, the movida's lack of formal political engagement disappointed
many on the traditional left. Some argued that the movida's "postmodern"
stylizations really masked the triumph of a yuppified consumer culture over
a more progressive political program.[26] In other words, it was thought of
as frivolous, hollow, and as a distraction from formal political participation.
Framed as a kind of "dumbed-down" culture, propagated largely by the mass
media, the intellectual left showed little enthusiasm for a new national collective identity connected to the movement.

CONCLUSION

By juxtaposing Tierno Galvan's project in Madrid with the PSOE's national
political and economic program of the 1980s, Spain's particular path to
democratic consolidation comes more clearly into focus. In contrast to the
more participatory and communitarian democratic model developed in the
capital between 1979 and 1986, the country was firmly put on a centralized
path to neoliberalism and full European integration in the second half of the
decade. Despite this eventual course, the example of Madrid nonetheless
demonstrates that there was at least one alternative to the PSOE's demobilized and centralized path to democratic consolidation in the 1980s.

Despite the fact that Tierno Galván's project encountered resistance from
a number of different sources and was never supported outside of the capital
or adopted on the national level, the success of a new civic identity in Madrid
represented a possible democratizing and unifying force for the country as
a whole. This civic identity, built on inclusion and on the democratic present (instead of on a shared cultural past), could have provided not only a
more participatory model for democratic consolidation, but also a unifying
piece to Spain's collective identity in the post-transition period. While not
representing a singular national identity, such an inclusive civic identity
might have soothed regional animosities and provided an alternative to the
"necessity" of European integration. In other words, a unique Spanish civic
identity could have provided an alternative to those who saw European integration as the only solution to Spain's national identity "problem" after the
experience of the dictatorship.

This civic identity would *not* have replaced the presence of multiple identities in Spain or eliminated the development of European supranational
affiliations, but it might have provided a cohesive layer in between the

divisiveness and fragmentation of regionalism, based on separate ethnic/ linguistic traditions, and the homogenization that came with supranationalism, based on an all-out bid for European integration. In short, the unique regional identity experiment in Madrid represented a road to democratic consolidation not taken by Spain's political leadership after 1986—the road to an inclusive civic identity, to increased mobilization and participation, to nonalignment, and to greater social equality and cohesion.

In many ways, then, history did come to an end in Spain—at least temporarily—by the close of the decade, as Francis Fukuyama predicted for the rest of the West. The end of the 1980s marked the end of the great ideological debates in Spain, especially on the left.[27] A single-minded drive for European "convergence" and neocapitalist economic growth, based largely on increased consumption, dominated other alternative forms of Socialist ideology. The decision to remain in NATO and pursue the narrow path of European integration ended any hope of the Socialists' promise of radicalism, collectivism, independence, or progressive spirit. As a result, a pro-market, neoliberal Socialist party governed the country while the historical neoliberals, the Partido Popular, represented the official opposition. By the beginning of the 1990s, it was almost impossible to imagine any alternative path to democratic consolidation for Spain, such as the one Madrid's old professor had proposed less than a decade earlier.

CONCLUSION

Madrid's transformation is easy to take for granted. It seems as though the vibrant and socially frenetic city we know today has always existed. This is not the case. Many of the attributes, specially related to culture, which appear "natural" or "essential," were actually the result of a conscious project in the 1980s to remake the city and its residents. But this transformation of the capital was not so much about physically catching up with modernity, or with the rest of Europe—the economic and, for the most part, the social modernization of Spain had already happened under Franco—rather it was about positively changing the habits and self-perception of all madrileños after the experience of the dictatorship. In other words, it embodied the successful consolidation of Spain's democratic transition at the center. During the first part of the decade, the "remaking" of Madrid and the formation of a new regional democratic identity signified the reconciliation of madrileños with the place in which they lived and with one another. And the second half of the decade represented a turn toward the perceived necessities of European integration and economic development. The democratic and dynamic Madrid of today—known as much for its business reputation as its cultural prominence—is thus the product of both halves of the 1980s.

Madrid's remarkable transformation also illustrates several important points about contemporary nationalism and regionalism, the uses of culture, and Spain's democratic transition. Despite the official end of regionalism in Madrid after 1986, the disconnect between the interests and motivations of the capital—articulated as a unique region—and the interests of the national political elite demonstrates that an official Spanish national identity and the "center" are not naturally or inexorably linked. Likewise, evidence of regionalism in Madrid demonstrates that every area of Spain, not just those on the so-called periphery, sought to define new forms of democratic identification, specifically on the regional level, in a context where nationalism was closely associated with the former authoritarian regime. Thus, in the decade and a half after 1975, new regional identities were not constructed simply "to legitimize a broad state-led political project," as some scholars have suggested.[1] Instead new regional affiliations were one of the important means by which democracy came to flourish in post-Francoist Spain.

Spain's "problem" of creating a new democratic identity in the post-Francoist period was thus ultimately solved by an embrace of both "the regional," in the first half of the 1980s, and "the international," in the second half. But it was not as simple as various regional identities replacing a defunct national identity, or as supranational affiliations taking the place of emerging regional and national affiliations. Instead, regional, national, and supranational identities came to exist all at the same time. In other words, Spanish "national" identity became plural and, as a result, what it meant to be Spanish changed in the 1980s. Instead of meaning identification solely with the nation-state of Spain, being "Spanish" meant identifying with a region, with Spain, and with Europe. These simultaneous affiliations presented no inherent contradiction; being Spanish became fundamentally defined by the acceptance of multiple and overlapping identities.

In this light, the almost universally accepted center-periphery model may not be the most accurate method for conceptualizing Spanish regional and national identity after 1975. From this alternative perspective, the formation of national identity, or the perceived imposition of a national identity by some regions, is not specifically related to Madrid as the "center" or to geography. It depends instead on the domination of institutions that yield power, and, subsequently, on the ability to articulate an overlaying national identity on all regions, including the capital itself. Similarly, the differences in the ways regional identities manifest themselves cannot be accurately described by a single model. Rather, regional difference depends on a variety of variables: the perception of geography, the ability to appropriate and reuse symbols and traditions from the past, the strength of local institutions, and the individual motivation of local elites.

So while the project in Madrid may not have been as strong or as clearly evident as those in Catalonia or the Basque Country, it is nonetheless clear that the promotion of a new civic identity in the capital between 1979 and 1986 did not represent official Spanish nationalism, a monolithic national identity, or a new Spanishness. Instead, the capital was part of a broad, parallel process, affecting every region in the country. In this regard, Madrid's transformation during the first half of the 1980s was not an example of an exception to the rule. Again, change in the capital fits squarely within the context of a broader process of defining new democratic collective identities within a new constitutional framework after 1978.

Yet, at the same time, regionalism in Madrid did exhibit some of its own unique characteristics. Although most regions employed traditional customs, and often times language, to stake out a new democratic identity, the political elite of Madrid chose a different path. Instead of embracing the peculiarities of past customs and traditions, the local and regional administrations undertook a wide-ranging project, which included urban renewal, cultural mobilization, and the promotion of a modern cultural identity based on the movida madrileña, in order to construct a more inclusive identity in Madrid. Because this project represented a "civic" rather than an "ethnic" identity, inclusion was not defined by a certain way of speaking, as was true in the case of Catalonia for example, or by familiarity with a set of traditional customs from the past. As a result, no one was marginalized in the capital on the basis of language or by having been born someplace else. Instead, inclusion was based on voluntary residence in the capital and on the assimilation of certain democratic values. Thus part of what made the project in Madrid unique was its openness to all segments of the population, to equality, to modernity, to cultural experimentation, and, most importantly, to the democratic future. Only those who wished to remain solely in the past would be left behind.

The case of Madrid was also unique because rather than using "culture" to construct a collective identity based on exclusion, the local and regional administrations used culture and the promotion of cultural activities to reinforce the creation of this new inclusive civic identity. Through the process of cultural mobilization, all madrileños—regardless of age, place of birth, economic status, or political affiliation—were encouraged to come together and actively participate in a variety of cultural activities that related specifically to Madrid. In addition, the promotion of a new official cultural identity based on the inclusive, participatory, optimistic, and modern symbols of the movida madrileña specifically reinforced the effort to create a new civic rather than an ethnic regional identity. It was believed that such a cultural program would help instill the democratic values of active participation and peaceful coexistence and provide the foundation for a new democratic sense of place in the capital.

In fact, the embrace of a new democratic regional identity had a profound effect both on Madrid and on madrileños. It served to distance the newly baptized democratic capital from its association with Francoism, in general, and from its reputation as the authoritarian center of Spain, in particular. At the same time, the creation of a new civic identity based on active participation and peaceful coexistence also served to "reeducate" madrileños after almost 40 years of dictatorship. While rock concerts, street festivals, and art exhibits may not have constituted traditional methods of teaching democratic principles and civic engagement, cultural mobilization and the promotion of a new modern cultural identity did, nonetheless, provide a break from the undemocratic past and created the means by which new behaviors and affiliations could be formed.

In this way, participation in cultural activities in Madrid was a struggle against the nondemocratic habits of the past and, eventually, became a daily exercise of emancipation. Spending time out on the city's streets, staying up all night, and creating "popular" art promoted feelings of liberty and the freedom of expression. For some, the cultural transformation was also a "magnificent screen to hide their changes of political attitude: from dogmatism to modernity, from the leather jacket clad political activist [*la zamarra guerrillera*] to the suit of a young functionary, from solid [*macizo*] democratic centralism to the soft theory of social fragmentation."[2] In other words, cultural change permitted social, and even political, transformations on both the left and the right after the experience of the dictatorship. Over time, new forms of cultural participation helped Madrid become the place for transitive democratic actions: passing freely through the streets, speaking openly, participating unconditionally, and coming together peacefully. Residents also passed from being passive receivers of culture to being active transmitters of culture. And, of course, integral to this change was the official embrace and widespread assimilation of the movida madrileña.

Even though few observers would now deny rock and roll's dynamism, its diversity, and its power to effect social change, no one has ascribed similar attributes specifically to the movida. While there is no question that the movement began on the margins of society, just as rock and roll had done in the United States, the movida gained legitimacy and full assimilation as Madrid's political elite officially co-opted and promoted its symbols in the mid-1980s. With the popular embrace of this "*contra-castizo*" movement, the movida increasingly provided the freedom for madrileños to enjoy themselves and interact with one another in new ways. At the same time, it also allowed the residents of Madrid to overcome their Franco-induced inferiority complex and to regain their self-confidence. Even more specifically, the widespread embrace of the movida helped madrileños overcome outdated social taboos and prejudices, including homophobia, negative youth stereotypes, and cultural elitism (who could be an artist and what should be considered art).

Thus, an embrace of the movida signified not only the rejection of Franco's conservative, religious, and backward-looking culture, it also helped reclaim many of the things that had been marginalized by the dictatorship: free expression, spontaneity, popular participation, and a feeling of pride for Madrid. Most importantly, the movida provided many residents of Madrid with something they could voluntarily identify with, as the movement represented something new, modern, and absolutely different from what had come before. Strange new haircuts, extravagant clothing, experimentation with "forbidden" drugs, and poorly sung pop music all formed part of the formula to create a unique sense of place in the capital.

Recalling the end-of-the-year party for *La Luna de Madrid* held at the elite Palace Hotel in 1984, the former editor of the magazine, Borja Casani, described this feeling of transformation associated with the movida:

> We hired the whole hotel and there were musicians everywhere, two or three thousand people drugged up and drunk lying on these gorgeous hand-woven carpets beneath crystal chandeliers smoking joints. It seemed like a miracle, as though we'd stormed the Winter Palace, a sensation of tremendous power, not economic or political power but a feeling of sheer physical force, as if to say: look at what's possible.[3]

With the help of the movida madrileña, almost anything seemed possible for madrileños in the mid-1980s, including the storming of the traditional symbols of power and hegemony. In fact, only a year and a half earlier, Felipe González had taken over the very same luxury hotel to celebrate the PSOE's national election victory. Greater cultural mobilization based on the movida had allowed the residents of Madrid to become something more than what they had been in their everyday lives under the dictatorship. Pedro Almodóvar, for example, worked for Telefónica during the day, while performing on stage and filming movies at night. Over time, these extracurricular activities that occurred after dark became more important than what was happening during the day. In 1986, Almodóvar summed up the transformative power of culture in the capital:

> [A]fter 1977, there was a true boiling over of ideas. Fresh, daring, spontane-ous, authentic, and immediate ideas rapidly reflected themselves and that could be easily savored by the people. It's not important that all has been reduced to a handful of records and fanzines. The decisive thing is that that [experience] has been incorporated into our biography: we lived it, we enjoyed it, and none of the unbelievers that attack the *movida* can take that from us . . . many things did happen with regard to fashion, music, behaviors, and to the mentality [of madrileños].[4]

In other words, residents of Madrid were able to redefine themselves through the cultural activity associated with the movida. In this way, the movement represented nothing less than a new way of life in the capital. It was exactly this new way of life that made up an important part of Madrid's new regional identity.

As the cultural activity related to the movida helped transform Madrid's residents, the movement also broke down prejudices abroad against Madrid. The cultural isolation of the Franco years did not merely exclude the capital from the merry-go-round of international exhibitions for more than three decades; it also prevented the world from developing an awareness and appreciation for what was going on in Madrid. The new popularity and prestige of "the Madrid of the *movida*" allowed for that to finally come to an end in the mid-1980s. This was particularly true with regard to art, music, and the capital's overall cultural scene. On account of the movida, for the first time since the civil war, a trip to Madrid represented something more than the classic visit to the Prado Museum. When told she had to return to Paris to continue her studies, the daughter of a French diplomat responded: "Paris? That city so boring where there is no one out at any place at 11:00 pm?"[5] The old stereotypes associated with Madrid simply no longer held up in the face of the movement's dynamism and novelty. Thus, to those outside of the capital, the movida madrileña represented a kind of passport to modernity and acceptability.

While Madrid's embrace of the movida served a symbolic function for the rest of the world that was as important as that of the 1978 Constitution, the decentralized framework of autonomous communities, and the newly elected Socialist government, there was an important difference between the development of the movement in the capital and those other symbols of post-Francoist Spain. Specifically, the movida madrileña was part of a process of defining a new democratic collective identity that related directly to Madrid, and was not a nationwide phenomenon. But because of Madrid's long-time position as the capital of the nation, the rest of the world understood the changes that were occurring in Madrid as the complete transformation of Spain, even though this was not the case. In fact, it could be said that the opposite was true. The official and popular acceptance of a new cultural identity based on the modern symbols of the movida actually helped to differentiate the region of Madrid from the rest of Spain during the 1980s.

But it should be noted that Madrid's "peculiarity" in the Spanish context was nothing more than an embrace of modern, plural, and democratic cultural currents that were common in most major metropolitan areas of the West. In other words, while differentiating Madrid from other regions in Spain, the changes taking place in the capital were part of the same processes that could be found elsewhere in Europe and in the United States. What occurred in Madrid over the course of the 1980s was thus a kind of "normalization" of its culture. But this normalization should not be understood as a sign of backwardness or of the need to "catch up." The development of multiple and flexible identities, greater acceptance of homosexuality, the worship of youth and youth culture, and the embrace of ethnic diversity and multiculturalism were all ongoing and openly contested developments that were occurring elsewhere in the West at this time. Put another way, these cultural and social changes were not fully solidified everywhere else, while they lagged behind in Madrid. In fact, Madrid was one of the leaders of these developments.

Madrid was so good at this "modernity" game during the first half of the decade because the region had little "traditional" identity to compete against. The contortions required by modernity (or by postmodernity, as some prefer to call it), or by a plural and democratic modern society, were more easily achieved in Madrid because of its specific historical context, as expressed through a set of unique characteristics: a large immigrant and youth population, no established bourgeois identity, the presence of a local political elite who wished to remake the region, and the experience of the Franco regime. This last aspect was particularly important. In contrast to Paris, New York, and London, what had come before in Madrid was clearly illegitimate because of the former regime's connection to authoritarianism and repression. Furthermore, the region's political elite deliberately assumed modern symbols and values as a part of its plan to redefine Madrid as a new democratic region. Thus, rather than being set in opposition to the establishment, the processes that produced modern cultural currents were actively incorporated within the official program to transform the capital.

Like all great transformations, however, this one did not come without certain costs. Madrid's new environment of tolerance and openness in the first half of the 1980s was often associated with sexual promiscuity and with greater use of marijuana, cocaine, and heroin.[6] A relaxing of sexual norms and increased drug use also opened the door for the spread of AIDS.[7] In addition, a deliberate emphasis on the culturally vibrant present produced a lack of interest in what had come before. Even though Madrid's new democratic regional identity was defined first and foremost by inclusion, there was little room for the history, culture, or traditions of the past in this new imagined community.

However, the main cost of the project to "reeducate" madrileños after the experience of the dictatorship and to create a new inclusive democratic identity in Madrid was the lack of interest in formal political participation. The capital's apparently apolitical, and, at times, chaotic transformation created an engaged, spirited, and peaceful public, but one that was not very interested in formal forms of associationalism or political participation. In other words, the promotion of active participation and peaceful coexistence through cultural activity came at a political price. Formal participation in politics was simply not a priority in the capital after the mid-1980s.

In no way, however, does this political "deficit" negate the fact that an important transformation took place in Madrid between 1979 and 1986. In an environment where people on both the left and the right feared mass political mobilization and polarization, broad cultural mobilization offered another path to a more participatory form of democratic consolidation. Based on this alternative path, Madrid was transformed from the home of oppression and bureaucratic centralism into an independent and democratic region with its own unique identity. And, just as importantly, madrileños transformed from passive subjects of the former dictatorship to active democratic citizens. Thus, while demobilization was the general outcome of Spain's top-down transition to democracy, this was not completely true for the region of Madrid in the mid-1980s. Between the first democratic municipal elections of 1979 and the death of Tierno Galván in 1986, citizens were encouraged to become more civically involved, participate more actively, and identify more closely with each other and with the capital.

Of course, this particular effort to transform Madrid did not last forever. As we have seen, the movida madrileña, and the broader project to create a new regional identity in Madrid, was crushed by the national PSOE's decision to elect Europeanization as the party's guiding "ideology" in the 1980s. Writing in 1991, John Hooper explained González's ultimate objective:

> What does explain the ideological flotsam and jetsam González has left in his wake is his readiness to cast aside anything that might hinder Spain's re-assumption of what he sees as its rightful place in the international community. A more idealistic socialist approach could have got in the way of the growth which has brought Spain within sight of a place at the big table.[8]

More than any other single solution, the PSOE sought European convergence to solve the country's problems. Joining the European "big table" was perceived as conferring respectability, national legitimacy, international prestige, and economic benefits on Spain. By the end of the decade,

Spain's integration into Europe appeared to be going so well that the goal of the PSOE was no longer just integration into the EC, but equality with its leading members. For the vice president, Alfonso Guerra, the PSOE's new aim was to place Spain "among those [countries] that are at the head of Europe."⁹

While offering certain benefits, this "European solution" favored economic development over the promotion of other activities, such as culture. It was exactly this change of priorities that helped bring an end to Madrid's regional identity project between 1986 and 1992. In addition, the PSOE's specific vision of Europeanization made greater popular mobilization unnecessary, and possibly even turned it into a threat. Beginning in 1982, but becoming especially evident after 1985, the national leadership of the PSOE discouraged higher levels of social and political mobilization in the capital and elsewhere in the country. This strategy was probably the result of many different factors: from political prudence and a fear of destabilizing tensions to simple convenience for a political party holding an absolute majority. Most importantly, however, the desire for economic prosperity and the necessity of following a strict policy line, which was required for European integration, discouraged any desire for greater mobilization. In other words, greater popular mobilization only threatened to rock the boat—a boat firmly on course to European convergence. In short, the PSOE found it easier to consolidate Spain's democracy based on European integration and economic prosperity than on the promotion of greater social equality and popular mobilization.

Although, clearly, not all forms of "participation" were equally marginalized in Spain, or specifically in Madrid, after 1986. The PSOE's emphasis on prosperity, again predicated largely on European integration, privileged economic activity over other forms of mobilization. As a result, economic consumption came to replace cultural mobilization in the capital. As madrileños relied less on culture and more on personal consumption to define themselves, the active form of democratic citizenship that developed during the first half of the decade was replaced by a more passive form of citizenship. Put another way, a pro-NATO, pro-European, proconsumption identity won out over a more participatory form of identity based on broad civic engagement. On account of this change, the old professor's death in 1986 marked, in many ways, "the end of the utopia" in Madrid.¹⁰

Despite this shift from culture to economics and the end of Tierno Galván's project in Madrid after 1986, one thing remained the same in the capital: the underlying feature of *political* demobilization stayed constant throughout the 1980s. Whereas Tierno Galván chose to use cultural mobilization in order to avoid political polarization and to construct new regional affiliations as the means of consolidating democracy after the transition, the national PSOE relied on economic development and the expansion of a consumer society to achieve the same ends. Put another way, Tierno Galván was willing to trade formal political mobilization for the chance to move toward an alternative form of participatory democracy centered on cultural activity. In contrast, the PSOE was prepared to give up political mobilization and greater social equality for economic prosperity and a chance at European convergence. Of course, the national PSOE's vision of democracy eventually won out. The idea of a socially equitable, nonaligned, and culturally mobilized capital simply could not be reconciled with the national PSOE's desire for a Europeanized Spain. After 1986, the PSOE settled on a neoliberal, consumer-focused, and demobilized path to democratic consolidation after leaving behind neutrality in foreign policy and populism in economic policy.

Perhaps, from this perspective, Spain's democratic consolidation in the 1980s represents yet another period in Spanish history, similar to the Restoration (and even the Franco regime), when stability and economic development were sought at the expense of popular mobilization and greater democratization. In 2000, Santos Juliá wrote that the Socialist era was a mixture of "lightness and darkness," but that it was too early to tell.[11] It may now be the time to acknowledge more of that darkness. The national leadership of the PSOE was seduced by Europeanization, neoliberalism, and material prosperity. Ultimately, the result was corruption, less social equality, decreased mobilization, and the willingness to favor stability and economic growth at almost any cost. While it is true that the PSOE's specific path in the 1980s achieved the primary goal of securing Spain's democratic transition, it was not, however, the only available path. The project to transform Madrid between 1979 and 1986 represented the possibility of at least one alternative form of Spanish Socialism and of an alternative path to democratic consolidation in Spain after the dictatorship.

NOTES

INTRODUCTION

1. Articles describing the transformation of Madrid appeared in such diverse news outlets as *Time*, *Newsweek*, *The New York Times*, *Le monde*, *Les Nouvelles Littéraires*, *National Geographic*, and *Rolling Stone Magazine*.
2. Bob Spitz, "The New Spain," *Rolling Stone Magazine*, June 6, 1985, 33.
3. Ibid., 34.
4. Michael Richards, "Collective Memory, the Nation-State and Post-Franco Society," in *Contemporary Spanish Cultural Studies*, ed. Barry Jordan and Rikki Morgan-Tamosunas (London: Arnold Press, 2000), 76. Also see Sebastian Balfour and Alejandro Quiroga, *The Reinvention of Spain: Nation and Identity since Democracy* (Oxford: Oxford University Press, 2007).
5. See Paloma Aguilar Fernandez, *Memoria y olvido de la guerra civil española* (Madrid: Alianza, 1996). Jeffery Herf makes a similar argument about democratization and the need to "forget" the past with regard to post-1945 Germany. See Jeffery Herf, *Divided Memory: The Nazi Past in the Two Germanys* (Cambridge, MA: Harvard University Press, 1997).
6. Here, and throughout the text, the term "local political and cultural elite" is used to refer specifically to the group of Socialists and Communists that came to power in Madrid after the death of Francisco Franco. Of course, there were other members of the political elite in the capital, particularly those on the right, who opposed any transformation of the capital after the end of the dictatorship.
7. Spain's Socialist party, or the PSOE (*Partido Socialista Obrero Español*— Spanish Socialist Worker's Party), was the national governing party in Spain from October 1982 to March 1996.
8. See, for example, Mary K. Flynn, "Constructed identities and Iberia," *Ethnic and Racial Studies* 24, no. 5 (2001); Xosé Manoel Núñez, "What is Spanish Nationalism Today? From Legitimacy Crisis to Unfulfilled Renovation (1975–2000)," *Ethnic and Racial Studies* 24, no. 5 (2001).

CHAPTER 1

1. Parts of this chapter in an earlier version appeared in "Reconsidering Spanish Nationalism, Regionalism, and the Center-Periphery Model in the Post-Francoist Period, 1975–1992." *International Journal of Iberian Studies* 20, no. 3 (2007): 171–185
2. Despite the foreseeable objections, I will use the term "regionalism" from this point forward to refer both to the three historical nationalities (Catalonia, the Basque Country, and Galicia) and to the other projects to create new regional

collective identities in other parts of Spain, for example in Valencia. This is done for clarity and consistency within the text.

3. The debates surrounding the definitions of "nationalism" and "regionalism" are extensive. Here and throughout the text, as a member of the "modernist school," I understand nationalism as a tool "for autonomy, unity, and identity of a population deemed to constitute a nation." John Hutchinson and Anthony D. Smith, eds., *Nationalism: Critical Concepts in Political Science*, vol. I (London: Routledge, 2000), 29. Likewise, just as I see nationalism producing nations and national identities, I use regionalism in this study to refer to the creation of an intrastate identity within the borders of a sovereign nation.

4. See Tom Nairn, *The Breakup of Britain: Crisis and Neo-Nationalism* (London: New Left Books, 1977).

5. Michael Hechter, *Internal Colonialism: The Celtic Fringe in British National Development, 1536–1966* (London: Routledge and Kegan Paul, 1975), 34.

6. Use of the center-periphery model in Spain was also based heavily on the later work of Stein Rokkan and D. W. Urwin. See Stein Rokkan and D. W. Urwin, eds., *The Politics of Territorial Identity* (Beverley Hills: Sage, 1982). Other important works on the center-periphery model in the Spanish context include: Xavier Arbós, "Central Versus Peripheral Nationalism in Building Democracy: The Case of Spain," *Canadian Review of Studies in Nationalism* XIV, no. 1 (1987); Michael Hebbert, "Spain—A Centre-Periphery Transformation," in *Unfamiliar Territory: The Reshaping of European Geography*, ed. Michael Hebbert and Jens Christian Hansen (Aldershot: Avebury, 1990).

7. David Corkill, "Multiple National Identities, Immigration and Racism in Spain and Portugal," in *Nations and Identity in Contemporary Europe*, ed. Brian Jenkins and Spyros A. Sofos (London: Routledge, 1996), 157.

8. Juan J. Linz, "Los nacionalismos en España: una perspectiva comparativa," in *El estado moderno en Italia y España*, ed. Elio d'Auria and Jordi Cassassas (Barcelona: Universitat de Barcelona, 1993), 82–83.

9. See Justo G. Beramendi, "La historiografía de los nacionalismos en España," *Historia Contemporánea* 7 (1992); Xosé Manoel Núñez, *Historiographical Approaches to Nationalism in Spain* (Saarbrucken: Breitenbach, 1993).

10. Xosé Manoel Núñez, "What is Spanish Nationalism Today? From legitimacy Crisis to Unfilfilled Renovation (1975–2000)," *Ethnic and Racial Studies* 24, no. 5 (2001): 719.

11. Ibid.

12. Núñez, *Historiographical Approaches to Nationalism in Spain.*

13. Ibid., 138.

14. While the post-1975 period continues to be overlooked, scholars have more recently begun to examine the development and functioning of Spanish nationalism in earlier periods. For example, José Álvarez Junco has argued that the appearance of the national idea of Spain, based in part on a distorted history of the Reconquest and of the Latin American Empire, did not occur until the late nineteenth century. See José Álvarez Junco, *Mater Dolorosa: la idea de España en el siglo XIX* (Madrid: Taurus, 2001). For a reappraisal of the intellectual origins and formation of Spanish nationalism under Franco, see Geoffrey Jensen, *Irrational Triumph: Cultural Despair, Military Nationalism, and the Ideological Origins of Franco's Spain* (Reno: University of Nevada Press, 2002).

15. Núñez, *Historiographical Approaches to Nationalism in Spain*, 148.
16. Stanley Payne, "Nationalism, Regionalism and Micronationalism in Spain," *Journal of Contemporary History* 26 (1991): 487.
17. Mary K. Flynn, "Constructed identities and Iberia," *Ethnic and Racial Studies* 24, no. 5 (2001): 712.
18. Ibid.
19. Hebbert, "Spain—A Centre-Periphery Transformation," 133.
20. Núñez, *Historiographical Approaches to Nationalism in Spain*.
21. Ibid., 144.
22. Ibid.
23. Despite the fact that most scholars discount the existence of Spanish national-ism and some kind of a Spanish national identity after 1978, empirical data show that the percentage of Spaniards that declare themselves to be opposed to a national Spanish identity has been very small. In fact, even in Catalonia, the Basque Country, and Galicia, the majority of a region's population claims loyalty to both a regional *and* a national identity. See for example Xosé Manoel Núñez, "The Reawakening of Peripheral Nationalisms and the State of the Autonomous Communities," in *Spanish History since 1808*, ed. José Alvarez Junco and Adrian Shubert (London: Arnold, 2000).
24. In addition to the works cited above, also see Miguel Platón, *La amenaza separatista. Mito y realidad de los nacionalismos en España* (Madrid: Temas de Hoy, 1994). In the realm of public opinion surveys, no one thought to ask the standard "dual identity" question in the region of Madrid until 1990, even though this question had been asked in practically every other region since the late 1970s, including in Andalusia, Valencia, and even Extremadura. For example, the question would read: "In general, do you feel more Valencian than Spanish, as Valencian as Spanish, or more Spanish than Valencian?" Public opinion researchers must have assumed, at least until 1990, that everyone living in Madrid simply felt Spanish; see, for example, Luis Moreno, *La federalización de España* (Madrid: Siglo XXI, 1997), 123–140.
25. By linking together the historical nationalities and newly created autonomous communities, it is not my intention to ignore some of the obvious differences between the two, nor is it to dismiss the claims for greater self-determination made by Catalonia, the Basque Country, and Galicia. Instead, my purpose here is to highlight the broad similarities in order to question the application of the center-periphery model in the Spanish context after the end of the dictatorship.
26. Michael Keating has suggested that, rather than representing something inherently new, such multiple geographical affiliations actually hearken back to the past: "These trends represent a step back in history, to an era of over lapping authority, multiple identity and complexity, before the rise of the modern state." Michael Keating, "The Minority Nations of Spain and European Integration: A New Framework for Autonomy?," *Journal of Spanish Cultural Studies* 1, no. 1 (2000): 31. It also should be noted that along with geographical identities, class and gender affiliations often make up part of this plural identity as well.
27. Jo Labanyi, ed., *Constructing Identity in Contemporary Spain* (Oxford: Oxford University Press, 2002), 257.
28. In contrast to this argument, many scholars, beginning with Juan Linz in the mid 1970s, have linked the persistence of regional identities and weak

Spanish nationalism in the late twentieth century to incomplete nation
building in the nineteenth century; see Juan J. Linz, "Early State Building
and Late Peripheral Nationalisms Against the State: The Case of Spain," in
Building States and Nations: Analysis by Region, ed. S. N. Eisenstadt and
Stein Rokkan (Beverly Hills: Sage, 1973). In this view, regional identities
in Spain, especially those manifesting themselves in the twentieth century,
are seen essentially as remnants of the past, mainly premodern, and opposed
to a "modern" national identity. Regionalisms thus represent a certain backwardness, caused by incomplete economic modernization and political consolidation in the nineteenth century. This incomplete nationalization thesis
has been supported by a wide range of authors, including: Borja de Riquer,
"La débil nacionalización española del siglo XIX," *Historia Social* 20 (1994);
Payne, "Nationalism, Regionalism and Micronationalism in Spain"; Juan
Pablo Fusi, *España. La evolución de la identidad nacional* (Madrid: Temas
de Hoy, 1999); José Álvarez Junco, "The Formation of Spanish identity
and Its Adaptation to the Age of Nations," *History and Memory: Studies in
Representation of the Past* 14, no. 1–2 (2002).

29. Eric Hobsbawm has persuasively argued that the emergence of new states
    and new forms of collective identity in this period was the result of "the
    weakening or collapse of previous states, and not as the product of some
    new wave of powerful nationalist movements or nationalist consciousness."
    Eric Hobsbawm, "Nation, State, Ethnicity, Religion: Transformations of
    Identity," in *Nationalism in Europe: Past and Present*, ed. Justo G. Beramendi
    and Xosé M. Núñez (Santiago de Compostela: University of Santiago de
    Compostela, 1994), 44.

30. Juan Linz has characterized the lack of an exclusively national or regional
    identity as a failure of both Spanish nationalism and the various regionalist
    projects within Spain. See Linz, "Los nacionalismos en España: una perspec-
    tiva comparativa."

31. For example, Núñez has described the rise of new regionalisms (besides the
    three historical nationalities) after 1978 as a "fundamental contradiction" within
    the structure of the Spanish state. See Xosé Manoel Núñez, "Region Building
    in Spain During the 19th and 20th Centuries," in *Region und Regionsbildung
    in Europa: Konzeptionen der Forschung und Empirische Befunde*, ed. Gerhard
    Brunn (Baden-Baden: Nomos Verlagsgesellschaft, 1996).

32. Eric Hobsbawm, *Nations and Nationalism since 1780* (Cambridge: Cambridge
    University Press, 1990), 185.

33. In his recent study of the 1992 Olympic Games, John Hargreaves offers a
    similar reading of the way multiple layers of identity—from the local to the
    national—can co-exist, and at times even reinforce one another, within the
    framework of a modern democratic nation-state. See John Hargreaves, *Freedom
    for Catalonia? Catalan Nationalism, Spanish Identity and the Barcelona
    Olympic Games* (Cambridge: Cambridge University Press, 2000).

CHAPTER 2

1. David Gilmour, *Cities of Spain* (Chicago: Ivan R. Dee, 1992), 192.
2. Antonio Gómez Rufo, *Madrid, bajos fondos* (Madrid: El Avapiés, 1987), 13.
3. For further information on the culture of repression during this early period
   of the Franco regime, see Michael Richards, *A Time of Silence: Civil War*

and the Culture of Repression in Franco's Spain, 1936–1945 (Cambridge: Cambridge University Press, 1998).

4. Ayuntamiento de Madrid, *Plan General de Ordenación de Madrid, 1985. Memoria de Participación* (Madrid: Ayuntamiento de Madrid, 1985), 61.

5. For further information on the urban and cultural history of Madrid from the turn of the century to the early 1930s, see Deborah Parsons, *A Cultural History of Madrid: Modernism and the Urban Spectacle* (Oxford: Berg, 2003).

6. Manuel Castells, *The City and the Grassroots: A Cross-Cultural Theory of Urban Social Movements* (Berkeley: University of California Press, 1983), 287.

7. No regional institutions existed under Franco, as the country was divided up into 50 fragmented local provinces. In addition, regional customs, languages, and education were all repressed. For an analysis of the Franco regime's educational policies with regard to the regional question, see Carolyn P. Boyd, *Historia Patria: Politics, History, and National Identity in Spain, 1875–1975* (Princeton: Princeton University Press, 1997), 232–301.

8. David Corkill, "Multiple National Identities, Immigration and Racism in Spain and Portugal," in *Nations and Identity in Contemporary Europe*, ed. Brian Jenkins and Spyros A Sofos (London: Routledge, 1996), 157.

9. Ibid., 158.

10. Mary Nash, "Towards a New Moral Order," in *Spanish History since 1808*, ed. José Alvarez Junco and Adrian Shubert (London: Arnold, 2000), 294.

11. Castells, *The City and the Grassroots*, 287.

12. See Deborah Parsons, "Fiesta Culture in Madrid Posters, 1934–1955," in *Constructing Identity in Contemporary Spain*, ed. Jo Labanyi (Oxford: Oxford University Press, 2002).

13. See Paloma Aguilar Fernandez, *Memoria y olvido de la guerra civil española* (Madrid: Alianza, 1996).

14. For a further discussion of the term "*castizo*," see Parsons, "Fiesta Culture in Madrid Posters, 1934–1955."

15. Michael Richards, "Collective Memory, the Nation-State and Post-Franco Society," in *Contemporary Spanish Cultural Studies*, ed. Barry Jordan and Rikki Morgan-Tamosunas (London: Arnold Press, 2000), 44.

16. Michael T. Newton and Peter J. Donaghy, *Institutions of Modern Spain: A Political and Economic Guide* (Cambridge: Cambridge University Press, 1997), 145.

17. Madrid's five mayors under the Franco regime included: Alberto Alcocer, José Moreno Torres, José Finat y Escrivá de Romaní, Carlos Arias Navarrro, and Miguel Angel Gracía Lomas.

18. Newton and Donaghy, *Institutions of Modern Spain: A Political and Economic Guide*, 145.

19. Bernard Bessière, "El Madrid de la democracia: comportamientos culturales y crisol de creación. Realidades y dudas," in *España frente al siglo XXI: cultura y literatura*, ed. Samuel Amell (Madrid: Cátedra, 1992), 54.

20. Municipal elections were held on April 19, 1979, 48 years after the last free municipal elections on April 12, 1931.

21. Ayuntamiento de Madrid, "Otra idea de Madrid," *Villa de Madrid*, 1983-II.

22. In addition to initially serving as the Concejal de Hacienda, Joaquín Leguina later became the first president of the new autonomous community of Madrid in 1983.

NOTES

23. For more biographical information on Enrique Tierno Galván, see Alex Masllorens, *La herencia y humana de Enrique Tierno Galván* (Barcelona: Tibidabo, 1986); Eduardo Chamorro, *Enrique Tierno: el alcalde* (Madrid: Cambio 16, 1986); Antonio Gómez Rufo, *Carta a un amigo sobre don Enrique Tierno Galván* (Madrid: Ediciones de Antonio Machado, 1986); Raúl Morodo, "Enrique Tierno: semblanza, aventura y compromiso político-intelectual," *Sistema*, no. 71–72 (1986); Mario Ruiz Sanz, *Enrique Tierno Galván: aproximación a su vida, obra y pensamiento* (Madrid: Universidad de Carlos III de Madrid: Dykinson, 1997); Antonio Rovira, *Enrique Tierno Galván: 1918–1986* (Madrid: Fundación Pablo Iglesias, 1987); Raúl Morodo, *Tierno Galván y otros precursores políticos* (Madrid: El País, 1987); César Alonso de los Ríos, *La verdad sobre Tierno Galván* (Madrid: Anaya & Muchnik, 1997). For the period up to 1978, also see the autobiography, Enrique Tierno Galván, *Cabos sueltos* (Madrid: Bruguera, 1981).
24. Angel de Río López, *Varas y bastones de la villa y corte* (Madrid: Temas de Hoy, 1994), 257.
25. Even while the mayor of Madrid, Tierno Galván regularly published articles and taught classes at the Universidad Autonoma de Madrid. See "Una vida a manos llenas," *Villa de Madrid*, January 21, 1986.
26. Some of Tierno Galván's diverse books included: *Los supuestos escotistas en la teoría política de Jean Bodin* (1951), *Diderot como pretexto* (1959), *Tradición y modernismo* (1962), *Ensayos sobre el cine* (1964), *Antología de escritores políticos del Siglo de Oro* (1965), *Introducción a la Sociología* (1967), *Baboeuf y la conspiración de los iguales* (1967), *Razón mecánica y razón dialéctica* (1969), *La rebelión juvenil y el problema en la Universidad* (1972), *Ensayos sobre la novela picaresca* (1975), *Qué es ser agnóstico* (1976), and *Galdós y el Episodio Nacional Montes de Oca* (1979). No complete bibliography of Tierno Galván's works exists at this time. However, for a more comprehensive listing of publications, see Chamorro, *Enrique Tierno: el alcalde*, 52–53; Gómez Rufo, *Carta a un amigo sobre don Enrique Tierno Galván*, 29–31; Ruiz Sanz, *Enrique Tierno Galván: aproximación a su vida, obra y pensamiento*, 288–304.
27. Jean Grugel and Tim Rees, *Franco's Spain* (London: Arnold, 1997), 71.
28. Tierno Galán was also made honorary president of the PSOE for a brief period of time in 1978 and was a representative in Congress until 1982.
29. After a late diagnosis, Tierno Galván underwent surgery for colon cancer in February 1985 and died less than a year later in January 1986, at 67 years old.
30. In the absence of official reform, local administrative authority in the capital was based on the previous *Ley de Bases de Régimen Local* and on Article 140 of the new Constitution: "The constitution guarantees the autonomy of the municipalities. They shall enjoy full legal status. Their government and administration are the responsibility of their respective town halls, made up of the mayors and councilors." Newton and Donaghy, *Institutions of Modern Spain*, 147.
31. Ayuntamiento de Madrid, "Otra idea de Madrid," 9.
32. Ibid.
33. Madrid was not the only uniprovincial Comunidad to be created under the new autonomous framework. Other uniprovincial Comunidades include Asturias, the Balearic Islands, Cantabria, La Rioja, and Murcia.

34. For a concise history of Madrid's process to become an autonomous community, see Pedro Fernández Vicente, *Madrid en Comunidad* (Madrid: Bitácora, 1989), 149–160.

35. See Castells, *The City and the*, 272–275.

36. Angel del Rio, "Diez años para cambiar realidades y enterrar utopias," *Alfoz*, no. 62–63 (1989): 79.

37. Bessière, "El Madrid de la democracia: comportamientos culturales y crisol de creación. Realidades y dudas," 59–60.

38. Ibid., 69.

39. Santos Juliá, "The Socialist Era, 1982–1996," in *Spanish History since 1808*, ed. José Alvarez Junco and Adrian Shubert (London: Arnold, 2000), 339.

40. For further analysis of the division between Tierno Galván and the PSOE, see Antonio García Santesmases, "Enrique Tierno: una luz en el tunel," *Leviatán*, no. 23–24 (1986); Masllorens, *La herencia y humana de Enrique Tierno Galván*, 111–116.

41. By the mid 1980s, the nation PSOE had clearly moved from a traditional socialist program to more of a pragmatic political platform. Focusing far less on the nationalization of industries and more on supporting the private sector of the economy, the PSOE pursued neo-liberal fiscal and monetary policies in order to promote economic development and widen its electoral appeal. The promise to create 800,000 new jobs also caused the party to break its promises to the country's trade unions. By the late 1980s, many of the PSOE's policies had become indistinguishable from the conservative neoliberal administrations in England or Germany.

42. Masllorens, *La herencia y humana de Enrique Tierno Galván*, 111–116.

43. See "El PSOE estudia una moción de critica contra Tierno por sus declaraciones a *El País*," *El País*, 11 March 1980.

44. Jesús Ceberio, "Tierno Galván: 'Vamos a dejar una ciudad limpia, culta y con una circulación libre'," *El País*, July 29, 1979.

45. Victoriano de Azúa, "Enrique Tierno: 'Donde había un castillo ahora una plaza, en la que nos reunimos todos para hablar'," *El País*, May 7, 1983.

46. In fact, when the PSOE eventually lost its absolute majority in the general elections of 1993, the party chose to form a governing pact with Catalan nationalists instead of with the far left.

47. See Julio Fernandez, "El alcalde reivindica independencia para el Ayuntamiento ante el próximo Govierno," *El País*, October 30, 1982.

48. Enrique Tierno Galván, "Un ajedrez con Enrique Tierno," *EPOCA*, 2 September 1985, 19. Also see "Tierno afirma que Felipe González tiene contradicciones profundas," *El País*, August 28, 1985.

49. See, for example, Tierno Galván, "Un ajedrez con Enrique Tierno," 20.

50. Comunidad de Madrid, *Comunidad de Madrid, 1983–1985: balance de gestión del primer gobierno regional madrileño en el ecuador de su mandato* (Madrid: Comunidad de Madrid, 1985), 9.

51. Ibid.

52. Ibid.

53. Ibid.

54. Comunidad de Madrid, *Comunidad de Madrid, 1983–1987* (Madrid: Comunidad de Madrid, 1987), 7.

55. See for example Joaquín Leguina, "El Socialismo y Humpty Dumpty," *El País*, December 14, 1985.

56. Cited in Masllorens, *La herencia y humana de Enrique Tierno Galván*, 131.
57. Editorial, "El homenaje de la calle," *El País*, January 22, 1986.
58. Ibid.

Chapter 3

1. The desire to remake the capital after the end of the dictatorship has already been identified in one of the most authoritative histories of Madrid. In the "Epilogue" to *Madrid, historia de una capital*, Santos Juliá, David Ringrose, and Cristina Segura briefly highlight the overwhelming need to "renovate [*recuperar*] the city" after the dictatorship. The reinstatement of Madrid's festivals, the rebirth of street life, and a renewed interest in the city's history and traditions were all part of a program to recuperate "the call signs [*las llamadas señas*] of identity" after the capital's extended association with Francoism. Santos Juliá, David Ringrose, and Cristina Segura, *Madrid, historia de una capital* (Madrid: Alianza Editorial, 2000), 572.
2. A good example of this kind of memory creation can be found in Carolyn Boyd's article on collective identity in the region of Asturias. Boyd's article describes how the memory of the Battle of Covadonga, fought in the eighth century, has been employed and contested, by both regionalists and nationalists, to claim a spectrum of collective identities throughout the twentieth century. See Carolyn P. Boyd, "The Second Battle of Covadonga: The Politics of Commemoration in Modern Spain," *History and Memory: Studies in Representation of the Past* 14, no. 1–2 (2002). For an excellent discussion of the uses and misuses of "memory" and "collective memory" in the context of cultural history, see Alon Confino, "Collective Memory and Cultural History: Problems of Method," *The American Historical Review* 102, no. 5 (1997).
3. José Luis Aranguren, "La vida como conducta y como función," *El País*, January 20, 1986. Cited in Elías Díaz, "Tierno Galván, entre el fraccionamiento y la totalidad," *Sistema*, no. 71–72 (1986): 19.
4. Jesús Ceberio, "Tierno Galván: 'Vamos a dejar una ciudad limpia, culta y con una circulación libre'," *El País*, July 29, 1979. For further information on Tierno Galván's conception of a Socialist utopia, see Enrique Tierno Galván, "Urbanismo y utopia," *Villa de Madrid*, July 1982; Sergio Vilar, "Tierno Galván y las utopias," *El País*, January 29, 1986.
5. For more on Tierno Galván's notion of a cultural revolution, see "Conferencias de Sanroma y Tierno sobre la Revolución Cultural," *El País*, April 29, 1980.
6. Antonio Gómez Rufo, *Carta a un amigo sobre don Enrique Tierno Galván* (Madrid: Ediciones de Antonio Machado, 1986), 32.
7. Victoriano de Azúa, "Enrique Tierno: 'Donde había un castillo ahora una plaza, en la que nos reunimos todos para hablar'," *El País*, May 7, 1983.
8. Tierno Galván's understanding of "culture" in this regard is similar to the E. Inman Fox's definition of the term: "the interpretation . . . of a way of thinking, feeling and behaving: an interpretation which is derived from the cultural products themselves—history, literature, art—which provide images and ideas for ordering behavior; or for defining ways of thinking and believing." E. Inman Fox, "Spain as Castile: Nationalism and National Identity," in *Modern Spanish Culture*, ed. David T. Gies (Cambridge: Cambridge University Press, 1999), 25.

9. de Azúa, "Enrique Tierno."

10. Ibid.

11. Ibid.

12. For a detailed discussion of Madrid's citizen movement in relation to different forms of democratic citizenship, see Pamela B. Radcliff, *Citizenship, Gender, and the Transition to Democracy* (New York: Palgrave Macmillan, forthcoming).

13. Enrique Tierno Galván, "El Primer Discurso del nuevo alcalde," *Villa de Madrid* 1979-II, 8.

14. Ibid.

15. In May 1983, a foreign journalist specifically highlighted Tierno Galván's unusually effective non confrontational style: "[He is] a man who has transformed non aggressiveness into a formidable political weapon." John Darnton, "The 'Old Professor' Rules Madrid Like an Old Pro," *The New York Times*, May 3, 1983.

16. Gómez Rufo, *Carta a un amigo sobre don Enrique Tierno Galván*, 130. For more on the creation of the 1978 Constitution, see Gregorio Peces-Barba Martínez, *La elaboración de la constitución de 1978* (Madrid: Centro Estudios Constitucionales, 1988).

17. de Azúa, "Enrique Tierno."

18. Ibid.

19. See Benedict Anderson, *Imagined Communities: Reflections on the Origins and Spread of Nationalism* (London: Verso, 1992).

20. David Brown, *Contemporary Nationalism: Civic, Ethnocultural, and Multicultural Politics* (London: Routledge, 2000), 126.

21. Brian Jenkins and Spyros A. Sofos, "Nation and Nationalism in Contemporary Europe: A Theoretical Perspective," in *Nations and Identity in Contemporary Europe* (London: Routledge, 1996), 14.

22. Brown, *Contemporary Nationalism*, 34.

23. Ibid., 126.

24. Jenkins and Sofos, "Nation and Nationalism in Contemporary Europe," 15.

25. For a further discussion about the predominance of ethnic nationalism over civic nationalism at the end of the twentieth century, see Chapter 6 in Eric Hobsbawm, *Nations and Nationalism since 1780* (Cambridge: Cambridge University Press, 1990); Jenkins and Sofos, "Nation and Nationalism in Contemporary Europe"; Brown, *Contemporary Nationalism*.

26. For a good example of how ethnic nationalism has been used to forge new collective identities in the Basque country, see Ludger Mees, "Between Votes and Bullets. Conflicting Ethnic Identities in the Basque Country," *Ethnic and Racial Studies* 24, no. 5 (2001).

27. Equipo Viajar and Ayuntamiento de Madrid, *Conocer Madrid* (Madrid: Ayuntamiento de Madrid, Oficina Municipal del Plan, 1982), 7.

28. Ibid., 111.

29. Ibid., 112.

30. Ibid., 7. This statement also echoed a common slogan from the period: "No one is an outsider in Madrid [*Nadie es forastero en Madrid*]."

31. Ramón Masats and Luis Carandell, *Madrid es más que Madrid* (Madrid: Comunidad de Madrid, Consejería de Cultura, 1984), 33.

32. Joaquín Leguina, "Madrid en la Autonomía," *Revista de Occidente*, no. extraordinario VII (1983): 14.

33. Comunidad de Madrid, *Consejería de Cultura y Deportes, 1983–1987* (Madrid: Comunidad de Madrid, 1987), 14.

34. Ibid.

35. Ibid.

36. Tierno Galván, "El Primer Discurso del nuevo alcalde." Also see Angel del Rio, "Diez años para cambiar realidades y enterrar utopias," *Alfoz*, no. 62–63 (1989): 76.

37. "'Ustedes también son vecinos de Madrid'," *Villa de Madrid*, July 1, 1985.

38. See Enrique Tierno Galván, "Convivir con los gitanos," *Villa de Madrid*, October 15, 1984.

39. *Villa de Madrid*, October 1982. Cited in "Nos queda su palabra," *Villa de Madrid*, January 21, 1986.

40. "Tierno Galván: 'El civismo aumenta'," *Villa de Madrid*, January 1, 1984.

41. "Tierno Galván recomienda a los jóvenes seguir 'el camino de la justicia y la paz'," *El País*, September 24, 1985.

42. Ayuntamiento de Madrid, *Plan Especial Villa de Madrid: cuatro años de gestión* (Madrid: Ayuntamiento de Madrid, 1986), 13.

43. Ibid.

44. Ibid.

45. Ayuntamiento de Madrid, *Plan General de Ordenación de Madrid, 1985. Memoria de Participación* (Madrid: Ayuntamiento de Madrid, 1985), 31.

46. Ibid.

47. Ayuntamiento de Madrid, *Madrid Avanza: 1983–1984, un año de gestión* (Madrid: Ayuntamiento de Madrid, Concejalía de Relaciones Institucionales y Comunicación, 1984), 7.

48. Carlos Otero, "Inversión sin precedentes," *Villa de Madrid*, January 1, 1982.

49. Ayuntamiento de Madrid, *Recuperar Madrid* (Madrid: Ayuntamiento de Madrid, Oficina Municipal del Plan, 1982), 85.

50. Ibid., 7.

51. The scale of the housing program was enormous. The *Plan General* called for the protection and rehabilitation of 7,000 housing units in the center and 25,000 units on the periphery, and the construction of 14,000 new units per year with a total of 112,000 after eight years. Ibid., 128.

52. Ibid., 128–133.

53. Ibid., 134–135.

54. Expansion of the public transportation system called for the creation of a network of suburban buses, with an "express" service, and the addition of 30 new kilometers and 42 new stations for Madrid's metro. Ibid., 137.

55. Ibid., 140.

56. The expansion of city services called for the construction of 111 daycare centers, 116 athletic centers, 43 healthcare clinics, 51 retirement centers, 47 cultural centers, and 11 urban parks. Ibid., 136–140.

57. Ibid., 139–140.

58. Ibid., 95.

59. Ayuntamiento de Madrid, *Madrid Proyecto Madrid: exposición* (Madrid: Ayuntamiento de Madrid, 1986), n. p.

60. Ibid.

61. For a list of projects, see ibid.

62. Ibid., n. p.

63. Ibid.

64. Ibid. Also, for example, investment in public works in the city of Madrid increased from \$29 million in 1979 to \$115 million in 1982. See Joaquín Leguina, "Duro Sevillano," *El País*, October 7, 1982.

65. Ayuntamiento de Madrid, *Programa de Actuación. Plan General de Ordenación de Madrid* (Madrid: Ayuntamiento de Madrid, 1985), 57. In fact, the size of Madrid's metropolitan area remained exactly the same as under the 1963 plan. See Ayuntamiento de Madrid, *Plan General de Ordenación de Madrid, 1985. Memoria de Participación*, 120.

66. Ayuntamiento de Madrid, *Programa de Actuación. Plan General de Ordenación de Madrid*, 57.

67. Ibid.

68. Ibid.

69. Ibid., 17.

70. Ibid., 18.

71. See Ayuntamiento de Madrid, *Madrid Proyecto Madrid: exposición*, n. p.

72. Ayuntamiento de Madrid, *Madrid Restaura: 1979–1981, exposición de mayo 1981* (Madrid: Ayuntamiento de Madrid, Delegación de Cultura, 1981), n. p.

73. Ibid.

74. Ibid.

75. Scholars have recently argued that the construction and restoration of monuments tended to promote local or regional affiliations, and not a cohesive national identity, during the Restoration period. It appears as though what weakened nationalism in the earlier period was useful for promoting regional identity in the post-Francoist period. See Boyd, "The Second Battle of Covadonga"; José Álvarez Junco, *Mater Dolorosa: la idea de España en el siglo XIX* (Madrid: Taurus, 2001), 545–565.

76. Ayuntamiento de Madrid, *Plan Especial Villa de Madrid: cuatro años de gestión*, 18. In addition, the total number of buildings undergoing conservation or restoration quadrupled from 597, in 1982, to 2,415, in 1984. See Ayuntamiento de Madrid, *Plan Especial Villa de Madrid*, 26.

77. Some other examples of the buildings restored included Banco Exterior de España (at Santa Catalina, 6), Residencia de Estudiantes (at Don Ramón de la Cruz, 4), Hemeroteca Nacional (Magdalena 10), and dozens of housing units (*viviendas*). For a comprehensive list of the restoration projects, see Ayuntamiento de Madrid, *Plan Especial Villa de Madrid*.

78. Ayuntamiento de Madrid, *Madrid Avanza: 1983–1987* (Madrid: Ayuntamiento de Madrid, 1987), 41.

79. Comunidad de Madrid, *Comunidad de Madrid, 1983–1985: balance de gestión del primer gobierno regional madrileño en el ecuador de su mandato* (Madrid: Comunidad de Madrid, 1985), 64.

80. Ibid.

81. Ibid.

82. Comunidad de Madrid, *Veintinueve propuestas de mejoras urbanas en la Comunidad de Madrid* (Madrid: Comunidad de Madrid, 1986), 7.

83. See ibid.

84. Ayuntamiento de Madrid, "Otra idea de Madrid," *Villa de Madrid* 1983-II, 10.

85. Otero, "Inversión sin precedentes."
86. The derogatory term "*banusadas*" came from the real estate developer, José Banús.
87. Ayuntamiento de Madrid, *Plan General de Ordenación de Madrid, 1985*, 74.
88. Ayuntamiento de Madrid, "Circulación y transportes: 'STOP' al caos," *Villa de Madrid*, no. 76 (1983-II): 89.
89. Ibid.
90. In 1960, the 2,028,091 residents of Madrid produced 252,427 metric tons of waste. In 1980, the city's 3,368,466 inhabitants created 810,147 metric tons of waste. The 20 year period saw a 320 percent increase in waste with only a corresponding 66 percent increase in population. Ayuntamiento de Madrid, *Plan de limpieza de la ciudad de Madrid* (Madrid: Ayuntamiento de Madrid, Área de Urbanismo e Infraestructuras, 1984), 129.
91. In all, more than 3,000 new solid waste containers and 5,000 public wastepaper cans were installed in Madrid. See Ayuntamiento de Madrid, "Madrid se lava la cara," *Villa de Madrid*, no. 76 (1983-II): 130.
92. Ibid.
93. Ibid.
94. Ibid.
95. Ayuntamiento de Madrid, *Plan de limpieza de la ciudad de Madrid*, 43–44.
96. Ibid., 113.
97. Ayuntamiento de Madrid, "Madrid se lava la cara," 130.
98. Ibid., 129.
99. "Iniciativas más drásticas para frenar la contaminación," *Villa de Madrid*, January 1, 1986.
100. Otero, "Inversión sin precedentes."
101. "Madrid, en obras," *Villa de Madrid*, September 18, 1984.
102. In conjunction with the PSI, the *Plan de Acción Sur* (PAS) also helped decrease the inequities of infrastructure and facilities between the northern and southern parts of the capital by giving pavement, lighting, and sewer systems to districts in the south. Ayuntamiento de Madrid, "Madrid se lava la cara," 122.
103. Ayuntamiento de Madrid, *Madrid Avanza: 1983–1984, un año de gestión*, 104–105.
104. Antonio Nieva, "Madrid recupera su río," *Villa de Madrid*, June 1, 1982.
105. Ayuntamiento de Madrid, "Madrid se lava la cara," 125.
106. Ibid., 126.
107. Javier Echenagusia, "Juan Barranco," *Alfoz*, no. 26 (1986): 17.
108. Ayuntamiento de Madrid, "Madrid se lava la cara," 128.
109. Enrique Tierno Galván, "Política de parques y jardines: no sólo estética," *Villa de Madrid*, February 1, 1983.
110. Ayuntamiento de Madrid, "Madrid se lava la cara," 128.
111. "Bando para una fiesta," *Villa de Madrid*, January 1, 1985. Tierno Galván even dedicated a *Bando* to tree planting in December 1984. See Enrique Tierno Galván, *Bandos del Alcalde* (Madrid: Editorial Tecnos, 1986), 105–110.
112. David Gilmour, *Cities of Spain* (Chicago: Ivan R. Dee, 1992), 194.
113. Tierno Galván, "Política de parques y jardines."

114. Enrique Tierno Galván, *Charlas de radio pronunciadas por el alcalde de Madrid* (Madrid: Ayuntamiento de Madrid, 1981), 22.
115. Ibid., 23.
116. Ayuntamiento de Madrid, "La descentralización: el nuevo papel de las juntas y de los vecinos," *Villa de Madrid*, no. 76 (1983-II): 133.
117. Ibid.
118. Ayuntamiento de Madrid, *Madrid Avanza: 1983–1987*, 23.
119. Ibid.
120. Comunidad de Madrid, *Comunidad de Madrid, 1983–1985*, 16.
121. Ibid.
122. Ayuntamiento de Madrid, "La cultura: cuatro años fecundos," *Villa de Madrid*, no. 76 (1983-II): 30.
123. Many Tierno Galván's early "chats" with the public were transcribed. See Tierno Galván, *Charlas de radio pronunciadas por el alcalde de Madrid*.
124. The *Bandos* were such a ubiquitous sight, in fact, that a political cartoon from the period likened their appearance on every available wall to out-of-control graffiti. Ayuntamiento de Madrid, *Bandos del Alcalde*, 23.
125. Ibid.
126. Ibid., 27–29.
127. Ibid., 31.
128. Ibid.
129. The four *Bandos* were from January 26, 1981; February 3, 1982; June 11, 1982; and November 16, 1982. Ibid., 41–44, 65–74.
130. For a further discussion of Tierno Galván's *Bandos*, see Alex Masllorens, *La herencia y humana de Enrique Tierno Galván* (Barcelona: Tibidabo, 1986), 35–40; Eduardo Chamorro, *Enrique Tierno: el alcalde* (Madrid: Cambio 16, 1986).
131. Enrique Tierno Galván, "Programa municipal para una enseñanza viva," *Villa de Madrid*, September 15, 1985.
132. Ibid.
133. Ibid.
134. Tierno Galván, *Charlas de radio pronunciadas por el alcalde de Madrid*, 23.
135. Ayuntamiento de Madrid, *Madrid Avanza: 1983–1984, un año de gestión*, 162.
136. Ibid.
137. Ibid.
138. Ibid.
139. Tierno Galván, "Programa municipal para una enseñanza viva."
140. Comunidad de Madrid, *Primer certamen escolar, "Conoce tu ciudad"* (Madrid: Comunidad de Madrid, 1983), 5.
141. Ibid.
142. See ibid; Comunidad de Madrid, *Segundo certamen escolar, "Conoce tu ciudad"* (Madrid: Comunidad de Madrid, 1985); Comunidad de Madrid, *Tercer certamen escolar, "Conoce tu ciudad"* (Madrid: Comunidad de Madrid, 1985).
143. Comunidad de Madrid, *Tercer certamen escolar*, 15.
144. Ibid., 5.
145. The regional government, in particular, sponsored numerous studies on everything from demographics and cultural demand, to how many pigs were being raised. See for example Comunidad de Madrid, *Informe sobre*

demanda latente de cultura y deporte (Madrid: Comunidad de Madrid, 1985). Also see the *Comunidad*'s *Anuario Estadístico* (Madrid: Comunidad de Madrid, 1983–1992).

146. Masats and Carandell, *Madrid es más que Madrid.* For another example, see Juan Luna Wennberg, *Nuestro Madrid* (Madrid: Lunwerg, 1986).

147. Masats and Carandell, *Madrid es más que Madrid,* 13.

148. Ibid., 11.

149. Ibid., 13.

150. Ibid., 14.

151. Ibid.

152. See Comunidad de Madrid, *Pensar en Madrid* (Madrid: Comunidad de Madrid, 1984).

153. See ibid.

154. Ayuntamiento de Madrid, *Madrid, único y múltiple, 21 crónicas periodísticas* (Madrid: Ayuntamiento de Madrid, 1987), 7.

155. See ibid.

156. Equipo Viajar and Ayuntamiento de Madrid, *Madrid* (Madrid: Editorial Tania, 1983), 4.

157. Ibid., 14–21.

158. Equipo Viajar and Ayuntamiento de Madrid, *Conocer Madrid.*

159. Fernando Jiménez de Gregorio, *Madrid y su Comunidad* (Madrid: El Avapiés, 1986), 255–279.

160. Ibid., 13.

161. Ibid., 278.

162. See Comunidad de Madrid, *Madrid y los Borbones en el siglo XVIII: la construcción de una ciudad y su territorio* (Madrid: Comunidad de Madrid, 1984); Fernando Aznar, *Madrid: una historia en comunidad* (Madrid: Comunidad de Madrid, 1987); Comunidad de Madrid, *Madrid en la sociedad del siglo XIX* (Madrid: Comunidad de Madrid, 1986).

163. See Comunidad de Madrid, *Consejería de Cultura y Deportes, 1983–1987,* 85.

164. Cayetano Rosell, *Crónica de la provincia de Madrid: Madrid 1865* (Madrid: Comunidad de Madrid, 1983); Pascual Madoz, *Madrid, Audiencia, Provincia, Intendencia, Vicaría, Partido y Villa (1848)* (Madrid: Comunidad de Madrid, 1984).

165. Equipo Viajar and Ayuntamiento de Madrid, *Conocer Madrid,* 109.

166. Michael T. Newton and Peter J. Donaghy, *Institutions of Modern Spain: A Political and Economic Guide* (Cambridge: Cambridge University Press, 1997), 145. According to Newton, because of the administrative neglect under the Franco regime, "the governments elected after 1977 were confronted not only with the need to democratize government at all levels but also with the necessity of over hauling an anachronistic system of local administration." Newton and Donaghy, *Institutions of Modern Spain,* 145.

167. Ayuntamiento de Madrid, *Madrid Avanza: 1983–1984, un año de gestión,* 11.

168. Ayuntamiento de Madrid, "Reforma administrativa: La burocracia pierde la guerra," *Villa de Madrid,* no. 76 (1983-II): 107.

169. Ibid., 107–108.

170. Ayuntamiento de Madrid, *Madrid Avanza: 1983–1984, un año de gestión,* 9.

171. Enrique Tierno Galván, "La carta del alcade," *Villa de Madrid*, February 1, 1982.

172. Ayuntamiento de Madrid, *Madrid Avanza: 1983–1984, un año de gestión*, 11–17.

173. Ibid., 15.

174. Ayuntamiento de Madrid, "Reforma administrativa," 108.

175. Ayuntamiento de Madrid, *Madrid Avanza: 1983–1984, un año de gestión*, 14–17.

176. Ayuntamiento de Madrid, *Madrid Avanza: 1983–1987*, 29.

177. Ayuntamiento de Madrid, *Madrid Avanza: 1983–1984, un año de gestión*, 8.

178. Ayuntamiento de Madrid, "Reforma administrativa," 108.

179. Ayuntamiento de Madrid, *Madrid Avanza: 1983–1984, un año de gestión*, 25.

180. Ibid., 26–27.

181. Tierno Galván, *Charlas de radio pronunciadas por el alcalde de Madrid*, 130.

182. Ibid., 129–130.

183. Ibid., 129.

184. Ibid.

185. Ayuntamiento de Madrid, "La cultura," 11.

186. Tierno Galván, *Charlas de radio pronunciadas por el alcalde de Madrid*, 130. It should be noted, however, that the local administration also created some new street names that appear to contradict this intention of recovering only traditional names. For example, such new names included Federico García Lorca, Antonio Machado, Pablo Iglesias, John Lennon, and Padre Llanos (the inventor of Esperanto).

187. Ayuntamiento de Madrid, "Seguridad y policía: se acabó el miedo," *Villa de Madrid*, no. 76 (1983-II): 111.

188. Ibid., 112.

189. Ibid., 111.

190. Ibid. Other material improvements to the police force included the addition of new vehicles and radios. More than 200 new vehicles were acquired in the first six months of the administration alone. Between 1983 and 1986 an additional 147 new cars and 256 motorcycles were acquired. Other improvements included the creation of a K-9 unit and the addition of off-road motorcycles for patrolling parks and open spaces. See Ayuntamiento de Madrid, "Seguridad y policía"; Ayuntamiento de Madrid, *Madrid Avanza: 1983–1984, un año de gestión*, 62–63; Ayuntamiento de Madrid, *Madrid Avanza: 1983–1987*, 115.

191. Ayuntamiento de Madrid, "Seguridad y policía: se acabó el miedo," 113.

192. Ibid., 115.

193. Ayuntamiento de Madrid, *Madrid Avanza: 1983–1984, un año de gestión*, 63.

194. Newton and Donaghy, *Institutions of Modern Spain*, 162.

195. Tierno Galván, "El Primer Discurso del nuevo alcalde," 7.

196. Ayuntamiento de Madrid, "La cultura," 29.

197. Enrique Tierno Galván, "La universalidad del vecino," *Ayuntamientos Democráticos*, June 1982, 14.

198. Tierno Galván, "La carta del alcade."

199. Ayuntamiento de Madrid, *Madrid Avanza: 1983–1987*, 16.

200. Ayuntamiento de Madrid, "La cultura," 30.

201. See for example José María Álvarez del Manzano, "Hemos hecho una oposición más constructiva que negativa," *Villa de Madrid*, January 1, 1983; José María Álvarez del Manzano, "Presentaremos proyectos alternativos para 1984," *Villa de Madrid*, January 15, 1984; José María Álvarez del Manzano, "No se ha mejorado en nada," *Villa de Madrid*, January 18, 1984; José María Álvarez del Manzano, "Falta rigor," *Villa de Madrid*, June 1/15 1985; José María Álvarez del Manzano, "La alternativa presupuestaria de la oposición," *Villa de Madrid*, January 1, 1986.

202. Tierno Galván, "La carta del alcade."

203. "Nota de la dirección," *Villa de Madrid*, January 1, 1986.

204. Enrique Tierno Galván, "Nueva visión del carnaval," *Villa de Madrid*, February 15, 1985.

205. Enrique Tierno Galván, "De la pasividad a la convivencia activa," *Villa de Madrid*, March 15, 1985.

206. Ibid.

207. Ayuntamiento de Madrid, *Participación Ciudadana: II Jornadas, del 3 al 15 diciembre 1982* (Madrid: Ayuntamiento de Madrid, Delegación de Relaciones Sociales y Vecinales, 1983), 14.

208. Ayuntamiento de Madrid, "La descentralización," 131.

209. Ibid.

210. Ayuntamiento de Madrid, *Participación Ciudadana*, 7.

211. Ayuntamiento de Madrid, *Madrid Avanza: 1983–1987*, 166.

212. Ayuntamiento de Madrid, *Participación Ciudadana*, 7.

213. Ibid.

214. Ayuntamiento de Madrid, "La descentralización," 132.

215. Ayuntamiento de Madrid, *Madrid Avanza: 1983–1987*, 166.

216. Ibid., 166–167.

217. Tierno Galván, "De la pasividad a la convivencia activa."

218. Ayuntamiento de Madrid, *Madrid Avanza: 1983–1987*, 165.

219. Ayuntamiento de Madrid, *Participación Ciudadana*, 11.

220. Ibid.

221. Ayuntamiento de Madrid, "La descentralización," 132.

222. See Ayuntamiento de Madrid, *Participación Ciudadana*.

223. Ayuntamiento de Madrid, *Participación ciudadana: I Jornadas, 17, 18, y 19 de enero 1986* (Madrid: Ayuntamiento de Madrid, Junta Municipal de Centro, 1986).

224. Enrique Tierno Galván, "Tres años de gestión: los Ayuntamientos democráticos han cumplido con su deber," *CEUMT*, no. 50 (1982): 66.

225. Ayuntamiento de Madrid, *Recuperar Madrid*, 169.

226. Ayuntamiento de Madrid, *Plan General de Ordenación de Madrid, 1985. Memoria General* (Madrid: Ayuntamiento de Madrid, 1985), 18.

227. "Hacia una ciudad distinta," *Villa de Madrid*, March 15, 1982.

228. Ayuntamiento de Madrid, *Plan General de Ordenación de Madrid, 1985*, 24.

229. Ayuntamiento de Madrid, *Recuperar Madrid*, 196–197.

230. Ibid.

231. Ibid., 199.

232. Ayuntamiento de Madrid, *Plan General de Ordenación de Madrid, 1985. Memoria General*, 17–21.
233. Ibid., 18.
234. Ibid., 17.
235. Ibid., 18.
236. Ayuntamiento de Madrid, *Recuperar Madrid*, 199.
237. Ayuntamiento de Madrid, *Plan General de Ordenación de Madrid, 1985. Memoria de Participación*, 26–27.
238. Ayuntamiento de Madrid, *Plan General de Ordenación de Madrid, 1985. Memoria General.*
239. Ibid., 27.
240. Ayuntamiento de Madrid, *Recuperar Madrid*, 198.
241. Ayuntamiento de Madrid, *Plan General de Ordenación de Madrid, 1985. Memoria General*, 17.
242. Ibid.
243. Ibid., 9.
244. Ibid.
245. Ayuntamiento de Madrid, *Recuperar Madrid*, 199.
246. For an exact breakdown of the suggestions by type, district, and organization, see Ayuntamiento de Madrid, *Plan General de Ordenación de Madrid, 1985. Memoria General*, 39–43. Also, according to a survey carried out in June and July of 1982, to gauge the effect of the information campaign, 66 percent of the population knew about the Preview of the *Plan General* and 75 percent knew that the Ayuntamiento wanted to "revitalize Madrid." Ayuntamiento de Madrid, *Plan General de Ordenación de Madrid, 1985. Memoria General*, 16.
247. Ibid., 52.
248. For a detailed summary of all claims filed, see ibid., 57–74.
249. For a complete list of suggestions incorporated into the *Plan General*, see ibid., 44–46.
250. Ibid., 9.
251. Tierno Galván, "La universalidad del vecino," 12.
252. Tierno Galván, "El Primer Discurso del nuevo alcalde," 7.
253. Ibid., 8.
254. "Siete años de transformaciones en la ciudad," *Villa de Madrid*, January 21, 1986.
255. The four *Bandos* related to traffic and transportation were posted on: September 8, 1980, April 22, 1981, November 16, 1982, and December 5, 1983. Tierno Galván, *Bandos del Alcalde*, 37–40, 53–56, 74–82, and 95–98.
256. "La 'bici,' protagonista," *Villa de Madrid*, November 1, 1983.
257. Gerardo Mediavilla, "La 'bici' dueña de Madrid," *Villa de Madrid*, November 1, 1983.
258. Ayuntamiento de Madrid, "La cultura," 24.
259. Tierno Galván, "Tres años de gestión," 66.
260. Fundación Villa y Corte, *Madrid, Objetivo Cultural: actas de la semana de estudios sobre el presente y el futuro de la cultura madrileña celebrada durante los días 6 al 11 de febrero de 1984* (Madrid: Caja de Ahorros y Monte de Piedad de Madrid, 1985), 1.

261. Ibid., 409.
262. Ibid.

Chapter 4

1. For a discussion of the myths and realities of Spain's democratic hangover, commonly known as the "*desencanto*," see Teresa M. Vilarós, "Los monos del desencanto español," *MLN* 109 (1994).

2. While the concepts of civic and ethnic nationalism make useful analytical categories, they do not reflect an objective social reality; nor do they perfectly describe particular nationalisms/regionalism. See Anthony D. Smith, *Nationalism and Modernism* (London: Routledge, 1998), 125–127; Bernard Yack, "The Myth of the Civic Nation," *Critical Review* 10, no. 2 (1996); Nicholas Xenos, "Civic Nationalism: Oxymoron?," *Critical Review* 10, no. 2 (1996).

3. Brian Jenkins and Spyros A. Sofos, "Nation and Nationalism in Contemporary Europe: A Theoretical Perspective," in *Nations and Identity in Contemporary Europe* (London: Routledge, 1996), 19.

4. Fernando López Agudin, "Enrique Tierno Galván: 'No tenemos una cultura para el pueblo ni hemos sabido tampoco asimilar una cultura del pueblo'," *Triunfo*, May 5, 1979, 29. Even as far back as in 1978, Tierno Galván had described how he wished to increase participation and revive Madrid's culture. See Enrique Tierno Galván, "Tierno Galván: 'Si yo fuera alcalde . . .'" *Triunfo*, February 18, 1978.

5. Ayuntamiento de Madrid, *Madrid Avanza: 1983–1984, un año de gestión* (Madrid: Ayuntamiento de Madrid, Concejalía de Relaciones Institucionales y Comunicación, 1984), 9.

6. Ibid., 142.

7. "El Gobierno municipal opina," *Villa de Madrid*, June 1/15, 1985.

8. Ayuntamiento de Madrid, *Madrid Avanza: 1983–1984*, 141.

9. Ayuntamiento de Madrid, *Madrid Avanza: 1983–1987* (Madrid: Ayuntamiento de Madrid, 1987), 80.

10. Enrique Tierno Galván, "Festejos populares," *Villa de Madrid*, May 1, 1982.

11. See Pedro Montoliú, "La construcción de un gran centro cultural Islámico junto a la M-30 comienza el lunes," *El País*, March 21, 1987.

12. Ayuntamiento de Madrid, *La experimentación en el arte: exposición, octubre 1983* (Madrid: Ayuntamiento de Madrid, Consejalía de Cultura, 1983), n. p.

13. Ibid.

14. Ignacio Julia, "Rock para el pueblo, votos para el partido," *Primera línea de la Actualidad*, August 1985, 67.

15. Ayuntamiento de Madrid, *Adquisiciones 1979–1983: Museo Municipal, exposición abril–junio 1983* (Madrid: Ayuntamiento de Madrid, Delegación de Cultura del Ayuntamiento, 1983), XIII.

16. Ibid.

17. Ayuntamiento de Madrid, *Madrid Restaura: 1979–1981, exposición de mayo 1981* (Madrid: Ayuntamiento de Madrid, Delegación de Cultura, 1981), n. p.

18. Ángeles García, "Madrid ha iniciado la recuperación de sus fiestas y concentra una oferta cultural de alto nivel," *El País*, April 28, 1983.

19. Ayuntamiento de Madrid, *Adquisiciones 1979–1983*, XIII–XIV.
20. Ayuntamiento de Madrid, *Madrid Restaura: 1979–1981*, n. p.
21. Ayuntamiento de Madrid, "La cultura: cuatro años fecundos," *Villa de Madrid* 1983-II.
22. Ayuntamiento de Madrid, *Madrid Avanza: 1983–1984*, 156.
23. Ayuntamiento de Madrid, *Madrid Avanza: 1983–1987*, 81–83.
24. Ibid., 82.
25. The situation was similarly desperate in the rest of Spain. In 1982, the country had 1,436 public libraries with just eight books for every 100 habitants, a lower figure than that of Morocco. John Hooper, *The New Spaniards* (London: Penguin, 1995), 340.
26. Ayuntamiento de Madrid, "La cultura: cuatro años fecundos."
27. Ibid.
28. Ibid.
29. Ibid.
30. Ibid.
31. Ayuntamiento de Madrid, *Madrid Avanza: 1983–1984*, 154.
32. López Agudin, "Enrique Tierno Galván: 'No tenemos una cultura para el pueblo ni hemos sabido tampoco asimilar una cultura del pueblo'," 30.
33. Ibid.
34. Ayuntamiento de Madrid, *Madrid Avanza: 1983–1984*, 158.
35. Working with the Concejalía de Cultura, Eduardo Huertas and Ramón Herrero were largely responsible for the drive to open new cultural centers across the capital. See Ibid.
36. Ibid., 157.
37. Anabel González, "'Madrid está a la vanguardia de la cultura'," *Villa de Madrid*, November 15, 1984.
38. Comunidad de Madrid, *Comunidad de Madrid, 1983–1987* (Madrid: Comunidad de Madrid, 1987), 70.
39. Comunidad de Madrid, *Comunidad de Madrid, 1983–1985: balance de gestión del primer gobierno regional madrileño en el ecuador de su mandato* (Madrid: Comunidad de Madrid, 1985), 64. Also see Comunidad de Madrid, *Comunidad de Madrid, 1983–1987*, 70.
40. Comunidad de Madrid, *Comunidad de Madrid, 1983–1987*, 71.
41. Comunidad de Madrid, *Comunidad de Madrid, 1983–1985*, 64.
42. Comunidad de Madrid, *Consejería de Cultura y Deportes, 1983–1987* (Madrid: Comunidad de Madrid, 1987), 27. To further promote participation and patronage, a new *Biblio-bus* program was even started. This program was designed to bring news and books to the smaller and more isolated towns of the Comunidad. An important step toward equal access to cultural resources was made with the introduction of five new *Biblio-buses* in 1985, and the number was expanded to 13 in 1986. Altogether, the network of *Biblio-buses* came to circulate more than 100,000 volumes and visited 160 different municipalities on over 38 routes. See Comunidad de Madrid, *Consejería de Cultura y Deportes, 1983–1987*, 27.
43. Comunidad de Madrid, *Consejería de Cultura y Deportes, 1983–1987*, 27.
44. Ibid.
45. Ayuntamiento de Madrid, *Madrid Avanza: 1983–1984*, 150–153.
46. Ayuntamiento de Madrid, "La cultura: cuatro años fecundos."
47. Comunidad de Madrid, *Consejería de Cultura y Deportes, 1983–1987*, 53.

48. Comunidad de Madrid, *Comunidad de Madrid, 1983–1987*, 71.

49. Comunidad de Madrid *Consejería de Cultura y Deportes, 1983–1987*, 53–55. For a complete list of expositions presented between 1983 and 1987, see ibid., 53–55.

50. For additional information on the development of the region's exhibit halls and expositions, see Alberto Mariñas, "Del cero al infinito," *Lápiz*, Summer 1991.

51. Ayuntamiento de Madrid, "La cultura: cuatro años fecundos."

52. Ibid.

53. Ibid.

54. Ayuntamiento de Madrid, *Madrid Avanza: 1983–1987*, 85.

55. Ibid., 86.

56. Ayuntamiento de Madrid, "Volcados en la cultura," *Villa de Madrid* 1982-I.

57. Ibid., 3.

58. For example, for the first time in the capital's history, the *Ayuntaminto* commissioned a survey in February 1981 to analyze and study Madrid's youth. See Ayuntamiento de Madrid, "El Ayuntamiento con los jóvenes," *Villa de Madrid* 1982-I.

59. José de la Paz, "Cambios demográficos recientes en la capital, el area metropolitana y la provincia," *Alfoz*, no. 7–8 (1984): 29. It was precisely in 1964–1965 that the most babies were born in Spain. Of course, in 1985, those individuals turned 20 years old. By 1988, there were 9.7 million young people between the ages of 15 and 29 in Spain, more than in any time in the country's history. See José Luis Zárraga, *Informe juventud en España: 1988* (Madrid: Instituto de la Juventud, 1989).

60. José Miguel Santos Preciado, "La población," in *Madrid, presente y futuro*, ed. José Estébañez Álvarez (Madrid: Editorial Akal, 1990), 65.

61. Enrique Tierno Galván, "1983, un año decisivo," *Villa de Madrid*, January 1, 1983.

62. Ayuntamiento de Madrid, *Madrid Avanza: 1983–1984*, 175.

63. For further information on Madrid's youth, see Amando de Miguel, "La juventud Madrileña de los años 80: la última invasión de los bárbaros," in *Madrid, años ochenta*, ed. Rafael Sierra (Madrid: Ayuntamiento de Madrid, 1989). For additional information about Spanish youth during this period, see Enrique Gil Calvo and Elena Menéndez Vergara, *Ocio y practicas culturales de los jóvenes* (Madrid: Ministerio de Cultura, Instituto de la Juventud, 1985); José Luis Zárraga, *Informe juventud en España: la inserción de los jóvenes en la sociedad* (Madrid: Instituto de la Juventud, 1985). Rafael Prieto Lacaci, *La participación social y política de los jóvenes* (Madrid: Instituto de la Juventud, 1985); Pedro González Blasco, *Jóvenes españoles 89* (Madrid: Fundación Santa María, 1989); Manuel Martín Serrano, *Historia de los cambios de mentalidad de los jóvenes entre 1960–1990* (Madrid: Instituto de la Juventud, 1994); Fundación Santa María, *Juventud española, 1984* (Madrid: Ediciones SM, 1985); and Zárraga, *Informe juventud en España: 1988*.

64. "Protagonistas, los jóvenes," *Villa de Madrid*, January 15, 1985.

65. Ayuntamiento de Madrid, *Madrid Avanza: 1983–1987*, 102. Also see "Pintura joven," *Villa de Madrid*, June 15, 1984.

66. Ayuntamiento de Madrid, *Madrid Avanza: 1983–1987*, 102.

67. Ayuntamiento de Madrid, "La cultura: cuatro años fecundos."
68. Ayuntamiento de Madrid, *Madrid Avanza: 1983–1984*, 173.
69. Ibid., 165.
70. Ibid., 166.
71. Ibid., 167.
72. Ibid.
73. Ayuntamiento de Madrid, "La fiesta somos nosotros," *Villa de Madrid* 1982-I, 18.
74. Enrique Moral, "Madrid, cita obligatoria," *Villa de Madrid*, January 1, 1984.
75. Ayuntamiento de Madrid, *Programa de San Isidro, 1985* (Madrid. Ayuntamiento de Madrid, 1985), n. p.
76. Tierno Galván, "Festejos populares."
77. Alaska, "La fiesta debe continuar," *Primera Linea de la Actualidad*, February 1986, 7.
78. Ibid.
79. Tierno Galván, "Festejos populares."
80. Ibid.
81. Ibid.
82. Ayuntamiento de Madrid, "Volcados en la cultura," 3.
83. Tierno Galván, "Festejos populares."
84. Ayuntamiento de Madrid, "La cultura: cuatro años fecundos."
85. Ayuntamiento de Madrid, "La fiesta somos nosotros," 18.
86. Ayuntamiento de Madrid, *Madrid Avanza: 1983–1984*, 146.
87. Ayuntamiento de Madrid, "La cultura: cuatro años fecundos."
88. Ibid.
89. Ayuntamiento de Madrid, *Madrid Avanza: 1983–1984*, 145.
90. Ibid.
91. Enrique Tierno Galván, *Charlas de radio pronunciadas por el alcalde de Madrid* (Madrid: Ayuntamiento de Madrid, 1981), 32.
92. Ibid.
93. "El Gobierno municipal opina."
94. Ayuntamiento de Madrid, "El Madrid total," *Villa de Madrid*, May 15, 1982.
95. Ayuntamiento de Madrid, *Madrid Avanza: 1983–1987*, 92.
96. Comunidad de Madrid, *Consejería de Cultura y Deportes, 1983–1987*, 75.
97. Comunidad de Madrid, *Festival de Otoño en Madrid: 1984–1988* (Barcelona: Iberia, 1988), n. p.
98. Comunidad de Madrid, *Consejería de Cultura y Deportes, 1983–1987*, 75–77.
99. The following year, 1985, 37 acts were held in the city and 58 in the rest of the region. Comunidad de Madrid, *Comunidad de Madrid, 1983–1987*, 74. For a comprehensive list of the events between 1984 and 1988, see Comunidad de Madrid, *Festival de Otoño en Madrid: 1984–1988*.
100. Comunidad de Madrid, *Comunidad de Madrid, 1983–1985*, 61.
101. Ricardo Martín, "2 de mayo, fiesta autonómica," *Villa de Madrid*, May 1, 1984.
102. Ibid.
103. See Deborah Parsons, "Fiesta Culture in Madrid Posters, 1934–1955," in *Constructing Identity in Contemporary Spain*, ed. Jo Labanyi (Oxford: Oxford University Press, 2002).

104. Ayuntamiento de Madrid, "La cultura: cuatro años fecundos."

105. Ayuntamiento de Madrid, "La fiesta somos nosotros," 18.

106. Ibid.

107. Ayuntamiento de Madrid, "La cultura: cuatro años fecundos."

108. Raul Herrero, "Nueve días intensos y variados," *Villa de Madrid*, May 1, 1982.

109. Ayuntamiento de Madrid, *Madrid y el Cine: Fiesta de San Isidro 1984* (Madrid: Ayuntamiento de Madrid, Filmoteca Española, 1984). Also see "Cine en San Isidro," *Villa de Madrid*, May 1, 1984.

110. Julio Pérez Perucha, "A la busqueda de un cine madrileñista," in *Madrid y el cine: Fiestas de San Isidro 1984*, ed. Ayuntamiento de Madrid (Madrid: Ayuntamiento de Madrid, Filmoteca Española, 1984), 5.

111. Ibid.

112. Ibid., 7. For a complete list of the films presented at *San Isidro* 1984, see Ayuntamiento de Madrid, *Madrid y el Cine: Fiesta de San Isidro 1984.*

113. Juan Pablo Fusi, "La cultura de la transición," *Revista de Occidente* 122–123 (1991): 63.

Chapter 5

1. Parts of this chapter appeared in an earlier version titled "Just a Teardrop in the Rain? The *movida madrileña* and Democratic Identity Formation in the Capital, 1979–1986." *Bulletin of Spanish Studies* 86, no. 3 (2009): 345–369.

2. The films of Pedro Almodóvar have been easily accessible for English-speaking academics. This, along with their colorful and provocative nature, has led to an overemphasis on his work. In reality, Almodóvar was just one small part of the movida. An example of this overemphasis can be seen in David Gies's assertion that Pedro Almodóvar was "the putative leader of the so-called *movida*"; David T. Gies, "Modern Spanish Culture: An Introduction," in *Modern Spanish Culture*, ed. David T. Gies (Cambridge: Cambridge University Press, 1999), 2. Other important works linking Pedro Almodóvar and the movida include Kathleen M. Vernon and Barbara Morris, "Introduction: Pedro Almodóvar, Postmodern *Auteur*," in *Post-Franco, Postmodern: The Films of Pedro Almodóvar*, ed. Kathleen M. Vernon and Barbara Morris (Westport, CT: Greenwood, 1995); Núria Triana Toribio, "A Punk Called Pedro: *La Movida* in the Films of Pedro Almodóvar," in *Contemporary Spanish Cultural Studies* (London: Arnold Press, 2000); Paul Julian Smith, *Desire Unlimited: The Cinema of Pedro Almodóvar* (London: Verso, 1994); Mark Allinson, "Alaska: Star of Stage and Screen and Optimistic Punk," in *Constructing Identity in Twentieth Century Spain*, ed. Jo Labanyi (Oxford: Oxford University Press, 2002); Mark Allinson, *A Spanish Labyrinth: The Films of Pedro Almodóvar* (London: Tauris, 2001); María Antonio García de León, *Pedro Almodóvar, la otra España cañí* (Ciudad Real: Biblioteca de Autores y Temas Manchegos, 1990).

3. Only a single book published in Spain before 2005 exclusively examines the movida: José Luis Gallero, *Solo se vive una vez. Esplendor y ruina de la movida madrileña* (Madrid: Adora, 1991). Up to this point, Gallero's popular oral history of the period served as the most important source of information

for scholars interested in the movida. Even though Gallero's book consists of nothing more than a series of interviews with former participants, nearly everyone has taken the words and interpretations of the movida's participants at face value, without any recognition or interrogation of the possible distortions, intentional or not, that may come from the recollection of a period close to a decade in the past. This situation changed recently with the twenty-fifth anniversary of the movida madrileña. Along with a series of retrospective expositions, film screenings, and round-table discussions sponsored by the regional government of Madrid, the years 2006 and 2007 saw the publication of a variety of new books addressing different aspects of the movida; see Silvia Grijalba, *Dios salve a la movida* (Madrid: Espejo de Tinta, 2006); Víctor Coyote, *Cruce de perras y otros relatos de los 80* (Madrid: Visual Books, 2006); Pablo Pérez Mínguez, *Mi movida madrileña: fotografías 1979–1985* (Barcelona: Lunwerg, 2006); J. D. Álvarez, *Ouka Lele: biografía* (Madrid: Neverland Ediciones, 2006); Héctor Foure, *El futuro ya está aquí* (Madrid: Velecio Editores, 2007).

4. In the preface to their 1995 ground-breaking work on Spanish cultural studies, Helen Graham and Jo Labanyi call attention to the lack of work on the topic and point out that the "history of the *movida* has still to be written"; see Helen Graham and Jo Labanyi, "Editors' Preface," in *Spanish Cultural Studies: An Introduction*, ed. Helen Graham and Jo Labanyi (Oxford: Oxford University Press, 1995), vii. Since that time, not a single scholarly monograph has been written on the movida to fill that gap.

5. See Santos Juliá, "History, Politics, and Culture, 1975–1996," in *Modern Spanish Culture*, ed. David T. Gies (Cambridge: Cambridge University Press, 1999). The movida has also been left out of many of the most important works of Spanish history covering the post-Francoist period. See for example Raymond Carr, ed., *Spain: A History* (Oxford: Oxford University Press, 2000); Adrian Shubert, *A Social History of Modern Spain* (London: Routledge, 1990); José María Jover Zamora, Guadalupe Gómez-Ferrer Morant, and Juan Pablo Fusi, *España: sociedad, política y civilización (siglos XIX–XX)* (Madrid: Areté, 2001); Paul Preston, *The Triumph of Democracy in Spain* (London: Muthuen, 1986); Víctor Pérez Díaz, *The Return of Civil Society: The Emergence of Democratic Spain* (Cambridge, MA: Harvard University Press, 1993); Kenneth Maxwell and Steven Spiegel, *The New Spain: From Isolation to Influence* (New York: Council on Foreign Relations Press, 1994); Bernat Muniesa, *Dictadura y Monarquía en España: de 1939 hasta la actualidad* (Barcelona: Editorial Ariel, 1996).

6. For an in-depth discussion of the historiography of the movida madrileña, see Hamilton Stapell, "Just a Teardrop in the Rain?"

7. Cited in John Hooper, *The New Spaniards* (London: Penguin, 1995), 345. Hooper correctly points out that this habit had caught on even before Franco's death.

8. Allinson, *A Spanish Labyrinth*, 18.

9. Teresa M. Vilarós, "Los monos del desencanto español," *MLN* 109 (1994): 232. The movida's lack of any major literary legacy is explained by Vilarós as a kind of cultural hangover resulting from the long dictatorship. From this perspective, the movida represents a cultural void rather than a cultural rebirth in the post-Francoist period.

10. Peter Scales, "La movida madrileña: una lagrima en la lluvia," in *Siete ensayos sobre la cultura*, ed. Federico Bonaddio and Derek Harris (Old Aberdeen: Aberdeen University Press, 1995), 47.

11. José Carlos Mainer, "1975–1985, Los poderes del pasado," in *La cultura española en el posfranquismo*, ed. Samuel Amell (Madrid: Playor, 1988), 22.

12. José Luis Gallero, *Solo se vive una vez. Esplendor y ruina de la movida madrileña* (Madrid: Adora, 1991), 314.

13. Ibid.

14. Ricardo de la Cierva, one of the early Ministers of Culture during the Transition period, has strongly criticized the left for their interventionism in matters of culture in the 1980s. See Ricardo de la Cierva, *España, la sociedad violada* (Barcelona: Planeta, 1989). Specifically see the chapter, "El frente popular de la cultura," pages 229–260.

15. José María Brunet, "José María Álvarez del Manzano," *La Vanguardia*, August 30, 1991.

16. Jesús Ordovás, *Historia de la música pop española* (Madrid: Alianza, 1987), 196.

17. Jesús Ordovás, *De que va el Rrollo* (Madrid: Las Ediciones de Piqueta, 1977), 80–84.

18. Ibid., 91.

19. For a detailed chronology of the movida, including bands, concerts, records, festivals, see Ordovás, *Historia de la música pop española*, 210–244.

20. See Jesús Ordovás, *De que va el Rrollo*.

21. For more on the relationship between music magazines and the movida, see Pepo Fuentes, "La prensa," in *La Edad de Oro del pop español*, ed. Carlos López (Madrid: Luca Editorial, 1992), 87.

22. For further information on fanzines, see F. Javier Astudillo, "Los Fanzines," in *La Edad de Oro del pop español*, ed. Carlos López (Madrid: Luca Editorial, 1992), 84–85.

23. Comics and graphic novel experienced an unprecedented explosion of popularity during this period. For more information on the development of comics in Madrid, see Ricardo Aguilera, "A ritmo de comic," in *La Edad de Oro del pop español*, ed. Carlos López (Madrid: Luca Editorial, 1992), 83; Mireia Sentís, "Cómic," in *Madrid, años ochenta*, ed. Rafael Sierra (Madrid: Ayuntamiento de Madrid, 1989).

24. For a detailed description of the success and failures of the early musical groups of the movida, see Fernando Márquez, *Música moderna* (Madrid: Las Ediciones Nuevo Sendero, 1981); Paco Martín, *La movida* (Madrid: n. p., 1982), 34–109; R. Abitbol and Ramón Trecet, "La nueva ola madrileña, ¿Mito o realidad?," *Disco Actualidad*, April 1981.

25. For further information on the popular music scene of the 1980s, see Jesús Ordovás, "Madrid Pop, 1979–1989," in *Madrid, años ochenta*, ed. Rafael Sierra (Madrid: Ayuntamiento de Madrid, 1989).

26. For a detailed chronology of the movida music scene (bands, records, etc.), see Carlos López, ed., *La Edad de Oro del pop español* (Madrid: Luca Editorial, 1992), 6–16. For a discography of the movida, see Ordovás, *Historia de la música pop española*, 245–260.

27. For further information on the early nightclubs and bars of the movida, see Márquez, *Música moderna*, 87–89; Martín, *La movida*, 24–30.

28. For a detailed description of the various bars and clubs of the movida, see López, ed., *La Edad de Oro del pop español*, 64–65; Acacia Domínguez Uceta, "Lugares de los 80," in *Madrid, años ochenta*, ed. Rafael Sierra (Madrid: Ayuntamiento de Madrid, 1989).

29. For a brief review of recording industry during this period, see Dario Vico, "La industria del disco: diez años de reconversión," in *La Edad de Oro del pop español*, ed. Carlos López (Madrid: Luca Editorial, 1992), 74–75.

30. For a description of early radio programming and the movida, see Márquez, *Música moderna*, 84; Martín, *La movida*, 12–17.

31. For further information on the development of Radio 3 in the 1980s, see Martín Sabas, *Radio 3. 20 años* (Valencia: La Máscara, 1998).

32. Pablo García, "Radio 3, 1982–1986," in *Radio 3. 20 años*, ed. Martín Sabas (Valencia: La Máscara, 1998), 332.

33. For more information on these early television programs, see Martín, *La movida*, 17–18.

34. For additional information about film in Madrid in the 1980s, see José Ramón Rey, "El cine: entre el amor y el odio a la Ley," in *Madrid, años ochenta*, ed. Rafael Sierra (Madrid: Ayuntamiento de Madrid, 1989).

35. For further information on photography and the movida, see Alberto Mariñas, "La ruptura y la seducción—Imagen gráfica en los 80," in *Madrid, años ochenta*, ed. Rafael Sierra (Madrid: Ayuntamiento de Madrid, 1989), 393–410.

36. For more on fashion during this period, see Merche Yoyoba, "De Sid Vicious a la chipie generation," in *La Edad de Oro del pop español*, ed. Carlos López (Madrid: Luca Editorial, 1992), 112–113.

37. Ordovás, *Historia de la música pop española*, 220.

38. For example, Alaska cohosted a television program, headlined a band, appeared in films, wrote for the alternative press, and took photographs. Paco Martín promoted the record label *Fonogram*, was part owner of the nightclub Marquee, and wrote about the movida. In addition to his film work, Pedro Almodóvar performed a live act at Rock-ola, wrote a column for the magazine *La Luna de Madrid*, and put out a record with Fabio McNamara, *Gran Ganga* (1982). The fluidity and overlapping of roles was so great that Pedro Almodóvar did not even consider himself a film director per se until the filming of his fourth movie, *Que he hecho yo para merecer esto?*, in 1984. See Rafa Cervera, "Prólogo-Entrevista: Pedro Almodovar," in *Alaska y otras historias de la movida* (Barcelona: Plaza & Janés, 2002), 22.

39. It is estimated that more than 1.1 million people turned out on the streets of Madrid in a show of solidarity after the attempted coup in February 1981. See Ramón Adell Argiles, "Madrid: capital de manifestaciones," *Alfoz*, no. 74–75 (1990): 105.

40. Martín, *La movida*, 19.

41. See *Diario 16*, September 27, 1980.

42. Although the coverage of popular music in a sports paper that primarily covered soccer may appear incongruous, Paco Martín reminds us, "Soccer [*el fútbol*] is pure rock and roll." Martín, *La movida*, 21.

43. For a brief history of radio and the movida during this period, see José Manuel Costa, "Radio Song," in *La Edad de Oro del pop español*, ed. Carlos López (Madrid: Luca Editorial, 1992), 78–80.

44. Rock-ola opened on April 3, 1981. The name came from the combination of the terms "Rock and Roll" and "Nueva ola." Pedro Almodóvar has called Rock-ola "the grand university of those years." Gallero, *Solo se vive una vez. Esplendor y ruina de la movida madrileña*, 214. For a brief history of Rock-ola, see Jorge Gonzalez, "Rock-ola," in *La Edad de Oro del pop español*, ed. Carlos López (Madrid: Luca Editorial, 1992), 72–73.

45. Vico, "La industria del disco: diez años de reconversión," 74.

46. See Rosa Olivares, "Una década tumultuosa," *Lápiz*, Summer 1991, 38.

47. For more on the popular press and the movida, see Javier Domingo, "*La Luna*, el *Madriz*, *El Paseante* . . . y otras especies de los 80," in *Madrid, años ochenta*, ed. Rafael Sierra (Madrid: Ayuntamiento de Madrid, 1989).

48. For further information on *La Luna de Madrid*, see Malcolm Allan Compitello, "Todavía en *La Luna*," *Arizona Journal of Hispanic Cultural Studies* 1 (1997); Domingo, "*La Luna*, el *Madriz*, *El Paseante* . . . y otras especies de los 80," 313–316.

49. For more information on Paloma Chamorro and "La Edad de Oro," see Santi Carrillo, "De la nada a la más absoluta miseria," in *La Edad de Oro del pop español*, ed. Carlos López (Madrid: Luca Editorial, 1992), 94–96.

50. Thus, contrary to the conservative interpretation, the cultural phenomenon described above was not the creation of a conscious effort by public institutions to win votes, to pacify the masses with bread and circuses, or to battle the so-called *desencanto*. In fact, prior to 1984, Tierno Galván and Madrid's other political elite had very little appreciation for or understanding of the movida. For example, there was no recognition of the movida in the many reports and studies put out by the *Ayuntamiento*, see, for example, Ayuntamiento de Madrid, "La fiesta somos nosotros," *Villa de Madrid* 1982-I; Ayuntamiento de Madrid, "La cultura: cuatro años fecundos," *Villa de Madrid* 1983-II; Ayuntamiento de Madrid, *Madrid Avanza: 1983–1984, un año de gestión* (Madrid: Ayuntamiento de Madrid, Concejalía de Relaciones Institucionales y Comunicación, 1984). In addition, the *Comunidad* of Madrid simply did not exist before the middle of 1983 to help promote the movida. To Tierno Galván and the rest of the political elite within the administration, the activity of the movida was just one part of Madrid's increasingly vibrant cultural scene. The administration was simply not responsible for initially conceiving or engineering the culture of the movida.

51. Ordovás, *Historia de la música pop española*, 220.

52. López, *La Edad de Oro del pop español*, 11.

53. Antonio Gómez, "El día más largo de la música," *El País*, January 29, 1984.

54. See, for example, ibid.

55. Elizabeth Nash, *Madrid: A Cultural and Literary Companion* (Oxford: Signal Books, 2001), 221.

56. Ibid., 222.

57. Fabio de Miguel, "Rock-ola 1981–1985," *Sur-Exprés*, May 1987, 59.

58. Alfredo Villaverde, "La movida madrileña," in *Madrid, único y múltiple, 21 crónicas periodísticas*, ed. Ayuntamiento de Madrid (Madrid: Ayuntamiento de Madrid, 1987), 111.

59. Carlos Berlanga's father was the famous Spanish film director, Luis García Berlanga.

60. José Tono Martínez, "Madrid: 2041," in *Madrid Hoy*, ed. Lolo Rico (Madrid: La Comunidad de Madrid, Consejería de Gobernación, 1987), 351.
61. García, "Radio 3, 1982–1986," 333.
62. Ibid., 332.
63. Ibid., 333.
64. See Gabriel Giorgi, "Madrid en tránsito: Travelers, Visibility, and Gay Identities," *GLQ: A Journal of Lesbian and Gay Studies* 8, no. 1 (2002). Also see Smith, *Desire Unlimited: The Cinema of Pedro Almodóvar*, 28–29; Allinson, *A Spanish Labyrinth: The Films of Pedro Almodóvar*, 16; Gema Perez-Sanchez, *Queer Transitions in Contemporary Spanish Culture: From Franco to La Movida* (Albany, NY: SUNY Press, 2007).
65. Gallero, *Solo se vive una vez. Esplendor y ruina de la movida madrileña*, 20.
66. Ibid., 21.
67. Alaska, "Declaraciones de Alaska," *Total*, no. 3, 1982, cited in Ayuntamiento de Madrid, *Dossier de exposición: "Madrid, Madrid, Madrid"* (Madrid: Ayuntamiento de Madrid, 1984).
68. In 1985, only 46.7 percent of the residents of the *Comunidad* of Madrid had been born in the region. Comunidad de Madrid, *Informe sobre demanda latente de cultura y deporte* (Madrid: Comunidad de Madrid, 1985), 21.
69. The fact that the movida's cultural elite was not from Madrid represents the historical norm, rather than the exception. The three authors most closely associated with the culture of Madrid in the past were not originally madrileños: the *aragonés* Pedro Laín Entralgo, the *segoviano* Anselmo Carretero, and the *sevillano* Antonio Machado.
70. Nacho García Vega, "Ni me consultan, ni me piden consejo," in *Madrid Hoy*, ed. Lolo Rico (Madrid: La Comunidad de Madrid, Consejería de Gobernación, 1987), 247.
71. For further information on some of the different sites of the movida, see Domínguez Uceta, "Lugares de los 80."
72. In 1982, for example, only approximately 20 percent of the musical groups in Madrid had made a record. Martín, *La movida*, 11.
73. Fernando Íñiguez, "Los músicos de la movida madrileña, contra la política cultural del alcalde," *El País*, 7 July 2002.
74. *11 fotógrafos españoles*, 1982, cited in Ayuntamiento de Madrid, *Dossier de exposición: "Madrid, Madrid, Madrid."*
75. Ibid.
76. See for example Juan Pablo Fusi, *Un siglo de España: la cultura* (Madrid: Marcial Pons, 1999), 157; Mainer, "1975–1985, Los poderes del pasado," 21; Hooper, *The New Spaniards*, 344.
77. Mark Allinson has specifically described the movida's optimism with regards to the singer Alaska, see Allinson, "Alaska: Star of Stage and Screen and Optimistic Punk."
78. There is no firm agreement over the exact origin this term. While some attribute the name to foreign journalists living in Madrid to cover the country's political transition to democracy, others claim it came from Madrid's drug culture, slang for scoring a hit. Even though both of these explanations place the origin of the term in Madrid itself, it appears as though the phrase was actually first applied to Madrid from the outside. Specifically, it came from a television program produced in Barcelona. In the summer of 1980, Ángel

Casas first used the phrase "*la movida madrileña*" on his program "Musical Express" (TVE) to describe the unique musical and cultural scene in Madrid, see Francisco Umbral, "El 'Rock/nenuco'," *El País*, July 6, 1980. Also see Márquez, *Música moderna*, 85; Martín, *La movida*, 18. Regardless of the actual origin of the phrase, the words, "movida" and "madrileña," did become inexorably linked together. In the press, the two words were almost always used together and soon it became impossible to think of the movida without thinking of Madrid.

79. See, for example, Moncho Alpuente, "Tu no tienes la culpa Federico," *Madrid Me Mata*, April 1985, 26.

80. Moncho Alpuente, "La Capital del Mundo en 1984," *El País Semanal*, January 15, 1984.

81. Miguel A. Rodríguez and José García Monge, "Cartas al Director," *La Luna de Madrid*, April 1984.

82. Ibid.

83. Antonio Gómez Rufo, *Carta a un amigo sobre don Enrique Tierno Galván* (Madrid: Ediciones de Antonio Machado, 1986), 34. For similar comments, see Antonio Gómez Rufo, *Madrid, bajos fondos* (Madrid: El Avapiés, 1987), 17. Alaska also commonly referred to Madrid as the "capital of the world." See, for example, Alaska, "La fiesta debe continuar," *Primera Linea de la Actualidad*, February 1986, 4.

84. See, for example, Borja Casani and José Tono Martínez, "Madrid 1984: ¿La Posmodernidad?," *La Luna de Madrid*, November 1983. Also see Éric Beaumatin, "Madrid, la la décennie prodigieuse," *Autrement* (1987).

85. See, for example, José Tono Martínez, ed., *La polémica de la posmodernidad* (Madrid: Editorial Libertas, 1986); Francisco Umbral, *Guía de la posmodernidad* (Madrid: Temas de Hoy, 1987). For a further discussion of Spain within the postmodern context, see José B. Monleón, *Del franquismo a la posmodernidad* (Madrid: Akal, 1995); Eduardo Subirats, "Postmoderna modernidad: la España de los felices ochenta," *Quimera* 145 (1996); Kathleen M. Vernon and Barbara Morris, *Post-Franco, Postmodern: The Films of Pedro Almodóvar* (Westport, Conn.: Greenwood, 1995).

86. Bernard Bessière, *La culture espagnole. Les mutatuins de l'après franquisme (1975–1992)* (Paris: L'Harmattan, 1992), 255.

87. See, for example, Antonio de Senillosa, "Modernidad o Postmodernidad: That Is the Question," *Primera Linea de la Actualidad*, September 1985.

88. According to Bessiére, the confusion surrounding the terms "modern," "postmodern," and "post modernity" was "without a doubt one of the most trivial aspects of the period." Bernard Bessière, "El Madrid de la democracia: comportamientos culturales y crisol de creación. Realidades y dudas," in *España frente al siglo XXI: cultura y literatura*, ed. Samuel Amell (Madrid: Cátedra, 1992), 64. Also see Bernard Bessière, "Le postmodernisme en Espagne dans les années 80," *Les Mélanges de la Casa de Velázquez* (1990).

89. This well known quote is attributed to Adolfo Domínguez. See Ordovás, *Historia de la música pop española*, 226.

90. The use of the word "*jóvenes*," both at the time and later in the historiography, has led to confusion and misunderstanding, especially for Hispanists working outside of Spain. Unlike in the United States and England, the terms *jóvenes* and *juventud* refer to a population between 15 and 25 or 15 and 30 years old, not strictly to teenagers. See EDIS, *La juventud de*

Madrid, 1985 (Madrid: Ayuntamiento de Madrid, Concejalía de Juventud, 1985); Fundación Santa María, *Juventud española, 1984* (Madrid: Ediciones SM, 1985). Young people (*jóvenes*) are even occasionally classified between 16 and 32 years old. See for example CIS, "La actividad de los jóvenes madrileños," *REIS*, no. 26 (1984).

91. The weeklong visit of the master of "pop" art to Madrid in 1983 had a significant impact on the movida in general and on some participants in particular. The movida singer Carlos Berlanga recalled, "To discover Warhol is like a Christian discovering God (*Descubrir a Warhol es como para un cristiano descubrir a dios*)." Comunidad de Madrid, *Andy Warhol y España: exposición* (Madrid: Comunidad de Madrid, 1987), 28.

92. Juan Barranco, "La 'movida' de Madrid," *Villa de Madrid*, March 15, 1986.

93. Fundación Villa y Corte, *Madrid, Objetivo Cultural: actas de la semana de estudios sobre el presente y el futuro de la cultura madrileña celebrada durante los días 6 al 11 de febrero de 1984* (Madrid: Caja de Ahorros y Monte de Piedad de Madrid, 1985), 410.

94. Ibid.

95. For further information on the creation of *Madriz*, see Ayuntamiento de Madrid, *Madrid Avanza: 1983–1984, un año de gestión*, 175; Ayuntamiento de Madrid, *Madrid Avanza: 1983–1987* (Madrid: Ayuntamiento de Madrid, 1987), 100; Sentís, "Cómic," 172–176; Domingo, "*La Luna*, el *Madriz*, *El Paseante* . . . y otras especies de los 80," 316–319.

96. "*Madriz*, un ensayo de historieta urbana," *El País*, January 3, 1984.

97. Ayuntamiento de Madrid, "Terzera," *Madriz*, January 1984, 3.

98. Ibid.

99. Ibid.

100. Antonio Machin, "*Madriz* exporta imaginación," *Villa de Madrid*, January 1, 1985.

101. Ibid.

102. Domingo, "*La Luna*, el *Madriz*, *El Paseante* . . . y otras especies de los 80," 318.

103. For more on *Madrid Me Mata*, see ibid., 318–321.

104. For example, see *La Luna de Madrid*, November 1983, no. 1. The journalist and writer Moncho Alpuente also confirmed the public support of these magazines through advertising in 1985. See Mariano Antolín Rato, "Historias de la movida: así nos la inventamos," *La Primera Linea de la Actualidad*, November 1985, 38.

105. See Sentís, "Cómic," 173.

106. Ayuntamiento de Madrid, *Madrid Avanza: 1983–1984, un año de gestión*, 175.

107. "Cables," *Villa de Madrid*, March 1, 1984. Also see Ordovás, *Historia de la música pop española*, 236.

108. Jesús Ordovás, "La fiesta del Rock," *Villa de Madrid*, June 15, 1984.

109. Ordovás, "Madrid Pop, 1979–1989," 100.

110. Jesús Ordovás has also speculated that the administration supported bars that hosted movida bands, see Javier Memba, "La movida, del infinito al cero," *Interviú*, April 23, 1990, 110.

111. Enrique Tierno Galván, "El significado de las fiestas de San Isidro," *Villa de Madrid*, May 1, 1984.

112. Ibid.
113. Javier Angulo, "'Los Madrileños han demostrado estos días que les va la marcha,' declara Enrique Tierno," *El País*, May 21, 1984.
114. Ibid.
115. Even the title of the exposition linked the movida with the identity of the capital. The title "Madrid, Madrid, Madrid" was taken from the chorus of Agustín Lara's 1951 song, "Madrid," which over the years had become Madrid's very popular unofficial anthem or hymn. With such a title, the exhibit, which almost exclusively featured the movida madrileña, was directly tied to a positive and long-standing symbol of Madrid, Lara's famous song.
116. Alicia Acebes, "La movida de Madrid en imagen," *Villa de Madrid*, July 1, 1984.
117. Ibid. Also see Ordovás, *Historia de la música pop española*, 237.
118. Acebes, "La movida de Madrid en imagen."
119. Ibid.
120. Ibid.
121. "'Viva el caos!'" *El País*, January 20, 1996.
122. However, with the official institutionalization of the movement came some restrictions and limitations. After a stabbing near the entrance of Rock-Ola, the movida's most famous bar was permanently closed by the *Ayuntamiento* on March 14, 1985. Coincidentally, Paloma Chamorro's popular television "La Edad de Oro" was canceled the same week. However, as the program aired on national television, TVE2, the cancellation of "La Edad de Oro" was not a municipal decision. After the closure of Rock-Ola, and an earlier fire at the disco Alcalá 20, other bars and concert halls, such as Sala Universal, had problems with the municipal administration and were forced to close. While the closure of these bars represented the local administration's desire to control some of the excesses of the movida, official support for the movement far outweighed the few restrictions placed on it.
123. Ordovás, *Historia de la música pop española*, 235.
124. Ignacio Aranda, "'Me gustaría hacer una película con el Alcalde'," *Villa de Madrid*, February 15, 1984.
125. See, for example, *Villa de Madrid*, May 15, 1985.
126. See Alaska, "La fiesta debe continuar."
127. Ordovás, *Historia de la música pop española*, 241.
128. See Ayuntamiento de Madrid, *Centro Cultural de la Villa: 1977–1987 diez años* (Madrid: Ayuntamiento de Madrid, Consejalía de Cultura, 1987), 7.
129. Anabel González, "Alaska, pregonera de las fietas navideñas," *Villa de Madrid*, December 4, 1985. Also see "La cantante Alaska pronunció el pregón de Navidad," *El País*, 21 December 1985.
130. "Nueve dias de 'Movida'," *Villa de Madrid*, May 15, 1985.
131. See Ayuntamiento de Madrid, *Programa de San Isidro, 1985* (Madrid: Ayuntamiento de Madrid, 1985).
132. "Nueve dias de 'Movida'."
133. "Más de dos millones de personas asistieron a los actos de San Isidro," *El País*, May 21, 1986.
134. Ayuntamiento de Madrid, *Programa de San Isidro, 1985*, n. p.
135. Ibid.
136. Ibid.

137. Comunidad de Madrid, *Consejería de Cultura y Deportes, 1983–1987* (Madrid: Comunidad de Madrid, 1987), 14.
138. Ibid.
139. Ibid.
140. See Comunidad de Madrid, *Festival de Otoño, programa 1985* (Madrid: Comunidad de Madrid, Consejería de Cultura, 1985); Comunidad de Madrid, *Festival de Otoño en Madrid: 1984–1988* (Barcelona: Iberia, 1988).
141. Joaquín Leguina, "Madrid en la Autonomía," *Revista de Occidente*, no. extraordinario VII (1983): 15.
142. Comunidad de Madrid, *Consejería de Cultura y Deportes, 1983–1987*, 53.
143. Three individuals in particular from the regional administration have been linked to the official sponsorship of *La Luna de Madrid*: the *Consejeros* Virgilio Cano de Lope and Agapito Ramos, and the Director General de Cultura, Juan Miguél Hernández de León. See Domingo, "*La Luna*, el *Madriz, El Paseante* . . . y otras especies de los 80," 315.
144. See, for example, Borja Casani, "Madrid: ciudad fronteriza," *Alfoz*, no. 7–8 (1984); Fernando Márquez, "Madrid no es el ombligo del cosmos," *Alfoz*, no. 7–8 (1984); Antonio Gómez Rufo, "Administración pública y cultura," *Alfoz*, no. 7–8 (1984).
145. For more on regional radio programming in Madrid during this period, see Eduardo García Matilla and Ortiz Miguel Angel, "Los jóvenes madrileños y la radio de los 80," in *Madrid, años ochenta*, ed. Rafael Sierra (Madrid: Ayuntamiento de Madrid, 1989).

CHAPTER 6

1. For an excellent treatment of the problems related to the issue of "reception," see Alon Confino, "Collective Memory and Cultural History: Problems of Method," *The American Historical Review* 102, no. 5 (1997): 1395–1397.
2. Luis Carandell, "Madrid vuelve a ser Madrid," *Villa de Madrid*, January 1, 1983.
3. See Diego Manrique, "Madrid se mueve, dicen en París," *Villa de Madrid*, November 15, 1986.
4. Rosa Olivares, "Una década tumultuosa," *Lápiz*, Summer 1991, 40.
5. Javier Tusell, "La cultura en España en la última década a través de las estadísticas," *Cuenta y Razón*, no. 19 (1985): 176.
6. For more information on the popularity of the large number of expositions in Madrid during this period, see Julián Gallego Serrano, "Diez años de exposiciones madrileñas," *Cuenta y Razón*, no. 35 (1988).
7. John Hooper, *The New Spaniards* (London: Penguin, 1995), 327.
8. In comparison to Madrid, Barcelona counted 182 galleries, Valencia 58, Zaragoza 39, Palma de Mallorca 38, and Bilbao 18. See Bernard Bessière, "El Madrid de la democracia: comportamientos culturales y crisol de creación. Realidades y dudas," in *España frente al siglo XXI: cultura y literatura*, ed. Samuel Amell (Madrid: Cátedra, 1992), 69.
9. Enrique Tierno Galván, "Madrid mejora," *Villa de Madrid*, June 1/15, 1985.
10. Ibid.
11. Bob Spitz, "The New Spain," *Rolling Stone Magazine*, June 6, 1985.

12. See, for example, Adela Gooch, "Madrid Falls Behind in Spain's Fierce War of Cities," *The Independent*, January 22, 1991.

13. Borja Casani, "[No title]," in *Madrid Hoy*, ed. Lolo Rico (Madrid: La Comunidad de Madrid, Consejería de Gobernación, 1987), 79.

14. For a discussion of CBS's experience with the *movida* music scene, see Jesús Ordovás, *Historia de la música pop española* (Madrid: Alianza, 1987), 205–208.

15. Amelia Castilla, "*Madriz* seguirá publicándose, pese a la oposición del Grupo Popular," *El País*, April 23, 1984.

16. Arturo Arnalte, "Cartas al director," *La Luna de Madrid*, April 1984.

17. Javier Memba, "La movida, del infinito al cero," *Interviú*, April 23, 1990, 110.

18. "Tribus Urbanas," *El País*, December 16, 1984.

19. Inmaculada de la Fuente, "Bárbara Allende, 'Ouka-Lele'," *El País*, January 17, 1985.

20. Ordovás, *Historia de la música pop española*, 235.

21. See, for instance, Alaska, "Morriña fin de siglo," *Primera Linea de la Actualidad*, November 1985.

22. Rafa Cervera, *Alaska y otras historias de la movida* (Barcelona: Plaza & Janés Editores, 2002), 348.

23. "Fiestas, fiesta, fiestas," *Alfoz*, no. 28 (1986): 6. Also see Tierno Galván, "Madrid mejora."

24. CIS, *Barómetro Comunidad Autónoma de Madrid I (Estudio 1503)* (Madrid: CIS, 1986).

25. Ministerio de Cultura, *Encuesta de comportamiento cultural de los españoles* (Madrid: Ministerio de Cultura, 1985), 315. For additional information on cultural demand in Spain during this period, see Ministerio de Cultura, *Demanda cultural en España* (Madrid: Ministerio de Cultura, 1978); José Luis Zárraga, *Encuesta, cultura y ocio* (Madrid: Ministerio de cultura, Secretaría General Técnica Subdirección General de Estudios y Coordinación, 1984); José Luis Piñuel Raigada, *El consumo cultural* (Madrid: Instituto Nacional de Consumo/Fundamentos, 1987).

26. Ministerio de Cultura, *Encuesta de comportamiento cultural de los españoles*, 315.

27. Ministerio de Cultura, *Encuesta de comportamiento cultural de los españoles: Autonomía de Madrid* (Madrid: Ministerio de Cultura, 1986), 249.

28. Ibid.

29. Ibid., 234.

30. CIS, *Municipales Madrid (Estudio 1546)* (Madrid: CIS, 1986).

31. Unfortunately, because this study was commissioned by the regional government of Madrid, instead of by the Ministry of Culture, similar statistics from other regions are not available for comparison. See Comunidad de Madrid, *Informe sobre demanda latente de cultura y deporte* (Madrid: Comunidad de Madrid, 1985).

32. Ibid., 63.

33. Additionally, as mentioned in Chapter 4, the overall use of Madrid's regional public library system also significantly increased during this period, with patronage increasing from 216,000 books checked out in 1983 to 536,500 in 1987, almost a two and a half fold increase. See Comunidad de Madrid, *Consejería de Cultura y Deportes, 1983–1987* (Madrid: Comunidad de Madrid, 1987), 27.

34. Comunidad de Madrid, *Informe sobre demanda latente de cultura y deporte*, 78.
35. Ibid., 65.
36. Paloma Aguilar Fernandez, "The Opposition to Franco, the Transition to Democracy and the New Political System," in *Spanish History since 1808*, ed. José Alvarez Junco and Adrian Shubert (London: Arnold, 2000), 311.
37. Carlos López, ed., *La Edad de Oro del pop español* (Madrid: Luca Editorial, 1992), 8.
38. See Ramón Adell Argiles, "Madrid: capital de manifestaciones," *Alfoz*, no. 74–75 (1990).
39. CIS, *Municipales Madrid (Estudio 1546)*.
40. Ibid.
41. Editorial, "El homenaje de la calle," *El País*, January 22, 1986.
42. Felix Santos, "Tierno Galván: un nuevo estilo de ser alcalde," *Ayuntamientos Democráticos*, February 1986, 6. Also see "Madrid llora a su alcalde," *Villa de Madrid*, January 21, 1986.
43. "Madrid llora a su alcalde."
44. "Una larga espera," *Villa de Madrid*, January 21, 1986.
45. Ibid.
46. Ibid.
47. Ibid.
48. Ibid.
49. Ibid.
50. Ibid.
51. "Condecorado con la Gran Cruz de Carlos III," *El País*, January 22, 1986.
52. "Homenaje a Tierno Galván, que murió hace hoy 10 años," *El País*, January 14, 1996.
53. Fernando García, "El pueblo de Madrid, pendiente de la salud del alcalde," 15 February 1985. Also see Editorial, "El Alcalde de Madrid," *El País*, February 11, 1985.
54. To celebrate its fiftieth anniversary, Radio Nacional de España asked listeners from all across Spain to decide the most popular person in each Autonomous Community. Tierno Galván was the overwhelming winner in the Comunidad of Madrid. See "El más popular de Madrid," *Villa de Madrid*, February 4, 1986.
55. "Miles de madrileños expresaron anoche en la calle su dolor por la muerte de Enrique Tierno," *El País*, January 20, 1986.
56. See, for example, "Escriben los madrileños," *Villa de Madrid*, March 15, 1986.
57. See "Escriben los Madrileños," *Villa de Madrid*, February 1, 1987.
58. This was only the second time the City Council granted its highest honor. The first time was to the Congress (*Cortes Generales*) after the attempted coup in 1981. See "El pleno concede por unanimidad la Medalla de Honor de Madrid a Enrique Tierno," *El País*, January 21, 1986.
59. The monument was eventually constructed in the Parque de las Delicias, later renamed Parque de Tierno Galván in the mayor's honor. See Carmen Santamaría, "El Parque de las Delicias llevará su nombre," *Villa de Madrid*, February 4, 1986.
60. Antonio Gómez Rufo, *Carta a un amigo sobre don Enrique Tierno Galván* (Madrid: Ediciones de Antonio Machado, 1986), 15.

61. José Antonio Vizcaíno, *Historia de la villa de Madrid: de los orígenes a la actualidad* (Barcelona: Óptima, 2000), 406–407.
62. On May 8, 1983, Tierno Galván and the PSOE won 29 of Madrid's 57 City Council seats, compared to 23 by the conservative coalition of AP-PDP-UL (Alianza Popular, Partido Demócrata Popular, Unión Liberal). Despite winning the absolute majority of the City Council seats, Tierno Galván's administration received just 49 percent of the overall vote, while 37 percent of *madrileños* voted for the Grupo Popular coalition. See Fernando García, "Los socialistas revalidan su triunfo," *Villa de Madrid*, May 5, 1983.
63. Ibid.
64. Ibid.
65. Ibid.
66. CIS, *Municipales Madrid (Estudio 1546).*
67. Ibid. Even as far back as 1982, the majority of the population supported the local administration's cultural program. See Julio Fernandez, "La cultura centra el mayor grado de satisfacción de los madrileños con la actuación de su Ayuntamiento," *El País*, October 7, 1982.
68. CIS, *Municipales Madrid (Estudio 1546).*
69. CIS, *Barómetro Comunidad Autónoma de Madrid I (Estudio 1503).*
70. Editorial, "Un cierto madrileñismo," *El País*, August 17, 1982.
71. Editorial, "El País más aburrido de Europa," *El País*, September 6, 1979.
72. Miguel Gato, "Se crece con la democracia," *Villa de Madrid*, January 1, 1983.
73. Borja Casani and José Tono Martínez, "Madrid 1984: ¿La Posmodernidad?," *La Luna de Madrid*, November 1983.
74. Pedro Almodóvar, "Autoentrevista," *La Luna de Madrid*, December 1983, 7.
75. Ibid.
76. "La Comunidad de Madrid es un símbolo del cambio español, según García-Pelayo," *El País*, October 26, 1984.
77. Ibid.
78. Antonio Gómez Rufo, "Administración pública y cultura," *Alfoz*, no. 7–8 (1984): 85.
79. Fundación Villa y Corte, *Madrid, Objetivo Cultural: actas de la semana de estudios sobre el presente y el futuro de la cultura madrileña celebrada durante los días 6 al 11 de febrero de 1984* (Madrid: Caja de Ahorros y Monte de Piedad de Madrid, 1985), 409.
80. Editorial, "El Alcalde de Madrid."
81. Ibid.
82. Moncho Alpuente, "Madrid 1975–1985: la década prodigiosa," *Villa de Madrid*, December 4, 1985.
83. Manuel Ariza, "Tierno y la Juventud," *Villa de Madrid*, February 4, 1986.
84. Cited in Alex Masllorens, *La herencia y humana de Enrique Tierno Galván* (Barcelona: Tibidabo, 1986), 131.
85. Cited in ibid., 132.
86. Cited in ibid.
87. Antonio J Ripoll, ed., *La gloriosa movida nacional* (Aviles: Casa Municipal de Cultura, 1988), 20.
88. Fernando Chacoa Fuertes, "Estereotipos regionales de los madrileños," *Papeles Psicólogos del Colegio*, no. 25 (1986): 28.

89. Ibid.
90. Ibid.
91. CIS, *Barómetro Comunidad Autónoma de Madrid I (Estudio 1503)*.
92. EDIS, *Las elecciones generales 1986: valores sociales y actitudes políticas, movilidad y motivación del voto* (Madrid: Fundación Friedrich Ebert, 1987), 78.
93. Ibid., 55.
94. Fernando Jiménez de Gregorio, *Madrid y su Comunidad* (Madrid: El Avapiés, 1986), 77.
95. José de la Paz, "Cambios demográficos recientes en la capital, el area metropolitana y la provincia," *Alfoz*, no. 7–8 (1984): 29.
96. José María Baviano, "'Yo no tengo futuro político; lo mío es concurrir con los vecinos'," *El País*, January 20, 1986.
97. See "'Hay que salir de la OTAN por patriotismo,' afirma el alcalde de Madrid, Enrique Tierno," *El País*, June 22, 1984.
98. Juan Barranco, "El Madrid de las libertades y los nuevos tiempos: conferencia en Club XXI," *Villa de Madrid Suplemento Informativo* 1986, 15.
99. Francisco Alvira Martín and José García López, "Los españoles y las autonomias," *Papeles de Economica Española* 35 (1988): 403. The decrease in regionalist sentiment in areas such as the Basque Country and Galicia was probably due to regional aspirations being fulfilled by the development of the system of autonomous communities during this period.
100. Ibid.
101. CIS, *Los españoles ante el segundo aniversario de la firma del tratado de adhesión de España a la Comunidad Europea* (Madrid: CIS, 1988).
102. Ibid.
103. Ibid.
104. For further information on sociological studies regarding national and regional identity in Spain, see José Jiménez Blanco, *La conciencia regional en España* (Madrid: CIS, 1977); José Luis Sangrador García, *Estereotipos de las nacionalidades y regiones de España* (Madrid: CIS, 1981); Eduardo López Aranguren, *La conciencia regional en el proceso autonómico español* (Madrid: CIS, 1983); Gonzalo Herranz Rafael, *La vigencia del nacionalismo* (Madrid: CIS, 1992); M. García Ferrando, *La conciencia nacional y regional en la España de las autonomías* (Madrid: CIS, 1994); José Luis Sangrador García, *Identidades, actitudes y estereotipos en la España de las autonomías* (Madrid: Centro de Investigaciones Sociológicas, 1996); Félix Moral, *Identidad regional y nacionalismo en el estado de las autonomías* (Madrid: CIS, 1998).
105. Luis Moreno, *La federalización de España* (Madrid: Siglo XXI, 1997), 130.
106. Ibid., 130–135.
107. Ibid., 130.
108. Ibid.
109. "Madrid honra a los reyes de Suecia," *Villa de Madrid*, April 1, 1983.
110. Gómez Rufo, *Carta a un amigo sobre don Enrique Tierno Galván*, 33.

CHAPTER 7

1. Carmen Santamaría, "La despedida a Enrique Tierno," *Villa de Madrid*, February 4, 1986.
2. Ibid.

3. "Hasta Siempre [Adversitment]," *ABC*, January 21, 1986.

4. Sebastian Balfour, "Spain from 1931 to the Present," in *Spain: A History*, ed. Raymond Carr (Oxford: Oxford University Press, 2000), 282.

5. Undoubtedly, the PSOE's program was also influenced to a degree by the general rise of neoliberalism during this period, symbolized by the successes of Margaret Thatcher (1979), Ronald Reagan (1980), and Helmut Kohl (1982), and by the general revitalization of the process of European integration across Western Europe in the 1980s.

6. James Petras has summed up the contradictions resulting from the PSOE's embrace of a neoliberal program: "[It was] a party that contested for power from a strong working-class base (after all, it is officially the Spanish Socialist Workers Party—PSOE) and that upon assuming power pursued a business orientation with a single-mindedness that would impress the most earnest Thatcherite; a party that promised comprehensive social changes and realized a capitalist transformation; a party that ascended to power on the back of rising working-class militancy and presided over a policy aimed at weakening working-class organization; a party whose ideologues and publicists subscribed to and promoted an ideology promising to extend the power of civil society against the state and that in power witnessed the extension of state power over civil society; a party that attracted a substantial number of anti-bureaucratic intellectuals and transformed them into functionaries of the state." James Petras, "Spanish Socialism: The Politics of Neo-liberalism," in *Mediterranean Paradoxes: Politics and Social Structure in Southern Europe*, ed. James Kurth and James Petras (Providence: Berg, 1993), 95. With regard to popular participation, Petras also argues: "Populist in style, plebeian in appearance, conservative and elitist in policy, it practices [the PSOE] the politics of great entertainment spectaculars and mass diversions to convert the critical public into Ortega's passive masses." Ibid., 99.

7. In fact, it has been argued that "the ideals of full participation in the process of European integration encompassed the 'cardinal and transcendent thought' to which the Socialists oriented themselves in formulating their hegemonic project" in the 1980s. Otto Holman, *Integrating Southern Europe. EC Expansion and the Transnationalization of Spain* (London: Routledge, 1996), 96.

8. "The Dark Side of Spain's Fiesta," *Time*, July 13, 1992, 55.

9. José María Jover Zamora, Guadalupe Gómez-Ferrer Morant, and Juan Pablo Fusi, *España: sociedad, política y civilización (siglos XIX–XX)* (Madrid: Areté, 2001), 819.

10. Michael T. Newton and Peter J. Donaghy, *Institutions of Modern Spain: A Political and Economic Guide* (Cambridge: Cambridge University Press, 1997), 306.

11. Full membership in the European Economic Community (EEC) was applied for in 1977, immediately after the first democratic elections were held. The Treaty of Accession was finally signed by King Juan Carlos in June 1985, and Spain officially entered the European Community (EC) on January 1, 1986.

12. John Hooper, "González and the Search for Greatness," *The Guardian*, May 7, 1991.

13. John Hooper, *The New Spaniards* (London: Penguin, 1995), 52.

14. Juan Luis Cebrián, "El Señor Presidente," *El País*, December 12, 1982. Cited in Xosé Manoel Núñez, "What is Spanish Nationalism Today? From

Legitimacy Crisis to Unfulfilled Renovation (1975–2000)," *Ethnic and Racial Studies* 24, no. 5 (2001): 736.

15. "El Gobierno disolverá las Cortes si pierde el referendum sobre la OTAN, según Javier Solana," *El País*, January 24, 1986.

16. It should be noted that the national NATO referendum was only held after the death of Tierno Galván, one of the most vocal opponents of the PSOE's proposal, and after Spain's official entry into the EC at the beginning of 1986.

17. For further information on Spain's economic development with regard to its integration into Europe, see K. G. Salmón, *The Modern Spanish Economy: Transformation and Integration into Europe* (London: Pinter, 1995); Holman, *Integrating Southern Europe*.

18. "Álvarez del Manzano califica al alcalde de 'centralista aprervi'," *El País*, January 9, 1987.

19. For example, Bob Spitz's article for *Rolling Stone Magazine* entitled "The New Spain" focused almost exclusively on Madrid. See Bob Spitz, "The New Spain," *Rolling Stone Magazine*, June 6, 1985.

20. Alfredo Villaverde, "La movida madrileña," in *Madrid, único y múltiple, 21 crónicas periodísticas*, ed. Ayuntamiento de Madrid (Madrid: Ayuntamiento de Madrid, 1987), 111.

21. For the best example of this phenomenon, see José Luis Gallero, *Solo se vive una vez. Esplendor y ruina de la movida madrileña* (Madrid: Adora, 1991).

22. Javier Memba, "La movida, del infinito al cero," *Interviú*, April 23, 1990, 109. It should be noted that not all of the artists, musicians, and designers of the movida were washed away and forgotten. There have been a few exceptions. As mentioned previously, Pedro Almodóvar has gone on to become the most famous child of the movida. The internationally famous director, and generally acknowledged enfant terrible, has won praise both at home and abroad for his films depicting the pleasures and perversions of post-Francoist society, even winning the Oscar for best foreign film in 2000 for *Todo Sobre Mi Madre*. The teenage singer, performer, and undisputed movida icon, Alaska, continues to pursue a musical career, and remains in the public's eye through her numerous appearances on television. The fashions of a handful of designers, including Agatha Ruiz de la Prada and Sybilla, also have retained their popularity. In comparison to these few successes, though, the hundreds of rockers, artists, and would-be cultural icons, along with the cultural movement they helped create, have faded into oblivion since the mid 1980s.

23. Javier Solana, *Perspectivas de política cultural. Comparencia del Ministro de Cultura ante la Comisión de Educación y Cultura del Congreso de los Diputados, 23 September 1986* (Madrid: Ministerio de Cultura, 1986), 10–11.

24. Ibid., 17–18.

25. Ibid., 18.

26. Ibid.

27. Ibid., 18–20.

28. Ibid., 18.

29. Speech in Congress, cited in Anabel Díez, "Javier Solana afirma que el PSOE no ha estatalizado la cultura," September 24, 1986.

30. See Javier Solana, *Informe ante la Comisión de Educación y Cultura del Congreso de los Diputados, 14 Abril 1983* (Madrid: Ministerio de Cultura, 1983).

31. Ministerio de Cultura, *L'Imagination Nouvelle: les anées 70–80, exposición Paris 1987* (Madrid: Ministerio de Cultura, 1987).

32. Ministerio de Cultura, *Epoca Nueva: Painting and Sculpture from Spain, Chicago office of Fine Arts* (Madrid: Ministerio de Cultura, 1988).

33. Under the administration of Javier Solana, the Ministry of Culture provided financial support for regional cultural activities everywhere from Catalonia to Andalusia. See Emiliano Fernández Prado, *La política cultural. ¿Qué es y par que sirve?* (Gijón: Ediciones Trea, 1991).

34. Alberto Mariñas, "La ruptura y la seducción—Imagen gráfica en los 80," in *Madrid, años ochenta*, ed. Rafael Sierra (Madrid: Ayuntamiento de Madrid, 1989), 408.

35. Bernard Bessière, "El Madrid de la democracia: comportamientos culturales y crisol de creación. Realidades y dudas," in *España frente al siglo XXI: cultura y literatura*, ed. Samuel Amell (Madrid: Cátedra, 1992), 68.

36. "Cultura destina a Madrid el 53% de sus inversions, según el estudio encargado por la Generalitat," *El País*, July 26, 1989.

37. Ibid. Also see Bessière, "El Madrid de la democracia: comportamientos culturales y crisol de creación. Realidades y dudas," 70. In light of this information, the minister of culture at the time, Jorge Semprún, promised to correct the inequalities between Madrid and the other regions. While the Ministry of Culture promised to protect the cultural interests of all of the country's autonomous regions in this example, the institution most often mirrored and reinforced the main priorities of the national PSOE between 1986 and 1991. See "Semprún admite que deben corregirse los desequilibrios entre Madrid y Barcelona," *El País*, July 27, 1989.

38. Conceived in 1985 by the Ministry of Culture of the EEC, the yearly designation of a European cultural capital was designed to improve the exchange and integration of the different cultures that constituted the EC. Athens was the first city to be selected in 1985. Subsequent nominations included Florence, Amsterdam, Berlin, Paris, Glasgow, Dublin, and finally, in 1992, Madrid.

39. Consorcio para la organización de Madrid Capital Europea de Cultura, *Madrid Capital Europea de Cultura 1992* (Madrid: Asisa, 1993), 30. In addition, the Junta of Castilla y León openly accused the national government of mounting a propaganda campaign that favored the nomination of the capital. See Bessière, "El Madrid de la democracia," 69.

40. "Madrid, elegida por la EC capital cultural de Europa en 1992," *El País*, May 28, 1988. Apart from the funding provided by the national administration, Madrid's program for its promotion as the Cultural Capital of Europe in 1992 relied heavily on support from the private sector. The four biggest sponsors, Caja Madrid, Telefónica, El Corte Inglés, and Leche Pascual, contributed more than $12 million. This figure was only slightly less than the total investment made by the Ayuntamiento of Madrid: $13 million. Consorcio para la organización de Madrid Capital Europea de Cultura, *Madrid Capital Europea de Cultura 1992*, 295.

41. In 1992, Barcelona celebrated Spain's first Olympic Games amidst much fanfare and Seville held an international exposition, Expo-92, to commemorate the quincentennial of America's "discovery."

42. Ayuntamiento de Madrid, *Madrid, cultura vive: candidatura a la capitalidad europea de la cultura 1992* (Madrid: Ayuntamiento de Madrid, 1988), 29.

43. Ibid., 1.

44. Ibid., 3.

45. Feliciano Fidalgo, "'Los bancos no son cultura en Suiza'," *El País*, November 3, 1991. For more on Madrid's official preparations for 1992, see Pedro Montoliú, "El Ayuntamiento concreta en casi 50 proyectos su infraestructura para la capitalidad cultural," *El País*, June 23, 1990.

46. Santos Juliá, "History, Politics, and Culture, 1975–1996," in *Modern Spanish Culture*, ed. David T. Gies (Cambridge: Cambridge University Press, 1999), 113.

47. See John Hargreaves, *Freedom for Catalonia? Catalan Nationalism, Spanish Identity and the Barcelona Olympic Games* (Cambridge: Cambridge University Press, 2000).

48. Ibid., 148–157.

49. Ibid., 107.

50. Ibid., 161.

51. Ibid., 162.

52. See Richard Maddox, *The Best of All Possible Islands: Seville's Universal Exposition, the New Spain, and the New Europe* (Albany: State University of New York Press, 2004).

53. Ibid., 5–6.

54. Ibid., 57.

55. Ibid., 203.

56. Ibid.

57. Ibid., 204–205.

58. Ibid., 217.

59. Ibid., 215.

60. Ibid., 220–221.

61. Ibid., 205.

62. Ibid., 47.

63. See, for example, Anabel Díez, "'Vamos a ganar estas y las próximas elecciones' asegura Felipe González," *El País*, June 8, 1987.

64. Despite the rivalry between Adolfo Suarez and Manuel Fraga, the CDS and the Partido Popular (PP) decided in 1989 to bring motions of censure in several cities across Spain where Socialists governed with only a simple majority. This strategy's most spectacular success came in Madrid, where Juan Barranco was deposed in June 1989 and Joaquín Leguina held on as president of the Comunidad of Madrid by only a single vote, averting the creation of a center-right regional government under the leadership of Alberto Ruiz Gallardón (PP). Despite the fact that the CDS only won 8 percent of the popular vote in the 1987 municipal elections, Barranco's replacement was the head of the CDS in Madrid, Agustín Rodríguez Sahagún. The center-right coalition lasted for two years, until 1991, when the PP's candidate, José María Álvarez del Manzano, won the absolute majority after the disintegration of the CDS. For more on the crisis related to the censure of Barranco, see Javier Echenagusia, "Galerna en el rompeolas," *Alfoz*, no. 64 (1989).

65. Javier Echenagusia, "Juan Barranco," *Alfoz*, no. 26 (1986): 17.

66. See Antonio Gómez Rufo, "Enrique Tierno, todavía," *El País*, 19 January 1988.

67. Ayuntamiento de Madrid, *Madrid, cultura viva* (Madrid: Patronato Municipal de Turismo, 1989), 12.

68. See Pedro Montoliú, "El Ayuntamiento de Madrid se prepara para desarrollar actividades propias del sector privado," *El País*, March 31, 1987.
69. Ibid.
70. Juan Barranco, "Madrid, símbolo de la España del futuro," *Alfoz*, no. 50 (1988): 36.
71. "El Ayuntamineto de Madrid crea una empresa de fomento," *El País*, February 16, 1987.
72. J. L. Regueira, "Barranco viaja a Francia para promocionar Madrid," *El País*, January 13, 1988.
73. "Barranco invitará a empresarios franceses a invertir en Madrid," *El País*, January 10, 1988. Also see Regueira, "Barranco viaja a Francia para promocionar Madrid."
74. "Barranco invitará a empresarios franceses a invertir en Madrid."
75. Juan Antonio Carbajo, "Madrid ha logrado ser la quinta ciudad mundial en número de congresos celebrados," *El País*, November 21, 1988.
76. Ibid.
77. See, for example, Juan Barranco, "La Capital Europea de la Cultura," *Villa de Madrid*, 1 February 1987.
78. Juan Barranco, "'Empezaremos a ver los frutos de las grandes obras'," *Villa de Madrid*, January 1, 1986.
79. Ibid.
80. Juan Barranco, "El Madrid de las libertades y los nuevos tiempos: conferencia en Club XXI," *Villa de Madrid Suplemento Informativo* 1986, 19.
81. Ibid.
82. Ibid.
83. Teresa Castro, "En 1992 puede multiplicarse la proyección internacional de Madrid," *Villa de Madrid*, February 1, 1987.
84. Juan Barranco, "Un proyecto ambicioso," *Villa de Madrid*, April 1, 1987.
85. Ayuntamiento de Madrid, *Madrid, cultura viva*, 12.
86. Ayuntamiento de Madrid, *Madrid, cultura vive: candidatura a la capitalidad europea de la cultura 1992*, 1.
87. Ibid., 11.
88. Ibid., 26.
89. Fernando Íñiguez, "Los músicos de la movida madrileña, contra la política cultural del alcalde," *El País*, July 7, 2002.
90. Feliciano Fidalgo, "Madrid," *El País*, June 5, 1988.
91. Plácido Domingo, *Pregón de las Fiestas de San Isidro, 1986* (Madrid: Ayuntamiento de Madrid, 1986).
92. "San Isidro '86: Madrid vive su fiesta," *Villa de Madrid*, May 1, 1986.
93. Ibid.
94. Carlos López, ed., *La Edad de Oro del pop español* (Madrid: Luca Editorial, 1992), 14.
95. Emilio Butragueño, *Pregón de las Fiestas de Navidad, 1986* (Madrid: Ayuntamiento de Madrid, 1986).
96. Mireia Sentís, "Cómic," in *Madrid, años ochenta*, ed. Rafael Sierra (Madrid: Ayuntamiento de Madrid, 1989), 173. Also see Amelia Castilla, "Desaparece la revista *Madriz*, financiada durante tres años por la Concejalía de Juventud," *El País*, February 12, 1987.
97. Castilla, "Desaparece la revista *Madriz*, financiada durante tres años por la Concejalía de Juventud."

98. See Eduardo García Matilla and Ortiz Miguel Angel, "Los jóvenes madrileños y la radio de los 80," in *Madrid, años ochenta*, ed. Rafael Sierra (Madrid: Ayuntamiento de Madrid, 1989).

99. See Pedro Montoliú, "El Ayuntamiento anuncia el cierre de 13 de las 91 terrazas situadas en el centro de Madrid," *El País*, July 23, 1987.

100. Anunchi Bremón, "El Ayuntamiento guarda silencio sobre la prohibición de acceso a la sala Universal desde el Martes," *El País*, December 15, 1987.

101. Ibid.

102. See Santiago Alconda, "De todo, menos 'punk'," *El País*, May 8, 1987; Pedro Montoliú, "La actuación de Tina Turner y Genesis costará al Ayuntamiento 80 milliones entre 'cachés' e impuestos," *El País*, May 7, 1987.

103. López, *La Edad de Oro del pop español*, 16.

104. "El Ayuntamiento gastará 150 millones en las verbenas y actos de San Isidro," *El País*, May 5, 1989.

105. Ibid.

106. "La Corporación socialista se despide con una exposición sobre sus logros," *El País*, March 18, 1987.

107. See "La Delegación del Gobierno prohibirá las manifestacions en el centro de la ciudad," *El País*, November 7, 1987.

108. See, for example, "Barranco se queja de la proliferación de manifestaciones en Madrid," *El País*, March 1, 1987.

109. The motion specifically outlawed demonstrations from the center of the city, even with prior authorization. In addition, no demonstrations were allowed between 8:00 a.m. and 8:00 p.m. during the workweek in the city center or on any of the city's major streets. Some of the prohibited streets included Castellana, Princesa, Gran Vía, and Alcalá. The local administration even went so far as to suggest the implementation of a "demonstration stadium" (*manifestódromo*) located away from the city. For more on limiting the right to protest in Madrid, see Rodolfo Serrano, "Los sindicatos rechazan la prohibición de manifestarse por el centro de la ciudad," *El País*, November 11, 1987. Also see "El Tribunal fija el recorrido de una manifestación," *El País*, November 21, 1987; "Sólo Izquierda Unida rechazó la propuesta del PSOE," *El País*, November 27, 1987; Ramón Adell Argiles, "Madrid: capital de manifestaciones," *Alfoz*, no. 74–75 (1990).

110. Adell Argiles, "Madrid: capital de manifestaciones," 110.

111. Javier Echenagusia, "Joaquín Leguina," *Alfoz*, no. 33 (1986): 15. Also see "Joaquín Leguina," *Alfoz*, no. 44 (1987); Joaquín Leguina, "La economía madrileña y los socialistas," *El País*, April 28, 1988; Joaquín Leguina, "Contra la sociedad perfecta," *El País*, May 26, 1988.

112. Echenagusia, "Joaquín Leguina," 15.

113. Emma Dent Coad, *Spanish Design and Architecture* (London: Studio Vista, 1990), 193.

114. Xosé Manuel Pereiro, "Madrid se escribe con V de Vigo," *El País*, September 12, 1986.

115. Ricardo Cantalapiedra, "El encuentro de las 'vanguardias' de Madrid y Vigo se dispersó en la algarabía de la fiesta," *El País*, September 22, 1986.

116. For further information on the events in Vigo, see ibid; José María Palmeiero, "Quietos, la movida!," *El País*, September 22, 1986; Santi Potros, "Vigo toma el testigo," *La Luna de Madrid*, October 1986; Emilio Alonso, "Encuentros en la tercera fase: Madrid-Vigo," *Rock de Lux*, November 1986.

117. José Ríos Longares, *Y yo caí—enamorado de la moda juvenil* (Alicante: Agua Clara, 2001), 26.
118. "50 artistas madrileños viajan a tres ciudades italianas para mostrar la 'movida'," *El País*, October 23, 1986.
119. Ibid.
120. Costus, *Valle de los Caídos, 1980–1987* (Madrid: Comunidad de Madrid, Consejería de Gobernación, 1987), n. p.
121. Lolo Rico, ed., *Madrid Hoy* (Madrid: La Comunidad de Madrid, Consejería de Gobernación, 1987).
122. Joaquín Leguina, "Madrid hoy," in *Madrid Hoy*, ed. Lolo Rico (Madrid: La Comunidad de Madrid, Consejería de Gobernación, 1987), 9.
123. "La Comunidad de Madrid reduce el presupuesto del Festival de Otoño," *El País*, February 11, 1987.
124. Comunidad de Madrid, *Anuario Estadístico. Comunidad de Madrid* (Madrid: Comunidad de Madrid, 1992), 542.
125. See ibid.
126. Ibid.
127. Ibid.
128. "Monografía: Ciencia y Tecnología: I+D una apuesta compleja," *Alfoz*, no. 94–95 (1992).
129. García Matilla and Angel, "Los jóvenes madrileños y la radio de los 80," 333.
130. Comunidad de Madrid, "Muy pronto, Ud. podrá venir al Parque volando [Adversitment]," *Alfoz*, no. 80 (1991): 6.
131. Javier Echenagusia, "Madrid cultural, escaparate y trastienda," *Alfoz*, no. 69–70 (1989): 37.
132. Ibid.
133. Íñiguez, "Los músicos de la movida madrileña, contra la política cultural del alcalde."
134. José Manuel Costa, "Radio Song," in *La Edad de Oro del pop español*, ed. Carlos López (Madrid: Luca Editorial, 1992), 80.
135. Other observers have been critical of the costs generally associated with the PSOE's emphasis on economic neoliberalism and consumption. John Trumpbour, for example, has criticized the national PSOE's particular brand of socialism: "Spain's *via thatcheriana* brought in its wake unemployment approaching 20 percent amidst vandalized public services, a ravaged physical environment, and large scale projects designed to slake the thirst for predatory over-consumption among the middle and upper classes." John Trumpbour, "Preface: Southern Europe Past and Present," in *Mediterranean Paradoxes: Politics and Social Structure in Southern Europe*, ed. James Kurth and James Petras (Providence: Berg, 1993), 10.
136. Hooper, *The New Spaniards*, 57.
137. Ibid.
138. For further information on Spain's economic development with regard to its integration into Europe, see Salmón, *The Modern Spanish Economy: Transformation and Integration into Europe*; Holman, *Integrating Southern Europe. EC Expansion and the Transnationalization of Spain*.
139. Newton and Donaghy, *Institutions of Modern Spain*, 339–341. Also see Holman, *Integrating Southern Europe*.
140. Santos Juliá, "The Socialist Era, 1982–1996," in *Spanish History since 1808*, ed. José Alvarez Junco and Adrian Shubert (London: Arnold, 2000), 337.

141. Leguina, "La economía madrileña y los socialistas."
142. Ibid.
143. Elizabeth Nash, *Madrid: A Cultural and Literary Companion* (Oxford: Signal Books Limited, 2001), 231.
144. Amando de Miguel, "La juventud Madrileña de los años 80: la última invasión de los bárbaros," in *Madrid, años ochenta*, ed. Rafael Sierra (Madrid: Ayuntamiento de Madrid, 1989), 56.
145. Spain's seven-year transition period came to an end in 1993, further exacerbating the country's post-1992 economic recession.
146. Hooper, *The New Spaniards*, 58.
147. de Miguel, "La juventud Madrileña de los años 80: la última invasión de los bárbaros," 56.
148. Ibid.
149. Patricia Godes, "Años 80: una década de Rock Español," *Rock de Lux*, June 1990, 22.
150. "El 66% de los vecinos no sabe que Madrid será Capital Cultural de Europa en 1992," *El País*, June 16, 1989.
151. "Madrid 92: ¿Qué hice yo para merecer esto?," *Alfoz* 64 (1989): 36.
152. García Matilla and Angel, "Los jóvenes madrileños y la radio de los 80," 341.
153. Ibid.
154. For a further discussion of the movida as kitsch, or *cursi*, see Noël Valis, *The Culture of Cursilería: Bad Taste, Kitsch, and Class in Modern Spain* (Durham: Duke University Press, 2002), 277–302. Also see Javier Navarro, "Notas kitsch del paisaje urbano madrileño," in *El Kitsch Español*, ed. Antonio Sánchez Casado (Madrid: Temas de Hoy, 1988).
155. Carmen de Posadas, *Yuppies, jetset, la movida y otras especies* (Madrid: Temas de Hoy, 1987), 96.
156. Ibid., 94.
157. Borja Casani, "[No title]," in *Madrid Hoy*, ed. Lolo Rico (Madrid: La Comunidad de Madrid, Consejería de Gobernación, 1987), 81.
158. Julio Iglesias de Ussel, "La movida: un análisis sociológico," in *Movida y sociedad*, ed. María Consolación Calderón España (Sevilla: Real Sociedad Económica, 1997), 63.
159. "80.000 personas asistieron al Festival de Otoño de Madrid," *El País*, November 28, 1990.
160. "La Comunidad de Madrid reduce el presupuesto del Festival de Otoño."; "80.000 personas asistieron al Festival de Otoño de Madrid."
161. Hooper, *The New Spaniards*, 326.
162. Ibid.
163. Rosa Olivares, "Una década tumultuosa," *Lápiz*, Summer 1991, 40.
164. Ibid.
165. Jesús Ordovás, "Madrid Pop, 1979–1989," in *Madrid, años ochenta*, ed. Rafael Sierra (Madrid: Ayuntamiento de Madrid, 1989), 119.
166. "Mañana, sondeo europeo de *El País/The Independent*," *El País*, November 18, 1989.
167. Ibid.
168. CIS, *Los españoles ante el segundo aniversario de la firma del tratado de adhesión de España a la Comunidad Europea* (Madrid: CIS, 1988), 36.
169. Ibid.
170. Ibid., 34.

171. Ibid.
172. For further information on Spanish public opinion data with regards to European integration, see CIS, *La opinion pública ante las Comunidades Europeas. Estudio 1776* (Madrid: CIS, 1988); CIS, *Opiniones y Actitudes CIS: La opinion pública española ante Europa y los europeos. Estudios y Encuestas 17* (Madrid: CIS, 1989); CIS, *Sentimiento europeista de los españoles. Estudio 2084* (Madrid: CIS, 1994).
173. Inmaculada Szmolka, *Opiniones y Actitudes 21. Opiniones y actitudes de los españoles ante el proceso de intregración europea* (Madrid: CIS, 1999), 73.
174. CIS, *Estudio 1984*, December 1991, cited in ibid., 74.
175. Ibid., 132.
176. By the end of the decade, the Comunidad of Madrid had become more European in another small but symbolic way. Between 1984 and 1989, the number of Europeans living in the region more than doubled, increasing from 14,852 to 33,574. Comunidad de Madrid, *Anuario Estadístico*, 148.
177. Newton and Donaghy, *Institutions of Modern Spain*, 345.
178. CIS, *Estudio 2023*, October 1992, cited in Szmolka, *Opiniones y Actitudes 21*, 16.
179. Once again, data from the years 1990 to 1995 must be used here for analysis because the "dual identity" question was not put to the residents of Madrid during the 1980s.
180. Luis Moreno, *La federalización de España* (Madrid: Siglo XXI, 1997), 130–135.
181. See Alberto Pérez Navarro, "Casa Regional para Madrid," *Villa de Madrid*, July 15, 1987; León Casado Fernandez, "Madrileñismo a tope," *Villa de Madrid*, September 15, 1987.
182. Pérez Navarro, "Casa Regional para Madrid."
183. Ibid.
184. See, for example, Juan Antonio Carbajo, "San Isidro, el santo del agua," *El País*, May 15, 1989.
185. For additional information on the *Partido Regionalista Independiente Madrileño* (PRIM), see Nicolás Piñeiro, *Regionalismo: Madrid, capital y region* (Madrid: Grafiprintin, 1991). Also see Nicolás Piñeiro, "El nuevo regionalismo," *El País*, March 20, 1991.
186. See "Ruiz Gallardón: 'El PRIM es un invento de Leguina'," *El País*, June 12, 1989.
187. For example, see José Ignacio Wert, "Las elecciones del 26 de Mayo: una interpretación," *Alfoz*, no. 81–82 (1991); Mikel Altuna and Javier Echenagusia, "Madrid es mucho Madrid," *Alfoz*, no. 81–82 (1991).
188. The PRIM even presented itself at the October 2003 regional elections, winning a total of 1,472 votes in a region of more than 5 million inhabitants. Moncho Alpuente, "Mínimos y anónimos," *El País*, October 20, 2003.
189. Javier Domingo, "Una decada de nueva cultura," *Alfoz*, no. 69–70 (1989): 72–73.
190. Ibid., 73.

CHAPTER 8

1. Francis Fukuyama, *The End of History and the Last Man* (New York: Free Press, 1992). While Francis Fukuyama and other conservatives interpreted

the apparent dominance of neoliberalism at the end of the 1980s in a decidedly positive light, the opposite interpretation is, of course, possible. The triumphalism of liberal democratic regimes and the unquestioned embrace of the " 'logic' " of the market can also be seen as limiting the possibility of pursuing political alternatives that would eventually lead to greater egalitarianism, social justice, and democratization. From this perspective, the perceived end of ideological alternatives represents not a victory for capitalism and the West, but a defeat for more progressive models of democracy.

2. See, for example, José Vidal Beneyto, "Volver a empezar o la ruptura ciudadana," *El País*, April 8, 1995. Cited in Pamela B. Radcilff, "Citizenship and the Transition," (San Diego: UCSD, 2003).

3. Geoff Eley, *Forging Democracy: The History of the Left in Europe, 1850–2000* (Oxford: Oxford University Press, 2002), 428.

4. For example, scholars such as Guillermo O'Donnell and Philippe C. Schmitter argue that while popular mobilization may promote democratization during the early stages of transition from authoritarian rule, highly active or militant political participation usually represents a threat to democratic consolidation in the long term: "[Popular mobilization] may be an efficacious instrument for bringing down a dictatorship but may make subsequent democratic consolidation difficult, and under some circumstances may provide an important motive for regression to an even more brutal form of authoritarian rule." Guillermo O'Donnell and Philippe C. Schmitter, *Transitions from Authoritarian Rule: Tentative Conclusions about Uncertain Democracies* (Baltimore: Johns Hopkins University Press, 1986), 65. For a good general discussion of the major lines of debate surrounding the democratic consolidation of former authoritarian regimes, see Diane Ethier, "Introduction: Processes of Transition and Democratic Consolidation: Theoretical Indicators," in *Democratic Transition and Consolidation in Southern Europe, Latin America, and Southeast Asia*, ed. Diane Ethier (London: Macmillan Press, 1990).

5. Radcliff, "Citizenship and the Transition," 4.

6. Ibid. In contrast to those who see demobilization as a prerequisite for a stable democracy, other scholars, such as Peter McDonough, Doh Shin, and José Álvaro Moisés, maintain that low levels of popular participation undermine "the quality of democracy." Peter McDonough, Doh Shin, and José Álvaro Moisés, "Democratization and Participation: Comparing Spain, Brazil, and Korea," *The Journal of Politics* 60, no. 4 (1998): 945. For a classic treatment of this issue, see Gabriel Almond and Sidney Verba, *The Civic Culture* (Princeton: Princeton University Press, 1963).

7. See Jürgen Habermas, "Historical Consciousness and Post-Traditional Identity," in *The New Conservatism: Cultural Criticism and the Historians' Debate*, ed. Shierry Weber Nicholsen (Cambridge, MA: MIT Press, 1989). Also see Jürgen Habermas, "Citizenship and National Identity: Some Reflections on the Future of Europe," *Praxis International* 12, no. 1 (1992).

8. See Sandie Holguín, *Creating Spaniards: Culture and National Identity in Republican Spain* (Madison, WI: University of Wisconsin Press, 2002).

9. Sandie Holguín argues that the Republican-Socialist insistence on a national identity based on the primacy of Castilian culture, which also failed to celebrate cultural diversity, led in part to the failure of the Second Republic. See ibid.

10. Ignasi Riera, "Autonomía de la cultura, cultura de la autonomía," in *Encuentros en Madrid 1985: por la renovación cultural, por la democratización*

de la cultura, ed. Fundación de Investigaciones Marxistas (Madrid: Fundación de Investigaciones Marxistas, 1986), 78.

11. Ibid., 76.
12. Enrique Tierno Galván, "Del Madrid de la dictadura al de 'la movida'," *Villa de Madrid*, December 4, 1985.
13. Antonio Gómez Rufo, "Madrid cultural: el lustro lustroso," *Alfoz*, no. 24–25 (1986): 19.
14. Fernando Martín Vicente, "¿Una mayoría para el cambio?," *El País*, September 24, 1982.
15. Enrique Rojas, *El hombre Light: una vida sin valores* (Madrid: Temas de Hoy, 1992).
16. Despite this ignoral by *ABC*, the *Ayuntamiento* of Madrid placed full-page advertisements in the newspaper promoting *San Isidro* 1985. See, for example, *ABC*, May 10, 1985.
17. See, for example, Ernesto Carvajal, "Tamames, los bares y el goatiné," *ABC*, January 11, 1986.
18. Pilar Bidagor Altuna was writing in response to the issue: *Alfoz*, no. 7–8, September 1984.
19. Pilar Bidagor Altuna, "La movida y la juventud," *Alfoz*, no. 13 (1985): 14.
20. Ibid.
21. Amelia Castilla, "*Madriz* seguirá publicándose, pese a la oposición del Grupo Popular," *El País*, April 23, 1984.
22. José María Álvarez del Manzano, "'Quisieramos ver mejorada la infraestructura de Madrid'," *Villa de Madrid*, January 1, 1986.
23. See for example Julio Sentien, in *Encuentros en Madrid 1985: por la renovación cultural, por la democratización de la cultura*, ed. Fundación de Investigaciones Marxistas (Madrid: Fundación de Investigaciones Marxistas, 1986).
24. José Tono Martínez, "Periodistas postmodernos," *El País*, April 15, 1987.
25. Juan Pablo Fusi, "La cultura de la transición," *Revista de Occidente* 122–123 (1991): 63.
26. Kathleen M. Vernon and Barbara Morris, "Introduction: Pedro Almodóvar, Postmodern *Auteur*," in *Post-Franco, Postmodern: The Films of Pedro Almodóvar*, ed. Kathleen M. Vernon and Barbara Morris (Westport, CT: Greenwood, 1995), 12.
27. Geoff Eley makes a similar argument about the general "deradicalization" of European socialist parties during this period in his recent book: "Profoundly deradicalized, they were separating rapidly from the political cultures and social histories that had sustained them . . . No one talked any longer of abolishing capitalism, of regulating its dysfunctions and excesses, or even of modifying its most egregiously destructive social effects. For a decade after 1989, the space for imagining alternatives narrowed to virtually nothing." See Eley, *Forging Democracy: The History of the Left in Europe, 1850–2000*, vii.

CONCLUSION

1. David Corkill, "Multiple National Identities, Immigration and Racism in Spain and Portugal," in *Nations and Identity in Contemporary Europe*, ed. Brian Jenkins and Spyros A. Sofos (London: Routledge, 1996), 168.

2. Borja Casani, "[No title]," in *Madrid Hoy*, ed. Lolo Rico (Madrid: La Comunidad de Madrid, Consejería de Gobernación, 1987), 80.
3. Elizabeth Nash, *Madrid: A Cultural and Literary Companion* (Oxford: Signal Books, 2001), 232. Also see "*La Luna de Madrid*, adelanta la fiesta de fin de año," *El País*, December 27, 1983.
4. Diego A. Manrique, "La entrevista definitiva," *Primera Linea de la Actualidad* (November 1986): 27.
5. Fernando Díaz-Plaja Contesti, *Madrid desde "casi" el cielo* (Madrid: Maeva, 1987), 230.
6. Beyond anecdotal evidence, it is difficult to link an increase of drug use directly with the *movida*. This task is made even more difficult by the fact that there is little information in general regarding drug use specifically in the capital during this period. However, one study from the mid-1980s showed that the proportion of young people in Madrid between the ages of 15 and 24 years that smoked marijuana on a regular basis increased from 19 percent in 1982 to 24 percent in 1985. See Amando de Miguel, "La juventud Madrileña de los años 80: la última invasión de los bárbaros," in *Madrid, años ochenta*, ed. Rafael Sierra (Madrid: Ayuntamiento de Madrid, 1989), 44.
7. In fact, with regard to those associated with the *movida*, AIDS claimed the lives of the writer Eduardo Haro Ibars, the gallery owner Fernando Vijande, and half of the artistic duo known as Los Costus.
8. John Hooper, "González and the Search for Greatness," *The Guardian*, May 7, 1991.
9. "Guerra dice que 10 años mas de mandato socialista pondrían a España en cabeza de Europa," *El País*, September 23, 1989.
10. Francisco Umbral, *Y Tierno Galván ascendió a los cielos* (Barcelona: Seix Barral, 1990), 165. Also see Angel del Rio, "Diez años para cambiar realidades y enterrar utopias," *Alfoz*, no. 62–63 (1989): 77–82. Referring to Tierno Galván's funeral, John Hooper has similarly remarked: "On that day Spain's Socialists buried the spirit of their young ideals along with the body of their old teacher." John Hooper, *The New Spaniards* (London: Penguin, 1995), 57.
11. Santos Juliá, "The Socialist Era, 1982–1996," in *Spanish History since 1808*, ed. José Alvarez Junco and Adrian Shubert (London: Arnold, 2000), 344.

BIBLIOGRAPHY

I. ARCHIVES, LIBRARIES, AND SPECIAL COLLECTIONS

Archivo de la Villa de Madrid. Madrid, Spain.
Archivo General de la Administración. Alcalá de Henares, Spain.
Biblioteca de la Comunidad de Madrid. Madrid, Spain.
Biblioteca del Ministerio de Cultura. Madrid, Spain.
Biblioteca Nacional. Madrid, Spain.
Centro de Investigaciónes Sociológicas (CIS). Madrid, Spain.
Fundación Pablo Iglesis. Alcalá de Henares, Spain.
Hermeroteca Municipal de Madrid. Madrid, Spain.

II. NEWSPAPERS, MAGAZINES, AND OFFICIAL PUBLICATIONS

ABC (Madrid)
Agenda Cultural (Madrid)
Ajoblanco (Madrid)
Alfoz (Madrid)
Análisis e Investigaciones Culturales (Madrid)
Boletín del Ayuntamiento de Madrid (Madrid)
Boletín Oficial de la Comunidad de Madrid (Madrid)
Boletín Oficial del Estado (Madrid)
Cambio 16 (Madrid)
Dezine (Madrid)
Diario 16 (Madrid)
Disco Actualidad (Madrid)
El Día (Madrid)
El Mundo (Madrid)
El País (Madrid)
Información Cultural (Madrid)
Interviú (Madrid)
La Luna de Madrid (Madrid)
Lápiz (Madrid)
La Vanguardia (Barcelona)
Madriz (Madrid)
Noticias Culturales (Madrid)
Primera Linea de la Actualidad (Barcelona)
Rock de Lux (Madrid)
Rock Espezial (Madrid)
Sur-Exprés (Madrid)

Triunfo (Madrid)
Vibora (Barcelona)
Vibraciones (Madrid)
Villa de Madrid (Madrid)
Ya (Madrid)

III. PUBLISHED SOURCES

Aguilar Fernandez, Paloma. *Memoria y olvido de la guerra civil española*. Madrid: Alianza, 1996.

———. "The Memory of the Civil War in the Transition to Democracy: The Peculiarity of the Basque Case." *West European Politics* 21, no. 4 (1998): 5–25.

———. "The Opposition to Franco, the Transition to Democracy and the New Political System." In *Spanish History since 1808*, edited by José Alvarez Junco and Adrian Shubert. London: Arnold, 2000.

Aguilera, Ricardo. "A ritmo de comic." In *La Edad de Oro del pop español*, edited by Carlos López. Madrid: Luca Editorial, 1992.

Allinson, Mark. "Alaska: Star of Stage and Screen and Optimistic Punk." In *Constructing Identity in Twentieth Century Spain*, edited by Jo Labanyi. Oxford: Oxford University Press, 2002.

———. "The Construction of Youth in Spain in the 1980s and 1990s." In *Contemporary Spanish Cultural Studies*, edited by Barry Jordan and Rikki Morgan-Tamosunas. London: Arnold, 2000.

———. *A Spanish Labyrinth: The Films of Pedro Almodóvar*. London: Tauris, 2001.

Almond, Gabriel, and Sidney Verba. *The Civic Culture*. Princeton: Princeton University Press, 1963.

Alonso de los Ríos, César. *La verdad sobre Tierno Galván*. Madrid: Anaya & Muchnik, 1997.

Alonso Fernández, Luis. "Madrid, capital mundial del pop." *Reseña*, no. 142 (1983): 40–42.

Alpuente, Moncho. "¿Hay vida despues de la movida?" In *Madrid Hoy*, edited by Lolo Rico. Madrid: La Comunidad de Madrid, Consejería de Gobernación, 1987.

———. "Y algo se movio 'Historia de una decada.'" In *Madrid, años ochenta*, edited by Rafael Sierra. Madrid: Ayuntamiento de Madrid, 1989.

Altares, Pedro. "Madrid, ni mas ni menos." In *Madrid Hoy*, edited by Lolo Rico. Madrid: La Comunidad de Madrid, Consejería de Gobernación, 1987.

Álvarez, J. D. *Ouka Lele: biografía*. Madrid: Neverland Ediciones, 2006.

Álvarez Junco, José. "The Formation of Spanish identity and Its Adaptation to the Age of Nations." *History and Memory: Studies in Representation of the Past* 14, no. 1–2 (2002): 13–36.

———. *Mater Dolorosa: la idea de España en el siglo XIX*. Madrid: Taurus, 2001.

———. "The Nation-Building Process in Nineteenth Century Spain." In *Nationalism and the Nation in the Iberian Peninsula. Competing and Conflicting Identities*, edited by Clare Mar-Molinero and Ángel Smith. Oxford: Berg, 1995.

Alvira Martín, Francisco, and José García López. "Los españoles y las autonomias." *Papeles de Economica Española* 35 (1988): 402–21.

Amell, Samuel, ed. *España frente al siglo XXI: cultura y literatura*. Madrid: Cátedra, 1992.

———. *La cultura española en el posfranquismo*. Madrid: Playor, 1988.

Amo, Montserrat del. *Historia mínima de Madrid*. Madrid: Avapies, 1987.

Anderson, Benedict. *Imagined Communities: Reflections on the Origins and Spread of Nationalism*. London: Verso, 1992.

Arbós, Xavier. "Central versus Peripheral Nationalism in Building Democracy: The Case of Spain." *Canadian Review of Studies in Nationalism* XIV, no. 1 (1987): 143–60.

Archilés, Ferran, and Manuel Martí. "Ethnicity, Region and Nation: Valencian Identity and the Spanish Nation-State." *Ethnic and Racial Studies* 24, no. 5 (2001): 779–97.

Arespacochaga, Juan de. "Prólogo." In *Madrid con soluciones*, edited by Enrique Villoría. Madrid: Azara, 1982.

Armstrong, John. *Nations before Nationalism*. Chapel Hill: University of North Carolina Press, 1982.

Asociación Cultural y Recreativa de Villanueva Sto. Adriano. *Primera Gran Semana Cultural: año 1988*. Oviedo: Caja de Ahorros de Asturias, 1988.

Asociación de Vecinos "L'Andecha." *La Movida Asturiana: febrero-marzo de 1984*. Avilés: Biblioteca Pública de la Luz, 1984.

Astudillo, F. Javier. "Los Fanzines." In *La Edad de Oro del pop español*, edited by Carlos López. Madrid: Luca Editorial, 1992.

Ayuntamiento de Madrid. *Adquisiciones 1979–1983: Museo Municipal, exposición abril–junio 1983*. Madrid: Ayuntamiento de Madrid, Delegación de Cultura del Ayuntamiento, 1983.

———. *Centro Cultural de la Villa: 1977–1987 diez años*. Madrid: Ayuntamiento de Madrid, Consejalía de Cultura, 1987.

———. *Dossier de exposición: "Madrid, Madrid, Madrid."* Madrid: Ayuntamiento de Madrid, 1984.

———. *La experimentación en el arte: exposición, octubre 1983*. Madrid: Ayuntamiento de Madrid, Consejalía de Cultura, 1983.

———. *Madrid Avanza: 1983–1984, un año de gestión*. Madrid: Ayuntamiento de Madrid, Concejalía de Relaciones Institucionales y Comunicación, 1984.

———. *Madrid Avanza: 1983–1987*. Madrid: Ayuntamiento de Madrid, 1987.

———. *Madrid, cultura viva*. Madrid: Patronato Municipal de Turismo, 1989.

———. *Madrid, cultura vive: candidatura a la capitalidad europea de la cultura 1992*. Madrid: Ayuntamiento de Madrid, 1988.

———. *Madrid Proyecto Madrid: exposición*. Madrid: Ayuntamiento de Madrid, 1986.

———. *Madrid Restaura: 1979–1981, exposición de mayo 1981*. Madrid: Ayuntamiento de Madrid, Delegación de Cultura, 1981.

———. *Madrid, único y múltiple, 21 crónicas periodísticas*. Madrid: Ayuntamiento de Madrid, 1987.

———. *Madrid y el Cine: Fiesta de San Isidro 1984*. Madrid: Ayuntamiento de Madrid, Filmoteca Española, 1984.

———. *Normas Urbanísticas I. Plan General de Ordenación de Madrid*. Madrid: Ayuntamiento de Madrid, 1985.

———. *Normas Urbanísticas II. Plan General de Ordenación de Madrid*. Madrid: Ayuntamiento de Madrid, 1985.

———. *Participación ciudadana: I Jornadas, 17, 18, y 19 de enero 1986*. Madrid: Ayuntamiento de Madrid, Junta Municipal de Centro, 1986.

———. *Participación Ciudadana: II Jornadas, del 3 al 15 diciembre 1982*. Madrid: Ayuntamiento de Madrid, Delegación de Relaciones Sociales y Vecinales, 1983.

————. *Plan de limpieza de la ciudad de Madrid*. Madrid: Ayuntamiento de Madrid, Área de Urbanismo e Infraestructuras, 1984.

————. *Plan Especial Villa de Madrid: cuatro años de gestión*. Madrid: Ayuntamiento de Madrid, 1986.

————. *Plan General de Ordenación de Madrid, 1985. Memoria de Participación*. Madrid: Ayuntamiento de Madrid, 1985.

————. *Plan General de Ordenación de Madrid, 1985. Memoria General*. Madrid: Ayuntamiento de Madrid, 1985.

————. *Programa de Actuación. Plan General de Ordenación de Madrid*. Madrid: Ayuntamiento de Madrid, 1985.

————. *Programa de San Isidro, 1985*. Madrid: Ayuntamiento de Madrid, 1985.

————. *Recuperar Madrid*. Madrid: Ayuntamiento de Madrid, Oficina Municipal del Plan, 1982.

Aznar, Fernando. *Madrid: una historia en comunidad*. Madrid: Comunidad de Madrid, 1987.

Balfour, Sebastian. "Spain from 1931 to the Present." In *Spain: A History*, edited by Raymond Carr. Oxford: Oxford University Press, 2000.

————, and Alejandro Quiroga. *The Reinvention of Spain: Nation and Identity since Democracy*. Oxford: Oxford University Press, 2007.

Beramendi, Justo G. "Identity, Ethnicity and State in Spain: 19th and 20th Centuries." In *Identity and Territorial Autonomy in Plural Societies*, edited by William Safran and Ramón Máiz. London: Frank Cass, 2000.

————. "La historiografía de los nacionalismos en España." *Historia Contemporánea* 7 (1992): 135–54.

Beramendi, Justo G., and Xosé Manoel Núñez. "Introduction." In *Nationalism in Europe: Past and Present*, edited by Justo G. Beramendi and Xosé Manoel Núñez. Santiago de Compostela: University of Santiago de Compostela, 1994.

————. *O Nacionalismo Galego*. Vigo: A Nosa Terra, 1995.

Berlanga, Jorge. "Madrid Babilonia." In *Madrid Hoy*, edited by Lolo Rico. Madrid: La Comunidad de Madrid, Consejería de Gobernación, 1987.

Bessière, Bernard. "El Madrid de la democracia: comportamientos culturales y crisol de creación. Realidades y dudas." In *España frente al siglo XXI: cultura y literatura*, edited by Samuel Amell. Madrid: Cátedra, 1992.

————. *Histoire de Madrid*. Paris: Fayard, 1996.

————. *La culture espagnole. Les mutatuins de l'après franquisme (1975–1992)*. Paris: L'Harmattan, 1992.

————. "Le postmodernisme en Espagne dans les années 80." *Les Mélanges de la Casa de Velázquez* (Madrid, 1990).

Bhabha, Homi, ed. *Nation and Narration*. London: Routledge, 1990.

Bonaddio, Federico, and Derek Harris, eds. *Siete ensayos sobre la cultura*. Old Aberdeen: Aberdeen University Press, 1995.

Boyd, Carolyn P. *Historia Patria: Politics, History, and National Identity in Spain, 1875–1975*. Princeton: Princeton University Press, 1997.

————. "The Second Battle of Covadonga: The Politics of Commemoration in Modern Spain." *History and Memory: Studies in Representation of the Past* 14, no. 1–2 (2002): 37–66.

Breuilly, John. *Nationalism and the State*. Manchester: Manchester University Press, 1985.

Brown, David. *Contemporary Nationalism: Civic, Ethnocultural, and Multicultural Politics*. London: Routledge, 2000.

Buero Vallejo, Antonio. *Pregón de las Fiestas de San Isidro, 1983.* Madrid: Ayuntamiento de Madrid, 1983.

Bustamante, Enrique, and Ramón Zallo, eds. *Las industrias culturales en España.* Madrid: Akal, 1988.

Butragueño, Emilio. *Pregón de las Fiestas de Navidad, 1986.* Madrid: Ayuntamiento de Madrid, 1986.

Cabezudo, Maria Dolores. "Los vinos de las cinco leguas, ayer, hoy y mañana." In *Vinos de Madrid, Son Nuestros Vinos: IV y V semanas del vino,* edited by Comunidad de Madrid. Madrid: Comunidad de Madrid, Dirección General de Política Alimentaria e Investigación Agraria, 1986.

Cagigo, José L., ed *España 1975–1980. Conflictos y logros de la democracia.* Madrid: Jose Porrúa Turanzas, 1982.

Carmen de Posadas. *Yuppies, jetset, la movida y otras especies.* Madrid: Temas de Hoy, 1987.

Carr, Raymond, ed. *Spain: A History.* Oxford: Oxford University Press, 2000.

———, and Juan Pablo Fusi. *Spain: From Dictatorship to Democracy.* London: Allen and Unwin, 1979.

Carrillo, Santi. "De la nada a la más absoluta miseria." In *La Edad de Oro del pop español,* edited by Carlos López. Madrid: Luca Editorial, 1992.

Casani, Borja. "[No title]." In *Madrid Hoy,* edited by Lolo Rico. Madrid: La Comunidad de Madrid, Consejería de Gobernación, 1987.

Castells, Manuel. *The City and the Grassroots: A Cross-Cultural Theory of Urban Social Movements.* Berkeley: University of California Press, 1983.

Cela, Camilo José. "Madrid, Tierno y yo." In *Así es Madrid,* edited by Antonio Gómez Rufo. Madrid: Temas de Hoy, 1988.

Cervera, Rafa. *Alaska y otras historias de la movida.* Barcelona: Plaza and Janés Editores, 2002.

———. "Prólogo-Entrevista: Pedro Almodovar." In *Alaska y otras historias de la movida.* Barcelona: Plaza and Janés, 2002.

Chacoa Fuertes, Fernando. "Estereotipos regionales de los madrileños." *Papeles Psicólogos del Colegio,* no. 25 (1986): 23–30.

Chamorro, Eduardo. *Enrique Tierno: el alcalde.* Madrid: Cambio 16, 1986.

Chatterjee, Partha. *The Nation and Its Fragments.* London: Zed Books, 1993.

Cierva, Ricardo de la. *España, la sociedad violada.* Barcelona: Planeta, 1989.

CIS. *Barómetro Comunidad Autónoma de Madrid I (Estudio 1503).* Madrid: CIS, 1986.

———. *Estudio 2014. Comunidad de Madrid.* Madrid: CIS, 1992.

———. "La actividad de los jóvenes madrileños." *REIS,* no. 26 (1984): 273–94.

———. *La opinion pública ante las Comunidades Europeas. Estudio 1776.* Madrid: CIS, 1988.

———. *Los españoles ante el segundo aniversario de la firma del tratado de adhesión de España a la Comunidad Europea.* Madrid: CIS, 1988.

———. *Municipales Madrid (Estudio 1546).* Madrid: CIS, 1986.

———. *Opiniones y Actitudes CIS: La opinion pública española ante Europa y los europeos. Estudios y Encuestas 17.* Madrid: CIS, 1989.

———. *Opinión pública y cultura política en las Comunidades Autónomas, Madrid. Estudio 2037.* Madrid: CIS, 1993.

———. *Sentimiento europeista de los españoles. Estudio 2084.* Madrid: CIS, 1994.

Clark, Robert P. *The Basque Insurgents: ETA, 1952–1980.* Madison: University of Wisconsin Press, 1980.

———. *Negotiating with ETA: Obstacles to Peace in the Basques Country, 1975–1988.* Reno: University of Nevada Press, 1990.

Coller, Xavier, and Rafael Castelló. "Las bases sociales de la identidad dual: el caso valenciano." *Revista Española de Investigaciones Sociológicas,* no. 88 (1999): 155–83.

Compitello, Malcolm Allan. "From Planning to Design: The Culture of Flexible Accumulation in Post-Cambio Madrid." *Journal of Hispanic Cultural Studies,* no. 3 (1999): 199–220.

———. "Todavía en *La Luna.*" *Arizona Journal of Hispanic Cultural Studies* 1 (1997): 153–68.

Comunidad de Madrid. *Andy Warhol y España: exposición.* Madrid: Comunidad de Madrid, 1987.

———. *Anuario Estadístico 1984.* Madrid: Comunidad de Madrid, 1984.

———. *Anuario Estadístico. Comunidad de Madrid.* Madrid: Comunidad de Madrid, 1992.

———. *Artistas en Madrid años 80.* Madrid: Dirección General del Patrimonio Cultural, 1992.

———. *Comunidad de Madrid, 1983–1987.* Madrid: Comunidad de Madrid, 1987.

———. *Comunidad de Madrid, 1983–1985: balance de gestión del primer gobierno regional madrileño en el ecuador de su mandato.* Madrid: Comunidad de Madrid, 1985.

———. *Consejería de Cultura y Deportes, 1983–1987.* Madrid: Comunidad de Madrid, 1987.

———. *Festival de Otoño en Madrid: 1984–1988.* Barcelona: Iberia, 1988.

———. *Festival de Otoño, programa 1985.* Madrid: Comunidad de Madrid, Consejería de Cultura, 1985.

———. *Informe sobre demanda latente de cultura y deporte.* Madrid: Comunidad de Madrid, 1985.

———. *Madrid en la sociedad del siglo XIX.* Madrid: Comunidad de Madrid, 1986.

———. *Madrid y los Borbones en el siglo XVIII: la construcción de una ciudad y su territorio.* Madrid: Comunidad de Madrid, 1984.

———. *Pensar en Madrid.* Madrid: Comunidad de Madrid, 1984.

———. *Primer certamen escolar, "Conoce tu ciudad."* Madrid: Comunidad de Madrid, 1983.

———. *Segundo certamen escolar, "Conoce tu ciudad."* Madrid: Comunidad de Madrid, 1985.

———. *Tercer certamen escolar, "Conoce tu ciudad."* Madrid: Comunidad de Madrid, 1985.

———. *Veintinueve propuestas de mejoras urbanas en la Comunidad de Madrid.* Madrid: Comunidad de Madrid, 1986.

———. *Vinos de Madrid, son nuestros vinos: IV y V semanas del vino.* Madrid: Comunidad de Madrid, Dirección General de Política Alimentaria e Investigación Agraria, 1986.

Confino, Alon. "Collective Memory and Cultural History: Problems of Method." *The American Historical Review* 102, no. 5 (1997): 1386–1403.

———. *The Nation as a Local Metaphor: Württemberg, Imperial Germany, and National Memory, 1871–1918.* Chapel Hill: University of North Carolina Press, 1997.

Consorcio para la organización de Madrid Capital Europea de Cultura. *Madrid Capital Europea de Cultura 1992.* Madrid: Asisa, 1993.

Conversi, Danielle. *The Basques, the Catalans and Spain: Alternative Routes to Nationalist Mobilisation*. Reno: University of Nevada Press, 1997.

Corkill, David. "Multiple National Identities, Immigration and Racism in Spain and Portugal." In *Nations and Identity in Contemporary Europe*, edited by Brian Jenkins and Spyros A Sofos. London: Routledge, 1996.

Costa, José Manuel. "Radio Song." In *La Edad de Oro del pop español*, edited by Carlos López. Madrid: Luca Editorial, 1992.

Costandina Titus, A. "Decentralization in Post-Franco Spain: The Andalusian Autonomy Movement." *Iberian Studies*, no. 1–2 (1983).

Coste, María Teresa. *Trovador de veras: vida de Agustín Lara*. Buenos Aires: Claridad, 1988.

Costus. *Clausura: exposición antológica*. Madrid: Comunidad de Madrid, 1992.

———. *Valle de los Caídos, 1980–1987*. Madrid: Comunidad de Madrid, Consejería de Gobernación, 1987.

Coyote, Víctor. *Cruce de perras y otros relatos de los 80*. Madrid: Visual Books, 2006.

Cruspinera, Joan. *Tauromaquia: grabado*. Madrid: Galeria Estampa, 1983.

"Datos de opinión: la CE." *REIS*, no. 50 (1990): 343–67.

de Anton, Jorge. "Onda 2." In *La Edad de Oro del pop español*, edited by Carlos López. Madrid: Luca Editorial, 1992.

de Miguel, Amando. "La juventud Madrileña de los años 80: la última invasión de los bárbaros." In *Madrid, años ochenta*, edited by Rafael Sierra. Madrid: Ayuntamiento de Madrid, 1989.

Delacampagne, Christian, ed. *Madrid, la la décennie prodigieuse*. Paris: Autrement, 1987.

Dent Coad, Emma. "Designer Culture in the 1980s: The Price of Success." In *Spanish Cultural Studies: An Introduction*, edited by Helen Graham and Jo Labanyi, 376–80. Oxford: Oxford University Press, 1995.

———. *Spanish Design and Architecture*. London: Studio Vista, 1990.

Desfor Edles, Laura. *Symbol and Ritual in the New Spain: The Transition to Democracy after Franco*. Cambridge: Cambridge University Press, 1998.

Deutsch, Karl. *Nationalism and Social Communication*. Cambridge, MA: MIT Press, 1966.

Díaz, Elías. "Tierno Galván, entre el fraccionamiento y la totalidad." *Sistema* no. 71–72 (1986): 19–42.

Díaz-Plaja Contesti, Fernando. *Madrid desde "casi" el cielo*. Madrid: Maeva, 1987.

Díez Medrano, Juan. *Divided Nations: Class, Politics, and Nationalism in the Basque Country and Catalonia*. Ithaca: Cornell University Press, 1996.

Domingo Iribarren, Florencio. *ETA. Estrategia organizativa y actuaciones, 1978–1992*. Bilboa: Universidad del País Vasco, 1998.

Domingo, Javier. "La Luna, el Madriz, El Paseante . . . y otras especies de los 80." In *Madrid, años ochenta*, edited by Rafael Sierra. Madrid: Ayuntamiento de Madrid, 1989.

Domingo, Plácido. *Pregón de las Fiestas de San Isidro, 1986*. Madrid: Ayuntamiento de Madrid, 1986.

Domínguez Uceta, Acacia. "Lugares de los 80." In *Madrid, años ochenta*, edited by Rafael Sierra. Madrid: Ayuntamiento de Madrid, 1989.

Donaghy, Peter J., and Michael T. Newton. *Spain: A Guide to Political and Economic Institutions*. Cambridge: Cambridge University Press, 1987.

EDIS. *La juventud de Madrid, 1985*. Madrid: Ayuntamiento de Madrid, Concejalía de Juventud, 1985.

————. *Las elecciones generales 1986: valores sociales y actitudes políticas, movilidad y motivación del voto.* Madrid: Fundación Friedrich Ebert, 1987.

Eley, Geoff. *Forging Democracy: The History of the Left in Europe, 1850–2000.* Oxford: Oxford University Press, 2002.

Equipo, Viajar, and Ayuntamiento de Madrid. *Conocer Madrid.* Madrid: Ayuntamiento de Madrid, Oficina Municipal del Plan, 1982.

————. *Madrid.* Madrid: Editorial Tania, 1983.

Estébañez Álvarez, José. *Madrid, presente y futuro.* Madrid: Editorial Akal, 1990.

Ethier, Diane. "Introduction. Processes of Transition and Democratic Consolidation: Theoretical Indicators." In *Democratic Transition and Consolidation in Southern Europe, Latin America, and Southeast Asia*, edited by Diane Ethier. London: Macmillan, 1990.

Europalia 85. *Programa, Europalia 85 España.* Madrid: Dirección General del Instituto Español de Emigración, 1985.

Evans, Martin. "Languages of Racism within Contemporary Europe." In *Nations and Identity in Contemporary Europe*, edited by Brian Jenkins and Spyros A Sofos. London: Routledge, 1996.

Evans, Peter. "Back to the Future: Cinema and Democracy." In *Spanish Cultural Studies: An Introduction*, edited by Helen Graham and Jo Labanyi. Oxford: Oxford University Press, 1995.

Feldman, Sharon G. "Scenes from the Contemporary Barcelona Stage: La Fura del Baus's Aspiration to the Authentic." *Theatre Journal* 50, no. 4 (1998): 447–72.

Fernández Prado, Emiliano. *La política cultural. ¿Qué es y par que sirve?* Gijón: Ediciones Trea, 1991.

Fernández Vicente, Pedro. *Madrid en Comunidad.* Madrid: Bitácora, 1989.

Ferrer, Manuel. "Aspectos geograficos." In *La España de las autonomías*, edited by Fernando Fernández Rodríguez. Madrid: Instituto de Administración Local, 1985.

Flynn, Mary K. "Constructed Identities and Iberia." *Ethnic and Racial Studies* 24, no. 5 (2001): 703–18.

Foure, Héctor. *El futuro ya está aquí.* Madrid: Velecio Editores, 2007.

Fox, E. Inman. *La invención de España.* Madrid: Cátedra, 1997.

————. "Spain as Castile: Nationalism and National Identity." In *Modern Spanish Culture*, edited by David T. Gies. Cambridge: Cambridge University Press, 1999.

Fuentes, Pepo. "La prensa." In *La Edad de Oro del pop español*, edited by Carlos López. Madrid: Luca Editorial, 1992.

Fukuyama, Francis. *The End of History and the Last Man.* New York: The Free Press, 1992.

Fundación Santa María. *Juventud española, 1984.* Madrid: Ediciones SM, 1985.

Fundación Villa y Corte. *Madrid, Objetivo Cultural: actas de la semana de estudios sobre el presente y el futuro de la cultura madrileña celebrada durante los días 6 al 11 de febrero de 1984.* Madrid: Caja de Ahorros y Monte de Piedad de Madrid, 1985.

Fusi, Juan Pablo. *España. La evolución de la identidad nacional.* Madrid: Temas de Hoy, 1999.

————. "La cultura de la transición." *Revista de Occidente* 122–23 (1991): 37–64.

————. *Un siglo de España: la cultura.* Madrid: Marcial Pons, 1999.

Gallego Serrano, Julián. "Diez años de exposiciones madrileñas." *Cuenta y Razón*, no. 35 (1988): 29–36.

Gallero, José Luis. *Solo se vive una vez. Esplendor y ruina de la movida madrileña.* Madrid: Adora, 1991.

Gangutia, Clara. *Otro Madrid.* Madrid: Medici, 1985.

García de León, María Antonio. *Pedro Almodóvar, la otra España cañi.* Ciudad Real: Biblioteca de Autores y Temas Manchegos, 1990.

García Ferrando, M. *La conciencia nacional y regional en la España de las autonomías.* Madrid: CIS, 1994.

García Matilla, Eduardo, and Ortiz Miguel Angel. "Los jóvenes madrileños y la radio de los 80." In *Madrid, años ochenta*, edited by Rafael Sierra. Madrid: Ayuntamiento de Madrid, 1989.

García, Pablo. "Radio 3, 1982–1986." In *Radio 3. 20 años*, edited by Martín Sabas. Valencia: La Máscara, 1998.

García Vega, Nacho. "Ni me consultan, ni me piden consejo." In *Madrid Hoy*, edited by Lolo Rico. Madrid: La Comunidad de Madrid, Consejería de Gobernación, 1987.

Gellner, Ernest. *Nations and Nationalism.* Ithaca: Cornell University Press, 1983.

Gies, David T. "Modern Spanish Culture: An Introduction." In *Modern Spanish Culture*, edited by David T. Gies. Cambribge: Cambridge University Press, 1999.

Gil Calvo, Enrique, and Elena Menéndez Vergara. *Ocio y practicas culturales de los jóvenes.* Madrid: Ministerio de Cultura, Instituto de la Juventud, 1985.

Gilmour, David. *Cities of Spain.* Chicago: Ivan R. Dee, 1992.

———. *The Transformation of Spain: From Franco to the Constitutional Monarchy.* London: Quartet Books, 1985.

Giorgi, Gabriel. "Madrid en tránsito: Travelers, Visibility, and Gay Identities." *GLQ: A Journal of Lesbian and Gay Studies* 8, no. 1 (2002): 57–79.

Gómez de las Roces, Hipólito. *El estado del Estado de las Autonomías.* Zaragoza: Diputación General de Aragón, 1988.

Gómez Rufo, Antonio. *Carta a un amigo sobre don Enrique Tierno Galván.* Madrid: Ediciones de Antonio Machado, 1986.

———. *Madrid, bajos fondos.* Madrid: El Avapiés, 1987.

———. "Un milagro llamado Madrid." In *Así es Madrid*, edited by Antonio Gómez Rufo. Madrid: Temas de Hoy, 1988.

González Blasco, Pedro. *Jóvenes españoles 89.* Madrid: Fundación Santa María, 1989.

Gonzalez, Jorge. "Rock-ola." In *La Edad de Oro del pop español*, edited by Carlos López. Madrid: Luca Editorial, 1992.

Graham, Helen, and Jo Labanyi. "Editors' Preface." In *Spanish Cultural Studies: An Introduction*, edited by Helen Graham and Jo Labanyi. Oxford: Oxford University Press, 1995.

———. "Glossary." In *Spanish Cultural Studies: An Introduction*, edited by Helen Graham and Jo Labanyi. Oxford: Oxford University Press, 1995.

Greenfeld, Liah. *Nationalism: Five Roads to Modernity.* Cambridge: Harvard Universty Press, 1992.

Grijalba, Silvia. *Dios salve a la movida.* Madrid: Espejo de Tinta, 2006.

Grugel, Jean, and Tim Rees. *Franco's Spain.* London: Arnold, 1997.

Guerra de la Vega, Ramón. *Madrid: nueva arquitectura (1980–1985).* Fuenlabrada: Graficinco, 1985.

Guibernau, Montserrat. "Globalization and the Nation-State." In *Understanding Nationalism*, edited by Montserrat Guibernau and John Hutchinson. Cambridge: Polity Press, 2001.

———, and John Hutchinson, eds. *Understanding Nationalism*. Cambridge: Polity Press, 2001.

Habermas, Jürgen. "Citizenship and National Identity: Some Reflections on the Future of Europe." *Praxis International* 12, no. 1 (1992): 1–19.

———. "Historical Consciousness and Post-Traditional Identity." In *The New Conservatism: Cultural Criticism and the Historians' Debate*, edited by Shierry Weber Nicholsen. Cambridge, MA: MIT Press, 1989.

Harding, Susan Friend. *Remaking Ibieca: Rural Life in Aragón under Franco*. Chapel Hill, NC: University of North Carolina Press, 1984.

Hargreaves, John. *Freedom for Catalonia? Catalan Nationalism, Spanish Identity and the Barcelona Olympic Games*. Cambridge: Cambridge University Press, 2000.

Haro Ibars, Eduardo. *Gay Rock*. Madrid: Júcar, 1975.

Hayek, Garí. "Los nacionalismos periféricos ante la construcción política europea: el caso del archipielago canario." In *Nationalism in Europe: Past and Present*, edited by Justo G. Beramendi and Xosé Manoel Núñez. Santiago de Compostela: University of Santiago de Compostela, 1994.

Hebbert, Michael. "Spain—A Centre-Periphery Transformation." In *Unfamiliar Territory: The Reshaping of European Geography*, edited by Michael Hebbert and Jens Christian Hansen. Aldershot: Avebury, 1990.

Hechter, Michael. *Internal Colonialism: The Celtic Fringe in British National Development, 1536–1966*. London: Routledge and Kegan Paul, 1975.

Herf, Jeffery. *Divided Memory: The Nazi Past in the Two Germanys*. Cambridge: Harvard University Press, 1997.

Hernández Bravo de Laguna, Juan. *Historia popular de Canarias. Franquismo y transición política*. Santa Cruz de Tenerife: Centro de la Cultura Popular Canaria, 1992.

Herranz Rafael, Gonzalo. *La vigencia del nacionalismo*. Madrid: CIS, 1992.

Herrero Martín, Ramón, and Inmaculada López Salvador. "Madrid años ochenta." In *Madrid, años ochenta*, edited by Rafael Sierra. Madrid: Ayuntamiento, 1989.

Hobsbawm, Eric. *Nations and Nationalism since 1780*. Cambridge: Cambridge University Press, 1990.

———. "Nation, State, Ethnicity, Religion: Transformations of Identity." In *Nationalism in Europe: Past and Present*, edited by Justo G Beramendi and Xosé M Núñez. Santiago de Compostela: University of Santiago de Compostela, 1994.

Holguín, Sandie. *Creating Spaniards: Culture and National Identity in Republican Spain*. Madison, WI: University of Wisconsin Press, 2002.

Holman, Otto. *Integrating Southern Europe. EC Expansion and the Transnationalization of Spain*. London: Routledge, 1996.

Hooper, John. *The New Spaniards*. London: Penguin, 1995.

Hroch, Miroslav. "From National Movement to the Fully-Formed Nation: The Nation-Building Process in Europe." *New Left Review*, no. 198 (1993): 3–20.

———. *Social Preconditions of National Revival in Europe*. Cambridge: Cambridge University Press, 1985.

Hutchinson, John. *The Dynamics of Cultural Nationalism: The Gaelic Revival and the Creation of the Irish Nation State*. London: Allen and Unwin, 1987.

———, and Anthony D. Smith, eds. *Nationalism: Critical Concepts in Political Science*. Vol. 1. London: Routledge, 2000.

Iglesias de Ussel, Julio. "La movida: un análisis sociológico." In *Movida y sociedad*, edited by María Consolación Calderón España. Sevilla: Real Sociedad Ecónomica, 1997.

Jenkins, Brian, and Spyros A. Sofos. "Nation and Nationalism in Contemporary Europe: A Theoretical Perspective." In *Nations and Identity in Contemporary Europe*. London: Routledge, 1996.

Jensen, Geoffrey. *Irrational Triumph: Cultural Despair, Military Nationalism, and the Ideological Origins of Franco's Spain*. Reno: University of Nevada Press, 2002.

Jiménez Blanco, José. *La conciencia regional en España*. Madrid: CIS, 1977.

Jiménez de Gregorio, Fernando. *Madrid y su Comunidad*. Madrid: El Avapiés, 1986.

Johnston, Hank. *Tales of Nationalism: Catalonia, 1939–1979*. New Brunswick: Rutgers University, 1991.

Jordan, Barry, and Rikki Morgan-Tamosunas. "Introduction: Part III." In *Contemporary Spanish Cultural Studies*. London: Arnold, 2000.

Jover Zamora, José María, Guadalupe Gómez-Ferrer Morant, and Juan Pablo Fusi. *España: sociedad, política y civilización (siglos XIX–XX)*. Madrid: Areté, 2001.

Juliá, Santos. "History, Politics, and Culture, 1975–1996." In *Modern Spanish Culture*, edited by David T. Gies. Cambridge: Cambridge University Press, 1999.

———. "The Socialist Era, 1982–1996." In *Spanish History since 1808*, edited by José Alvarez Junco and Adrian Shubert. London: Arnold, 2000.

———, David Ringrose, and Cristina Segura. *Madrid, historia de una capital*. Madrid: Alianza Editorial, 2000.

Keating, Michael. "The Minority Nations of Spain and European Integration: A New Framework for Autonomy?" *Journal of Spanish Cultural Studies* 1, no. 1 (2000): 29–42.

Kitromilides, Paschalis. "'Imagined Communities' and the Origins of the National Question in the Balkans." *European History Quarterly* 19, no. 2 (1989): 149–92.

Labanyi, Jo, ed. *Constructing Identity in Contemporary Spain*. Oxford: Oxford University Press, 2002.

———. "Introduction: Engaging with Ghosts; or, Theorizing Culture in Modern Spain." In *Constructing Identity in Contemporary Spain*, edited by Jo Labanyi. Oxford: Oxford University Press, 2002.

Leguina, Joaquín. "Madrid en la Autonomía." *Revista de Occidente*, no. extraordinario VII (1983): 11–17.

———. "Madrid hoy." In *Madrid Hoy*, edited by Lolo Rico. Madrid: La Comunidad de Madrid, Consejería de Gobernación, 1987.

———. "Tierno Galván: el alcalde." *Sistema*, no. 71–72 (1986): 161–63.

Linz, Juan J., ed. *Conflicto en Euskadi*. Madrid: Espasa-Calpe, 1986.

———. "Early State Building and Late Peripheral Nationalisms against the State: The Case of Spain." In *Building States and Nations: Analysis by Region*, edited by S. N. Eisenstadt and Stein Rokkan. Beverly Hills: Sage, 1973.

———. "Los nacionalismos en España: una perspectiva comparativa." In *El estado moderno en Italia y España*, edited by Elio d'Auria and Jordi Cassassas. Barcelona: Universitat de Barcelona, 1993.

Llera, Francisco J. "Conflicto en Euskadi Revisited." In *Politics, Society, and Democracy: The Case of Spain*, edited by Richard Gunther. Boulder: Westview, 1993.

López Aranguren, Eduardo. *La conciencia regional en el proceso autonómico español*. Madrid: CIS, 1983.

López, Carlos, ed. *La Edad de Oro del pop español*. Madrid: Luca Editorial, 1992.

Luna Wennberg, Juan. *Nuestro Madrid*. Madrid: Lunwerg, 1986.

Madoz, Pascual. *Madrid, Audiencia, Provincia, Intendencia, Vicaría, Partido y Villa (1848)*. Madrid: Comunidad de Madrid, 1984.

Mainer, José Carlos. "1975–1985, Los poderes del pasado." In *La cultura española en el posfranquismo*, edited by Samuel Amell. Madrid: Playor, 1988.

Máiz, Ramón. "Democracy, Federalism, and Nationalism in Multinational States." In *Identity and Territorial Autonomy in Plural Societies*, edited by William Safran and Ramón Máiz. London: Frank Cass, 2000.

Mann, Michael. "Explaining Murderous Ethnic Cleansing: The Macro-Level." In *Understanding Nationalism*, edited by Montserrat Guibernau and John Hutchinson. Cambridge: Polity, 2001.

Maravall, José María. *La política de la transición*. Madrid: Taurus, 1985.

Mariñas, Alberto. "La ruptura y la seducción—Imagen gráfica en los 80." In *Madrid, años ochenta*, edited by Rafael Sierra. Madrid: Ayuntamiento de Madrid, 1989.

Márquez, Fernando. *Música moderna*. Madrid: Las Ediciones Nuevo Sendero, 1981.

———. *Todos los chicos y chicas/Historias de la nueva ola*. Madrid: Las Ediciones de Banda de Moebius, 1980.

Martín, Paco. *La movida*. Madrid: n. p., 1982.

Martín Serrano, Manuel. *Historia de los cambios de mentalidad de los jóvenes entre 1960–1990*. Madrid: Instituto de la Juventud, 1994.

Masats, Ramón, and Luis Carandell. *Madrid es más que Madrid*. Madrid: Comunidad de Madrid, Consejería de Cultura, 1984.

Masllorens, Alex. *La herencia y humana de Enrique Tierno Galván*. Barcelona: Tibidabo, 1986.

Mateo, Cristina. "Identities at a Distance: Markers of National Identity in the Video-Diaries of Second-Generation Spanish Migrants in London." In *Constructing Identity in Twentieth Century Spain*, edited by Jo Labanyi. Oxford: Oxford University Press, 2002.

Maxwell, Kenneth, and Steven Spiegel. *The New Spain: From Isolation to Influence*. New York: Council on Foreign Relations Press, 1994.

McDonough, Peter, Doh Shin, and José Álvaro Moisés. "Democratization and Participation: Comparing Spain, Brazil, and Korea." *The Journal of Politics* 60, no. 4 (1998): 919–53.

Medina, Antonio. "Estudio sociologico de las clases dirigentes en Madrid." In *Madrid, Objetivo Cultural: actas de la semana de estudios sobre el presente y el futuro de la cultura madrileña celebrada durante los días 6 al 11 de febrero de 1984*, edited by Fundación Villa y Corte. Madrid: Caja de Ahorros y Monte de Piedad de Madrid, 1985.

Mees, Ludger. "Between Votes and Bullets. Conflicting Ethnic Identities in the Basque Country." *Ethnic and Racial Studies* 24, no. 5 (2001): 798–827.

Ministerio de Asuntos Exteriores. *Madrid: años 80, imágenes de la movida*. Madrid: Ministerio de Asuntos Exteriores, 1994.

Ministerio de Cultura. *Acción cultural de los organismos internacionales euopeos*. Madrid: Ministerio de Cultura, 1979.

———. *Animación socio-cultural*. Madrid: Ministerio de Cultura, 1980.

———. *Cuatro años de política cultural, 1982–1986*. Madrid: Ministerio de Cultura, 1986.

———. *Demanda cultural en España*. Madrid: Ministerio de Cultura, 1978.

———. *Desmitificación de la Cultura*. Madrid: Ministerio de Cultura, 1979.

———. *Dos años de política cultural: 1983–1984*. Madrid: Ministerio de Cultura, 1984.

———. *Encuesta de comportamiento cultural de los españoles.* Madrid: Ministerio de Cultura, 1985.

———. *Encuesta de comportamiento cultural de los españoles: Autonomía de Madrid.* Madrid: Ministerio de Cultura, 1986.

———. *Epoca Nueva: Painting and Sculpture from Spain, Chicago Office of Fine Arts.* Madrid: Ministerio de Cultura, 1988.

———. *5 artistas españoles / 5 Spanish Artists: exposicón 1985, New York City.* Madrid: Ministerio de Cultura, 1985.

———. *Guia de servicios culturales.* Madrid: Ministerio de cultura, 1985.

———. *Hacia una democracia cultural.* Madrid: Ministerio de Cultura, 1979.

———. *L'Imagination Nouvelle: les anées 70–80, exposición Paris 1987.* Madrid: Ministerio de Cultura, 1987.

———. *Los derechos culturales como derechos humanos.* Madrid: Ministerio de Cultura, 1979.

———. *Memoria 1982.* Madrid: Ministerio de Cultura, 1982.

———. *Metodos y objetivos de la planificación cultural.* Madrid: Ministerio de Cultura, 1979.

———. *Política cultural, 1982–1986.* Madrid: Novatex, 1986.

———. *Políticas culturales en Europa.* Madrid: Ministerio de Cultura, 1980.

———. *Sociedad y Cultura. Una política de promoción sociocultural a debate.* Madrid: Ministerio de Cultura, 1985.

Monge Casado, Javier. "La inversión pública en cultura." *Economistas,* no. 34 (1988): 22–39.

Monleón, José B. *Del franquismo a la posmodernidad.* Madrid: Akal, 1995.

Montoliú Camps, Pedro. *Madrid: villa y corte.* Madrid: Sílex Ediciones, 1996.

Moral, Felíx. *Identidad regional y nacionalismo en el estado de las autonomías.* Madrid: CIS, 1998.

———, and Araceli Mateos. *La identidad nacional de los jóvenes y el estado de las autonomías.* Madrid: CIS, 1999.

Morán, Fernando. "Recuerdo de Tierno Galván." *Sistema,* no. 76 (1986): 49–57.

Morán, María Luz. *La cultura política de los espanoles: un ensayo de reinterpretación.* Madrid: CIS, 1995.

Moreno, Luis. *La federalización de España.* Madrid: Siglo XXI, 1997.

Morodo, Raúl. "Enrique Tierno: semblanza, aventura y compromiso político-intelectual." *Sistema,* no. 71–72 (1986): 5–18.

———. *Tierno Galván y otros precursores políticos.* Madrid: El País, 1987.

Muniesa, Bernat. *Dictadura y Monarquía en España: de 1939 hasta la actualidad.* Barcelona: Editorial Ariel, 1996.

Nairn, Tom. *The Breakup of Britain: Crisis and Neo-Nationalism.* London: New Left, 1977.

Nash, Elizabeth. *Madrid: A Cultural and Literary Companion.* Oxford: Signal, 2001.

Nash, Mary. "Towards a New Moral Order." In *Spanish History since 1808,* edited by José Alvarez Junco and Adrian Shubert. London: Arnold, 2000.

Navarro, Javier. "Notas kitsch del paisaje urbano madrileño." In *El Kitsch Español,* edited by Antonio Sánchez Casado. Madrid: Temas de Hoy, 1988.

Newton, Michael T., and Peter J. Donaghy. *Institutions of Modern Spain: A Political and Economic Guide.* Cambridge: Cambridge University Press, 1997.

Núñez, Xosé Manoel. "Autonomist Regionalism within the Spanish State of the Autonomous Communities: An Interpretation." In *Identity and Territorial*

Autonomy in Plural Societies, edited by William Safran and Ramón Máiz. London: Frank Cass, 2000.

———. *Historiographical Approaches to Nationalism in Spain*. Saarbrucken: Breitenbach, 1993.

———. "The Reawakening of Peripheral Nationalisms and the State of the Autonomous Communities." In *Spanish History since 1808*, edited by José Alvarez Junco and Adrian Shubert. London: Arnold, 2000.

———. "The Region as *Essence* of the Fatherland: Regionalist Variants of Spanish Nationalism (1840–1936)." *European History Quarterly* 31, no. 4 (2001): 483–518.

———. "Region Building in Spain During the 19th and 20th Centuries." In *Region und Regionsbildung in Europa: Konzeptionen der Forschung und Empirische Befunde*, edited by Gerhard Brunn. Baden-Baden: Nomos Verlagsgesellschaft, 1996.

———. "What is Spanish Nationalism Today? From Legitimacy Crisis to Unfulfilled Renovation (1975–2000)." *Ethnic and Racial Studies* 24, no. 5 (2001): 719–52.

O'Donnell, Guillermo, and Philippe C. Schmitter. *Transitions from Authoritarian Rule: Tentative Conclusions about Uncertain Democracies*. Baltimore: Johns Hopkins University Press, 1986.

Ordovás, Jesús. *De que va el Rrollo*. Madrid: Las Ediciones de Piqueta, 1977.

———. *Historia de la música pop española*. Madrid: Alianza, 1987.

———. "Madrid Pop, 1979–1989." In *Madrid, años ochenta*, edited by Rafael Sierra. Madrid: Ayuntamiento de Madrid, 1989.

Orizo, Francisco Andres. *España, entre la apatía y el cambio social*. Madrid: Mapfre, 1983.

Parsons, Deborah. *A Cultural History of Madrid: Modernism and the Urban Spectacle*. Oxford: Berg, 2003.

———. "Fiesta Culture in Madrid Posters, 1934–1955." In *Constructing Identity in Contemporary Spain*, edited by Jo Labanyi. Oxford: Oxford University Press, 2002.

Payne, Stanley. "Nationalism, Regionalism and Micronationalism in Spain." *Journal of Contemporary History* 26 (1991): 479–91.

Peces-Barba Martínez, Gregorio. *La elaboración de la constitución de 1978*. Madrid: Centro Estudios Constitucionales, 1988.

Pérez Díaz, Víctor. *The Return of Civil Society: The Emergence of Democratic Spain*. Cambridge, MA: Harvard University Press, 1993.

Pérez Mínguez, Pablo. *Mi movida madrileña: fotografías 1979–1985*. Barcelona: Lunwerg, 2006.

Pérez Perucha, Julio. "A la busqueda de un cine madrileñista." In *Madrid y el cine: Fiestas de San Isidro 1984*, edited by Ayuntamiento de Madrid. Madrid: Ayuntamiento de Madrid, Filmoteca Española, 1984.

Perez-Sanchez, Gema. *Queer Transitions in Contemporary Spanish Culture: From Franco to La Movida*. Albany, NY: State University of New York Press, 2007.

Petras, James. "Spanish Socialism: The Politics of Neo-Liberalism." In *Mediterranean Paradoxes: Politics and Social Structure in Southern Europe*, edited by James Kurth and James Petras. Providence: Berg, 1993.

Piñeiro, Nicolás. *Regionalismo: Madrid, capital y region*. Madrid: Grafiprintin, 1991.

Piñuel Raigada, José Luis. *El consumo cultural*. Madrid: Instituto Nacional de Consumo / Fundamentos, 1987.

Piqueras, Andrés. *La identidad valenciana. La difícil construcción de una identidad colectiva.* Madrid: Escuela Libre, 1996.

Pi Sunyer, O. "Catalan Politics and Spanish Democracy: An Overview of a Relationship." *Iberian Studies*, no. 1–2 (1988).

Platón, Miguel. *La amenaza separatista. Mito y realidad de los nacionalismos en España.* Madrid: Temas de Hoy, 1994.

Preston, Paul. *The Triumph of Democracy in Spain.* London: Methuen, 1986.

Prieto Lacaci, Rafael. *La participación social y política de los jóvenes.* Madrid: Instituto de la Juventud, 1985.

Radcliff, Pamela B. *Citizenship, Gender, and the Transition to Democracy.* New York: Palgrave Macmillan, forthcoming.

———. "El estado y la sociedad civil en la España del siglo XX." Madrid· 2002.

———. *From Mobilization to Civil War: The Politics of Polarization in the Spanish City of Gijón, 1900–1937.* Cambridge: Cambridge University Press, 1996.

Revilla, Fidel. *Historia breve de Madrid.* Madrid: La Libería, 1994.

Rey, José Ramón. "El cine: entre el amor y el odio a la Ley." In *Madrid, años ochenta*, edited by Rafael Sierra. Madrid: Ayuntamiento de Madrid, 1989.

Richards, Michael. "Collective Memory, the Nation-State and Post-Franco Society." In *Contemporary Spanish Cultural Studies*, edited by Barry Jordan and Rikki Morgan-Tamosunas. London: Arnold, 2000.

———. *A Time of Silence: Civil War and the Culture of Repression in Franco's Spain, 1936–1945.* Cambridge: Cambridge University Press, 1998.

Rico, Lolo, ed. *Madrid Hoy.* Madrid: La Comunidad de Madrid, Consejería de Gobernación, 1987.

Riera, Ignasi. "Autonomía de la cultura, cultura de la autonomía." In *Encuentros en Madrid 1985: por la renovación cultural, por la democratización de la cultura*, edited by Fundación de Investigaciones Marxistas. Madrid: Fundación de Investigaciones Marxistas, 1986.

Río López, Angel de. *Varas y bastones de la villa y corte.* Madrid: Temas de Hoy, 1994.

Ríos Longares, José. *Y yo caí-enamorado de la moda juvenil.* Alicante: Agua Clara, 2001.

Ripoll, Antonio J, ed. *La gloriosa movida nacional.* Aviles: Casa Municipal de Cultura, 1988.

Riquer, Borja de. "An Analysis of Nationalisms in Spain: A Proposal for an Integrated Historical Model." In *Nationalism in Europe: Past and Present*, edited by Justo G. Beramendi and Xosé Manoel Núñez. Santiago de Compostela: University of Santiago de Compostela, 1994.

———. "La débil nacionalización española del siglo XIX." *Historia Social* 20 (1994): 97–114.

Rojas, Enrique. *El hombre Light: una vida sin valores.* Madrid: Temas de Hoy, 1992.

Rokkan, Stein, and D. W. Urwin, eds. *The Politics of Territorial Identity.* Beverley Hills: Sage, 1982.

Rosell, Cayetano. *Crónica de la provincia de Madrid: Madrid 1865.* Madrid: Comunidad de Madrid, 1983.

Rovira, Antonio. *Enrique Tierno Galván: 1918–1986.* Madrid: Fundación Pablo Iglesias, 1987.

Ruiz del Arbol, Antonio. *Prensa local madrileña: 1970–1980.* Madrid: Comunidad de Madrid, 1987.

Ruiz Sanz, Mario. *Enrique Tierno Galván: aproximación a su vida, obra y pensamiento.* Madrid, Universidad de Carlos III de Madrid: Dykinson, 1997.

Sabas, Martín. *Radio 3. 20 años.* Valencia: La Máscara, 1998.

Safran, William, and Ramón Máiz, eds. *Identity and Territorial Autonomy in Plural Societies.* London: Frank Cass, 2000.

Salmón, K. G. *The Modern Spanish Economy: Transformation and Integration into Europe.* London: Pinter, 1995.

Sangrador García, José Luis. *Estereotipos de las nacionalidades y regiones de España.* Madrid: CIS, 1981.

———. *Identidades, actitudes y estereotipos en la España de las autonomías.* Madrid: Centro de Investigaciones Sociológicas, 1996.

Santesmases, Antonio García. "Enrique Tierno: una luz en el tunel." *Leviatán,* no. 23–24 (1986): 189–200.

Santos Preciado, José Miguel. "La población." In *Madrid, presente y futuro,* edited by José Estébañez Álvarez. Madrid: Editorial Akal, 1990.

Scales, Peter. "La movida madrileña: una lagrima en la lluvia." In *Siete ensayos sobre la cultura,* edited by Federico Bonaddio and Derek Harris. Old Aberdeen: Aberdeen University Press, 1995.

Schröder, Manfred. "Testimonio: esta ciudad ya está acostumbrada . . . " In *Manifiesto por Madrid,* edited by Adrián Piera. Madrid: Cámara Oficial de Comercio e Industria de Madrid, 1993.

Sentien, Julio. In *Encuentros en Madrid 1985: por la renovación cultural, por la democratización de la cultura,* edited by Fundación de Investigaciones Marxistas. Madrid: Fundación de Investigaciones Marxistas, 1986.

Sentís, Mireia. "Cómic." In *Madrid, años ochenta,* edited by Rafael Sierra. Madrid: Ayuntamiento de Madrid, 1989.

Serrán Pagán, Francisco. *Cultura española y autonomias.* Madrid: Ministerio de Cultura, 1980.

Shubert, Adrian. *A Social History of Modern Spain.* London: Routledge, 1990.

Sierra, Rafael. *Madrid, años ochenta.* Madrid: Ayuntamiento de Madrid, 1989.

Smith, Anthony D. *The Ethnic Origins of Nations.* Oxford: Blackwell, 1986.

———. *National Identity.* Harmondsworth: Penguin, 1991.

———. *Nationalism and Modernism.* London: Routledge, 1998.

Smith, Paul Julian. *Desire Unlimited: The Cinema of Pedro Almodóvar.* London: Verso, 1994.

———. *The Moderns—Time, Space and Subjectivity in Contemporary Spanish Culture.* New York: Oxford University Press, 2000.

Solana, Javier. "Discurso de clausura." In *Sociedad y Cultura. Una política de promoción sociocultural a debate,* edited by Ministerio de Cultura. Madrid: Ministerio de Cultura, 1985.

———. *Informe ante la Comisión de Educación y Cultura del Congreso de los Diputados, 14 Abril 1983.* Madrid: Ministerio de Cultura, 1983.

———. *Perspectivas de política cultural. Comparencia del Ministro de Cultura ante la Comisión de Educación y Cultura del Congreso de los Diputados, 23 September 1986.* Madrid: Ministerio de Cultura, 1986.

Soto Carmona, Alvaro. *La transición a la democracia. España, 1975–1982.* Madrid: Alianza Editorial, 1998.

Stapell, Hamilton M. "Just a Teardrop in the Rain? The *movida madrileña* and Democratic Identity Formation in the Capital, 1979–1986." *Bulletin of Spanish Studies* LXXXVI, no. 3 (2009): 345–69.

———. "Reconsidering Spanish Nationalism, Regionalism, and the Center-Periphery Model in the Post-Francoist Period, 1975–1992." *International Journal of Iberian Studies* 20, no. 3 (2007): 171–85.

Subirats, Eduardo. *Después de la lluvia: sobre la ambigua modernidad española*. Madrid: Temas de Hoy, 1993.

———. "Postmoderna modernidad: la España de los felices ochenta." *Quimera* 145 (1996): 11–18.

Sullivan, John. *ETA and Basque Nationalism: The Fight for Euskadi, 1980–1986*. London: Routledge, 1988.

Suñer, Eugenia. "Kitsch firmado español." In *El Kitsch Español*, edited by Antonio Sánchez Casado. Madrid: Temas de Hoy, 1988.

Szmolka, Inmaculada. *Opiniones y Actitudes 21. Opiniones y actitudes de los españoles ante el proceso de intregración europea*. Madrid: CIS, 1999

Terán, Fernando. *Madrid*. Madrid: Mapfre, 1992.

Tierno Galván, Enrique. *Bandos del Alcalde*. Madrid: Editorial Tecnos, 1986.

———. *Cabos sueltos*. Madrid: Bruguera, 1981.

———. *Charlas de radio pronunciadas por el alcalde de Madrid*. Madrid: Ayuntamiento de Madrid, 1981.

———. *Europa y el fin de la utopía*. Madrid: Centro Madrileño de Estudios Socialistas, 1978.

———. *La España Autonómica*. Barcelona: Bruguera, 1985.

———. "Madrid." *Revista de Occidente*, no. extraordinario VII (1983): 19–23.

———. "Socialismo y Revolución." *Leviatán*, no. 5 (1981): 97–106.

———. "Tres años de gestión: los Ayuntamientos democráticos han cumplido con su deber." *CEUMT*, no. 50 (1982): 64–66.

Tono Martínez, José, ed. *La polémica de la posmodernidad*. Madrid: Editorial Libertas, 1986.

———. "Madrid: 2041." In *Madrid Hoy*, edited by Lolo Rico. Madrid: La Comunidad de Madrid, Consejería de Gobernación, 1987.

Triana Toribio, Núria. "A Punk Called Pedro: *La Movida* in the Films of Pedro Almodóvar." In *Contemporary Spanish Cultural Studies*. London: Arnold, 2000.

Trumpbour, John. "Preface: Southern Europe Past and Present." In *Mediterranean Paradoxes: Politics and Social Structure in Southern Europe*, edited by James Kurth and James Petras. Providence: Berg, 1993.

Tusell, Javier. "La cultura en España en la última década a través de las estadísticas." *Cuenta y Razón*, no. 19 (1985): 175–81.

Ucelay, Enric. "Catalan Nationalism: Cultural Plurality and Political Ambiguity." In *Spanish Cultural Studies. An Introduction*, edited by Helen Graham and Jo Labanyi. Oxford: Oxford University Press, 1995.

Umbral, Francisco. *Diccionario cheli*. Barcelona: Grijalbo, 1983.

———. *Guía de la posmodernidad*. Madrid: Temas de Hoy, 1987.

———. *Y Tierno Galván ascendió a los cielos*. Barcelona: Seix Barral, 1990.

Valis, Noël. *The Culture of Cursilería: Bad Taste, Kitsch, and Class in Modern Spain*. Durham: Duke University Press, 2002.

Vernon, Kathleen M. "Culture and Cinema to 1975." In *Modern Spanish Culture*, edited by David T. Gies. Cambridge: Cambridge University Press, 1999.

———, and Barbara Morris. "Introduction: Pedro Almodóvar, Postmodern *Auteur*." In *Post-Franco, Postmodern: The Films of Pedro Almodóvar*, edited by Kathleen M. Vernon and Barbara Morris. Westport, CT: Greenwood, 1995.

————. *Post-Franco, Postmodern: The Films of Pedro Almodóvar*. Westport, CT: Greenwood, 1995.

Vico, Dario. "La industria del disco: diez años de reconversión." In *La Edad de Oro del pop español*, edited by Carlos López. Madrid: Luca Editorial, 1992.

Vilarós, Teresa M. "Los monos del desencanto español." *MLN* 109 (1994): 217–35.

Vilar, Sergio. *Proyección internacional de España*. Madrid: Tecnos, 1981.

Villaverde, Alfredo. "La movida madrileña." In *Madrid, único y múltiple, 21 crónicas periodísticas*, edited by Ayuntamiento de Madrid. Madrid: Ayuntamiento de Madrid, 1987.

Villoria, Enrique. *Así cambiamos Madrid*. Madrid: Fundación Cuidad, 1996.

————. *Madrid con soluciones*. Madrid: Azara, 1982.

Vinuesa Angulo, Julio. *La población de Madrid*. Madrid: Comunidad de Madrid, Consejería de Política territorial, 1994.

Vizcaíno, José Antonio. *Historia de la villa de Madrid: de los orígenes a la actualidad*. Barcelona: Óptima, 2000.

Williams, Mark. *The Story of Spain*. Fuengirola, Spain: Ediciones Santana, 2000.

Xenos, Nicholas. "Civic Nationalism: Oxymoron?" *Critical Review* 10, no. 2 (1996): 213–31.

Yack, Bernard. "The Myth of the Civic Nation." *Critical Review* 10, no. 2 (1996): 193–211.

Yoyoba, Merche. "De Sid Vicious a la chipie generation." In *La Edad de Oro del pop español*, edited by Carlos López. Madrid: Luca Editorial, 1992.

Zárraga, José Luis. *Encuesta, cultura y ocio*. Madrid: Ministerio de cultura, Secretaría General Técnica Subdirección General de Estudios y Coordinación, 1984.

————. *Informe juventud en España: la inserción de los jóvenes en la sociedad*. Madrid: Instituto de la Juventud, 1985.

————. *Informe juventud en España: 1988*. Madrid: Instituto de la Juventud, 1989.

INDEX